MATERIAL CULTURE IN EUROPE AND CHINA, 1400–1800

Also by S. A. M. Adshead

CENTRAL ASIA IN WORLD HISTORY

CHINA IN WORLD HISTORY

PROVINCE AND POLITICS IN LATE IMPERIAL CHINA

SALT AND CIVILIZATION

THE MODERNIZATION OF THE CHINESE SALT
ADMINISTRATION

Material Culture in Europe and China, 1400–1800

The Rise of Consumerism

S. A. M. Adshead
Professor of History
University of Canterbury
Christchurch
New Zealand

First published in Great Britain 1997 by
MACMILLAN PRESS LTD
Houndmills, Basingstoke, Hampshire RG21 6XS and London
Companies and representatives throughout the world

A catalogue record for this book is available from the British Library.

ISBN 0–333–69082–6

First published in the United States of America 1997 by
ST. MARTIN'S PRESS, INC.,
Scholarly and Reference Division,
175 Fifth Avenue, New York, N.Y. 10010

ISBN 0–312–17285–0

Library of Congress Cataloging-in-Publication Data
Adshead, Samuel Adrian M. (Samuel Adrian Miles)
Material culture in Europe and China, 1400–1800 : the rise of
consumerism / S.A.M. Adshead.
p. cm.
Includes bibliographical references and index.
ISBN 0–312–17285–0 (cloth)
1. Consumption (Economics)—Europe—History.   2. Consumption
(Economics)—China—History.   3. Material culture—Europe—History.
4. Material culture—China—History.   I. Title.
HC240.9.C6A38 1997
339.4'7'094—dc21   96–45195
                                                    CIP

This book is printed on paper suitable for recycling and made from fully managed and
sustained forest sources.

10   9   8   7   6   5   4   3   2   1
06 05 04 03 02 01 00 99 98 97

Printed and bound in Great Britain by
Antony Rowe Ltd, Chippenham, Wiltshire

For Laura

Contents

Preface

This book first took such shape as it has in the course of a long day's shopping at Harrods, just before Christmas 1991. It developed out of the growing conviction that the phenomenon of consumerism is highly significant for world history as I have tried to expound it in two previous books, that it has been widely misconceived and misjudged, and that, despite many excellent previous studies of particular commodities, it needed to be approached in longer perspective and from a higher viewpoint. It is these which I hope to provide.

In such an enterprise my debts, intellectual and otherwise, are necessarily large and many. Most must remain unacknowledged, since my notes refer, for the most part, only to quotations and the bibliography is only a summation of the notes. Any other scheme of acknowledgement would have extended both to intolerable lengths. Three overriding debts, however, cannot be left unacknowledged. First, to my friend Professor Mark Francis who first suggested the topic to me as an extension to other commodities of my previous work on salt and has continued to provide a stream of stimulation. Second, to Rosemary Russo, who has wrestled with my handwriting, kept errant notes and aberrant spellings in order, and never quailed before a request for a new draft. Third, to my colleagues in the Department of History, and, in particular, to Professor David McIntyre, who has given me the time and space to write. My greatest debt, however, is to the person named in the dedication, who not only made critical comments on much of the text, but by her resolution reawakened mine.

S. A. M. ADSHEAD
Christchurch, New Zealand

1 Material Culture

Between 1400 and 1800, the four primary civilizations of Western Eurasia, China, Black Africa and Meso-America lost their former isolation and were transformed. As a result of the Mongolian explosion, the Great Discoveries, and concomitant or subsequent renaissances, reformations and enlightenments, the cultural monads ceased to be windowless and began to reflect a wider reality. Among these developments, which may be said to have founded the modern world, was a change in material culture, not yet adequately studied, which will be called the rise of consumerism. This change went furthest in Europe, because it was rooted in Christian materialism, that sacramental sense of this world which Michael Novak has emphasized in his recent writings. However, because it was propagated through a new globalization of commodities, consumerism may also be found to some extent in China, Islam, Black Africa and Meso-America, in roughly that order. Consumerism, like science and democracy, has become part of the modern world order, and shares with them an intellectual dimension. The rise of consumerism involved not merely an increasing number and variety of available commodities and, as emphasized by Braudel, the emergence for the first time of genuine choice for consumers, but also, concomitant with that wider choice, a deeper penetration of the physical by the psychological and the intellectual: Popper's World 1 by his World 2 and World 3.[1] This penetration brought with it profound social consequences which, as extended by the industrial revolution and mass consumption, are with us still and are only beginning to receive due attention from social analysts. Increasingly consumerism commands the economy as much as technology.

This book studies the rise of consumerism. It investigates it through the histories of a number of commodities used everyday in food, dress, shelter, utilities, communication and symbolization. The commodities have been selected, partly because of their inherent interest and importance, but also necessarily because of the availability of monographic material. Other commodities might have been selected, but it is hoped that the choice is sufficiently illustrative of the underlying process: the extension of the materialization of culture, that *Geist in Welt*, which Karl Rahner saw as the defining characteristic of the human condition.[2] The first step in the investigations must be a consideration of the notion of material culture. This will be the subject of Chapter 1. The first section examines the structure of material culture. The second section outlines its conjuncture: the three main changes material culture has undergone since classical antiquity in both the West and China. Section 3 focuses on the changes in material culture between 1400 and 1800. In particular, it highlights the phenomenon of globalization: the acquisition of oriental commodities by the West, of occidental commodities by the East, and the influence on both of commodities coming from the North and South. Centres of reception as well as points of origin will need to be considered, since commodities are essentially consumed. Finally, section 4 delineates consumerism. It is seen, not as a complete social system, as some have made it, but as an independent set of values and institutions, compatible with many social and economic systems, but born in the courtly cities of early modernity and now most mature in meritocracy and market economy.

(1) THE STRUCTURE OF MATERIAL CULTURE

Lévi-Strauss regarded the distinction of nature and culture as uniquely and definingly human. While he may have rejected too easily the claim of beavers, burrowing animals, nest-making birds, and even some insects to be making a similar distinction, there can be little quarrel with the notion that it is characteristic of human beings to convert natural resources into cultural objects. Sometimes the resources are raw, as in the case of blackberries picked from a hedgerow and either eaten at once, hand to mouth, or put into a container for subsequent direct consumption. More often, resources have to be processed to become cultural objects. Salt occurs spontaneously in nature, but brine, much commoner, must be evaporated to produce sodium chloride. Processed resources in turn fall into two categories: materials, processed for intermediate use and further elaboration, and commodities, processed for final use and ultimate consumption. Commodities, of course, are frequently confections of materials and the same substance can figure both as a material and a commodity. Salt, for example, is a material in a chemical factory or on an icy road, while it is a commodity, specifically an alimentary commodity, on a dining-room table. Commodities are the particular sphere of material culture, because it is with them that physical resources come closest to the human psyche and intellect. 'Men get how they can', wrote Lord Dacre, 'it is in their spending that they illustrate their philosophy'.[3] Consumption is a more humane activity than production or distribution, which are often experienced as alienation. Though people must consume to survive, consumption is seldom regarded as dehumanization except by anorexics or Manichaean *perfecti*. Material culture therefore lies at the interface of mind and matter. It cannot, however, be reduced to either of its components, whatever Marxists or Hegelians may wish to say. Mind is more than the subjectivity of matter; matter is more than the objectification of mind. Nor can Melanie Klein's neutral monism of projection and introjection eliminate their duality. Yet the two are obviously in frequent relationship, congnitively in knowledge and creatively in the various fields of material culture.

For the purposes of this study, material culture will be divided into six fields. These were six areas where, in the period under review, consumers, both in Europe and China, had some choice and therefore were effectively free to express a scale of values. The first three fields: food, dress and shelter, arise from basic physiological, specifically thermoregulatory, needs. The fourth field, the utilities of heat, light and water, is an extension of shelter, and to a lesser extent, via cooking, of food. Field five, communications, will here be taken to refer not to physical locomotion, but to intellectual diffusion. Information has been called the ultimate resource on account both of its role in processing and its ability to substitute for scarce natural raw materials.[4] Beyond that, information also plays a crucial role in consumption. Without menus, fashion magazines, realtors' windows, bookshop catalogues, television commercials and advertisement generally, modern levels of material culture would be impossible. Such communication, moreover, is not merely modern. Already in the eighteenth century, advertisement played a notable part in consumption, particularly in the field of dress, always the area most sensitive to the butterfly effect of movements in consumer preference. The birth of the floating world of fashion is indeed one of the major topics of this study. Finally, the sixth field, to be termed symbolization, covers the messages conveyed by consumer commodities which have entered widely into language as figures of speech: simile, metaphor, metonym and synecdoche. Here commodities function as semantic counters. All material culture is impregnated indirectly by thought, but in the field of symbolization it serves as its direct vehicle. Lévi-Strauss's argument in his study of totemism that animals are not only good to eat but also good to think, may be extended to other commodities.

In the following chapters, each of the six fields is subdivided into essentials, accessories and extras. This subdivision, drawn initially from the field of dress, was found to have useful application in other fields as well. In the field of food, for example, Sidney W. Mintz has argued that between the neolithic revolution and the changes brought by early modernity, most human diets involved a dualism of essential carbohydrates (bread, spaghetti, rice, noodles, porridge, and so on) accompanied by accessory protein, fats or vegetables (garum, bolognese, pomodoro, dal, sweet and sour pork, pickled beancurd), to which one might add an extra component of drinks (beer, wine, mead, tea, coffee, cocoa) to arrive at a trichotomy.[5] Similarly, in the field of shelter, to the essentials of thermoregulation and protection from the weather (cold, heat, humidity) may be added accessory comforts (floor coverings, furniture, blankets and bed linen, windows, privacy) and extra distinctions (napery, cutlery, tableware, pictures, flowers). Indeed, such a triple subdivision may be inherent in any scheme of evaluation. For the basic problem of axiology, the science of values, is not so much the dichotomy of good and bad as the continuum of better and worse. Thus Max Scheler, perhaps the foremost modern philosopher of axiology, argued in favour of a hierarchy of values: sensible, vital, personal and absolute or transpersonal, of which the last, as the valuation of values, may be regarded as lying beyond material culture, though always encompassing it as *summum bonum*. Scheler's axiological scheme is more convincing as a cognitional analysis of evaluation than its main rivals in Aristotelian eudaimonism, Enlightenment utilitarianism or Kantian universalism, while putting the personalism of thinkers as different as J. E. M. McTaggart and G. E. Moore in a wider context. Essentials, accessories and extras may therefore be regarded as an a priori structure which material culture imposes on commodities and consumption.

Material culture imposes value on objects. How does it do this? It has frequently been suggested that it does so because it is a language, a set of signs from which, together with its grammar and syntax, meaningful expression may be drawn. The analogy of material culture with language, sign or codes is useful in drawing attention to aspects of consumer behaviour which are often neglected. Nevertheless, it is only an analogy in the classic Thomist definition in which there is a preponderance of unlikeness over likeness.

First, material culture is less often directly propositional than natural language. It seldom states a meaning defined by internal connotation and external denotation. It is more often non-referential, performative or declaratory. An artefact *may* make a direct statement, or be regarded as such by an audience – as a farmer in Fermanagh, who having unthinkingly painted his gateposts green had them repainted orange overnight by his neighbours, found out – but is uncommon.

Second, material culture is both supralinguistic and infralinguistic. On the one hand, its signs are clearer than speech. Natural language is inexact in its description of sensation and perception. It is difficult to describe symptoms to a doctor, shades of discomfort to a dentist or the cadences of a robin's song in an English January. Even the language of wine, sophisticated though it is, often falls into inanity. Phenomenalism, implausible as a theory of language, is more convincing as a theory of material culture. Thus a couturier can cut to the requirements of a particular figure with an exactness that would baffle the crudities of natural speech to prescribe. Similarly, an interior decorator can assemble a synaesthesia of perspective, colour and light that would be difficult to specify verbally in advance of its implementation. Even in cooking, while recipes specify, there is a difference in results between amateur and professional. In these areas, material culture is superior to language, as some claim sign is superior to speech. On the other hand, material culture is inferior to language. It is inexact in relation to concepts and judgement. Visible to the senses, it may be invisible to the mind, not because it has no meaning, but because it has too many. Signification requires exclusion as well as inclusion. Besides positive logical content, there is negative information content, and every meaning is no meaning. Moreover, in artefacts, the disjuncture between authorial intention, artwork and audience, is wider than it is in texts. Material culture is more open to misunderstanding than language. Hence mindless vandalism, more principled iconoclasm and systematic hostility to materialization as idolatry. Language is polychromatic: it lives in the light, the world of clear and distinct ideas. Material culture is chiaroscuro and crepuscular: it lives in the twilight before dawn or darkness, the world which shows itself because it cannot be spoken of. In these areas, material culture is inferior to language, as some have claimed the unconscious is inferior to the conscious.

Third, material culture is paralinguistic or parabolic. Besides expression in objects, it also operates by impression, receiving objects by which language enriches itself in figures of speech. Owen Barfield argued that much language is congealed metaphor, thus reviving Vico's theory that poetry, which abounds in figures of speech, is older than prose. Commodities are a fecund source of metaphor: daily bread, the whole armour of God, the house built upon a rock, the light of the world, the book of life, the salt of the earth, to take only Biblical examples. In Islamic historiography, metaphor and simile are carried to excess, while a text like the *Mathnavi* of Jelal ad-Din Rumi abounds in parables, such as the Bedouin's gift of rainwater to the Caliph. In China too, material objects entered into the language. Official perquisites were rice bowls, a literati family had 'had the smell of books in it for generations', the red chamber is metonymy for the world of women, peasants eat bitterness, mandarin ducks become images of conjugal happiness, a bell echoes the impermanence of all things. To parallels in speech correspond sacramentals in action: Muslim ablutions, Chinese filial rites, Christian sacraments, though these are perhaps unique in requiring a combination of words and action. Significant gestures join figures of speech in defining material culture's paralinguistic contribution to conceptualization.

Fourth, material culture is at times non-linguistic. It may be non-semiotic, in the sense of having no signification beyond itself, even of a non-propositional kind. It is simply food, shelter or dress, the satisfaction of physiological need with what is closest to hand, even if a choice exists. Buridan did not suppose his ass starved to death. It simply showed that choice need not be based on utilitarian calculus and may entirely lack significance beyond itself. Much material culture, especially in conditions of underdevelopment, is of this kind: behavioural rather than semiotic. Moreover, material culture lacks the necessary articulation of language. Sidney Mintz writes: 'we can eat without meals, but we cannot speak without grammar'.[6] Thus meals are not really a grammar or syntax, food not really a language, though not without sense. Unlike spoken words, the concrete instances of material culture in food, dress and shelter, need not be *paroles* related to a *langue*. They may be simply morphemes which may or may not become the *paroles* which constitute a language, just as not all uttered phonemes become words. Robinson Crusoe, if born on his island, could not have created a language, even if he produced a system of significant patterned sounds, but he would, if he had survived, have produced a material culture in the sense of a mentally ordered set of consumed commodities. Mentality does not equal verbality. Children think before they speak, and material culture can be compared to other forms of pre-verbal or non-verbal mental activity, such as play or art-creation.

By these means, material culture imposes value on objects. What kind of value does it impose, what sort of messages does it send through its quasi-linguistic apparatus? The answer must be a great variety, a polysemia of signification, partly verbalizable, partly not, which runs the whole gamut of Scheler's axiology with its hierarchy of values and corresponding spheres of being.

Take, for example, the field of dress as a quasi-language, with clothes as its speech and actual wardrobes its recorded words. First, dress is sensible. It is thermoregulatory in a pattern relative to other forms of thermoregulation in food, shelter and climate. To some extent one form of thermoregulation may be substituted for another, and important differences of civilization stem from such substitution. Second, dress is vital. It conveys and receives messages to and from the living social group. Passively it conforms to or rejects basic canons of modesty and propriety. Swimwear is acceptable on the beach, but not in Piccadilly even in the hottest summer. Going topless may be acceptable on one beach, unacceptable on another. Actively, dress on the one hand proclaims age and gender distinctions while occasionally defying them. Mutton should not be dressed to look like lamb and his should not be hers, but granny shoes and glasses may be chic and unisex styles enhance femininity. On the other hand, dress asserts social status and creates social distance. Clothes make the man and cloth caps and bowler hats define social identities. Uniform, essentially an invention of the seventeenth century, displays social function in the military, the police and the clerical collar. Even the doctor's white coat is as much declaratory as utilitarian. Third, dress is personal. It projects variously the personage – the judge, the graduate, the bride; the personal – the yuppie, *bon chic bon genre*, the slick chick, the dumb blonde, country tweeds and Savile Row; and the person – extrovert ostentation and introvert understatement, the black and white of thought, the red or pink of feeling, the green of sensation and the blue of intuition. Clothes reveal: furs for Dianas who get what they go for, florals for Persephones who go for what they get, two-toned shoes for Don Giovannis, country brogues for Don Ottavios. Persons are complex, so clothes can simultaneously project the prostitute and proclaim the lady or combine the bimbo and the bluestocking. Perfumes may be signatures or altered to suit the mood.

Finally, dress at least points to the suprapersonal. Cavalier exuberance, Roundhead or Jansenist sobriety, the veil in Islam, the Quaker's hat, the skull cap of the Orthodox Jew, express values beyond the individual. In sixteenth-century Algiers, as in twentieth-century Nigeria, change of dress was a mark of conversion, even a motive for it. The Inquisition in places like Palermo took the wearing of Muslim clothes as prima facie evidence of renegation. The barber who shaved the renegade was often the surgeon who circumcised him, and converts admitted to being attracted by the bright colours then fashionable in the Maghreb. In the seventeenth century, the Manchus imposed a particular hairstyle, the queue, on their Chinese subjects as a mark of loyalty to the new mandate of heaven vested in the Ch'ing dynasty. In the nineteenth century, the Taiping rebels, who regarded Manchu rule as unnatural and demonic, wore their hair long and suffered death for it when their capital, Nanking, fell in 1864. In early twentieth-century China, the cutting off of the queue became a sign of both republicanism and modernity, just as in Turkey, Ataturk's secularism was expressed through the outlawry of the Islamic fez. Even in Christendom, it is not long since hat and gloves were *de rigueur* in Anglican churches, black lace in Catholic, while Mormon missionaries indicate themselves by their suits and Rastafarians by their dreadlocks. In politics we have seen Mao suits and Nehru jackets, Sukarno caps, Arafat *keffiyas*, and Anthony Eden hats, appeasement umbrellas and prime ministerial handbags. Thus religious or ideological orientations are readily expressed in dress codes and clothing choices.

Through both its semiotic form and semantic content material culture conveys a wide range of meanings, especially evaluations. It does this even in situations of economic scarcity or social constraint. Signification through material objects is no privilege of modernity. Grave goods and standards of dying are the stock in trade of the archaeology of mind as far back as the palaeolithic, as Marshall Sahlins has shown. For later periods ceramics and building sites provide silent but telling evidence to the presence or absence of social stratification and political centrality. Material culture was a natural field for peer polity interaction and emulation, just as in classical antiquity, building and utilities, especially baths, were fields for competitive philanthropy. Nevertheless, it can be accepted that material culture can provide more meaning where greater choice is economically possible and socially permitted. Here the discussion must advance from the structure of material culture to its conjunctures.

(2) THE THREE CONJUNCTURES OF MATERIAL CULTURE

Between classical antiquity and the present, consumption in both China and the West has been subject, at the highest level of generalization, to three major revolutions: the *limes* lifestyle, globalization and mass consumption. This section outlines this progression as a whole against the background of consumption patterns in antiquity.

Despite the splendour of its archaeology, antiquity till its last act was fundamentally an age of scarcity where the consumer had little choice. The splendour, characteristically in buildings in the Graeco-Roman West and in clothes in China, together with the brilliance of culture, was concentrated in cities which did not diffuse their lifestyle to the countryside, indeed remained largely unrelated to it. This element of scarcity appears in every field of consumption.

In food, the basic carbohydrates most widely used: barley, oats, rye in the West, foxtailed and panicled millet in China; were not the highest yielding or the most nutritious. Wheat and rice, today's more appetizing basics, were then only for a minority. Food accessories, too, were limited. In the Mediterranean, fish, fish products such as *garum*, and olives were the most important, but fishing was purely inshore and Western antiquity would not have known the herring and the cod except episodically. In China, still essentially the northern provinces in the valley of the Yellow river, there may, paradoxically in view of later history, have been more meat under the Han than in the West, but since Chinese agriculture had already rejected pastoralism in favour of exclusive intensive arable farming, the best of it would have been from refuse-fed pigs. Food luxuries were few and far between. Sugar was still confined to Southeast Asia. The West had no oranges, China, till the reign of Han Wu-ti (187–140 BC) no grapes. The West had no coffee, China as yet little tea. Neither had cocoa or chocolate or, in the case of alcoholic drinks, any spirits. Poets praised the wines they had, but they would not have been much appreciated by modern connoisseurs. In dress, though China produced and exported silks and Egypt produced and exported high grade damask linens, most of north China was clad in hemp cloth, just as most of the West was clad in rough flax cloth. Wool was known in both areas, but in default of more pastoralism, and selective breeding which later produced the Cistercian clip, and the merino, and greater availability of fuller's earth, it remained neither abundant nor of good quality. In shelter, it was the same. Augustus may have found Rome in brick and left it in marble, but this applied to public rather than private buildings. Neither he, nor his successor in urban renewal Trajan, did much for rural housing. In China, the Han capitals of Ch'ang-an and Lo-yang were palace cities, without even the great *insulae* or rookeries of the classical West. North China, short of timber, was poorly housed and the northwest remained into the twentieth century the part of the world where the highest percentage of the population was lodged in caves.

In utilities, antiquity did better. It produced the beginnings of domestic hydraulics with the urban aqueduct, cisterns, *cloaca*, baths and fountains in the West, and the beginnings of hydraulic agriculture with the embankment, barrage and spillway in the East, but neither used coal to any extent domestically. Vegetable oils were available for lamps, but candles were dependent on animal fats or beeswax, neither abundant. In information technology, China did not invent paper till the second century AD and the West could not grow papyrus anywhere else except Egypt and, to a much lesser extent, Sicily. Inscription on stone, wood or waxed tablet was the primary method of recording data, as silk, parchment or slate for writing remained in short supply. The basic scripts, alphabetical and ideographic, had long been invented and accepted as part of civilized living, but in the West literacy remained subordinate to oralcy. Plato felt one should know Homer by heart rather than read him. For a long time too in the West, to read meant to read aloud. The young Augustine was surprised to find Ambrose reading silently to himself. China, with a largely non-phonetic script, separated literacy and oralcy much earlier and never developed a tradition of oratory and rhetoric. Still, in both East and West literacy was minoritarian, almost by intention, held back by the preference for the scroll over the book which inhibited ready reference. Against this background of scarcity in commodities, their use in symbolism, though perhaps for that very reason highly sophisticated, could rest only on a limited repertoire of images.

The relative backwardness of antiquity, despite its intellectual brilliance, has been long debated. Long ago, Gordon Childe and the Marxists blamed slavery, which, it was argued, inhibited technological innovation and application. In fact, slavery was not a major institution in ancient China or ancient Egypt, whether Pharaonic or Ptolemaic, indeed was not a *dominant* institution anywhere in antiquity. Slavery may have been less inhibiting economically than marriage endogamy which impeded the flow of information between social micro-units. Household slavery at least enlarged the family circle and widened technological horizons. As in the case of Christian renegades in the Ottoman empire, slavery was not the disease, but an attempt at cure. Technologically, the backwardness of antiquity has been exaggerated. Ancient China had notable achievements to its credit in the iron and steel industry which underpinned its agriculture. In the West, it now seems, thanks to the work of Amouretti and others, that the development of efficient equine harness, formerly attributed to introduction from outside in the Dark Ages, should be attributed to antiquity.[7] If innovation was not always followed through in application, this is the common lot of invention in all civilizations. In fact, late antiquity in both East and West, far from stagnating technologically, shows signs of accelerating, with such things as the invention of paper in China AD *c.*100 and the advance of the woollen industry shown in Roman Pompeii. Indeed, it might be argued that antiquity declined because outmoded by its own technological advances.

More recently, Paul Kennedy and post-Marxists have argued that empires decline because of military and political overextension and consequent neglect of investment in social, economic and educational infrastructures. In the case of China and Rome, such neglect is not easy to demonstrate. Indeed, the massive investment in new religions might suggest the opposite. Nor is the overextension self-evident. Both Han China and the Roman empire might have done better to have occupied more barbarian territory rather than less as originally envisaged by both Han Wu-ti and Augustus. Not overextension, but exclusivity, autarchy, cultural isolationism and the attempt to be windowless were the faults of the classical empires. Barbarians, after all, fought to get in, not to keep out. Not too much but too little of the waters of the Orontes flowed into the Tiber. If this analysis is correct, it is easier to understand the first two consumer revolutions, the *limes* lifestyle and globalization, since both of them involved what may be called disenclavement: an opening of compartments.

The *limes* was a major institution in both Eastern and Western antiquity, as was first observed by Sir Aurel Stein. Rooted in the distinction between civilization and barbarity, a *limes* implied demarcation, control of persons and things, communication by signal and road, and fortification. Fortification did not necessarily mean continuous walls, as recent research on the so-called Great Wall of China has shown, but it did mean prearranged battlefields, troop concentrations and the requisite commissariat.[8] Some *limes* were supposed to be self-supporting. The Chinese in particular were addicted to the notion of *t' un-t'ien*, or military agricultural colonies, as a means of avoiding costly long distance supply. In practice, few *limes* were or could be self-supporting. As both the Vindolanda tablets and the Etzingol strips indicate, *limes* were areas of high consumption. Armies are naturally extravagant and men in danger feel entitled to give themselves special treatment. They therefore imposed a burden on their rear areas and homelands, which gave rise to political frictions, especially in the third century AD. *Limes* were also areas of different consumption. Enemies exchange more than weapons. While barbarians were excluded at one level, that of formal military attack, they were included at another, as traders, servants, prostitutes, informers, recruits, *foederati*, local specialists of one kind or another. Similarly, both the Romans and the

Chinese developed spies and barbarian experts. *Limes* were places of cultural osmosis. They developed a distinctive lifestyle in food, dress and shelter, sometimes symbolized by a new religion or ideology, such as, in the case of the Roman West by the pseudo-oriental freemasonry of Mithraism. From the third century AD, as a result of the militarization of politics and interventions of the frontier in the capitals, this lifestyle began to be adopted by an elite at least of the civil population of the homelands. This process was carried further by the so-called barbarian invasions of the fourth and fifth centuries in both China and the West: invasions of armies rather than peoples, a sort of inversion of the *limes*. It was carried furthest by the greatest inversion of the *limes*, the Muslim invasions of the seventh and eighth centuries. The result was a radical change in the consumption pattern of antiquity: the revolution of the *limes* lifestyle.

Limes were diverse. They were conditioned by what they faced. In the West, the northern *limes* faced the forest or the sea. Forest society, based on mixed arable and pastoral agriculture, was culturally deprived, but technologically little inferior to the Graeco-Roman world, especially in metallurgy. In the south, on the other hand, from Mauretania to Mesopotamia, the *limes* faced the desert. Desert society, based on oasis agriculture and camel-centred nomadic or transhumant pastoralism, was provincial rather than deprived, but, till the coming of Islam, lacked cohesion of its own.[9] In the East, the Han and its successor states, the San-kuo and Western Chin, were involved in four *limes*. First, a northern *limes* faced the steppe: a society based on Turco-Mongol horse-centred nomadic pastoralism, whose political instability as much as its economic needs pushed it towards trade or raid relations with China.[10] Second, in the northwest, a *limes* faced a combination of steppe, desert, oasis and plateau. This was the interface society of Koko-nor, Ninghsia and the Kansu panhandle, where intensive agriculture and ranch herding coexisted with two kinds of nomadic pastoralism. Third, a southern *limes* faced mountain and forest, the haunted and malarial worlds of pre-Chinese aboriginals, who spoke variants of Malay, Vietnamese, Thai, Burmese and Lolo. It was a pre-state world for the most part, whose resistance to sinicization continued to the nineteenth century, when it was finally reduced to quarantinized enclaves. Finally, in the southwest, a *limes* faced a combination of mountain, plateau, upland valleys and immense gorges. This was the interface society of Yunnan, western Szechwan and eastern Tibet, where organized mini-states, based on agriculture and pastoralism, both posed a threat to China and provided a gateway to Tibet, India and Southeast Asia.

Despite this diversity, the various contributions were sufficiently convergent to justify speaking of a single *limes* lifestyle. First, in food, the *limes* lifestyle shifted the balance from carbohydrates to proteins and fats. One indication of this was an increase, successively in China, Islam and Western Christendom, in the consumption of salt. In the Dark and Early Middle ages, it rose from 5lb a head to 7½lb a head. In pre-modern societies, the level of salt distribution is an index of the consumption of meat, fish, cheese and butter. The carbohydrate eater may need salt more physiologically, but it is the protein and fat eater who will consume more of it. The *limes* ate meat, particularly on the northern *limes*, but also on the Islamic frontiers. Bedouin may not have been great meat eaters in the normal course of nomad living, but Arab soldiers encamped in classical antiquity as a result of Islam were and they passed the habit on to their Turkish slaves and supplanters. It was the *limes* which put the roast at the centre of the meal, not every meal of course, but on high days and holidays. The roast, built up to and built away from, provided an alternative structure to the classic carbohydrate centrepiece with accessory side dishes or the Chinese model of several concurrent side dishes superimposed on a base or supplement of rice. The influence of the *limes* modified both content and form.

Second, in dress, the *limes* lifestyle shifted the balance from vegetable or insect fabrics (hemp, linen, silk) to animal fabrics, wool, hair, and especially as accessories, fur. The end of antiquity meant an enlargement of agriculture to include a larger pastoral component. Hence there were more animals both to eat and wear. Access was increased to the fur-bearing wild animals of the steppe, the marsh, the desert and the various degrees of forest – fringe, middle and deep. The *limes* lifestyle involved a certain militarization: the wearing of battledress in civilian life; the increased use of trousers, appropriate to horsemen, less appropriate to citizens and mandarins; and the adoption of long Hunnic hair styles in both east and west. In form, clothes became tighter rather than looser, more tailored and less draped. As a result, there was an accentuation of gender differences and an increase in the carrying of weapons, as much as a dress accessory as a means of private security. In China, where the *limes* lifestyle went less far than in Islam or Christendom, personal weapons never became a normal part of dress and gender dimorphism was less marked.

Third, in shelter, the *limes* lifestyle shifted the balance from the palace and the town house to the villa, the castle and the hunting lodge. The villas of northern France and southern Britain, though they might receive the same name as the pleasure houses of Roman aristocrats in Italy, performed different roles in the organization of rural space. They were no longer simple appendages of the city, but suppliers of the *limes*, autarchic units in their own right, or points of defence which could survive the fall of both city and *limes*. Similarly in China, in the period following the fall of the Han empire, a militarized aristocracy, served by a host of specialized retainers whom it protected from taxation and conscription by the state, formed self-sufficient estates which were kingdoms in themselves. In both west and east, form followed function in emphasizing storage, workshops and fortification in layout rather than social amenity. The castle grew out of the *castrum* rather than out of the city.

Finally, to all kinds of consumption, the *limes* lifestyle brought a new lavishness, an enhanced propensity to consume, and, in most cases, an actual increase in consumptivity, that is, consumption per head. On northern *limes*, where barbarian invasions were really armies in search of a state, generals and aristocrats, officers and gentlemen, distinguished themselves from common soldiers and native civilians by standards of consumption in life or death. In China, when the northern Wei, strongest of *limes* dynasties, built a new capital at Loyang in the late fifth century, it far outdid in magnificence and urban sophistication the Han capitals it replaced. To season the food, and in particular the meat it consumed, the salt works at An-i *hsien* (salt) lake just across the Yellow river, was redeveloped by the new technique of successive basin solar evaporation. Salt consumption per capita in the area doubled. In the West, a century and a half later, when one of the weakest of *limes* dynasties wished to celebrate a royal funeral in East Anglia, it could produce the unparalleled splendour of the Sutton Hoo treasure. In the south, Islam was born in scarcity, but it lived in luxury. It was a desert feast *en permanence* at the expense of the sedentarists initially, though these increasingly participated as slaves, clients, renegades and mercenaries. If the decline and fall of the ancient empires produced consumer contraction in some directions, it produced consumer expansion in others, and broke out of a circle of scarcity. It was a first consumer revolution.

The enlargement of ancient consumption begun by the *limes* lifestyle was extended more radically by the second consumer revolution: globalization between 1400 and 1800. Globalization is the subject of the next section and forms the ongoing theme of the subsequent chapters. Here only its role in the triple series of consumer revolutions needs to be established. Globalization brought a whole range of new resources, materials and commodities within the horizons of consumers. It unified east–west and north–south, different temperate zones and temperate zones and the tropics. The enlargement of consumer horizons was considerable everywhere, and greatest in Europe, but it none the less remained subject to limitations. The most serious of these were problems of transportation and corruption and the limited possibilities of acclimatization for exotic flora and fauna. Corruption could sometimes be dealt with by drying or salting, as in the case of farshore fisheries, but in most cases it could not. The full effects of globalization could not be felt until refrigeration in the nineteenth century and air freight in the twentieth. Till then, globalization, for the consumer, was to a considerable extent a matter of time- and distance-resistant vegetable substances. Consequently, it affected food and dress more than shelter, utilities less than information and symbolism.

For globalization affected the imagination and the mind as well as the body. The old Aristotelian cosmos had been exploded, as José de Acosta realized as he shivered on a mountain in Ecuador on a Christmas day in the 1590s and for the first time laughed at the *Meteorology* of the Stagyrite. Globalization not only satisfied old needs in a new way, it also suggested entirely new needs, especially in accessories and luxuries. Herein it laid the foundations for the third consumer revolution, that of mass consumption underpinned by industrialization in the nineteenth and twentieth centuries. The explosion of the global revolution prepared the way for the implosion of the industrial revolution.

The relationship between the global revolution and the industrial revolution, however, is not easy to define exactly. First, a distinction needs to be made between the economic flowering of the eighteenth century, based on existing resources and sources of energy and producing traditional materials and commodities in greater abundance, and the economic transformation of the nineteenth century, based on new resources and sources of energy and producing hitherto unknown materials and commodities. Mantroux's commercial revolution, extended by Yen-p'ing Hao to China, which linked globalization to industrialization, applies much better to the efflorescence than to the transformation, but it fails to take account of basic discontinuities. The entrepôt cities of the commercial revolution were not the smokestack cities of the industrial revolution. London was not Manchester. Venice was not Milan. Canton and Shanghai were not Mukden and Harbin. Moreover, in both Europe and China, the rise of mass consumption was accompanied by a change in dominant macroregion.

Second, recent research indicates that the notion of primitive accumulation as a necessary base of the industrial revolution and a link between it and the antecedent oceanic revolution must be abandoned.[11] The early industrial revolution did not require massive investment. It needed different investment and the eye of the entrepreneur to see markets where none had seen them before. Capital came from a variety of sources, among them no doubt overseas commerce, but there is no reason to think it was specially privileged. For example, some of the capital of the Trieste company passed into early Belgian industrialization, but more came from Mendel's rural proto-industrialization. A similar pattern may be found with regard to industrialization in Turin and Milan. J. A. Williamson supposed that the capital for the industrial revolution in Britain came from the spoils of India, but F. L. Furber showed that there were no spoils, that the nabobs, who anyway played a minuscule role in industry, exploited not the Indian peasant but the English taxpayer, and that the *raj*, like most imperialisms, cost more than it paid.

Third, consumer globalization was not necessarily favourable to industrialization at all. Contemporary mercantilists in Europe believed that the drain of specie to the East to pay for exotic consumer commodities was injurious to Europe's economic development. It reduced liquidity, raised interest rates and capped investment at home. Similarly, modern historians such as Jean Delumeau and Bartolomé Bennassar, have diagnosed overconsumption, unproductive investment, and borrowing to spend on high living and spectacle, as reasons for the decline of Baroque Catholic civilization in the Mediterranean.[12] The external expansion of Europe, they argue, pre-empted the internal development of Europe. Only when consumption had been restrained by seventeenth-century depression and redirected by eighteenth-century enlightenment could serious industrial implosion take place. Nevertheless, if the Baroque world in Rome, Valladolid and Naples did live beyond its means, its extravagance was not entirely in vain. For if globalization was related to industrialization, it was most likely through its long-term effects on consumption. Globalization set in motion trends in demand which it could not satisfy. By naturalizing exotics it created a potential for import substitution, especially in textiles. By limited foreign variegation of commodities, it opened the way to unlimited domestic diversification. Over and above this or that commodity, it altered the notion of consumption and the character of consumers. The combination of these effects produced consumerism which is a necessary institutional component in industrial mass economies and modern fashion-led societies. Globalization was not the sufficient reason for industrialization; but the significance of the consumerism it generated justifies further consideration of what globalization really consisted in.

(3) GLOBALIZATION 1400–1800

At first sight, globalization appears clearly defined and already well studied. It refers primarily to the Great Discoveries, from Prince Henry the Navigator's capture of Ceuta in 1415 to the death of Captain Cook in Tahiti in 1779, which formed the basis for the expansion of Europe. Further denotations are suggested by the titles of J. H. Parry's brilliant textbook *Europe and a Wider World* and Donald Lach's incompleted programme *Asia in the Making of Europe*. More abstractly, J. A. Williamson wrote of these developments as the Oceanic Revolution. None of these definitions, however, is sufficient when globalization is used to refer to the second revolution in the history of consumption.

First, globalization was not exclusively European. Besides the history of the establishment of European links with Black Africa, America, East Asia, Southeast Asia and Central Asia, there is the history of Chinese relations with Western Eurasia, Black Africa, America, Central Asia and Southeast Asia. Globalization had more than one point of origin. Even the expansion of Europe, which became the dominant centre, was in part initiated by events outside Europe, in particular the Mongolian explosion and its subsequent diffusion of information. Second, while most attention has been directed to commodities moving east and west between developed economies, less attention has been paid to commodities moving north and south from relatively backward economies to more advanced ones; from the frigid north in the case of Europe, from the torrid south in the case of China. Third, while geographers have long been aware that discovery is not the same as incorporation into cartography, commodity historians have been less aware that points of origin are not the same as centres of reception. Supply is not automatically followed by demand, and for a resource to become a material or a commodity it must be consumed. Consumption is an independent not a dependent variable, with a history of its own. Globalization of commodities must refer to the consumers as well as to the producers or distributors. These three necessary enlargements of the notion of globalization will be addressed below in more detail.

First, globalization was not wholly European. There was also the expansion of China which played a significant role in the establishment of a world commodities market. This expansion has often been overlooked, for two reasons. First, like the expansion of Rus and Muscovy in the West, it was an expansion by land contiguously, whereas the expansion of Western Europe was by sea discontiguously. It was less expansion than manifest destiny on the American model. Second, the expansion within China proper, the traditional 18 provinces, was at the expense of, for the most part, pre-political peoples, who did not form distinct states. Its record therefore consisted not of conquests and conquistadors, but of the suppression of rebellions and mutinies by Han Chinese officials, the last major instance of these episodes occurring in the mid-nineteenth century.[13] The Chinese expression for the imposition of direct rule on aboriginals was *kai-t'u k'uei-liu*, 'reform the local, return to the regular', in appearance a reversion to normalcy, whereas in fact it meant a replacement of local rajahs and headmen by Chinese bureaucrats.

Within the area now covered by China south and east of the Wall, two long-term historical tendencies can be seen: centripetal and centrifugal. Archaeologists at one time interpreted the pre-history of Chinese space in terms of a centrifugal movement from what was called the Chinese nuclear area in Shensi, Shansi and Honan. Such a movement did exist and was the basis of the expansion of dynastic China, both pre-imperial (Hsia, Shang and Chou) and imperial (Ch'in, Han and subsequent dynasties). More recent archaeology, however, has shown that this centrifugal movement was preceded by a centripetal movement from the coastal circumference of Chinese space, where the language would not have been even proto-Chinese, but rather Thai, Vietnamese or Malay. The bronze age of the early dynastic or San-tai period was based on these coastal neolithics which combined onshore fishing with an arable crop: soya beans, millet, rice in one of two forms, yams and taro. Behind this agriculture in turn lay the concentration of population and information produced by the rise in sea levels at the end of the last ice age which swamped the ancient Indonesian continent of Sunda-land and converted it into an archipelago. China therefore was built on Southeast Asian foundations and its subsequent centrifugal movement was a reflux of an antecedent centripetal movement. Similarly, in long perspective, the growing importance of the maritime provinces, the seas and the ocean in recent Chinese history may be seen as the harbinger of a new centripetal flood. A future China must be built not merely on Southeast Asia but on global foundations.

The centrifugal movement, the conquest of China by the Chinese and the projection of Chinatowns overseas, took place in three overlapping stages. First, there was the assimilation of the Lower and Middle Yangtze, which by 1300 had become the dominant macroregion, with two-thirds of the population.[14] This assimilation may be compared in European history to the conversion of Germany and Central Europe. It, too, was a product of an inversion of the *limes*, barbarian invasions and the establishment of new kingdoms; in this case that of Sun Ch'uan and his successors in Wu, followed by the Eastern Chin, Liu Sung, Ch'i, Liang and Ch'en. Though under the T'ang, 618–960, the Yangtze macroregion had only a quarter of China's population, its impact, amplified through the Grand Canal, was considerable in terms of resources. It has been compared to the partial assimilation of America by the Europeans in the sixteenth century. Next, there was the assimilation of coastal China south of the Nan-shan; Kwangtung, Kwangsi and Fukien. This, too, was achieved by 1300, but more slowly, erratically and less completely, so that to this day, there is a substantial Chuang or Thai community in Kwangsi. To Han China, the whole coastal macroregion was Yueh, or Viet as it would then have been pronounced; the land of non-Chinese people speaking proto-Vietnamese, some cooked or civilized who practised wet-rice agriculture, some raw or barbarian who did not. The First Emperor's viceroy Chao T'o had to go native to survive after the fall of the Ch'in, and as late as the T'ang, Canton, though superficially sinified, was a Southeast Asian shantytown and estuarial emporium rather than a Chinese mandarin city. Kwangtung only became fully Chinese under the Southern Han, one of the ten kingdoms in the interdynastic disorder between the T'ang and the Sung, Fukien only under the Sung, and Kwangsi in its entirety never.

Finally, there was the projection of Chinatowns overseas in Southeast Asia and beyond; not only in Sydney, San Francisco and Vladivostok, but everywhere where there are cities and where Singaporean and Taiwanese finance can establish itself. The process began with the expansion of Chinese shipping and overseas commerce under the Southern Sung. Visiting merchants turned into resident businessmen as local opportunity attracted and the unsympathetic attitude to private commerce of the early Ming repelled. Cheng Ho's voyages in the early fifteenth century, among their several purposes, sought to control rather than promote this commerce. They initiated a series of routs and rallies for the overseas Chinese communities, as one alien thalassocracy succeeded another in Southeast Asia. Despite occasional appalling losses of people and capital, on balance these communities were left in 1900 in a commanding position in Manila, Jakarta, Saigon, Bangkok and Singapore. In the nineteenth and early twentieth centuries, remittances home from these communities more than equilibrated the mainland's deficitary balance of visible trade. In effect, they financed China's early modernization, as well as supplying in Sun Yat-sen one of its most notable political leaders. These communities would still be performing this function today had they and their world not been repudiated by the Chinese Communists.

Second, globalization involved not only movements east and west, but also north and south. In the West, the movement north towards Russia and Canada took two forms. On the one hand, there was the movement by land into the *taiga* and *tundra* in search of fur-bearing animals, notably the sable.[15] This movement was initiated by the republic of Novgorod in response to Hanseatic demand for high-quality fur for the princely courts of fourteenth- and fifteenth-century Western Europe. Subsequently, it was taken over and consummated by the grand duchy of Muscovy, which sold as much via Cracow and Leipzig as via the Baltic ports. This extension of the fur catchment area had significant effects on European dress, and also, when extended to eastern Siberia, on that of China via the trade at Kiakhta after 1727. On the other hand, there was the movement by sea into cold sub-Arctic waters in search of fish and later whales. Laurier Turgeon has shown that at the end of the sixteenth century, the volume of shipping involved in the northern fisheries was little less than that of the *Carrera de las Indias*.[16] European diet was changed by cod, whether fresh, salted, dried or smoked. Whale oil in candles and lamps enlarged the utility of light, while whale bone for a time stiffened fabrics in fashion. Moreover, the movements north could subsequently be transferred south to become the sealing and whaling phase in the early histories of Australia, New Zealand and the sub-Antarctic islands.

In the East, Chinese expansion south was a factor in the development of Java, the first major commercial centre below the equator.[17] Java is first mentioned in Chinese sources in the fifth century when it was visited by Buddhist monks returning by sea from pilgrimage to India. In 721–5 the Tantric astronomer I-hsing visited the island to measure latitudes south of the equator. In 1079 a Sumatran ruler restored a Taoist temple at Canton and in 1129 the Southern Sung emperor conferred a title on a king of Java. The considerable number of Chinese shards, from the fifth to the twelfth centuries, found on the northern coast of Java, indicate both the volume of the trade and one of China's contributions to it. In return for porcelain, silks and copper cash, China imported aromatics, pepper and fine spices. In a well-known passage, Marco Polo noted that for every ship which went from Christendom to Alexandria for pepper, a hundred went from Zaiton (Ch'uan-chou in Fukien) to Java. From these contacts came resident communities, a Chinese consul being mentioned in a Javanese copper inscription as early as 860. These communities, the *hua-ch'iao* or flowery bridge, however, did not really take off until the Sung-Yüan period. They reached their *floruit* in the late Ming when the trade of Southeast Asia was dominated by Sino-Islamic sultanates: Demak, Japara, Gresik, Cirebon and Bantam on Java, Acheh in Sumatra and Malacca on the Malay peninsula. The sultanates survived Portuguese attempts at hegemony in the sixteenth century, but succumbed to more aggressive Dutch attacks in the seventeenth century. The massacre of the Chinese in Batavia in 1740 was one of the worst disasters ever suffered by the *hua-ch'iao*. Yet the community rose again to be massacred once more in 1965 in the wake of the failed Communist coup. By 1992, however, the Chinese community, now under Catholic rather than Muslim, Confucian or Marxist colours, was once more an economic force. The Huang family, former sugar kings, now ran conglomerates from New York, Amsterdam, Bangkok and Singapore.

Denys Lombard has emphasized the Muslim character of early Chinese expansion to the far south; what he calls the Islamic moment in Chinese history. For most Muslims, the Mongolian explosion was a disaster, only absorbed with difficulty and at the price of post-traumatic stress and sclerosis. For Islam in China, however, both Turkish speaking and Chinese speaking, it was an opportunity. Muslims served Qubilai as military engineers, fiscal experts and bankers both when he was an Il-khan in Tibet and west China and when, after 1260, he became Great Khan. His conquest of Nan-chao, which implanted the once substantial Muslim community of Yunnan, was designed not only to outflank the Southern Sung, but also to create a springboard for an independent *ulus* for Qubilai in Southeast Asia. Muslims in China generally benefited from Qubilai's patronage. Ibn Battuta found large, well-organized communities in all the major cities. It was from these that the religious and commercial leaders of the mercantile sultanates, in Java and elsewhere, came. Islam in Indonesia spread from east to west, just as, at the same time, the Ottoman empire spread from west to east. Once Islam became established, particularly when it was adopted by the inland empire of Mataram, the connection between China trade and Muslim mission was relaxed. The Chinatowns reverted to Confucianism or the typical Chinese mix of Buddhist, Taoist and family cults. The former Sino-Islamic connection therefore tended to be overlooked until it was rediscovered by Lombard. It was active, however, when the southbound trade from China had its greatest impact on world trade by communicating its dynamism to the newcomers: Arabs, Portuguese, Dutch and English. For the West did not simply bring capitalism to the East. It also learnt it from the East, especially as regards consumption.

Third, globalization must refer to the consumers as well as the producers or distributors, the centres of reception as well as the points of origin. As a result of the expansions of Europe and China, east and west, north and south, the range of commodities everywhere increased. American food plants, tobacco and specie went to China. Chinese silk, tea, porcelain and rhubarb went to Europe. Indian raw cotton went to China, Indian finished cottons went to Europe. Sugar for Europe and China was multiplied in the Caribbean and Java, in Brazil and Thailand. The search for fur for Europe and China was extended from Siberia to the Pacific, both north and south. It remains, however, to ask: where were these commodities received and by whom consumed? Beyond the structure of discovery and transportation, the familiar *ports*, *routes*, *traffics* of the French series, there was also a structure and conjuncture of consumption.

The most general answer must be that initially the new commodities were received in courtly capitals and were consumed by aristocrats or bureaucrats. The sixteenth century saw the rise in both Europe and China of cities which set new levels of high and conspicuous consumption. These cities owed their original impetus to government. Nanking began as a military headquarters and naval dockyard. Naples only took off as the capital of Spanish viceroys. Their subsequent development, however, owed more to the societies, secreted no doubt by royal administrations, but increasingly independent of them. Nanking, having ceased to be more than a second capital in the fifteenth century, became instead the playground of the Kiangnan scholar gentry. Valladolid, abandoned by the Habsburg court in favour of Madrid in the sixteenth century, became instead the parade ground of judges, ecclesiastics and nobility. In Rome, it was the cardinals rather than the austere Counter-Reformation court who set standards of consumption. In Naples, urban renewal, begun by the viceroys, was completed by the barons and the religious houses. In Constantinople, spending power was concentrated, not in the Seraglio or the Porte, but in the *waqfs*, the charitable foundations established by members of the Ottoman ruling institution to safeguard their accumulations from confiscation. In Algiers, capital of the Maghreb, the big spenders were not so much the beylebeys or the pashas, but the *rais*, the corsair captains, and the Janissary chiefs of the military corps.[18] Whatever the precise political arrangements, consumption was everywhere dominated by aristocracies. It was part of their self-image, their class pride, their demand for recognition from superiors, peers and inferiors; what Francis Fukuyama has called their *megalothymia*.[19]

This dominance was not altered by the universal crisis of the princely state in the seventeenth century. Whether the court won, as in the Habsburg lands and France, or the country won, as in the Netherlands, or whether there was a compromise, as in England, or a rationalization, as in China, the aristocracy retained its leadership in society. The most striking manifestation was the great aristocratic mansion: Vaux Le Vicomte, the Belvedere, Blenheim, Stowe, the *yali* on the Bosphorus, the villas of the *rais* in Algiers, the princely *fu* in Peking or the fictional Ningkuofu at Nanking in the *Dream of the Red Chamber*. Besides the shelter they provided, these mansions were the stage for prestige advertising in food, dress, utilities, information and symbolism for the aristocracy and their clients and for demonstration effect to the rest of society.

The courtly cities were never fully aware of the sources of the wealth which they spent so lavishly. They therefore lived beyond their means, 'outside reality' as a contemporary critic of Valladolid put it.[20] Consequently, they failed to save or invest, sterilized enterprise and entombed liquidity. In this way they precipitated the worldwide depression of the seventeenth century, a crisis essentially of overconsumption and underinvestment. From this depression, some of the courtly cities, among them Nanking and Valladolid, never fully recovered. Nevertheless, the courtly cities and their artistocracies were not entirely sterile even in purely economic terms. They displayed new levels of consumption and implanted new needs. Valladolid pioneered the secular theatre, Rome the oratorio, Naples the opera. Their increased propensity to consume may have exhausted their own fortunes, but it stimulated others to save and invest. Lyon, the hands of France, developed by supplying black velvet to Paris, its heart and brain. They multiplied literacy, amassed information and established communication networks. The very concept of news comes from sixteenth-century Rome. Networks, news and novelty laid the infrastructure for the virtually new phenomenon of fashion. By surcharging and redirecting consumption, fashion became the mother of consumerism in its modern form.

(4) CONSUMERISM

If material culture in Europe and China was transformed in the period of globalization, it was chiefly by the agency of consumerism. Consumerism appeared first in China, under the Sung, especially the Southern Sung. It is evident already in Marco Polo's astonished description of

Quinsai (Hsing-ts'ai, the temporary Southern Sung capital of Hang-chou) and Zaiton (Ch'uan-chou in Fukien) the Sinoport from which Chinese enterprise south was conducted. Hang-chou was the largest city in the world. From Polo's account, it may have had a population of six million. His description of its wealth and lifestyle is confirmed by Chinese evidence and the testimony of Ibn Battuta. With the possible exception of the Northern Sung capital of K'ai-feng, it was the first city to be dominated by consumerism. But what is meant by this? Here, consumerism will be characterized in terms first of conceptual connotation and then of empirical denotation. Characterization, however, must be distinguished from preconditions, causes and consequences, which will be examined briefly at the end of this section.

First, then, consumerism as connotation and concept. In the encyclical *Centesimus Annus*, in which he brought Catholic social teaching up to date, John-Paul II wrote: 'A given culture reveals its overall understanding of life through the choices it makes in production and consumption. It is here that *the phenomenon of consumerism* arises.' Consumerism is more than consumption. It is consumption at a high level and on the basis of particular scales of values. Thus in another passage, the Pope spoke of 'the affluent society or consumer society'. The Pope was critical of the values on which he supposed consumerism to be based, but he did not deny that they existed. On the contrary, their existence was essential to consumerism: 'These criticisms are directed not so much against an economic system as against an ethical or cultural system.'[21] Consumerism is not the same as consumption and consumers, just as capitalism is not the same as capital or capitalists. There is the difference, however, that, while capitalists frequently oppose capitalism in the sense of a free market, consumers seldom oppose consumerism, though ecologists sometimes encourage them to do so. Consumption need not imply consumers. It may refer to the final state of production, whether in use, waste or unusability. Consumers do imply consumption, but in conditions of scarcity and limited choice, their degree of conscious activity might be minimal. Consumerism connotes a different state of affairs; one where consumers follow a scale of values and where production is shaped by those values. For consumerism was a matter of more or less. It was not a total system, as Marxists supposed slavery, feudalism and capitalism to be. It was a more or less dominant cortex on the process of production, distribution and consumption. Consumerism was not necessarily materialistic. On the contrary, it was the imposition on material processes of non-material values. It was an extension of the kingdom of mind into the realm of commodities. Materialism was an abuse of consumerism, not its essence.

Second, consumerism as denotation and fact. Here it may be defined ostensively as a set of interlocking, social institutions and concomitant attitudes shaping the economy. The set consisted of four members. In the first place there were retail institutions. Although economic historians must have spent much time in shops and are willing to recognize that early modern England was a nation of shopkeepers, they have been slow to investigate the significance of retail in the final fruition of the traditional economy and the first blossoming of the modern. Consumerism required more retail. In food, in addition to the traditional butchers, bakers, grocers, fishmongers, fruiterers and vintners, it required specialist services: cafés, teashops, patisseries, delicatessens, rosticerias, wine merchants, sandwich bars, fast fooderies and off-licences, not to mention an extended range of ethnic restaurants. In dress, in addition to traditional tailors, cobblers, dressmakers and milliners, it required boutiques, accessory shops, street markets, second hand dealers and eventually department stores, as well as ancillaries in hairdressing, repair, alteration, maintenance and laundry. In shelter, in addition to traditional masons, carpenters, bricklayers and glaziers, it required interior decorators, paperhangers, carpetlayers, window cleaners and French polishers. In utilities, in addition to traditional chimney sweeps, it required plumbers, electricians, gas experts and central heating firms. These retail services were more than prerequisites for consumerism. Consumerism was impossible without them, it fostered their development, and its progress led to their further diversification.

Next, there were more consumerists: new categories of active consumers who made conscious choices on the basis of a scale of values, and were the customers of the new retail facilities. In Europe, the two chief groups of new, or bigger customers, were women and servants, often of course the same people. Early European consumerism involved both feminization and inferiorization. In China too, where the chief groups of new consumers were merchants and urban gentry, nevertheless both women's independence and servants' imitation of their masters were on the increase, though to a lesser extent than in Europe. In both East and West, however, the greater spending power of women and its degree were related to marriage patterns. In both, the basic principle was male hypergamy. Women were the carriers of status and nobility was nubility. Larger dowries, more investment in female education, and greater spending for and by women were means of enhancing family prestige and establishing social distance. Nobility was thus put in a better position to attract, via marriage, power and wealth which, along with land, formed the quadrilateral of family fortune. In both early modern China and Europe, marriage was strengthening its position *vis-à-vis* other factors in family strategy. In Counter-Reformation Rome, St Carlo Borromeo took great pains with the marriages and weddings of his sisters. In T'ung-ch'eng county in Anhwei, the home of some of the most renowned mandarin families in mid-Ch'ing China, the search for marriage prestige took precedence over the struggle for examination success, office, commercial monopolies or land.[22] Between Europe and China, however, there was one significant difference. Endogamy, as a means of not dissipating family wealth, was relatively easier to practice in China than in Europe. The tightening of the rules of exogamy by the Council of Trent meant that families could no longer pass off their daughters cheaply to relatives, but must invest to compete in a wider market. Women were the shop window of families. Exogamy favoured feminization of consumption. By enlarging family experience, attitudes and information, it also encouraged consumption generally.

Feminization in turn favoured inferiorization. In pre-modern society, women were closer to their servants than men. Female servants were in a better position to observe, learn, imitate, receive cast-offs, give advice even, than male. If, as in northern, unlike Mediterranean Europe, domestic service was not perpetual, but only an episode in a life cycle, the demonstration effect would be all the greater. In consumption, the important development of early modern Europe was not the rise of the middle classes, who were often hostile to consumerism in various kinds of Puritanism, but the rise of the service classes. This is the situation portrayed by the *Marriage of Figaro*. The opera is not prophetic of the French Revolution. Figaro and Susanna are not rising bourgeoisie. As valet and lady's maid, they are rising servants who claim the aristocratic privilege of virginity before marriage. The opera is not an attack on aristocratic values. Rather, it is a celebration of them, their extension to new groups, and the social reconciliation this effects. If *Figaro* is prophetic of anything it is of the consumerist revolution which brought liberty, equality and fraternity more genuinely than the French Revolution. Consumerism was born in the courtly cities of the sixteenth century. It came to maturity in the aristocratic societies of the eighteenth century, especially where, as in England, aristocratic tastes were diffused to wider circles in places like Bath and to the countryside by life-cycle servants.

Third, to join retailers and consumers in early modernity, there were publicity and advertising institutions. The increased demand of consumerism was not simply self-generating. It was also managed, even manipulated, by a new flow of written information. This information supplemented, extended and eventually supplanted example, word of mouth, gossip and rumour in the formation of taste. In food, cook books appeared; in dress, patterns, model dolls, magazines; in housing, design books, style manuals, garden plans, prototypes for furniture and ceramics. Advertising is commonly understood in terms of product promotion. That may be the intentio n of the advertiser, but authorial intent is an insufficient guide to the meaning of a text, and the growth of advertising should be seen as the rise of a more informated and mediated form of society.

Consumerist literature is best documented for dress, especially for eighteenth-century France, through the work of Daniel Roche.[23] Some of it was medical: a new emphasis on air and breathing, and hence on less constricting clothes. Some of it was philosophical, as in the cult of nature which culminated in Rousseau. More, however, was commercial. Roche notes 20 journals devoted to dress between 1700 and 1793, most of them ephemeral, but evidence of a reading public. Many of them were owned or edited by women, and were evidently designed for reading in the boudoir, perhaps in company with a lady's maid. Roche refers to this literature as the specifically feminine component of the Enlightenment and heads one of his sections, *liberté, égalité, frivolité*. In addition to clothes, these journals also recommended books and plays and it was in this period that the theatre, both the actors and the audience, began to set new trends in dress. Pepys, for example, frequently noted what Lady Castlemaine was wearing at the theatre. In the East, advertisement for restaurants and tea houses was common in eighteenth-century Edo, a true consumerist city. The famous prints of well-dressed courtesans were less advertisement for themselves than for their clothes and style. In Edo, too, the theatre played a part in publicity. Hokusai began his career as an apprentice to a leading designer of prints of *kabuki* actors in costume. When his landscapes became so popular, they too became the subject of advertisement. Hokusai was arguably the world's first commercial artist.

Finally, there was fashion and its institutions which energized retail, consumers and publicity alike. Fashion has not always existed. Its birth was one of the most important developments of the period 1400 to 1800. Before fashion, there was protocol, which prescribed the appropriate consumer behaviour for the different ranks and classes of society, variegated according to age, season and occasion. It was protocol which legislators sought to enforce through sumptuary laws. Protocol survives: in Lord Mayors' banquets, at weddings and funerals, in the diplomatic service, in law courts, and above all in the armed services. Modern cities have been designed in accordance with protocol; Canberra with its suburbs calibrated according to civil service salaries. Nevertheless, protocol has generally been fighting a losing battle. Breach of protocol, however, is not the same as fashion. It may be counterfeit, which does not challenge the currency of the coin it imitates. Fashion is not the same as luxury which remains within the constraints of protocol. It is not identical with fad or fancy, idiosyncrasy or eccentricity which are only limited, temporary revolts from the authority of protocol. Again, fashion is to be distinguished from style, which is collective, and taste which is individual. Both style and taste are compatible with protocol.

Fashion, however, was different. Its nature was paradoxical. First, fashion exhibited a kind of quantum reality. It was both particle and wave; an act of individual choice, yet part of a collective trend. If fashion became universal, then it ceased to be fashion and became protocol or style. Second, in Fukuyama's terms, fashion was both megalothymic and isothymic. It was both exclusive and inclusive. It sought to create an elite, yet prevented no one from joining. The elite it sought to create was its own, a new glamorati, but frequently it was annexed by existing elites of status, power and wealth. Third, once launched, fashion continued, but fashions constantly changed. Fashions, says Daniel Roche, always die young, but it would also be true to say that they live young. One of its functions in fact is to divide the young from the old and to prevent a daughter being mistaken for her mother. Fashions must change as generations succeed each other. Another French historian calls fashion 'the empire of the ephemeral'.[24] Yet, whether in food, dress or shelter, it has a structure, whose permutations change less frequently than the code in which they are expressed. Finally, fashion fought protocol in the name of appearance against reality, a meontology against an ontology. Yet increasingly appearance became reality. Fashion became constituent of social topography. Because it was ephemeral and endless, it opened an infinite horizon to consumption and turned it into consumerism.

Fashion first appeared, not in Western antiquity where what Seneca and Chrysostom denounced was not fashion but luxury, but in T'ang China. It appeared at the court of Emperor Hsüan-tsung when it was dominated by the 'beloved consort' Yang Kuei-fei, the Madame de Pompadour of China and the tragic heroine of Po Chu-i's poem *The*

Everlasting Wrong. Her intelligence and taste for exotics turned fads and fancies into genuine fashions in a court which aimed to fascinate. Fashion resurfaced in the Valois, Plantagenet and Burgundian courts of late medieval Europe, especially in dress. Among the items fashionable was the tall T'ang headdress known in French as the *hennin* and transmitted to Europe via the Lusignan court of Cyprus. Later, the Renaissance itself, in the sense of an emphasis on the non-technical literature of antiquity, may be regarded as a fashion, earlier renaissances or revivals, such as the Carolingian or twelfth century, being no more than fads or idiosyncrasies. The courtly cities of the sixteenth century readily embraced fashion. St Carlo Borromeo caught this when he said that to be a success in Rome, one must love God and have a carriage. In China, the *wa-tzu* or pleasure quarters of Hang-chou had continued the pursuit of the ephemeral begun by Ch'ang-an, but in more bourgeois mode. After the austerities of the early Ming, fashion reappeared in the sixteenth century in the raffinate *kulturstadt* of the Lower Yangtze. Thence it passed to Japan where it became the *ukiyoe* or floating world of Tokugawa Edo and Osaka. Protocol might rule in Kyoto, the city of the emperor, but fashion led in the cities of the shogun. Japan's precocity in fashion was a significant factor in its subsequent precocity in modernization. It was the vanguard institution in the character of consumerism, the play which preceded the work.

We may conclude briefly with some preconditions, causes and consequences of consumerism. The chief precondition was a high level of consumption, such as was provided by the courtly cities of the Renaissance and their aristocracies. This sufficed for the growth of retail and consumptivity, but, for publicity and fashion, a further development was required which occurred in the seventeenth century. This was the emergence, beyond the court and the restricted circles of the aristocracy of what has been called public space; an extension of information beyond the immediacy of the corridors of power to a public opinion whose database was mediated by the written word. Public opinion, of course, could be agitated by more than advertising and fashion. It was used for religion and against taxation, in defence of privilege and against the abuse of prerogative. When these preoccupations relaxed, however, civil concern in the ephemeral could use the networks so created.

The causality of consumerism – what brought the institutions into conjuncture – falls under two heads. On the one hand, there were internal factors; the political, social and economic histories which lay behind the rise of courts, aristocracy and public opinion. In the West, there was the rise of the new imperial monarchies and the subsequent appearance of country opposition to them. In the East, there was the decline of the Ming corporate state and the subsequent return of Confucian society as an autonomous entity in the body politic. On the other hand, there were external factors, the chief of which was globalization. Many of the modest luxuries of early consumerism were exotics: in food, tea, coffee, cocoa and tobacco; in dress, silks, calicoes and furs; in building, pavilions, kiosks and summer palaces. Exoticism imparted a taste for novelty which could then be exploited by domestic innovation. Even a reaction against modernism could foster a consumerism of nostalgia.

Finally, the consequences of consumerism. Without consumerism, it is difficult to see happening either the final efflorescence of the old technology or the first advances of the new. Import substitution for exotics was an element of both, especially in the area of dress. The successful application of water power to silk manufacture in Bologna, the Veneto, Piedmont and the Pennines was the last triumph of the old technology. The successful application of steam power to cotton manufacture in Lancashire and Belgium was the first triumph of the new technology.[25] Beyond prompting import substitution, consumerism created the climate in which entrepreneurs could market new products, as well as make old ones more cheaply. The third consumer revolution, the age of mass consumption, was more about new products than old. Its characteristic goods – the automobile, the refrigerator, the television, the microwave and the word processor – not only were unthought of in 1800, but fulfilled needs that were then har dly felt. Consumerism not only initiated the first industrial revolution, but maintained it into a permanent revolution of revolutions. For consumerism was less the continual expansion of human material culture than its constant mutation and refinement. It was the never-ending materialization of mind.

2 Consumerism and Food

Niels Bohr was in the habit of saying that a great truth was a statement of which the opposite was also a great truth. In this chapter, it is hoped to reverse Ludwig Feuerbach's dictum, *Der Mensch ist was er isst*, into its consumerist opposite: man eats what he is, if being may be social and evaluative as well as individual and psychological.

To begin a study of consumerism in material culture during the age of globalization with food is not as obvious as might first appear. It is often assumed that food is the most exigent of human needs, its provision the core of anthropic ecology. In fact, food only became a problem with the numbers and immobility generated by the neolithic revolution and agriculture. Before, thanks to the relative generosity of natural food resources (palaeolithic man, it has been reckoned, only had to devote four hours a day to their acquisition), the central problem was not food, but clothing and shelter: external hypothermia rather than internal. To go without food for a day would cause discomfort. To go without clothing or shelter for a night could cause death. As humankind advanced from the tropics to the temperate and frigid zones, the threat of external hypothermia became more pressing. Its reduction demanded specialized hunting, clothes of animal or vegetable provenance, caves and arbours, and fire. These postulated the essential human specification: speech, which in turn prompted further development of the brain. Yet, as every urban charity knows, even today the threat of external hypothermia can all too easily return.[1]

If food is taken first, it is less because of its ecological priority than because it affords the earliest accessible instance of culture in nature, the foundation of consumerism in culture. For, as Lévi-Strauss emphasized, if language was universal to humankind, so too was cooking. In the New England clambake, he saw a survival of one of the bases of culture: the afterglow of the primal theft of celestial fire for the terrestrial oven.[2] For, if cooking extended the range of resources from raw to processed, it was not simply an act of nature, but also of culture. It grounded the dichotomy of common fare and feast, low cooking and high cooking, plain and fancy. It erected the notion of commensality or table-fellowship. It encouraged a number of gender roles. It provided the material for the expression of a variety of rationalities when consumerism raised cooking to cuisine. Like other aspects of consumerism, cuisine had its preconditions in a sufficiency of commodities, in pleasure cities and in public space. It had its own institutions in restaurants, chefs and gourmets, recipes, reputations and good food guides. Through these institutions came the logic of eating which underlay the actual consumption of basics, accessories and extras in Europe and China between 1400 and 1800.

PRECONDITIONS, INSTITUTIONS, LOGIC

In the preconditions for consumerism in food, China held the priority over Europe. Public space is first described in the Southern Sung capital of Hang-chou by observers both Chinese and foreign. One such indication is that the Southern Sung emperor Hsiao-tsung (1165–90) sometimes dined out in the public market or sent out for specialties from well-known restaurants rather than rely solely on his palace chefs. The *Meng-liang lu*, an account of the city in 1274, emphasized the independent life of its 20-odd *wa-tzu* or pleasure quarters. It noted in particular that 'the tea-houses are a rendez-vous for young men of wealthy families, and for lower-grade officials from the various ministries, who practise on musical instruments and sing all sorts of airs and refrains'.[3] Though reduced to provincial status by the Mongol conquest, Hang-chou continued to be the largest city in China: perhaps the first non-capital megapolis in history and definitely a sign of its independent urban vitality. Marco Polo describes it as a pleasure city: 'For the people of this city think of nothing else, once they have done the work of their craft and their trade, but to spend a part of the day with their womenfolk, or with hired women, in enjoying themselves either in their barges or in riding about the city in carriages . . . For their minds and thoughts are intent upon nothing but bodily pleasure and the delights of society.'[4]

In Europe, the first indications of this kind of public space came from Renaissance Rome, from Valladolid after it had ceased to be a royal capital in the mid-sixteenth century, and from Amsterdam which never served as a capital. In Rome, Cardinal Bernardo Salviati (1508–68), a grandson of Lorenzo de Medici and a former captain-general of the pontifical galleys, a retired admiral in effect, used to entertain a dozen or so guests a month in the period 1562–5. Presumably, he received hospitality in return, since most of the names were his social equals: cardinals, counts, marquises, governors, ambassadors, as well as members of his own family.[5] Such networks of commensality and conviviality, however, were still restricted. It was inter-private space rather than fully public and much of it revolved round the papal court. In Valladolid, a well-fed city of parades and spectacles, society was more broadly based on an appeal court, a cathedral chapter, a tribunal of the Inquisition and a university, but it remained compartmentalized between those professions. A fully public space had to await developments in the north, Amsterdam above all. Like Hang-chou, Amsterdam was not a seat of government, at least not of princely government. It too was a pleasure city, with a wide range of commodities available to its citizens: Descartes' inventory of all that is possible. Like Hang-chou again, Amsterdam was a city of refugees and cultural convergence where world, street and home interpenetrated, not least in a constant round of civic, group and family banquets. Like Hang-chou, Amsterdam had outgrown its antecedents and environs, cuckoos in their respective nests. The Dutch, it is said, became a nation to avoid being a state, and Amsterdam, one might say, became a megapolis to avoid being a polis.[6] It was a city, less in the classic sense of a place for politics and civic virtue, than in the modern sense of business opportunity and consumer enjoyment. More than Rome or Valladolid, Amsterdam was the prototype for Paris and London as centres of consumerism.

A remoter prototype, however, was China. Within its public space, Hang-chou was well equipped with the institutions of consumerism in food. Marco Polo was particularly struck by the vast establishments on the islands of the West Lake, which catered for private parties. He wrote: 'Furthermore in the middle of the lake there are two islands, in each of which is a marvellous and magnificent palace, with so many rooms and apartments as to pass belief ... when anyone wishes to celebrate a wedding or hold a party, he goes to this palace ... on occasion the need may arise to cater for a hundred clients at once, some ordering banquets, others wedding-feasts; and yet they will all be accommodated in different rooms and pavilions so efficiently that one does not get in the way of another.' The *Meng-liang lu*, on the other hand, remembered specialist restaurants: 'sweet soya soup at the Mixed-Wares market, pig cooked in ashes in front of the Longevity-and-Compassion Palace, the fish-soup of Mother Sung outside the Cash-reserve gate, and rice served with mutton' (this last probably from a northern ethnic chef from Kaifeng, of whom there were many in the city).[7]

From Kaifeng came another consumerist institution: prestige advertising. 'The restaurants of the capital city of Kaifeng were in the habit of hanging up famous pictures so as to catch the attention of passers-by and attract customers. Nowadays, the tea-houses in the town of Hang do the same: they make arrangements of the flowers of the four-seasons, hang up paintings by celebrated artists, decorate the walls of the establishment, and all year round sell unusual teas and curious soups.'[8] In addition to the prestige restaurants, there were pie carts, snack bars, fast fooderies, barrow boys and street pedlars to supply the 'small eats', *hsiao-shih*, so beloved of the Chinese consumer. Thir-teenth-century China had definitely passed beyond the level where inns provided food for travellers.

The example of consumerism in food afforded by Southern Sung and Yüan Hang-chou was taken up, after the intermission of the aus-tere early Ming corporate state, by late Ming and early Ch'ing Nan-king. Early Ming Nanking had been a fortress, a dockyard, a party headquarters set on the edge of the Yangtze delta to control its elite in the interests of the Ming revolution. With the removal of the capital to Peking, the decline of the imperial navy, and the relaxation of corpo-ratism, however, Nanking was taken over by that elite, and became, like Hang-chou, a pleasure city. Father Semedo, who was in China from 1613 to 1658, except for home leave between 1637 and 1644, described it as 'the perfection of the whole realm . . . both for the form of the building, the largeness of the streets, the manners and dealings of the people, and for the plenty and excellency of all things', going on to observe that, 'Much time and money is consumed by the Chi-nese in their Banquets by reason they are almost continually at them.'[9] By the middle to late Ch'ing, Yang-chou, now a consumer as well as a commercial centre, had taken over from Nanking as the gastronomi-cal capital of China. A guide to the city dated to around 1775 records a battery of teahouses, taverns and restaurants, where tourists ordered meals before setting out on river trips to view the famous local gar-dens of the rich salt merchants.[10]

In Europe, restaurants came later than in China.[11] We know the names of 72 three-star establishments in Northern Sung Kaifeng, but in Eu-rope named restaurants are hard to find before the seventeenth cen-tury. Restaurants should be distinguished from inns, eating houses and alehouses. Inns, as old as human movement in both Europe and China, catered essentially for travellers, shelter being the primary provision rather than food. Chaucer's Tabard, and even a more upmarket hos-telry like the Goldenes Adler at Innsbruck, were not places of high gastronomy. The Tabard gave the pilgrims supper and Harry Bailey was sufficiently confident of his wife's cooking to offer the winner of the stories competition a festive meal on their return, but the Five Guildsmen took a cook along with them in apprehension of the inns along the way. The cook himself was probably the proprietor of an eating house rather than a professional chef. Though proficient – he could roast, seethe, boil and fry, as well as make 'blankmanger' – he does not sound *cordon bleu*, but no doubt the guildsmen had eaten satisfactorily at his establishment, just as Pepys and his friends three centuries later frequently dined out at noon. Alehouses, on the other hand, provided not food for travellers but liquid refreshments for residents, though cakes were early added to ale, and the line between an alehouse and an eating house was fine. A tavern, indeed, was an alehouse which provided reasonable quantities of food. Pepys mentions a total of some 125 inns, eating houses, alehouses and taverns. Only some offered food, more only snacks, and in only a few, such as the Great James in Bishopsgate, where Pepys dined on mackerel on 30 June 1664, was the food of high quality. Only the Dolphin in Tower Street, where Pepys attended an expensive naval dinner on 20 June 1665 to celebrate the recent victory over the Dutch at Lowestoft, really sounds like a restaurant.

If restaurants developed late, it was because eating out and gastronomy had different origins. Eating out was English and middle-class. It was the product of urban size, the disjuncture of home and work, and the need for business relationships. In traditional cities, residence and workplace were often identical or within walking distance of each other. Pepys frequently went home to Seething Lane to dine at midday, before returning to the Navy office or going to a matinée. In his early days, his most frequent place of dining out was the more or less open board of his patrons, the Earl and Countess of Sandwich at the Wardrobe: a relic of medieval hospitality, delivery and maintenance. As his acquaintance widened, however, Pepys dined out more at eating houses and taverns. He enjoyed food and drink, but it was the company and gossip he enjoyed more. Since his successful cutting for stone, he worried about his health and diet and was never a gastronome. Gastronomy, on the other hand, was French and aristocratic, even royal, with borrowings from Italy via the invasions and the Medici marriages. Francis I ordered his first plates, as opposed to trenchers in 1536. Henry III insisted on forks and replaced metal cups with Murano glass. In 1651, François Pierre, chef to the Marquis d'Uxelles, published *Le Cuisinier Français*, the first French cook book. Pierre found imitators. Between 1651 and 1691, it has been estimated, 100 000 copies of various cook books were in circulation in France. Gastronomy had ceased to be royal, but it remained domestic. Louis XIV was a gourmet, but he preferred to dine privately rather than in the public spectacles his duties compelled him to. Unlike the Sung emperor, he did not dine out.

Gastronomy and eating out only came together in the restaurant in the late seventeenth century, first in London, then in Paris, as consumerist public space developed. *Le Cuisinier Français* was translated into English as early as 1683 and French chefs began to find employment outside France. André Noel, for example, was employed by Frederick the Great in Berlin from 1755. In 1780, Antoine Beauvilliers opened *La Grande Taverne de Londres* on the English model in the rue de Richelieu. By 1789, there were said to be 100 restaurants in Paris. The Revolution multiplied them by extending public space, by encouraging a new style of consumerism, and by forcing chefs out of aristocratic houses to serve a wider clientele. Thus Méot, former chef to the Prince de Condé, set up a restaurant in the rue de Valois. In 1803, there were 500–600 Parisian restaurants, and by 1815, after Napoleonic military consumerism, 3000. In the field of gastronomy, Danton defeated Robespierre. In London, few surviving restaurants go back beyond the middle of the nineteenth century. Bellamy's, to whose meat pies the thought of the dying younger Pitt turned, ended its life soon after the fire of 1834. Dr Johnson's Cheshire Cheese is still happily with us, and George IV is reported to have visited an earlier version of Simpson's. The ancestors of the restaurants which once adorned Soho may go back to the late seventeenth century. Then it became the destination for both Huguenots and immigrants from the Ottoman empire who gave their name to Greek Street. Until this time, there was less inter-ethnic movement in Europe compared to China, where northerners and southerners have always mingled in the imperial capitals. Exoticism and nostalgia have always been motives for eating out and eating well.

If Europe and China differed in the speed with which they developed the preconditions and institutions of consumerism in food, they also differed in the logic they imparted to food in menus and meal organization.

The logic of eating may be divided into two parts: grammar and syntax, terms and their integration. In grammar, Europe and China did not much differ. In thirteenth-century Hang-chou, as in seventeenth-century London, three meals a day were the norm. In addition to this three-fold norm, both medieval Chinese and early modern English were addicted to between-meal snacks: the stock in trade of street vendors, market stalls, alehouses and later tea and coffee houses. Europe and

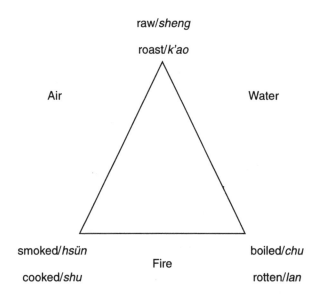

China too shared the basic food preparation techniques. Chaucer's cook was accomplished in roasting, seething (stewing), boiling and frying, and no doubt was familiar with grilling, baking, steaming and smoking. Most of these terms have Chinese equivalents: *k'ao* (roast), *tun* (stew), *chu* (boil) and *cha* or *ch'ao* (fry); *ao* (bake), *cheng* (steam), *hsün* (smoke).[12] Finally, since the raw and the cooked, the unprocessed and the processed, are as basic to Chinese thought as to the mythologies studied by Lévi-Strauss, it is possible to put his culinary triangle into Chinese (see above).[13]

On the horizontal axis, between culture and nature, it is significant that the Chinese characters for *shu* and *lan* are both classified under the fire radical. *Lan*, no doubt, originally meant overcooked, and only assumed its meaning of rotten as the concept of nature developed in apposition to that of culture: confirmation of Lévi-Strauss' surmise that, conceptually, culture has priority over nature. Lastly, in China as in Europe, the category of processing by water, that is, the various forms of boiling, needs to be enlarged to include other liquids, notably fats, in the various forms of frying (stir-fry, *ch'ao*, deep-fry, *cha*), which were of particular importance in Chinese cuisine.

The culinary triangle provides an excellent food grammar. It is much less satisfactory as a syntax: how dishes were integrated and actual meals were constructed. It is at this level that differences between Europe and China become significant.

First, as Françoise Sabban shows, although acceptable Chinese trans-
lations of familiar basic food preparation techniques may be given,
Chinese recipes use them in a less precise but more inclusive and
situational way. This is in accordance both with the open-textured genius
of the Chinese language and also with the actual operation of food
preparation. Chinese cooking does not privilege a particular moment
in an often complex culinary process. Of course, such complexity exists
in European recipes: an oxtail may be lightly fried before it is stewed;
but the underlying assumption is of a single act of cooking. Things
are either roasted, boiled or steamed. Chinese cooking language is less
pinpointed and more processual.

Second, there was a difference of emphasis within the culinary triangle. European cuisine, affected by a single, northern *limes* (to which
Islamic influence was secondary and in the same direction here), gave
pride of place to roasting and its modalities, such as grilling and baking. The oven, the grill or the barbecue were primary in Europe. Chinese cuisine, affected by a multiplicity of diverse *limes*, gave pride of
place to frying, especially stir-frying. The fry pan, *kuo* (*wok* in Cantonese), was primary in China. Primary, that is, in the side dishes (*ts'ai*)
whose multiplication was the hallmark of Chinese cuisine. Cereal staples were either boiled like rice or steamed like wheat dumplings and
noodles: again in contrast to the baked bread of Europe. Where Europe emphasized the perpendicular of the culinary triangle, China
emphasized its sides.

Third, Europe and China followed different principles of meal organization. In Europe, the organizer was the hostess and her principle
was catenary. A meal consisted of a succession of courses, generally
building towards and away from a central roast. Dinners were characteristically described as consisting of so many courses, the number
seldom large. The order of eating did not vary among the diners, and
a guest who replied to a suggestion of a second helping of turkey by
requesting more smoked salmon, would seem eccentric. In China, the
organizer was the guest and his principle was reticular. A meal consisted of a simultaneity of dishes, no one dish being considered piv-
otal. Dinners were characteristically described as consisting of so many
dishes, the number frequently large. The order of eating varied among
the diners and a guest who followed his host exactly would seem eccentric and failing to exercise his proper role as a discriminating gourmet. A European guest should be passive, putting himself in his hostess'
hands and only declining courses under extreme constraints of diet or
taste. A Chinese guest should be active in selecting from the *embarras*

de richesses provided by his host. The European hostess prescribed a path to follow. The Chinese host opened a garden in which to wander. The European meal was a command economy with a plan. The Chinese meal was an open market for shopping around.

Finally, whether commanded by the host or selected by the guest, eating followed different imperatives in Europe and in China. A European meal may readily be traced against the background of the culinary triangle, with its double dichotomy of unprocessed and processed, culture and nature. Thus a meal of raw oysters, *prosciutto con melone*, *caneton à l'orange*, gooseberry fool, stilton, port and nuts progresses from unprocessed nature to processed culture, processed nature, and back to unprocessed nature. The particular pattern is not invariant, but the variants too are relatable to the contours of unprocessed and processed, culture and nature. A European meal follows the curvature of a well-defined culinary space–time. A Chinese meal, on the other hand, is less easy to trace against the background of the culinary triangle, if only because the diners follow individual meanders. The quality most prized by Chinese gourmets is *ts'ui*, 'crispness'. To Western ears this suggests the fresh and natural, but in fact, Chinese cooks are often at pains to disguise the original flavour of substances, and some substances, such as sharks' fins, are valued precisely because of their lack of flavour and ability to receive it. What the Chinese cook seeks to provide and the gourmet hopes to find is a synaesthesia where taste, texture, aroma, colour and arrangement all play a part. In a garden, say Kew in May, someone may successively enjoy the perfume of disordered wisteria, the colour of ordered tulips, the modulation of bluebells in grass at one's feet, the serried ranks of various rhododendrons above eye level, the scent of different coloured lilacs, while his ears take note of robin, blackbird, thrush and willow warbler. But there is no particular order for doing these things, and though a line may be charted from the gate, it is no horticultural inconsistency to depart from it on impulse or reconsideration. So it is with a Chinese banquet. The culinary triangle is further in the background, the patterns more spontaneous, the order less clockwork than cloud.

To explain these differences between Europe and China in food syntax one must go beyond the culinary to the philosophical. Though equally rational, European and Chinese meals, it may be argued, embody different moments of rationality.

A European meal may be compared to a scientific or historical argument, which progresses through well-defined stages. It opens with enquiry, the formulation of a question, to which the culinary parallel would be aperitifs to arouse the palate and tempt it to further exploration. Enquiry is followed by investigation, the preliminary assemblage of relevant material. Here the culinary parallel might be hors d'oeuvres, with its variety of gustatory experience, or pasta and sauce, to remove the immediate hunger which inhibits gourmet enjoyment. Investigation is succeeded by conceptualization: the discrimination of evidence, as in an entrée, provided, say, by the subtle flavour of fish. Finally, there is judgement: the *eureka* of the scientist, the certainty of the historian that, on the evidence, such and such must have been the case. Here the culinary parallel is the triumphant roast: a turkey with all its trimmings – chipolatas, two kinds of stuffing, bread and cranberry sauces, potatoes, vegetables, salad – which recapitulate the meal so far. But judgement is not the end of the argument which now runs back on itself. Certainty is succeeded by certitude and conceptual enrichment, as the newly acquired knowledge reveals its implications, simple or complex. Similarly, the roast is succeeded by dessert, which may be simple in raspberries and cream or complex as in *tirami-su*. Conceptual enrichment is followed by reflections on the evidence, to which the culinary parallel might be cheese or fruit: natural counterparts to the earlier hors d'oeuvres or pasta. At the end, there is repletion, as the results of the successful enquiry are digested, and the meal concludes with after dinner mints, liqueurs or brandy: cultural, eupeptic counterparts to the opening aperitifs. Just as successful method invites to further research, so the perfect meal suggests the possibility of further perfection another day when we are ready for it. In both cases, a reality has been appropriated.

A Chinese meal, on the other hand, may be compared to a rational moral decision. Here too a judgement is involved: that I ought to do such and such. If it is to be rational, it must follow an enquiry, investigation and conceptualization. But the intention is different. A scientific or historical argument intends a recognition of fact. A moral argument intends a creation of fact by action. Because action modifies the universe, however slightly, moral argument necessarily involves a universal reference, as Kant saw. However, because the variables and the imperatives are more situational, moral decision is personal too. Personal decision is not absent from scientific and historical argument, as Newman and Michael Polanyi saw, but it is present to greater degree in moral argument because it intends creation and not just recognition. The active Chinese diner, surrounded by a multiplicity of choice, is in the position of a moral agent. Moreover, not only may the decision alter the lives of those who make it, but also, before that, the decision itself may require or effect an antecedent personal change. We are our decisions in a way that we are not our knowledge. Further, not only does the decision change the decider, but that person may be aware of this and that change become part of the matter to be decided. Moral judgement is self-discovery as well as discovery. Consequently, the second half of the argument – enrichment, reflection and assimilation – will be as much concerned with the actor as the act. Similarly, the active Chinese diner is involved in a process of self-definition and identification. He eats what he is or would like to become. To eat is to construct something both within the meal as within oneself. For both the moral agent and the Chinese diner, there is a reality to be created.

The Chinese meal, therefore, followed the paradigm of a moral decision, where the European meal followed the paradigm of a factual argument. The first reflected the strong post-scientific and meta-ethical bias of Chinese civilization, just as the second reflected the strong scientific and metaphysical bias of European civilization. The former pursued the good, the latter the true. Chinese philosophy recognized the analogy between gastronomy and epistemology. Ch'eng Yi-ch'uan (1033–1107), the founder of the *li-hsüch* or rationalist school of Neo-Confucianism, once deflated a sanctimonious, or excessively Kantian critic, with a reference to food: 'Ch'en Kuei-yi, questioning Yi-ch'uan, said: "As I see it, all that fills heaven and earth is my nature; I no longer know that my body is me." Yi-ch'uan said with a smile: "when someone else has a good meal, aren't you hungry any more?"'[14] Subsequently, a leader of the alternative *hsin-hsüeh* or intuitionist school of Neo-Confucianism, the ex-salt merchant Wang Ken (1483–1541), took as his leading principle *an-shen* 'pacify the self' which in other contexts might have been translated as 'satisfy the body'. The *hsin-hsüeh*, with its subjectivist, almost existential emphasis on the personal element in knowledge and action, was particularly influential in the great consumerist centres of Kaifeng, Hang-chou and Nanking at a time when society achieved a certain independence of the state and individuals could feel themselves self-constituting. Commensality in China expressed a community of self-discovery, just as commensality in Europe expressed a community of discovery, whether of nature, culture, or ultimately, the *Selbstmitteilung* of God between the first bread and the last cup.

ESSENTIALS: SORGHUM INSIDE CHINA, RICE OUTSIDE CHINA

We need to set the context before the age of globalization. Ever since the neolithic revolutions of *c.*10 000 BC, the essential in food has been the carbohydrates provided by domesticated plants. To this day, most human calories have been provided by the vegetable kingdom from cereals and tubers. As M. S. Swaminathan puts it: 'We live in this world as guests of green plants.'[15] If all human societies, from the neolithic revolutions, became parasitic on plant photosynthesis, it was, however, on different plants: maize in pre-Columbian America, millet and yams in Black Africa, barley, wheat and rye in Western Eurasia, millet and rice in East Asia. This pattern of localized monocultures was not, except in the case of the wider diffusion of rice in China, affected by the *limes* lifestyle, which referred more to the relations between the arable and pastoral components of different neolithic agricultures. It was not until globalization that significant exchanges were made between the primary civilizations in the matter of basic carbohydrates. Then the impact was considerable, not least in providing the infrastructure for consumerism. The best known of these exchanges is the introduction of American food plants – maize, sweet potatoes, peanuts, potatoes, cassava – to Europe, China and Africa, with revolutionary effects in all these areas. Less well known, but equally significant, were two earlier instances of exchange: the introduction of African sorghum to China, and the diffusion of rice outside East Asia.

Sorghum Inside China

The millet *Holcus sorghum* (in Chinese *kao-liang* or tall millet, as opposed to *hsiao-mi*, small or fox tail millet), and *huang-mi*, yellow or panic millet, played a part in the consumerist development of Szechwan, China's first colony, the metropolitan province of Chihli, and of Manchuria, China's last colony.

Sorghum was first domesticated in Ethiopia.[16] It was the crop of the Afro-Asiatic language family and it expanded westward with its Chadic and Hausa branch to become one of the major crops of ancient and medieval West Africa. Its expansion eastward came later and may be associated with the rise of Axumite power in southwest Arabia and along the southern sea route to the east whose ultimate destination was China. The earliest Chinese name for sorghum is *Shu-mi*, or millet from western Szechwan, a term first used in a work attributed to the third-century scholar Chang Hua. It reached Szechwan either over-land from India via Tali and Ning-yuan, or, perhaps more likely, by sea from the Yemen, via Tongking, K'un-ming and Hsü-chou. There, however, *kao-liang* remained until the Yüan period when it penetrated extensively into North China. Under the Ming, it reached Fengtien in southern Manchuria and under the Ch'ing it became the staple food crop of the whole area, the northern provinces of Kirin and Heilungkiang as well as the south. In Szechwan, Chihli and Manchuria alike, *kao-liang*, eaten as porridge or, like rice, whole-grain, or processed into spirits, was a key adjunct in the development of a more consumerist economy.

The exact circumstances of the introduction of sorghum to Szechwan are unclear. The general context, however, can be established. As a province, Szechwan developed by fits and starts, leaps forward and sudden catastrophes.[17] One such leap forward was the period 200 to 400. Then, under the leadership of the Taoist theocracy of the five pecks of rice sect, the Shu Han dynasty with its celebrated prime min-ister Chu-ko Liang, and, under the Chin, its own native aristocracy, Szechwan expanded. It expanded beyond its nucleus in the artificially created delta of the Chengtu plain, whose resources had turned Ch'in into China and given Liu Pang victory over Hsiang Yü, into the hill country surrounding the plain. This provided tea, wax, varnish and medicines for export to the rest of the empire, tea especially being one of the consumer discoveries of the T'ang period. On the plain, large colonial latifundia were based on paddy fields, fishponds and salt wells, but in the hills where small, market-oriented family farms predomi-nated, sorghum was a useful pioneer's crop. Its high yield per seed and per acre and the relatively low input of labour it required made it ideal for providing both subsistence and time for more valuable cash crops. Not a consumerist crop in itself, indeed a coarse grain rather disliked by its consumers, it made possible consumerism in other directions.

In North China, particularly the metropolitan province of Chihli where *kao-liang* found its second home, the millet from Szechwan also func-tioned as a subsistence crop alongside cash crops.[18] It was first intro-duced in the thirteenth century as part of the post-Mongol conquest reconstruction. Its ecology, however, was quite different from that in Szechwan. In Szechwan, *kao-liang* was and is a hillside crop, the plain being too valuable for such a purpose. In Chihli, where waterlogging by rivers coming out of the Western Hills was the problem, *kao-liang* was and is a wet-land crop, special damp-resistant strains being used for this purpose, the hills and well-drained areas being required for more valuable crops such as wheat, the regular millet, and, in the nineteenth century increasingly, cotton for local looms, Tientsin and export to Japan. As in Szechwan, sorghum supported a system of small-holders in a market economy, which, whatever its deficiencies in the circulation of information, provided its family-oriented members with real social satisfactions, as well as contributing to higher living standards elsewhere. In Chihli, thanks to sorghum, sociological conservatism could thus be combined with economic progress.

In Manchuria, whither *kao-liang* was brought by Chinese settlers in the late Ming period, both the ecology and the sociology were different. Here, neither a hill-country nor a wet-land crop, sorghum used another of its admirable qualities, its ability to adapt to a short growing season, to establish itself centrally in the valleys of the Liao and middle Sungari. These were areas of Chinese settlement in sizeable family units from Chihli and Shantung, where the grain was familiar if not loved and the multiple utility of the long stalks was appreciated. As Peter Fleming wrote in the 1930s: 'Practically everything in Manchuria is made of *kaoliang*. It serves as raw material for many manufactured articles, from hats to houses; also as fodder and fuel. Men eat it as a form of flour, and drink a spirit distilled from it.'[19] Even rural politics were shaped by the protective cover given by *kao-liang* to the *hung-hu tzu* or 'red-beards', the *mafiosi* who preyed on the Manchurian routes. For Manchuria's was not a subsistence economy. If in Szechwan, *kao-liang* was linked to tea and in Chihli to cotton, in Fengtien and Kirin, it was linked to the soya bean, the Manchurian wonder crop which will figure in the next section, and the region's most valuable product. With its huge fortified backcountry distilleries, its bean curd processing plant and bean vermicelli manufacture, Manchuria, underpinned by *kao-liang*, was a prime example of Franklin Mendels' rural proto-industrialization before becoming, with Russian and Japanese investment in railways, coal and iron, China's first industrial base. For industry too, *kao-liang* provided the demographic infrastructure.

If *kao-liang* made Manchuria, then Manchuria made modern China. It was from Manchuria, whence so many conquest dynasties had come, that the Ch'ing emerged to use its rising population to build a new kind of Sino-Manchu state. It was Manchuria which provided the military reserves and extra manpower which allowed the dynasty to defeat the Taiping northern expedition and so survive another 60 years. It was China's defeat in Manchuria in the Sino-Japanese war of 1894–5 which showed the world that Japan had modernized while China had not and convinced the Chinese elite that something radical must be done. It was Russia's defeat in Manchuria in the Russo-Japanese war of 1904–5 which showed the world that an Asian power could develop further politically than a European one and turned China to its long search for constitutional government. It was the lure of Manchuria which tempted Japan into continental expansion and Chiang Kai-shek into selling space to buy time: a policy which lost intelligentsia support and gave the Chinese Communists an easy propaganda victory. It was fear that the Manchurian industrial base would prove decisive in Communist hands that tempted Chiang Kai-shek into the fatal overextension which cost him the initiative in the last round of the civil war after 1946. It was with the resources, human and technical, of Manchuria, especially those of the Sungari-Ussuri triangle centred on Harbin, that Lin Piao delivered the counterstroke which destroyed the flower of the Kuomintang armies at Mukden in the fall of 1948.[20] It was with the support of the massive garrisons, the party organization, and the sun-set industrial proletariat of Manchuria that the Communist regime survived the revolt of key-board skilled Peking and commercial Shanghai in the second 4 May movement of 1989. All these contributions of Manchuria to Chinese history would not have been possible without the golden grain from western Ethiopia.

Rice Outside China

Though less in total production in 1982 than wheat or maize, ever since the paddy boom in the lower Yangtze in the late T'ang period rice has fed more human beings than any other source of carbohydrates.[21] The origins of the domestication of *Oryza sativa* are disputed between India and China and archaeology has not given its last word. Currently, opinion suggests that the first domestication occurred in what is now China, but was then Southeast Asia. The earliest grains, hulls and straw found in a human habitation site are those of Ho-mu-tu, *c*.8000 BC, near Yü-yao in eastern Chekiang. Wild relatives of the cultigen, however, are found further south in the valley of the West River, western Kwangtung, and on Hainan. Rice domestication probably began here, as the value of what had been seen as a weed in a patch of taro, began to be realized. At all events, in both areas at that time, the language was probably Austro-Asiatic rather than Sinitic. The credit for domestication should therefore go to neither the Indians nor the Chinese, but to the Vietnamese: the coastal Yüeh as the Chinese called them, whose territory extended at one time nearly to Shantung, and perhaps even to Japan. It was the Chinese, however, who carried rice cultivation to its greatest development: first, in Szechwan following Li Ping's irrigation scheme of *c.*250 BC; subsequently, in the Yangtze delta, especially after the introduction of early ripening Champa rice by Sung emperor Chen-tsung in 1012; and finally, in the middle Yangtze, the provinces of Anhwei, Hupei and Hunan. For the Chinese, northerners by background, rice was an exotic, a modest luxury, preferable to the millets with which they started or the wheat which they acquired, because of its ease of de-husking, susceptibility to boiling and palatability. Hence the elaborate arrangements, from the middle T'ang, to ensure that the court and the elite were always supplied via the grain tribute service with its barges on the Grand Canal. In China rice was a southern crop appropriated by northerners. Shanghai was its supermarket.

The expansion of rice outside China began early. Husks are reported from Mohenjodaro *c.*2500 BC, probably an import from the middle Ganges. Here the Buddhist kingdom of Magadha became a centre of rice cultivation in the period prior to the invasion of Alexander the Great. Yet rice remained in India only for a considerable period. Neither Ancient Egypt, nor the Bible, nor Aristotle know anything of rice, nor is there much sign of it in Achaemenid Persia. It was probably the conquests of Alexander themselves which brought rice beyond India. Diodorus Siculus, who used the lost work of Aristobulus, one of Alexander's staff officers, describes it as a crop of India. Theophrastus, Aristotle's successor, also has an account of rice in India. One of his successors says rice was cultivated in Egypt: probably an attempted acclimatization by Ptolemy Soter, always concerned for the agricultural development of his new kingdom, but one which did not take. For this is the last we hear of rice in Egypt for several centuries. Rice, however, did spread westward in the Hellenistic period. Chang Ch'ien, Han Wu-ti's explorer–ambassador to the West *c.*100 BC, mentions rice as a crop of Ta-yüan (Ferghana), An-hsi (Parthia: probably Merv and Herat) and Tiao-chih (Mesopotamia). Rice followed the routes of the Hellenistic armies, but it did not always transplant. Rome knew it only as an import from the East; and even Egypt continued to import, probably from India.

A second advance of rice was effected by the expansion of Islam. Islamic tradition represented Alexander and his conquests as a forerunner of those of the Prophet, the sultans of Rum, Malaya and China all being descended from the Macedonian, and in the case of rice it was correct. Islamdom, the revelation of Muhammad put into practice and expressed in institutions, was consumerist. Born on the *limes* as a provincial counter-culture, it represented a release from the desert rather than its extension. Lavishness in food as well as permissiveness in sex were part of its appeal from the beginning. Rice, picked up no doubt on the Sassanian *limes* in Mesopotamia, along with butter and sugar, were foods of paradise already available to the faithful on earth. Its cultivation was therefore extended by the Islamic armies: to Egypt, where by the Fatimid period it had become the principal crop in the Fayum; to northern Iraq and Syria under the Hamdanids of Aleppo; to Spain, notably Murcia and Valencia, where *paella* remains as testimony; to Turfan and Uighuristan to make *pilau* the local specialty; and, in the days of the Qajars, to the Caspian provinces of Persia, Gilan and Mazanderan. In Islamdom, rice was generally a luxury. When the governor of Alexandria wished to honour the Venetian ambassador in 1513 what he gave him was lamb, chicken, goose, rice, citrus and loaf sugar. Similarly, in 1860, Edward William Lane reported from Cairo that, 'Rice is too dear to be an article of common food for the fellaheen.'[22] Only in particularly favoured areas of the Middle East was rice a staple.

After the Ottoman occupation of Cairo in January 1517, rice, along with wheat, sugar and lentils, became part of the *Irsaliyye-i Hazine* or Egyptian remittance sent by the Pasha to Constantinople. These imports contributed to the change from the austere courts of the sultans up to Suleiman to the more lavish lifestyle of his successors. The Egyptian remittance stimulated the taste for rice. It began to be grown in the valley of the Meander and in coastal Cilicia for export to Constantinople and to be consumed in the army as well as the Seraglio. Busbecq, imperial ambassador 1554–62, noted: 'There are two things from which, in my opinion, the Turks derive the greatest advantage and profit, rice among cereals and camels among beasts of burden; both are admirably adapted to the distant campaigns which they wage.'[23] He went on to say that when the sultan went on campaign, he was accompanied by 40 000 camels loaded with rice. In the seventeenth century, rice, along with cotton and tobacco, became a characteristic market crop of the *çiftliks* or managerial estates of Ottoman Rumelia, notably the upper Maritsa valley round Plovdiv. Rice was also developed on the coastal plain of northern Anatolia and exported to the Ottoman satellite state of Crimea. Rice dishes, *dolmasi* and *pilav* were an important part of Ottoman cuisine.

In Europe, rice cultivation appeared first in extremities in contact with Islamdom: in the Lower Volga in the Jewish Khazar kingdom in the tenth century, and in the kingdom of Aragon, which eventually acquired the paddy fields of Valencia, not long afterwards. From Aragon, rice passed to Lombardy in the fifteenth century when canal building by Bertola da Novate, engineer to the Sforza dukes, made irrigation more feasible. From Lombardy, rice was introduced to the Veneto, though it is possible that the Venetians acquired seed and skills direct from Egypt through their contact with the Mamluk sultans. Whereas in Islamdom rice was a luxury, sometimes in the central place in a meal, in Christendom its status was more ambiguous. Risottos and rice puddings belonged to pre- and post-central positions in the menu and rice was plebeian as well as patrician, or simply exotic. In the *Winter's Tale*, for example, it figures in the Clown's speech in Act IV, scene 3 in a list of spices, 'specials' for a sheep shearers' feast, along with sugar, currants, saffron, mace, dates, nutmeg and ginger. Most likely, the ambiguity was sociological. Braudel associated rice in Lombardy–Venetia and Valencia–Murcia with latifundia which projected an image of extremes of wealth and poverty. Similarly in northern Europe, rice was colonial. Rice therefore was polarized: native food or food for children, but also food for those who had been east of Suez and were therefore allowed to eat it with a spoon. Moreover, there was already the pre-existing hierarchy of boiled, steamed and fried rice.

In Black Africa, the history of rice is puzzling. Africa has its own subspecies, *Oryza glaberrima*, and archaeology has shown that it was cultivated in the interior Niger delta of Jenno-Jenne as early as the first century AD. Most rice cultivated in West Africa today, however, is the familiar *Oryza sativa* from East Asia. As it is grown on the coast, it has been assumed that it was introduced by the Portuguese, either from Portugal or from the Indian Ocean. Two other possibilities, however, suggest themselves. First, that it was introduced from Egypt by African pilgrims returning from the *haj* in the tenth or eleventh centuries, when pagan Jenno-Jenne lost its predominance to Muslim states lower down the Niger or into the Chad depression. Mai Ume Jubu of Bornu was converted to Islam in 1080 and his successors maintained a hostel in Cairo for pilgrims and scholars. *Sativa* would then have come along the *sahel* route rather than from the sea or across the Sahara. Second, there is the possibility that *sativa* came even earlier from the Malay refugee colony of Madagascar where rice was and still is the major cereal. Madagascar and Bantu cultures were in touch in what is now Tanzania and Uganda, and if sorghum could travel from Ethiopia, so could rice from Lake Victoria. If either of these possibilities is correct, then the Portuguese will not have brought rice to West Africa, but found it there and taken it to America in the mid-sixteenth century, with their first slaves for the sugar plantations in Brazil.

In America, rice was first introduced to Alagoas and Sergipe half-way between the sugar colonies of Pernambuco and Bahia. Subsequently cultivation was extended south to Espirito Santo to serve Rio, north to Maranhao and Para to serve Belem, and inland to São Paulo. Each stage in the development of the Brazilian economy – from sugar to gold to coffee, rubber and beyond – was paralleled by an extension of rice cultivation as a significant element in its infrastructure. In 1986 Brazil was the largest producer of rice outside Asia. In North America, rice was introduced to Virginia by the royalist-governor Sir William Berkeley in 1646/7, but the acclimatization did not take. In 1696, it was reintroduced, to South Carolina, by governor Thomas Smith, who, having himself been in Madagascar, is said to have taken a bag of Madagascar rice off a Dutch ship returning home which touched at Charleston. In South Carolina, the acclimatization did take and until 1861 the Carolinas were responsible for three-quarters of the rice grown in the United States. After the Civil War, Louisiana took up rice in its abandoned sugar plantations, being joined in the early twentieth century by Texas, Arkansas and eventually California. Much of the crop was exported, under the mercantilist system via London, to the Mediterranean, and the world's biggest exporters of rice today are the United States and Thailand. In the domestic market, the long-grained *indica* of the Mississippi states went into babyfoods, while the short-grained *Japonica* of California went into breakfast cereals: another indication of the peripheral place of rice in Western menus – in infancy and early in the morning. In the United States too, as in Europe, there was exoticism, but it came characteristically from the West via the Chinese restaurant rather than from the East via the Indian restaurant. In London, Bombay and Calcutta cast an afterglow; in Los Angeles, Shanghai and Saigon. In both, *sushi* bars, Thai take-aways, and Korean barbecues heralded a new dawn of a different *raj*.

ACCESSORIES: FISH AND SOYA BEANS

From the neolithic revolution to the age of mass consumption, a meal for most people consisted of basic carbohydrates conjoined to accessory side dishes of protein and fat: bread and butter, pasta and sauce, meat and potatoes, curry and rice. In China too, a meal was *fan-ts'ai*:

fan, literally cooked rice, being the carbohydrates, and *ts'ai*, literally vegetables, being the side dishes. Everywhere, consumerism meant the predominance of the accessories over the essentials, whether by multiplication of side dishes as in China or by enhancement of the central roast as in the West. It was a victory of changeable culture over relatively unchangeable nature. Yet there was a paradox here. Consumerism was also a return to the palaeolithic: to Marshall Sahlin's first affluent society. For game, fish, fruit and vegetables, even some kinds of meat, were continuations of hunter-gathering into the age of neolithic agriculture. Culture, therefore, had deep roots, back to the primaeval clambake. To emphasize this continuity, this section focuses on the fisheries in the age of globalization and on the soya bean, that unique mixture of carbohydrate, protein and fat, both inside China and beyond.

The Fisheries in the Age of Globalization

Palaeolithic humanity took much of its food from the water, maybe especially so in the period just before the neolithic revolution when the Pleistocene megafauna rarefied. Not only was water, in the remarkable reproductive capacity of fish, more prodigal than earth, but unlike the forest, the sea, lakes and rivers offered food without the requirement of dispersal. Stable fishing communities, late palaeolithic proto-urbanization, concentrated intellectual resources, reduced infant mortality, and provided leisure for experimentation with plants. The earliest rice cultivation, in particular, is associated with coastal or aquatic sites. The wife at the hearth and the husband gone fishing not only provided a model of gender collaboration with a division of roles, but also fuller utilization, if not always recognition, of female initiative and intelligence. Moreover, as fishermen ventured upon hollowed logs in the West and bamboo rafts in the East, such primitive messing about in boats was laying the nautical foundations for globalization itself.

Fisheries fall into five categories.[24] First, there was on-shore fishing, by line, handnet or trap. Here the characteristic catch was shellfish: crays, crabs, lobsters, shrimps, snails, prawns, oysters; but also, in favoured places, such as Oregon, runs of salmon. Second, there was in-shore fishing, with boats, sampans or less primitive craft but within pre-1975 territorial waters of 12 miles, by drift net for pelagic or surface species and by trawl for demersal or sea-floor species. Here the characteristic catch was sardines and anchovies in Mediterranean waters, mackerel, sole and plaice in northern. Third, there was off-shore fishing, also by drift net or trawl, but in international waters and in-

volving an absence of days or weeks away from the home port. Here
the characteristic catch was herring in the North Sea, yellow croaker
in the South China Sea. Fourth, there was far-shore fishing on the
coastal shelf of another continent. Here the characteristic catch was
Grand Banks cod for Europeans, South Pacific squid for Taiwanese
and Japanese. Finally, there was non-shore fishing: fresh-water fishing
in rivers, lakes and fishponds, natural and artificial. Here the characteristic catch was eels and carp, significant in both medieval Europe
and China.

Within this spectrum, the fisheries of Europe and China followed a
similar trajectory, though at separate times in different directions and
to varying degrees. Both began with palaeolithic on-shore pursuit of
molluscs and crustaceans. Both advanced in antiquity to in-shore fishing of the kind still found in the Mezzogiorno, or the Greek islands,
the Yangtze delta, the Inland Sea, and the coastal waters of Hong Kong.
Then, from the Han in China and the early Middle Ages in Europe,
there was simultaneous development of fishpond pisciculture in Szechwan,
the Lower Yangtze, eastern France and Central Europe, and off-shore
fishing for herring and yellow croaker. In the age of globalization,
there was a leap outwards to far-shore fishing: an earlier, short leap in
the case of China to the South China Seas, the waters of Hainan and
the continental shelf of Indonesia; a later, long leap in the case of
Europe to the waters of Iceland, the Barents Sea and the continental
shelf of North America. Finally, with the acceptance from 1975 of
200-mile territorial waters, that latest if possibly Pyrrhic victory of the
nation-state, fisheries in both Europe and East Asia have been forced
back from far-shore to off-shore, and with the growth of inhibitory
conservation and changes in taste, to in-shore and on-shore. Thus contemporary fisheries return to the palaeolithic.

In both Europe and China, the extension of the fisheries in the age
of globalization was based, as Laurier Turgeon has pointed out, on a
variant of Franklin Mendels' rural proto-industrialization.[25] Communities specialized, fisheries capitalized, fishermen proletarianized, labour
was more divided, markets widened, and output rose. Though fisher
ports took on some of the cultural characteristics of mining communities, in society at large, a new alimentary consumerism of the not so
well-to-do was made possible. Provided, that is, that the problem of
distribution could be overcome. Fish is one of the most perishable of
foodstuffs: useless when rotten, best fresh, but acceptable on a scale
of less and more processed. Here salt was a crucial factor. In Ningpo,
the greatest fishing port of pre-modern China, the junkmen fought a

continual battle with Liang-che salt division, which was frightened that unused fishery salt would be smuggled inland. In Newfoundland waters, a greater availability of salt was a reason why French fishermen focused on the more heavily salted, less processed and more profitable 'green' cod catch on the outer banks, while English fishermen focused on the less salted but more dehydrated 'dry' salt catch on the inner waters with drying stations ashore. The long-term answer was refrigeration, but, while the Chinese made some progress with their deep ice houses and ice boats accompanying the fleets, this solution was not available to Europeans till the late nineteenth century. Fish, therefore, tended to be fresher in Shanghai than in Paris.

In *ancien régime* France, fish was either a coastal or an urban food. In maritime towns, hospitals, schools and convents were regular buyers. Paris, however, supreme here as in other consumerisms, consumed 12 kg per head per annum as against a national average of 2 kg. A list of people who ate fish there included coopers, tailors, surgeons, domestics, religious, school children, soldiers, sailors, shopkeepers, minor civil servants and clerks: a cross-section of the new service classes who, more than the bourgeoisie, were the carriers of consumerism. Consumer preference put fish in a hierarchy. First came fresh fish, either direct from the coast or from fishponds. Next came lightly processed salted 'green' cod, which sold best in the wealthier part of France north of the Loire. Last came the more highly processed 'dry' cod, which could withstand the cost and wastage of transport to the poorer part of France south of the Loire. In Europe as a whole, 'dry' cod, in which English and New England fishermen specialized, found its best market in southern Europe: Portugal, Spain and Italy, which, from the seventeenth century, was becoming relatively poorer than the north. Protestant fishermen thus provided Friday and Lenten fare for Catholic abstinence, just as Huguenot milliners in Wandsworth made cardinals' hats for their eminences in Rome. Abstinence originally envisaged a diet of bread and water, but Aquinas permitted fish and, except in Lent, cheese and eggs, and subsequently the exception was relaxed. What started as anti-meat became pro-fish, in a context where, as Le Roy Ladurie has shown, abstinence in general and Lent in particular were popular and well-observed lay pieties. However, when the rigorist Counter-Reformation church and state tried to turn a voluntary into an enforced observance, its popularity declined, and fish suffered by association with discipline. Consumers shifted to alternative cheap protein in cheese and eggs. With the exception of 'King' Roquefort, most French cheeses, such as Brie, Camembert, Port Salut and Saint-Paulin, date only from the eighteenth or early nineteenth centuries. Port Salut was the product of the Cistercians of the strict observance, the Trappists, for whom life was a perpetual Lent, but it did not carry the same rebarbative image as salt or dried cod.

In England, the ranking of fish was similar. Pepys probably ate herrings and cod, but they were not worthy of mention. His most commonly referred-to seafoods were oysters, either as a snack with a business associate or girlfriend or as a first course at a midday dinner, and lobsters, either out at midday or at home for supper. Thus Pepys shared some with his greatest patron, Lord Sandwich, and, on another occasion, was annoyed with himself when he left some behind in a coach on the way home. Cheese was humbler fare, and the only one Pepys names is the Parmesan he took care to move out of Seething Lane during the Fire. As in France, most of the famous English cheeses date from the eighteenth century when better roads diffused knowledge of local specialties. Thus Stilton, related to the Great North Road, was praised by Pope and familiar to Jane Austen. In Holland, the dialectic of fish and cheese began earlier. In the seventeenth century, pickled herring, cod, Edam and Gouda were all common parts of the diet. In 1636 the admiralty of Amsterdam guaranteed to common sailors half a pound of cheese, half a pound of butter and a fresh five-pound loaf a week, in addition to rougher food. In the eighteenth century, an English traveller described the Dutch as epicures in fish who would only eat the freshest varieties. Increasingly, the pickled herrings, on which the greatness of Amsterdam had been founded, were for export only. Some of them went to Russia where they joined dried roach or perch from the Caspian and the sea of Azov, not to mention sturgeon caught off Mazanderan and pickled with Astrakhan salt. By the 1880s average annual fish consumption in Russia had risen to more than 7 kg a year, well above *ancien régime* France, and by the mid-twentieth century to 14 kg a year. By the 1980s, the Soviet Union's fish catch was second only to that of Japan and double that of the United States.[26]

In China, the major marine fishing grounds – in-shore, off-shore and far-shore – were those fished from eastern Ckekiang. In the 1930s, 100 000 families and 17 000 boats participated directly, but it was reckoned that three million people were dependent indirectly.[27] The fish business was highly organized. Besides the actual fishing vessels which might remain at sea for several months, there were ice boats and salt boats to prevent the catch rotting, and on shore a battery of fish warehouses (*yü-chan*), fish factories (*yü-ch'ang*), fish guilds (*yü-hang*), wholesalers and retailers: a subdivision of function to increase speed from producer to consumer. The catch was varied: crabs, jellyfish, eels, sharks, hairtails, pomfret, shad, flounder. But the most important catch, the equivalent of herring or cod in Europe, was croaker: large yellow (*ta-huang yü*) and small yellow (*hsiao-huang yü*). Much of this went to the Yangtze delta, Shanghai in particular, or down the coast to Foochow and Amoy. Aquatic food was esteemed. In 1730, Li Yu, a minor liter- ary figure, wrote: 'as far as crabs are concerned, my mind is addicted to them, my mouth enjoys the taste of them, and not a single day in my life have I ever forgotten about them'.[28] In Shanghai, as in Paris, preference went to fresh fish, but despite the ice boats and the fishponds, this was not always available at an acceptable price. Recourse there- fore was had to processed fish, especially croaker, as with cod in Eu- rope, salted or dried to various degrees. Chinese taste did not run to strong flavours: salmon, tuna and swordfish, all popular in Japan, were rejected. It was to obviate such flavours in croaker, that sweet-and- sour fish was developed at Cheng-chou, in northern Honan, an inland town without water transport. In China, fish at least did not have to compete with cheese. Chinese agriculture did not combine arable with pasture and Chinese people had little taste for milk products. What did compete with fish as a food accessory was the soya bean: the equiv- alent in China of milk products in Europe and Islam.

The Soya Bean within China and Beyond

In 1906 the customs commissioner at Newchwang in South Manchu- ria, C. A. V. Bowra, wrote: 'It is said that in South China the natives like to eat "sweet"; in the North they like to eat "salt". Salted veg- etables are eaten in enormous quantities; salted fish, shrimps, beef and pork, and the favourite pickled beancurd all form articles of diet in universal use.'[29] Beancurd, a vegetable cream cheese or solidified yoghurt, widely used for fat or flavouring in a variety of stir-fry side dishes, was the most characteristic food product of the soya bean. So called from the Japanese *sho-yu*, soy sauce, a version of the Chinese *chiang- yü*, the soya bean is a concentrated and balanced source of calories: 42 per cent carbohydrate, 38 per cent protein, 20 per cent fat. A pound of soya beans has twice the protein of a pound of beef-steak. Soya beans are not difficult to grow, and, like so many *leguminosae*, have nitrogen fixing qualities so they are virtually self-fertilizing. If the excavations at Hung-shan in the 1980s are correct, they were first cul- tivated in Central Manchuria *c*.3000 BC, as the basis of an indepen- dent Tungusic neolithic nucleus. Adopted and diffused in North China under the Han, they were eventually implanted in many parts of the sub-continent – Szechwan, for example – and even among the overseas Chinese communities of Indonesia. But Manchuria remained the best and largest source of supply, and as late as the 1920s produced 60 per cent of the world's total. In China, soya beans were a frontier crop, part of *limes* lifestyle, however well-absorbed.

Soya beans, similar to our broad beans, were used in several ways. First, they might be eaten whole as part of a side dish. Second, they might be transformed into beancurd and given a number of additional flavourings. Third, they might form the raw material out of which soy sauce was manufactured. Fourth, their oil might be expressed and used for cooking, as an illuminant, or as raw material in the production of soap, paints, varnishes and lubricants. It was this industrial use which in the late nineteenth and early twentieth centuries led to international trade in Manchurian beans and bean oil. Much of this was directed to the nascent German chemical industry. In 1918, Manchuria exported 600 000 tons of whole beans, 750 000 tons of bean oil, and 1 000 000 tons of bean cake. Fifth, beans might be used as fertilizer, in the form of bean cake, that is, beans from which oil had been expressed, because of its nitrogen content. In China, Manchurian bean cake was used, especially from the mid-eighteenth century, in the cotton fields of Kiangsu and the sugar plantations of Fukien. These in turn added to the consumerism of Peking and Mukden with textiles and sugar. Already at the beginning of the nineteenth century, there were 3500 junks engaged in the traffic between Manchuria and the Lower Yangtze.[30] It was one of the major maritime articulations of the Chinese empire, and its volume increased when to the junks were added steamers, foreign and Chinese, the famous 'beancakers' which formed a kind of rock bottom for firms like Butterfield and Swire. Just as *kao-liang* provided Chinese immigrants from Chihli, Shantung and Honan with a subsistence crop, soya beans and bean products provided Manchuria with an export crop. With their aid, Manchuria could walk on two legs from a population of one million in 1787 to one of over 40 million in 1953. Thanks to this economic and demographic infrastructure, Manchuria was able to become, apart from the Lower Yangtze, the most heavily urbanized region of China, with, except for Shanghai, the highest levels of consumption.

Outside China, soya beans found their greatest success in the United States, followed by Brazil where the crop was strongly developed after 1960. The West first heard about soya beans from the Jesuits and botanists began to experiment with them in the late eighteenth century.

Thus, they were being grown by the Jardins des Plantes in 1781, at Kew in 1789, in Philadelphia, perhaps as a result of Benjamin Franklin's advocacy, in 1804, and in Cambridge, Massachusetts in 1829. There was a second introduction to the United States from Japan by Commodore Perry. By the beginning of the twentieth century, North Carolina was the leading American soya state, but production was not large. It was not until the interwar period that soya beans entered the corn belt, but by 1942, the United States was number one producer, outdistancing Manchuria, a kind of vegetable parallel to the battle of Midway. A lobby of enthusiasts for human consumption was active, of whom the most notable was Dr Harry W. Miller (1879–1976), an ex-Seventh Day Adventist medical missionary to China from Ohio, but its success was limited. Most of the crop went as food for pigs and poultry in the form of meal. After the war, half was exported for similar consumption elsewhere, notably to Europe via Rotterdam. At times soya beans were the largest single US export. In Europe, bean meal competed with fish meal, both imported from Peru and produced locally by Norway and Denmark, and with the newly developed rape seed industry in Europe. Such competition between animal foodstuffs frequently formed part of the tortuous GATT negotiations of the early 1990s. A source of protein itself, the soya bean makes a major contribution to the production of animal protein which is still, despite the devotees of fish or cheese, the world's preferred food accessory. If, however, the world ever turns vegetarian, in some super-green or animal rights revolution, the soya bean will be a prime beneficiary. China's Manchurian frontier could turn out to be everyone's frontier. As an enthusiast put it: 'soybeans can be the cream in your coffee, the dog in your bun, the chow for your cat, and then some'.[31]

In taking fish and soya beans as instances of consumerism in food accessories in the age of globalization it might seem that we have neglected the essential in favour of the peripheral. The essential, one could argue, was the growth of great cattle ranches in the New World to feed the slaughterhouses of Chicago and Buenos Aires, the conquest of Australia by sheep as much for the freezing works as for the woolshed, and the expansion of pigs in Szechwan or poultry in the United States, all of which increased the protein and fat content in the diet. Meat surely was the centre. Yet fish, cheese and beans were important at the lower levels and outer edges of consumerism, which were also its growing points. In the mid-1980s, Japan, hardly the least progressive of economies, obtained 50 per cent of its protein intake from vegetable products as against 27 per cent from meat and 22 per cent from fish. Fish and beans fully deserve their place in the history of consumerism.

EXTRAS: TEA AND COFFEE

In both Europe and China between 1400 and 1800, three meals a day was the assumed norm. Within these meals, the duality of carbohydrate and side dish, *fan* and *ts'ai*, pasta and sauce, potatoes and meat, was still basic, despite the impact of the *limes* lifestyle which in the West centralized the meal round a roast and in the East decentralized it to a multiplicity of side dishes. In both areas, however, snacks between meals, *hsiao-shih* ('small eats'), were frequent, as supplied by taverns, teahouses and street sellers. Moreover, this structure left room for consumerist extras, valued as much for culture as for calories, *bene esse* rather than *esse*. Structurally, extras took four forms. They might accompany meals, as with many drinks. They might add a new course, as in the case of puddings and desserts. They might create a new meal (or rather *two* new meals), as was the case with tea in England. They might reconstitute snacks, as was the case with coffee almost everywhere except, as yet, China. In every form, the extras were spearheads of consumerism.

The category of extras was created, no doubt, by fruit and wine, closely associated. In the Middle Ages and early modernity, however, a central place within it was taken by sugar, with which the newcomers of the age of globalization, tea, coffee and chocolate, were to make firm alliances, and on whose foundations they built. Sugar created dessert which could never be adequately sustained by honey. It extended food consumerism to more women and most children. It provided carbohydrate in a highly concentrated form. By the middle of the eighteenth century, it had become indispensable everywhere to civilized living. 'Sugar, Sugar, Sugar, Mr Speaker, Who will laugh at sugar now?' declaimed Pitt in the House of Commons on 9 March 1759, and we, like the members, must be cowed by his vehemence.[32] In particular, sugar forms part of the prehistory of tea and coffee because it allowed what were bitter drinks in the lands of their origin to become sweet drinks in the lands of their reception.

Sugar cane was first domesticated in New Guinea: an unexpected origin for a major constituent of culture. Neither the Han nor Graeco-Latin antiquity knew sugar. The earliest literary reference is in the writings of Buddhaghosa, a Theravada scholastic of around AD 500, who operated in the Buddhist maritime network which linked Burma, Ceylon and Indonesia. A Byzantine account of the capture of Ctesiphon by Emperor Heraclius in 627 refers to sugar as an Indian luxury. Cane may then have been cultivated in the deltas of the Indus and the Tigris-Euphrates. Here the Muslims discovered it, as they discovered rice, and thereafter sugar followed the Koran: to Egypt, Cyprus, the Maghreb, Spain, Sicily and Central Asia. Meanwhile, in China, Buddhism brought sugar cane from Magadha to Szechwan and eventually to the Yangtze delta and to Fukien, where Marco Polo commented on the great scale of its production. Christendom followed suit: first on the islands of the eastern Mediterranean, then on the Atlantic islands, the launching pad for Columbus' venture, and finally on the Caribbean islands and the continental island of northeast Brazil. If the first Atlantic of Seville was based on silver, the subsequent Atlantics of Lisbon, Amsterdam and London were based on sugar: hence Pitt's rhetorical question. Sugar, moreover, did not stop with tropical cane. When Napoleon wrote off French seapower and France's colonial empire, in his windowless common market, cane began to be rivalled by temperate beet. By the end of the nineteenth century as much sugar was being produced by beet as by cane. Per capita consumption continued to rise, not only in the West, but also in China, where the production of Fukien, though encouraged by exports to Europe and energized by beancake fertilizer, had to be supplemented by the cane fields of Thailand and Java initiated by Chinese enterprise. Sugar from New Guinea pioneered the consumerist market for extras which tea from China and coffee from Ethiopia were to exploit. It was the prototype of the superfluous but highly agreeable.

Tea from China

The tea plant came from the Nan-shan, the mountain divide which separates China from greater India and Southeast Asia. Commercial production of tea began in Szechwan in the second half of the T'ang period when tea-drinking became fashionable in the capital. There it was associated with the Yang family, the relatives of Emperor Hsüan-tsung's mistress and the feoffees of Szechwan, and with the aristocratic Ch'an (Zen) monks who valued it for keeping alert in meditation. Tea production soon expanded from the hills southwest of Chengtu to the hills southwest of the Yangtze delta and to the Wu-i divide between Kiangsi and Fukien. Under the Sung, tea ceased to be elitist. It was an extra, but hardly a luxury extra, save in its superior brands. At the end of the thirteenth century, Wu Tzu-mu noted that 'the things that people cannot do without every day are firewood, rice, oil, salt, soybean sauce and tea'. Nevertheless, tea, drunk without milk or sugar of course, was not without values. It belonged to the cooling category of foods and was associated with Ch'an Buddhism which was intellectually respectable, while sugar belonged to the heating category and was associated with Pure Land Buddhism which was not. The official, the first to taste the world's sorrow, the last to taste its joy, as Mencius put it, would embrace the bitter rather than the sweet. Confucian highmindedness therefore could make tea its own, and Confucian values were after all widely diffused in traditional China, especially under the Ming and Ch'ing.

Outside China and its satellites, tea consumption first appeared in eastern Islamdom: the three Turkestans, Afghanistan and Persia. There is in fact an interesting line across Islamdom dividing tea drinkers and coffee drinkers. It corresponds roughly to the line between Persians and ex-Persians, and Arabs, with the Turks in Central Asia and Anatolia being divided by the line. Morocco, however, is anomalous, having taken to tea, not early through the caravan trade, but late through contact with the European East Indiamen.

In Europe, tea first came to public notice in the mid-sixteenth century. Around 1550, the Italian travel writer Giambattista Ramusio met, at a dinner party in Venice, a Persian rhubarb merchant who had been to China. The merchant told him that the Chinese said that they had another drug, called *ch'a*, which, if the Europeans knew about it, would make them forget rhubarb. The Jesuits brought further information about tea and its use. Athanasius Kircher wrote in his *China Illustrata*: 'It is of a diuretic faculty, much fortifies the stomach, exhilarates the spirits, and wonderfully openeth all the Nephritick passages or Reins. It freeth the head by suppressing of fuliginous vapours, so that it is a most excellent drink for studious and sedentary persons to quicken them in their operations.' Tea first appeared in Holland in 1610 and in 1637 the directors of the East India Company ordered their agents in the East to send back a few jars with every ship. Dutch physicians – Leiden was then the medical centre of Europe – began recommending tea as a tonic, especially for women. From Holland, tea passed to England and France. In 1657, an enterprising café proprietor, Thomas Garraway, opened the first teashop in London. The same year, Cardinal Mazarin, a highly studious and sedentary person, began to take tea for his gout. On 25 September 1660, Pepys wrote: 'I did send for a cup of tee (a China drink) of which I never had drunk before.' From 1661, Queen

Katherine of Braganza introduced its use, already fashionable in Portugal, ex-Macao, to the English court. In 1664, the English East India Company brought some home as a present for Charles II. In 1701, the directors noted in their instructions to the ship *Northumberland* about to sail for Canton that, 'Tea does very much obtain in reputation among persons of all qualities.' In 1717, they instructed that each ship take in, 'Tea as much as the ship can conveniently stow.'[33] The tea trade had started, as tea ceased to be a medicine and became a drink.

Louis Dermigny has traced the rise of that trade from an export from Canton in 1720 of 10 000 cwt, to one of 400 000 cwt in 1833.[34] The trade was directed largely to England. On the supply side, two sets of factors lay behind this growth. First, there was the competition to the English East India Company by a protean consortium of English Jacobites and Continental Huguenots which embodied itself successively in a line of Continental East India companies and smuggling networks to bring down the price in England and expand sales. Second, there was the younger Pitt's Commutation Act of 1784, which, by drastically reducing the tax on tea (and hence the profits of smuggling), enabled the English East India Company to recapture the trade from its competitors and further expand sales. In 1833, in a further instalment of liberalization, the Whig government of Lord Grey abolished the East India Company's monopoly of tea import to Britain. Free trade, in the depressed 1830s and 1840s, at first made little difference. Then, with the onset of high Victorian prosperity, tea made a third leap forward: from 500 000 cwt in 1847 to 1 200 000 cwt in 1867, and to 1 800 000 cwt in 1886. By this time, exports of tea, if the overland trade be included, amounted to one-third of China's total production. For the Sino-British connection, however, 1886 was the high point: Assam and Ceylon were joining the suppliers. By 1905, England received over 1 million cwt from India, nearly 700 000 cwt from Ceylon, and only 50 000 cwt from China. In 1950 the world market for tea was still dominated by the United Kingdom which imported, mainly from India and Ceylon, nearly 4 million cwt, half the total traded internationally.

On the demand side, behind this trajectory lay two distinct developments in England: afternoon tea and high tea, the first a new meal, the second a mutation of the traditional supper. Afternoon tea preferred China to Indian. Its chief function was not alimentation – keeping body and soul together at appropriate temperature by means of calories – but social entertainment, especially by and for women, even when sandwiches and cake came to accompany it. As social entertainment, tea and tea parties may be associated, as both cause and effect, with a rise in the status, independence and affluence of women which, although general in eighteenth-century Western Europe, was, nevertheless, most prominent in England. By its demands for special facilities, furniture, ceramics, clothes and the opportunity to use them, the tea party promoted a feminization of domestic space and time via the drawing room and the tea hour. This promotion formed part of the more general feminization of consumption which preceded the industrial revolution and which was, so it will be argued in the chapter on dress, the chief long-term, demand-side, cause of it. England's precocity in tea was a sign of its overall economic, social and cultural precocity. Coffee and chocolate were still too expensive to play the role of middle-class, feminine, social beverage. Moreover, in the eighteenth century, the coffee house was still male-oriented, a place of business as much as recreation, and affiliated more to the street than to the home. Afternoon tea, a superfluous meal, born of affluence, leisure and domestic sociability, was the ideal expression of a particular social conjuncture.

High tea was the less than ideal expression of a different social conjuncture. It preferred Indian to China, because it was cheaper and stronger. It was not an extra, superfluous meal. Rather, it was a substitute, in the circumstances of early industrialization in the north of England, for both the heavy midday dinner and the light evening supper of Pepys' day. Its time was dictated by the return of the male from work and it presupposed a divorce between workplace and home. Since the male was further presupposed to have had an early breakfast and only a light, cold lunch of bread and cheese, its aim was to convey hot, concentrated calories quickly: hence the closer alliance between tea and sugar, strong Indian being better suited to the combination than weak China. Sugar also figured in the jam which made the basic carbohydrate palatable, and in the cakes which added a note of feminine culinary skill. Meat was frequently a male prerogative. Women and children shared in it only as dripping, confining themselves to the carbohydrates, diffused and concentrated, and to the tea. Where afternoon tea represented a feminization, high tea represented a remasculinization of domestic time and space. It was eaten at a time convenient for the husband with the wife in the background doing the work. It took place as often in the kitchen round the range as in a dining-room. High tea expressed a new social reality: the unity of the family at night, its division by day – at work, school, domestic service or back at home. Probably of rural origin, since one found it in Yorkshire farmhouses as well as in back-to-back dwellings, high tea became the alimentary infrastructure of the early industrial revolution in England. Though, like other aspects of early industrialization, it represented an albeit temporary fall in social standards to meet the economic needs of capital formation, it nevertheless preserved the values of the neo-local, nuclear family for future advance. In terms of consumerism, it was a *reculer pour mieux sauter*.

Coffee

If sugar added a new course and tea added two new meals, coffee revitalized snacks. At times it threatened to disrupt the order of meals and courses altogether and restore demand feeding in a succession of coffee breaks. For this reason, its empire, more universal than that of tea, made least progress in China, where the importance of snacks was already established. Even in East Asia, however, French and Spanish example secured the dominance of coffee over tea in Vietnam and the Philippines, in 1985 South Korea consumed more coffee than Egypt, and by the end of the twentieth century Japan was expected to surpass the United Kingdom in per capita consumption. Coffee was the global consumerist extra.[35]

Coffee, like sorghum, came from the Horn of Africa, but from its southwestern rather than northwestern escarpment, probably from the present Ethiopian province of Kaffa. From Ethiopia, coffee cultivation passed to the Yemen, most likely during the occupation of South Arabia by the Negus between 525 and 575. Apart from Ethiopia itself, where production was not large, the Yemen retained a world monopoly of coffee supply until the seventeenth century. The drink, more as a medicine than a beverage, is first mentioned by the Persian physician Rhazes (850–922) and then by that universal man Avicenna (980–1037). In the Yemen, coffee was associated with the dervish orders or *tarikats* established in the hill country south of the Holy Places, notably Zabid. In their pilgrim hostels and study centres, the dervishes used coffee to keep alert during their *dhikr* or special services, which sometimes lasted several hours: a use comparable to that of tea by the Ch'an monks in their meditation halls. In the period after the Mongol invasions when the dervish orders became the dynamic force in Islam and the Holy Places succeeded to the caliphate, pilgrims and scholars returning from the Yemen diffused the use of coffee to the rest of the Muslim world.

It was diffused first to Mamluk Egypt, the protector of the Holy Places. Here it was introduced in the fifteenth century under the patronage of the Shadhiliyya, the most aristocratic and intellectual of the dervish orders in Egypt, and was accepted as legitimate for Muslims by the consensus-minded Shafiite law doctors of al-Azhar.[36] Edward Lane noted 1000 coffee-shops in Cairo, but coffee, drunk strong without sugar or milk, remained a luxury, which was subsequently, under British influence presumably, challenged by tea.[37] From Cairo, coffee passed to Aleppo, the northern Mamluk capital. It first appeared in Constantinople in the first half of the sixteenth century, no doubt as a result of the Ottoman conquest of Syria and Egypt. Consumption was encouraged by the imposition of firm Ottoman rule in South Arabia by Yemeni Fatih Sinan Pasha in 1568. How sugar got added is not clear, but it may have been through the near contemporary conquest of the Venetian sugar island of Cyprus in 1571. From Constantinople, coffee passed, via the Turkish fleet, to Algeria, which is today a much bigger consumer of coffee than Egypt. In Constantinople, the reaction to coffee was not always favourable. Not all *tarikats* approved and some *ulema*, especially of the Hanbalite school, opposed it as falling under the Koranic ban against alcohol and stimulants. Sultan Murad IV (1623–40) issued decrees against both coffee and tobacco. Yet the prohibitions had little effect. Of the leading dervish orders, the Mevleviyya and the Bektashiyya were relatively liberal in their interpretation of the *sharia*, Islamic canon law, as were the marabouts in North Africa. Moreover, the greatest of the dervish orders, the Naqshbandiyya, despite its devotion to the *sharia*, never showed any systematic hostility to coffee. Coffee houses, therefore, became numerous in Constantinople, periodically closed, as by Grand Vizier Mehmet Koprulu in 1656, but more as centres of rumour and ructions than for ideological reasons. Turkish coffee had come to stay.

From the Ottoman empire, coffee passed to Christendom, a Dr Rauwolf who had been in Aleppo in 1573 being the first European to mention it. Clement VIII (1592–1605), a relaxed ecumenical pope, the friend of St Filippo Neri, gave it his approval, rejecting the argument that being black and Muslim it must be devilish. Christian clerics valued it for the same properties as Muslim or Buddhist. Rhazes and Avicenna were still medical authorities in seventeenth-century Europe. Italy, especially the north, was the pioneer of European coffee drinking, with Venice, through its contacts with the Levant, being the chief diffusion point. In France, an ally of the Ottoman empire, coffee advanced from Marseille to Lyon to Paris, where it was being sold in 1582. When Richelieu began building the Palais Cardinal in 1636, a number of places selling coffee grew up in its vicinity. In 1669, Suleiman Aga, ambassador of Mehmet IV, introduced Turkish coffee to the court of Louis XIV. In 1672, an Armenian named Pascal opened a café in the

Foire St Germain to cater to a wider public. By the early eighteenth century, Vienna was full of coffee houses, consumption surcharged by the quantity of beans abandoned by the Ottoman army after the siege of 1683. In Russia, coffee was being imported by 1726, though here it did not make headway against the dominant tea. In 1735, du Halde reported coffee being sold by Armenians at Sining in northwest China, probably brought from India via Tibet, but here too it came up against a tea barrier unbreakable till the twentieth century. In England, the first coffee drinker was Nathaniel Conopius, from Crete (then Venetian territory), who came to Oxford in 1638 as part of the scholarly exchanges arranged by Archbishop Laud, and the ecumenically minded Cretan patriarch of Constantinople, Cyril Lucaris.[38] The first coffee house was opened in 1650, in Oxford, by a Sephardic Jew named Jacob from the Ottoman empire, possibly an exile from Sabbatai's movement, who took advantage of Cromwell's philosemitism. In 1652, another Ottoman subject, variously described as a Greek or Armenian, opened the first coffee house in London near St Michael's, Cornhill. Pepys has several mentions of coffee houses, but he does not say what he drank in them, so that one wonders whether it was not just a fashionable name for an eating house or tavern.

As consumption expanded, so too did production. All early European coffee came from the Yemen, either indirectly via the Levant, or directly via the Dutch East India Company which traded at Mocha and sent coffee home via the Cape route. In the early seventeenth century, coffee was acclimatized in Mysore by a returning *hajji*, probably a dervish. In 1658 the Dutch began cultivation in Ceylon and in 1696 they brought plants to Java to inaugurate what was to become a massive set of plantations. The first crop arrived in Amsterdam in 1706. The Dutch also took coffee to Surinam in 1718 and French botanists, who obtained plants from Amsterdam, sent them to Martinique in the 1720s. In 1723 the first coffee was planted in Brazil in the province of Para and in 1760 it was brought to Rio, the initial credit being given to a Capuchin and Archbishop Joachim Bruno. From this point, Brazil, whether at Rio or São Paulo, rapidly obtained the dominance of the world coffee market which, despite competition earlier from Java and later from Columbia, Ivory Coast and Angola, it has never looked like losing. Apart from slaves, coffee was Africa's greatest contribution to America in return for manioc, maize and yellow fever.

On the demand side, coffee in Europe followed different imperatives from those of tea. Where tea, whether in silver pot or iron samovar, was feminine, coffee initially was masculine, as befitted its Islamic and clerical origins. When Pepys went on a *süsses Madel* crawl, it was to taverns and eating houses that he took them, not to coffee houses. Where tea belonged to the home, coffee belonged to the street. It was part of that quickening of business activity which followed the ending of the seventeenth-century depression and the definite victory of quarantine over plague in Western Europe. The origins of the London insurance market in 1688 in Lloyds coffee house in Tower Street, later moved to Abchurch Lane, is a case in point. Coffee houses, better than taverns, provided facilities for business. They were a sign of the growing importance of brokers in business and the primacy of information in the market. Where tea provided gossip over the table, coffee provided news round it. Consequently, coffee was most consumed, not in the Latin south where it was most esteemed, but in the more literate and commercialized north. In 1879, the leading consumers of coffee per capita were Holland, Belgium and Denmark. In 1987, the position was not so different. Sweden consumed 12 kg per capita per annum, Holland 8 kg, Belgium 7 kg, as against France 5 kg, Italy 2 kg and the United Kingdom 3 kg, though here allowance should be made for concentration in the southeast.

Serious coffee drinking only began in the United Kingdom after the Second World War. In 1879, the United Kingdom, like the United States, only consumed $1/2$ kg per capita per annum, as compared to four or five of tea. A century later, consumption had multiplied six times, maybe more in the capital and home counties. By 1989, tea and coffee divided England almost equally as regards per capita consumption. They also divided it geographically and even politically, the frontier lying roughly along the Fosse Way. Tea England to the north was Labour. Coffee England to the south was Conservative. Lady Thatcher's long ascendancy could have been predicted from the beverage figures alone. The chief agency of the rise of coffee was the post-war London coffee bar. The coming of *espresso* and *cappuccino* represented a partial feminization of business space: secretaries did not go to taverns and girlfriends could no longer, as in Pepys' day, be taken there. Its subsequent eclipse by the wine bar and the licensed pizza house represented the next stage in female emancipation, though they too were overtaken by the reaction against alcohol and tobacco. Another factor in the progress of coffee in the capital was the explosion of ethnic restaurants outside Soho from the 1960s: Italian, Spanish, Greek, Turkish, West Indian. Coffee was democratized and demystified. A feature of British coffee consumption was that, to a greater extent than any other country, it was composed of soluble, that is, instant, coffee. Coffee snobbery never established itself to the extent wine snobbery did. Speed and uniformity were what was required. It was an expression of the age of the typewriter, the photocopy, and the big bang. How coffee will fare in the age of the word processor, when bachelor girls and Sloane rangers have become unisex executives, remains to be seen, but the information on the screen would seem to demand just that alertness for which its devotees have always prized coffee.

Both tea and coffee were implicated in one of the major factors behind the rise of consumerism: the greater recognition of women's needs, tastes, initiative and intelligence; what might be called the feminine cutting edge of consumerism. For if consumerism is the imposition of mind on matter, the humanization of objects, then the humanity in question, the mind doing the imposing, has been increasingly female. This conclusion will be reinforced in the next chapter which follows the fortunes of dress.

3 Consumerism and Dress

In the history of consumption, dress forms a natural transition between food and shelter. All three relate to thermoregulation and choices in one affect choices in the others. Thus Europe's option for the heavy house, with its insulated microclimate and high diffused heat, affected European dress with its distinction of indoors and outdoors. Similarly, Chinese dress with its multiple layers in winter was related to the Chinese option for the light, uninsulated house with its low heat concentrated in the *k'ang* or thermo-bed. Consumerism, however, is more than consumption. It is consumption directed by *mentalité*: mind mattering in an incarnation of values. In the period 1400 to 1800, dress was the leading sector of consumerism in this sense, because, more than food or shelter, it was surcharged – in Europe strongly, in China weakly – by fashion, especially feminine fashion. Whereas in food, the Chinese were as consumerist as the Europeans, possibly more so, in dress comparison leads to contrast: a China dominated by male protocol, a Europe dominated by female fashion. Although the contrast requires attenuation, if only because the Chinese really invented fashion in dress, it remains true that Lipovetsky's empire of the ephemeral – an empire not only *over* the ephemeral but *by* it over other departments of life – went further in Europe than in China. It was round Europe, therefore, that consumerism as a world institution initially constructed itself.

This chapter, like the last, falls into two parts: an introduction to the logic of fashion, followed by successive sections on dress essentials, accessories and extras, as they came under the empire of fashion in the age of globalization.

THE LOGIC OF FASHION

It is often supposed that the logic of fashion is that it has no logic. In this view, fashion belongs to the kingdom of the irrational: either the whims of a few Paris moguls or the *non sequiturs* of an international youth culture. Fashion, in the expressive phrase of Lipovetsky (though he does not share this view) is a 'cascade of little nothings'.[1] In fact, it will be argued here, the truth is almost the exact opposite. Not only does fashion have a logic, indeed a succession of logics, but in the past its rationality has anticipated those of science and scholarship. If humankind eats what it is, it often thinks what it wears. Thus the logic of fashion has developed from the systematic to the unsystematic, from deterministic chaos to interdeterministic chaos, as the empire of the ephemeral has expanded its domain. 'Non-existent' fashion may be 'le rien qui fait tout', but illogical it is not.[2]

Let us start with linguistic conventions. First, in what follows, dress will be used as the most general term to comprise the production, distribution and consumption of clothes together with the finalities and functions which govern them. Dress is the *langue* of which clothes, as possessed and worn, are the *paroles*. Next, within the category of clothes, it is useful to make a distinction between wardrobe and wear. What shall I buy follows different imperatives from what shall I wear. Things bought with great care may never leave the wardrobe, or, alternatively, may virtually reduplicate items already there, whether used or not. Third, within both wardrobe and wear, a distinction may be made between outfits, which correspond to meals in the food series, and garments, which correspond to their component dishes. Daily meals correspond to the whole clothes performance of a person in a day: at breakfast, in the office, back home and out in the evening. Dress and clothes, wardrobe and wear, outfits and garments: these are the grammatical elements of the subject. Beyond grammar, however, is syntax into actual sentences: indicative, imperative, interrogatory, optative, conditional. Here a distinction should be made between protocol, prescription by another, as most characteristically in military uniform, and fashion, choice by oneself with others only as points of reference. Thus one way to describe the change from premodernity to modernity in dress is to say that protocol has been overcome by fashion. Both protocol and fashion, however, serve similar finalities and functions in dress, though fashion has added itself to their number.

The functions of dress have often been enumerated. In 1930, J. C. Flügel, writing from an early psychoanalytic point of view, named them as decoration, modesty and protection. Protection he dismissed as a rationalization mainly on the score of the quasi-nakedness observed by Darwin in Terra del Fuego. Modesty he regarded as negative decoration or resistance to self-display. Decoration was thus left as the basic function, though always in conflict with resistance: 'This essential opposition between the two motives of decoration and modesty is, I think, the most fundamental fact in the whole psychology of clothing.'[3] In 1978, Robert Delort, focusing on fur in late medieval Europe, listed thermoregulation, modesty, decoration, status and fashion as the finalities of dress.[4] Leaving aside his analysis of fashion to which we shall return, Delort's list amounts to a reiteration of Flügel's, with greater acceptance of protection as more than rationalization, and a more sophisticated differentiation of decoration into sexual and social. In 1981, Alison Lurie in her linguistic analysis of dress, clothes as semiotic rather than semantic, accepted implicitly Delort's pluralism of irreducible functions. She distinguished more sharply, however, decoration used in youth to proclaim attraction and acclaim time and decoration used in age to conserve dignity and defy time.[5] In 1987, Lipovetsky returned to a more unitary approach, though one quite different from Flügel's. Focusing on fashion, he argued that all the other functions of dress were obsolescent and in retreat before the dominance of fashion as self-expression and celebration of novelty. Under the rule of fashion, dress became the kingdom of Proteus, clothes a secular sacrament of the present moment. He concluded: 'Telle est la grandeur de la mode qui renvoie toujours plus l'individu à lui-même, telle est la misère de la mode qui nous rend de plus en plus problématique à nous-mêmes et aux autres.'[6] Where Flügel referred dress to a Freudian ego, Lipovetsky refers it more to a Jungian self.

Against this background, first the history and then the logic of fashion may now be examined. First, fashion has not always existed. It is not the same as luxury or extravagance. Its motto has always been more taste than money, though even in the form of anti-fashion, it costs, as with the case of Radcliffe beatnik or Bonwit tat in the 1960s or Grunge in the 1990s. It is doubtful if fashion existed in antiquity whether Graeco-Roman or Han. In the West, Cleopatra's see-through dresses at the summit with Antony at Tarsus in 41 BC, their display in the reign of Nero which so upset Seneca, and their widespread revival in Constantinople where Chrysostom preached against them, were a mixture of shock, exoticism and luxury. Shock, that is the outrage of deliberate if controlled immodesty, is not fashion but only a temporary departure from protocol, while exoticism, if not mutated, remains only potential fashion. In Graeco-Roman antiquity, neither was pursued to the point where protocol broke down. In China, the most famous Han costumes were not those of the living but of the dead: the jade suits of incorruptibility described in texts and recently recovered from tombs.[7] Though confined to a time span – the Western Han to the San-kuo Wei – they were protocol rather than fashion. The design was uniform, there were no gender distinctions, the use of gold, silver or copper thread was regulated according to rank in the imperial house or favour among China's foreign clients. Similar uniformity is found in surviving Han garments for the living, except for status differences in the quality of silk. While in both Europe and China, the *limes* lifestyle revolution brought increased use of 'barbarian' trousers and a general move from draped to shaped, this was a secular shift in style rather than an ephemeral change in fashion. Protocol, defied or modified, remained in command.

Lipovetsky sees three ages in the empire of fashion: premodern (1350–1850), which may be divided into medieval and *ancien régime*; modern (1850–1950), the age of the Paris fashion houses beginning with Worth and ending with Dior; and postmodern, 1950 plus, the decentralized age of designer boutiques (Quant, Ashley, Kenzo, and so on). Lipovetsky puts the origin of fashion in the interlocked courts of France, England and Burgundy in the late Middle Ages, a view shared and well documented by Delort. But in fact, Europe's permanent initiation of fashion was preceded by its temporary initiation in China in the reign of the T'ang emperor Hsüan-tsung (713–56). In the second half of the reign, dominated by his celebrated consort Yang Kuei-fei and the aristocratic minister Li Lin-fu, fashion, in the sense of frequent novelty in music, dance and dress, was a feature of court life. Emperor and consort imitated not only the steps of the Central Asian dance groups who came with tribute missions, but also their exotic costume. Head dress in particular changed frequently, but there were also variations in line.[8] Two unusual styles originating in the T'ang court, and known to us from both literary sources and the Tun-huang paintings, subsequently reappeared in late medieval Europe. First, there was the tall conical feminine head-dress, to which veils were attached, known as the *hennin*. Second, there was what may be called the 'back right-angled triangle' or 'front hypotenuse' line for women: that 'pregnant' look worn by Jeanne de Chenany as portrayed by van Eyck in the *Betrothal of the Arnolfini*. Giovanni Arnolfini's immense 'masculine' hat which, as Flügel observes, balances Jeanne's 'feminine' look, may also owe something to Chinese example. Since Islamdom was not a good conveyor of feminine fashions, both the *hennin* and the front hypotenuse were probably conveyed from China to Europe via the Manichaean Uighurs of Turfan, the pre-Muslim Il-khanate, Armenia, and the Lusignan court of Cyprus.

Behind the efflorescence of feminine fashion under the T'ang was a political, indeed social, even intellectual, conjuncture. T'ang government worked through fascination. To enlist the aristocracy which had subverted previous dynasties, it offered cosmopolitan glamour to offset the provinciality with which China was constantly threatened. At the same time, the dynasty began to shift its basis from hereditary aristocracy to bureaucracy recruited by imperial examination. In the transition from magnates to mandarinate (and only then), there was room for a 'madamate': mediation by educated imperial princesses and consorts. This potential was exploited most fully by Empress Wu and her female secretariat, partially by her successors, Empress Wei, the An-lo and T'ai-p'ing princesses, and, finally, by Yang Kuei-fei, the Chinese Pompadour. Feminization was not confined to politics. An increase in farm size and a shift from cereals to silk, enhanced women's role in the household, especially in Szechwan whence Yang Kuei-fei came. Finally, fashion in dress may have been encouraged by the latest intellectual currents at court: Tantric Buddhism with its stress on non-verbal communication in gesture (*mudras*), spell (*mantras*), logo (*mandala*) and initiation (*abhisheka*), and Ch'an Buddhism with its cult of wordless but meaningful performance.[9]

In China, fashion did not last. Yang Kuei-fei was put to death by court eunuchs, Hsüan-tsung had to abdicate, Ch'ang-an was sacked more than once by puritan provincials. The moment of the madamate passed. Estate management was re-masculinized, foot binding reduced female mobility, Tantrism was rejected and Ch'an was marginalized. Protocol resumed its sway under the Confucian Sung. Chinese dress, except for its massive use of silk, gets slight mention in Marco Polo. Nevertheless, when fashion reappeared, like some subterranean Greek river, in late medieval Europe, it bore marks of its Chinese origin, not only in the details mentioned above, but also in its circumstances.

The birth of fashion in Western Europe took place in what Delort has called the palatine milieu: a flamboyant but unstable court society where personal monarchy was unconsolidated by bureaucracy; where strong-minded royal women like Isabella of Bavaria, Margaret of Anjou, Margaret of York, Margaret of Austria, manoeuvred between aristocratic factions; where religion oscillated between empty gesture and non-verbal mysticism, both often inspired by women. In the competing peer polities of France, England and Burgundy, fascination became again an instrument of government within and without, 'show' a means of survival in cannibalistic conditions. On the one hand, as Delumeau has shown, the Black Death gave Europeans in that macabre age a heightened sense of the ephemeral quality of life. On the other hand, as Lipovetsky argues, Christian sacramentalism sought to incarnate itself in that very ephemerality: 'Un lien intime, bien que paradoxal, unit *l'homo frivolus* et *l'homo religiosus* du cas spécifique chrétien.'[10] Plague, it has been suggested, killed more women than men. It gave them and their reproductive power a new scarcity value. It contributed therefore to the proliferating cult of the Virgin, often portrayed in this

period in the height of fashion. Delumeau has called particular attention to the cult of the Virgin's (metaphorical) cloak at this time.[11]
Dress came to the forefront of sensibility. This laid the foundation for
the specificities of late medieval fashion: the shifts from squirrel to
ermine to sable, the fantastic head-dresses, the exaggerated length of
the *houppelandes*, the extreme shortness of doublets, the excessive points
of shoes. It was a new departure in European culture, set off by
globalization, by light from the long dead star of the T'ang court.

The transition from the medieval to the *ancien régime* phase of
premodern fashion occurred without breach of stylistic continuity, but
with a temporary geographical and a permanent social displacement.
First, in the sixteenth century, the centre of fashion was displaced from
the England–France–Burgundy triangle to the court of Spain, first at
Valladolid and then at Madrid. From Spain came monstrous ruffs, a
shift from colour to black and white, and the farthingale, the exagger-
atedly wide skirt, with understructure: fashions illustrated in El Greco's
Burial of Count Orgaz and in Velasquez's portraits of Infantas. Spanish
predominance, here as elsewhere, could not be sustained. In the seventeenth century leadership returned to Paris. Louis XIV used fashion as
an instrument of policy to support French textiles and to project a
different, more secular glamour. In the eighteenth century, Parisian fashion
dolls and magazines, going all over Europe, set the tone in women's
clothes. For men's clothes, the less formal English country styles predominated, just as in equestrian styles the English pioneered hacking,
trotting and the thoroughbred.

Second, from the sixteenth century, leadership was everywhere displaced from the court to aristocratic public space: from Whitehall to
Mayfair, from Versailles to the Rive Droite, from capitals to ex-capitals
like Valladolid or Nanking, semi-capitals like Naples or Brussels, non-
capitals like Amsterdam, Soochow or Osaka. Everywhere, in the genesis of public space, the theatre was a considerable ingredient, as a
place to see and be seen. Late Ming Nanking was famous for its gor-
geously arrayed geishas, and in the novel *Chin-ping mei* published in
1617 as a satire of yuppy hedonism, professional thespians regularly
formed part of banquet entertainment.[12] In the sixteenth century,
Valladolid became a city of theatres, resident troupes, and long running shows. Similarly, in Pepys' London, the theatre was a point of
contact between court and city, where each could observe the other as
well as the play and its costumes. Another ingredient in public space
was the spa: Bath where in Pump Room, assembly rooms, parade and
abbey, city met provinces in an atmosphere of relative equality. In

Northanger Abbey, Catherine Morland finds that Mrs Allen took no chances: 'Dress was her passion. She had a most harmless delight in being fine; and our heroine's entrée into life could not take place till after three or four days had been spent in learning what was mostly worn, and her chaperon was provided with a dress of the newest fashion.'[13] Even Mr Tilney felt it expedient to profess an expertise in muslins. Finally, according to circumstance, public space was variously constituted by bull fights, *autos da fé*, dragon boat festivals, Easter parades, official entries, race meetings, balls and dances, all of which provided opportunities for displays of dress.

For Lipovetsky, the modern age of fashion is the period of the dominance of the great Paris fashion houses from Worth to Dior. Accordingly, postmodernity began with the eclipse of that dominance by the rise of designer boutiques such as Quant and Kenzo, and the emergence of centres other than Paris. By the 1990s, as fashion became less standardized and more personal, almost every developed country produced designers who competed in an increasingly pluralistic and non-centred market. As with much of the world order, however, the polar attraction of old centres persisted long after their trumpeted overthrow. It was still worth watching Paris.

Lipovetsky's outline of the empire of the ephemeral was advanced, justifiedly, with a Eurocentric eye. For it would be hard to deny that fashion in dress went furthest initially in Europe. Indeed, one may ask whether it has any applicability outside Europe, if, for example, fashion existed in China after the T'ang and before the Parisian fashion houses burst into Shanghai between the wars.

Early European travellers were reticent about Chinese dress. Andrea Corsali, the Florentine spice merchant who was in the East under Portuguese auspices in 1515, described the Chinese as *di nostra qualità*. Did this extend to dress? The Portuguese Dominican Gaspar da Cruz in 1569, in the first European book devoted exclusively to China, says only that the everyday costume was a long gown with ultralong sleeves. His successor, the Spanish Augustinian, Juan Gonzalez de Mendoza, whose *Great and Mighty Kingdom of China* (1585) was based on a wider range of sources, gave even fewer details. He noted the wide use of silk, as common in China 'as in Europe to wear linen'. He marvelled at a piece of Chinese embroidery which caused Philip II, 'a person that little wondreth at things', much amazement. He noted too the wide use of furs, especially sable. But this was about as far as his interest or information extended. Even Matteo Ricci in his *History of the Christian Expedition to China* (1615) confined himself to generalities.

More informative is the Portuguese Jesuit Alvaro de Semedo whose *History of that Great and Renowned Monarchy of China*, originally written in Italian, was translated into English in 1655. He noted first: 'their garments, as also the furniture of their chambers and houses, they make of wool, linen, silk and cotton, which they make great use of and weave thereof many fair and curious stuffs'. He observed, though, that China avoided 'luxury in apparel and excess in diet which are the irreparable ruin of commonwealths'. Next, he noted the absence of gender differences: 'They wear breeches generally, both men and women . . . The rest of their undergarments are the same both in men and women.' Third, he remarked on the absence of local differences: 'This is the habit of this ample kingdom, being as large almost as all Europe, which hardly keepeth constant to its own fashions in any of its smallest provinces.' Finally, Semedo argued that the real differences in Chinese dress were those of age, status, season and wealth. Thus he says, 'The young men wear indifferently all sorts of colours, but the ancient men do wear always the most modest. The common people for the most part are clothed in black, as are all sorts of servants, who are bound not to alter that colour.' Again, he continues: 'The rich men change their garments at all the four seasons of the year, and the inferior sort (although poor) twice a year, at winter and summer . . . The rich and better sort of the people wear hose of damask or satin, or any sort of white silk; the rest, of white cotton.' The picture is one of affluence, but without consumerism, protocol rather than fashion.

Yet at one point Semedo does admit the existence of fashion in China. Speaking of urban transport, he remarks: 'Coaches were formerly much in use with them, and growing out of fashion there, we took them up, being first used, in Italy and Spain, in the year 1546.' The marginal existence of fashion is confirmed by later authors. Richthofen, the pioneer modern geographer of China, had this to say of nineteenth-century Szechwan: 'the people appear to retain a considerable surplus of their earnings, which they are able to dispose of for purchasing articles of luxury. These consist in foreign piece-goods, chiefly of woollen cloth, furs and many fancy articles. The general diffusion of a moderate wealth, as we find it in Sz'-chwan, appears to be particularly adapted to secure to such articles a wide and growing range of distribution.'[14] To the term piece-goods, a note is appended: 'Foreign piece-goods, perhaps with the exception of T cloth, are considered by Chinese of all inland countries as an article of luxury. I have heard it invariably stated by the natives, in many provinces, that as for durability, and cheapness in the long run, foreign cotton goods cannot compete with native cloth, although their price by the square yard may be lower. It is the greater elegance, the evenness and finish which have made the wearing of foreign cotton cloth "fashionable".' A similar note is appended to woollen cloth: 'In no province is the taste for these so conspicuous as in Sz'-chwan. Broadcloth is highly appreciated and much in demand, not for protection against the cold but on account of its outward appearance, and because it is not within reach of everybody.' Though Richthofen may not distinguish sufficiently between luxury, exoticism and fashion, his remarks strongly suggest the presence of the last in some form in nineteenth-century Szechwan.

If fashion went thus far but no further in China, an explanation must be sought. Semedo supplies a clue. He was much struck by the seclusion of women in China: 'The retirement of the women is very great. There is not a woman to be seen in the streets, although in years or never so blameless in her life, neither are men suffered to visit them at their houses. That part of the house where they inhabit is, as it were, a sacred place, for their sakes. It is enough to tell anyone who entereth unwittingly *That there are women there*, to make him stop presently.' Subsequently, Semedo qualifies, but only a little: 'Notwithstanding in so large a country as China, this custom cannot equally be observed everywhere, so that in some parts, as I have above mentioned, the ordinary women go abroad as among us, but the women of quality always observe that style of retirement.' In Europe, as has been shown by Daniel Roche, fashion was not only principally *for* women, but also increasingly *by* women as designers, entrepreneurs, journalists and boutique operators. In China, the partial exclusion of women from public space as buyers and sellers was a major factor in limiting the empire of the ephemeral. What distinguished Europe was not high consumption or consumerism in general (for it certainly existed in food in China), but the specifically feminine-powered consumerism of fashion in dress. It was the great input of female intelligence in Europe which gave it pre-eminence in consumption and then, via the industrial revolution, in production too.

Intelligence intends an intelligibility. We must now deal directly with the logic of fashion. If illogicality and randomness be rejected, two kinds of interpretation may be advanced: transitive, where fashion is given an external reference and denotational meaning; and intransitive, where the reference is solely internal and the meaning purely connotational. J. C. Flügel and Alison Lurie both advanced transitive interpretations.

Flügel believed that the primary function of dress was decoration. Modesty was only inverted decoration and protection was mainly rationalization. His approach was early psychoanalytic. Though subsequently his best-known work was on morals, he made little effort to integrate aggression or the super-ego into his work on clothes. He saw the mutation of fashion as a succession of emphases, whether by decoration or modesty, on the different erogenous zones of the body: 'the most obvious and important of all the variations of fashion is that which concerns the part of the body which is most accentuated'.[15] Thus the Renaissance emphasized the phallus and procreation in males by huge hats and cod-piece exhibitionism and the abdomen and pregnancy in females by extending dresses and skirts forward. In the late *ancien régime*, when the cult of nature was at its height, the emphasis, whether in Beau Brummel understated elegance or in high waisted *Directoire* décolletage, was on the whole body. High Victorians emphasized the waist and hips in the crinoline; later Victorians the posterior in the bustle; and Edwardians both bosom and posterior in the figure-of-eight silhouette of the *fin de siècle*. After the First World War, with shorter skirts and higher sleeves, came an emphasis on the limbs rather than the trunk, the female rotundities being put into the modest, androgynous retreat of the flapper. At all times, clothes revealed or concealed.

In his account of the mechanism of the mutations, Flügel was less psychoanalytic. If Freud had attempted a theory of fashion, he would have tried to find a parallel between ontogeny and phylogeny: between the individual's development in erotic interest – oral, anal, phallic and genital – and that of society. Flügel did not attempt this, either because he was too rooted in the assumptions of anthropology, or because he foresaw the difficulties, particularly with regard to the theory of the female castration complex, the centrepiece of the master's 'dark continent'.[16] Instead he advanced a sociological explanation. The lower classes imitated the higher to gain status. The higher defended themselves, first with sumptuary laws, and then, when these proved ineffective, with frequent changes of fashion. Mimesis from below, mutability from above were the essence: 'It is this double movement which essentially constitutes fashion, and it is the true ground of the perpetual variation to which "Modish" costume is subject.'[17] Fashion therefore 'implied a certain fluidity of the social structure of the community': and Flügel asked whether in a classless society it would continue. In particular, he wondered if, as women entered the workforce, their clothes might not become as fixed, as opposed to modish, as those of men. On the whole, he concluded, given female narcissism and the advertising industry, they would not. Flügel hoped for universal nudity, plus central heating. Bodies had greater reality than clothes. Dress was only an episode in illusion. Sartorial crutches would be discarded in accordance with the reality principle, to the greater, ultimate satisfaction of the pleasure principle.

Lurie saw more functions in dress than Flügel. Dress was a language, a semiotic system, in which many kinds of message could be sent: social, sexual, geographical, political; even the negative message 'I don't care a damn what I look like today.'[18] To explain the evolution of this language, she adopted, like Flügel, a sociological approach, though with the emphasis on strategy rather than tactics, and with the protagonists youth and age rather than inferiors and superiors.

Three cycles of youth to age and back again are outlined. *Directoire* represented return to childhood. The 1820s saw the 'silly little girl' look: Lawrence's *Pinkie* or, in the novel, David Copperfield's child-wife Dora Spenlow. The 1830s replaced this by the 'drooping adolescent', less juvenile but still blinkered in her poke bonnet, represented in fiction by Jane Eyre and in fact by the young Victoria. Next, for both women and men, came mid-Victorian maturity: Victoria, the plump, crinolined matron, and Albert, the bearded top-hatted man of substance. Finally, the angel in the house became a goddess, ostrich plumed, bustled, larger than the male: Junoesque in the paintings of Sargent or the illustrations of Gibson. Beyond this age could not go. Juvenility returned in asexual flappers and boys in plus fours: Edward VII and Lily Langtry were discarded in favour of Edward P. and Clara Bow. In the 1930s playful children were replaced by competent adults. Clara Bow gave way to Greta Garbo and Peter Pan Edward VIII to uxorious George VI. The 1940s demanded even more competence: squared shoulders, short skirts, battle dress and utility. Post-war brought successful adulthood: the New Look, the Man in the Grey Flannel Suit, and the baby boom. This time, however, there was no apotheosis. The cycle was cut short in the 1960s by the return of youth, even childhood, in the Twiggy look: big eyes, long thin legs, asexuality, dressing up in Granny shoes and glasses. Spring was in the air, but Quant's adolescent was soon ousted by Ashley's debutante, as the King's Road led into the Sloanes. In the 1980s, as the scene moved upmarket towards the city, Sloanes ceased to range and became two-job young married yuppies. Finally, in the 1990s, skirts lengthened again for the post-depression MBA, as a conservative ascendancy stretched into a future which might not belong to youth.

What is most interesting about Lurie's cycles, whatever one may think of the rather primitive sociology used to support them, is that they are true endogenous cycles, not a mere succession of happenings as in Flügel. They suggest that fashion has a motion of its own. Illogical only on the surface, fashion turns out to have sense below it: first in Flügel's body accentuation and class tactics, and then, at a deeper, demersal level, in the intergenerational strategy of Lurie's long cycles. Yet this triple order is not self-explanatory, which suggests that there may be a fourth, fundamental level of rationality still to be unearthed. Here an intransitive interpretation, a *Modologique* modelled on Lévi-Strauss' *Mythologiques* may be helpful.

Lévi-Strauss familiarized us with the notion that myths do not have a meaning in the sense of an external reference. Myths are not primitive science, as the Victorian anthropologists supposed. Nor are they dreams, personal or collective, as the depth psychologists supposed. Myths were directed to neither external nor internal reality, nor to any branch of constituted reason. What they were directed to was the mind itself in its constituent activity. Myth provided categories for thinking, but it was connotational not denotational. It was intransitive. The bedrock of fashion too, it may be argued, is of this character, though, as a formal system, it has features which myth does not.

First, the similarities. The categories which myth provided were, in Lévi-Strauss' analyses, mainly dichotomistic. These categories were then developed along two pre-established fault lines: the paradigmatic or metaphoric line of likeness, and the syntagmatic or metonymic line of contiguity. In the last chapter of *Mythologiques IV*, Lévi-Strauss compared these developments to the evolutionary transformations of fish, as these had been analysed by the English biologist Sir D'Arcy Wentworth Thompson in terms of the variation of the parameters of a set of geometrical coordinates: a hypothesis subsequently carried much further by Rupert Sheldrake in his theory of formative causation.[19] Lévi-Strauss concluded: 'Le biologiste anglais a montré qu'en faisant varier les paramètres d'un espace de coordonnées, on pouvait, par une série de transitions continue, passer d'une forme vivante à une autre forme vivante.'[20]

Fashion, it may be suggested, proceeds similarly. The late Middle Ages in Europe dichotomized male and female silhouette: rectangular for males, triangular for females. Subsequent female fashion took the form of permutations of the triangle: the back right-angled triangle of Jeanne de Chenany's 'pregnant' look in the *Betrothal of the Arnolfini*; the equilateral triangle of the Spanish farthingale; the front right-angled triangle in the French styles of the early seventeenth century, as popularized in England by Henrietta Maria. Similar, if more complex, permutations may be traced in the long sweep from the French Revolution to the First World War: the isosceles triangle of the *Directoire* and *Pinkie*; the equilateral triangle of the crinoline; the front right-angled triangle of the bustle; the double triangle, front and back, of the Gibson Girl; the inverted triangle of the hobble. What Flügel took to be changes in sexual interest and Lurie saw as movement of generation may really have been spontaneous mutations in a priori coordinates, to which sex and age adapted rather than initiated. There is no need to look for the causes of fashion beyond fashion itself.

Second, the dissimilarities. Fashion went beyond myth in a number of respects. It was more like the unstable morphogenetic fields formulated by Sheldrake. First, where the chaos of myth was closed and deterministic, the chaos of fashion was open and indeterministic. Myth, Lévi-Strauss argued, was essentially transformative and its changes followed a principle of fractality: 'une figure topologique se prête à des déformations aussi petites que l'imaginationé se plaît à les concevoir'.[21] Nevertheless, Lévi-Strauss emphasized the selectivity of the transformations and the immobility of the grid. Myths, he said, were machines for the suppression of time. Fashion, on the other hand, was not subject to these limitations. Within the functions of dress, it could change its coordinates as well as their content. In its quest for novelty, it exhilarated in time and proclaimed a Heraclitean flux rather than a Parmenidean one. Second, in its pursuit of infinite personalized fractality, fashion enjoyed greater resources than the dichotomizing repertoire of the *Mythologiques*. Silhouette was only one of its dimensions. Besides the dichotomies of long and short, tight and loose, shaped and draped, there were the alternatives of work and play, day and evening; the gamut of colour which Lurie unwisely tries to reduce to transitive symbolism; and the different texture effects of various fabrics – velvet, leather, mohair, fur and so on. Finally, where myth, by providing categories of thought in various codes, looked to the group which it sometimes constituted, fashion, by substituting itself for protocol looked to the person, the I within the We, whose existence it presumed. It is for this reason that Lipovetsky associates the advance of the empire of the ephemeral with the progress of democracy. Both rest on the correlation of creativity and community.[22]

To conclude: fashion, at the deepest level of analysis, is an intransitive formalism. As such, it is a pack of cards rather than a game though one to which jokers, trumps, and even whole new suits may suddenly be added. With these cards, a number of games may be played (thermoregulative, normative, seductive, dignifying, snobbish) and a succession of *personae* may be created (*ingénue*, sophisticate, romantic, politically correct or critical). Intransitive thought, like transitive, seeks a variety of intelligibilities: systematic as in Newtonian or Einsteinian physics; non-systematic as in quantum mechanics or some chaos theory. Fashion too has been plural. It emerged from protocol to become a series of classicisms: Burgundian, Spanish, French, and eventually exclusively Parisian. These systems, however, were prevented from ossifying by the non-systematic elements of frivolity, fantasy and folly which were part of fashion from the beginning. With the collapse of the Parisian dictatorship into polycratic chaos, these elements now take centre-stage not least in Grunge. They prefigure new forms of unsystematic rationality. Fashion is not only part of reason: it sometimes leads it. A cascade of fractalities, a new praise of folly, the nothing which does all, fashion invokes a fuller development of chaos theory, looks to a fresh physics of time, and invites science to join history in a principle of insufficient reason.[23]

ESSENTIALS: SILK IN EUROPE, COTTON IN CHINA AND EVERYWHERE

As food was arranged successively as breakfast, lunch and dinner, so dress was arranged spatially as overwear, middle wear and underwear. Either a single fabric or several fabrics might be involved. In China, several layers of cotton fabric might be worn in winter. In Europe, a Gibson girl might wear cotton underclothes, a silk dress and a fur coat, not to speak of leather shoes and an ostrich feather in her hat. Whether single or several, fibres, fabrics and finishing – via mordants, dyes, cutting and sewing – were the essentials of dress. Here the age of globalization saw three major developments: a further appropriation of Chinese silk in Europe and the conquest by Indian cotton first of China and then, via the Levant, the American South, Tsarist and Soviet Uzbekistan – of everywhere. In Europe silk was an initial facilitator of fashion, in China cotton was a promoter of inter-regional uniformity, while cotton everywhere extended fashion from the elite to the generality and made it a universal instrument of consumerism. Today, despite the progress of synthetics, most human clothes are made from cotton.

The history of fabrics since 1400 is largely that of the relationship between silk, cotton and wool. Before that time, however, it should be noted, all three were relative luxuries, even in their homelands. Prehistorians have been slow to investigate the means of dress available for creating the mobile microclimates without which the extension of humankind beyond the tropics is hardly conceivable. The common assumption that palaeolithic hunter-gatherers dressed in fur is not plausible. More likely, vegetable materials were used even before the neolithic revolution and may indeed have been one of its points of origin. Subsequently, flax in Europe and the Levant, hemp in India and China, were probably the source of most clothes before the Middle Ages. Wool was only widely available where arable and pastoral farming were practised together. Moreover, without plentiful supplies of fuller's earth, it was not an easy fibre to use.[24] The conjuncture of wool and fuller's earth was part of the *limes* lifestyle, but sheep only became really abundant with the great runs of the Cistercians and Premonstratensians remarked on by Pegolotti. Wool was an early privilege of the West, but it could not compare in significance to silk or cotton.

Silk in Europe

The initial transfer of sericulture from China to the West in the reign of Justinian through the Nestorian connection has often been discussed. Less often investigated are the stages through which the industry progressed till in the eighteenth century it became the pre-industrial prototype for the take-off of industrial cotton manufacture. Five such stages may be recognized.

First, there was a Byzantine stage. The tenth century *Book of the Eparch*, or city perfect, provides an account of the guilds of the capital. It describes a complex silk industry, reminiscent, in its subdivisions, of China itself. *Prandiopatrai* imported raw silk from Syria. *Metaxopratrai*, wholesale brokers, bought and sold raw silk. *Katartarioi* processed and dressed it ready for weaving. *Serikarioi* wove and dyed it in state and private factories. *Vestiopratai* dealt in silk cloth, which they supplied to the tailors who produced the cloaks, *sagia*, and sleeved tunics, *skaramangia*, which were the staples of elite Byzantine overwear and middle wear. Each guild was forbidden to perform the functions of another. Consumption was controlled by protocol and sumptuary law. Export was by diplomatic gift (again, very Chinese), rather than by trade. Silk was a status symbol of association with the *basileus* to be doled out carefully to those worthy of it. John VIII Palaeologus, as portrayed by Benozzo Gozzoli in his *Journey of the Magi to Bethlehem*, was the last embodiment of this imagery when his clothes made a powerful impression on the occasion of his visit to the Council of Florence in 1439 to seek help against the Ottomans.

Second, there was a central Italian stage. In the tenth century, sericulture spread from Syria to mainland Greece. Thessalonika, Thebes, Athens and Corinth became weaving centres. Next, Calabria took up silk growing and weaving is reported as early as the eleventh century at Lucca. In the twelfth century, Roger II of Sicily brought Greek weavers and growers to Palermo. From Calabria, growing spread to Naples, and from Lucca, weaving passed to Emilia and Tuscany. Yet European supply was inadequate to a demand which with Genoese marketing was breaking out of protocol, into private luxury. Down to the nineteenth century, China remained the world's biggest and best source of supply. Opportunity for import was opened with the Mongol conquests. Chinese silk was first mentioned at Genoa in 1257–9. It had been bought at Ayas in Armenian Cilicia and had come via Sivas and Tabriz. Subsequently, Tana at the head of the sea of Azov, the terminus of the northern land route, became the principal source for Chinese silk. Some Genoese went all the way to Peking. Antonio Sarmone made his will there in 1330, and in 1372, when China itself had become inaccessible, a member of the Adorno family bought seven camel loads of Chinese goods at Mazar-i-sherif in the Timurid empire.[25] Genoa supplied Lucca and Bologna and marketed their finished products. In 1372, a Luccan introduced to Bologna a hydraulic machine, based on Chinese prototypes, for spinning, or more accurately reeling or 'throwing', raw silk. Not very efficient since not imitated elsewhere till 1538, it was, nevertheless, the model for all subsequent powered textile machinery in Europe: an early example too of import substitution.

Next, there was a stage which focused on Lyon.[26] With the birth of fashion in the north, demand took the lead from supply. The fairs of Lyon became an isthmus between the Italian producer and the French consumer. In the sixteenth century, between one-third and a half of French imports passed through Lyon. At Lyon, textiles amounted to 75 per cent of what was traded. Silk led wool, cotton, linen and hemp and amounted to 25 per cent of market value. Within silks, velvet led satin, damask and taffeta and amounted to 10 per cent of market value. Half the velvet was supplied by the Genoese for whom Lyon was a shop window. *Velours de Gênes* – 'de loin le secteur prédominant du grand commerce lyonnais' – was the market leader. But the demand came from Paris, where the aesthetic possibilities of black velvet for women was one of the discoveries of the Late Renaissance. Subsequently, Lyon became a producer rather than a shop window: indeed the greatest of producers outside China; but, before that happened, there were further stages.

Fourth, there was a north Italian stage.[27] It represented a supply-side response to the increased demand from fashion. In the seventeenth century, an improved *molino bolognese* was transferred from the Appenines to the Alps, first of Venetia and then of Piedmont. The first Venetian mill was opened in 1604. By 1644, 15 mills were in operation and imports of reeled silk ceased. By 1700, there were 89 mills exporting to Lyon as well as supplying local weavers. In 1767, there were 227 Venetian mills, but by this time an even better mill had been developed in Piedmont, which now took the lead as the chief European producer of raw and semi-prepared silk. Between 1860 and 1910, silk constituted 25 per cent of all Italian exports. Venice by now had lost its pre-eminence as a port. Exports were directed to Lyon via Genoa which was thus able to retain its position better than its ancient rival.

Finally, there was an English stage.[28] Demand once more led supply. Silk weaving was brought to Britain by the Huguenot refugees who settled in Spitalfields and Wandsworth. In the early eighteenth century, Spitalfields became the first major English centre. Its demands put pressure on suppliers of reeled and thrown silk. In 1717, after two years of industrial espionage, John and Thomas Lombe of Derby erected a *molino piedmontese* on the River Derwent at a capital cost of £30 000 and a workforce of 300. Though water was a traditional source of energy, the Lombes' factory has not unreasonably been regarded as the first modern British textile mill. Following the expiry of the Lombes' patent in 1732 and an exhibition of a model of their machine in the Tower of London, similar mills were constructed along the Pennines at sites which might be further from Spitalfields and the public space of fashion, but where better water supply was available.

One of these sites was Macclesfield, where silk buttons had been made since 1649 and twist produced by hand since the end of the seventeenth century. In 1743, Charles Roe, described as a gentleman, established the first hydraulic mill, using a tributary of the Bollin to operate it. Further mills followed, notably that of Dainty and Ryle in 1775, some of them larger than Roe's. About 1790, hand weaving was introduced, operatives being imported from Spitalfields to teach locals. In 1817, there were a total of 28 throwing mills and 12 manufacturers of woven silk. By this time, steam was being used in the throwing sector. A further 20 new mills were added between 1819 and 1826. Power looms, however, were only introduced gradually in the 1830s. So long as English silk was protected and trade with France was frequently interrupted by war, the 5000-odd looms of Macclesfield prospered. But the ending of the Napoleonic wars and then Cobden's free trade treaty with France in 1860, showed that it could not compete in the long run with Lyon, with its 15 000-odd looms, greater expertise and closer access to raw silk in Italy. Except for the largest, or most efficient firms, the old weavers, as they were called, gradually went out of business, some of them in time to transfer capital to the new growth consumer industry of brewing. Macclesfield now sought to rival Burton on Trent.

Silk in Europe never entirely escaped its initial dependence on China. Indeed the expansion of the industry under the impetus of consumerism and fashion increased that dependence. In the first half of the nineteenth century, half the silk processed in Europe came from China. Before the rise of the tea trade, silk was the most valuable item imported from China, and it was so again after 1884. Between 1864 and 1904, the value of silk exported from China increased from 10 million taels to 70 million taels. In 1900, H. B. Morse reckoned that 'the West was supplied with silk, 27 per cent from China, 28 per cent from Japan, 25 per cent from Italy, and 20 per cent from all other countries'.[29] In 1895–7, Lyon, which bought over half the raw silk exported from Shanghai, sent a commission of enquiry to west China to investigate the possibility of increasing the import. The commissioners were favourably impressed by what they saw, and, if China had been able to improve the health of its silk worms it might, like Japan, have been able to finance a modernization programme by exports of raw and thrown silk. By the time such improvements came to be made, however, silk everywhere was under attack from the new family of synthetics heralded by the invention of rayon in 1891. Yet silk retains its position at the upmarket end of fashion as much as when Cleopatra wore it for the Tarsus summit with Antony in 41 BC. It is unlikely that the story of this strange fibre, pre-processed by worms out of leaves, is ended.

Cotton in China

In 1990, with only some exaggeration, Philip Huang wrote: 'In 1350, no one in China wore cotton cloth; by 1850, almost every peasant did.'[30] Earlier, in 1955, the first Five Year Plan had stated: 'In 1952, cotton piece-goods made up 98.8 per cent of the total national output of textile goods of all kinds: silk, woollen and linen fabrics made up the other 1.2 per cent.' Silk, which had given its name to the Seres, had been marginalized, and hemp, once the predominant fabric there, had disappeared. The conquest of China by cotton was not the least of the conquests of the age of globalization.

The beginnings of the conquest went back further than Philip Huang supposed. Edward Schafer, following an extensive discussion, came to the conclusion that cotton cultivation was introduced to Kwangtung in the late T'ang period: that is, the ninth century. Cotton was derived everywhere in the Old World from northern India. In many languages the name for it too is derived from the Sanskrit *karpasa*, as with our word kapok. Cotton goods came to China in the T'ang period from India by both the land and sea routes. Cotton cultivation was also introduced in the then Iranian-speaking Chinese satellite kingdom of Qoco or Turfan. In Kwangtung, cultivation came mediately from some Southeast Asian country such as Champa. Cotton was also grown in the Thai or Lolo state of Nan-chao in present-day Yunnan. Like sugar, cotton in East Asia was a gift of Buddhism. It established a bridgehead for itself as part of a *limes* lifestyle. Yet, under the T'ang, a bridgehead was all it established. Kwangtung was only marginally part of China and Canton was still a half Southeast Asian estuarial city. Moreover, cotton likes a longer dry season than most of tropical China can provide. Progress continued to be slow under the Sung. At the beginning of the thirteenth century, cotton cultivation was introduced to Fukien from Hainan. In his account of Chien-ning, 'a very large and splendid city subject to the Great Khan', in the northwest of the province, Marco Polo says, 'so much cotton cloth is woven here of dyed yarn that it supplies the whole province of Manzi', that is, the territories of the former Southern Sung. Yet this is his only mention of cotton in China – whether grown, processed or worn – so it must be presumed that the industry was still a secondary one. As late as the early fourteenth century, Ibn Battuta reported that cotton goods in Hang-chou were more expensive than silk: no doubt because of the high labour inputs which everywhere impeded its progress.

What brought about the conquest of China by cotton which was at least half complete by the advent of the Ch'ing? On the demand side, it was an expression of affluence and consumerism: first, in the late Yüan, in the towns; second, in the early Ming, in the countryside when rural taxation was reduced and an ethos of egalitarianism prevailed; third, in the middle to late Ming, in both town and country, with the prosperity generated by further reductions in taxation and by the influx of American silver which paid for the export of silk via the Acapulco galleon. Silk in Europe thus helped to activate cotton in China, but it was what the contemporary Shanghai scholar Lu Chi (*fl. c.*1540) called the 'custom of extravagance' which was the primary demand factor. On the supply side, the cultivation preparation, spinning, and in some cases, weaving of cotton represented for the farmer a more intensive application of man-hours, and more particularly wife-hours and children-hours, to a given plot of land. Philip Huang calls this involutionary commercialization. He regards it as ultimately a blind alley because *per horam* labour productivity fell. However, he takes insufficient account of the rise in household productivity and overlooks the fact that without cotton many of the hours would not have been worked at all: that is, there would have been considerable female and child unemployment. Moreover, cotton not only brought money to producers, but it also brought the social benefit of keeping the family farm and household viable and secure. In China, cotton was not a plantation crop, as in antebellum America, or a factory product, as in Victorian Lancashire. It was a household crop and product based on family solidarity, intelligent management, and market information, relayed to and from the brokers, guilds and teahouses of the gridlike system of rivers and canals of the Yangtze delta.

Cotton cultivation, spinning and weaving began there in the late thirteenth century in Sung-kiang prefecture. A certain Huang Tao-p'o is credited with being the first entrepreneur to respond to a perceived demand for an upmarket, exotic fibre then associated with the Muslim *ortaq* plutocracy. At first, no doubt, cotton was a subsistence farmer's market sideline: what was later known as *chia-t'ing fu-ye*. Subsequently, such households gave up rice, hemp and silk altogether to concentrate on cotton for the market. Eventually, a rough geographical pattern asserted itself in the Su Wu-shu: the five jurisdictions depending on Soochow. Silk and rice were in the middle round the lakes or lowlands which appeared when the delta outlets were obstructed by irrigation or land reclamation. Cotton was produced and processed on the slightly higher rim, especially to the east before the coast. Other businesses, such as tea, timber and fishponds found their place in the hills to the west, or, in the case of salt, on the coast. Though some spinning and weaving took place in Soochow, Wu-hsi and Sung-kiang town, most cotton processing, finishing and marketing, unlike silk, were entirely rural. Not the least remarkable aspect of the Su Wu-shu was its character as an inter-peasant commodity network independent of urban management. It was rational, but with a diffused brain: capitalism, but without capitalists or big capital; a market but without a central market-place. This was possible because of the unique concentration and diffusion of information in the delta. The Su Wu-shu looked to the teleworking mode of production of the twenty-first century.

In the course of the Ming, the Su Wu-shu began to supply other

parts of China. Under the Cheng-te emperor (1506–21), it was said
that 'Sung-kiang clothes the whole empire.' Given the character of the
system, no great entrepreneurial dynamism is required to explain this
expansion. Unlike silk in Europe, cotton in China did not need the
Genoese to promote it. Micro-enterprise, familial or mercantile, suf-
fices to explain a phenomenon which proceeded on the periphery by
inches and drops. As the system expanded it began to produce provincial replicas of itself: cotton cultivation in the Han valley of Hupei;
spinning and weaving in Hankow and Shasi; export from both river
ports to Szechwan where cotton could not be grown because of its
damp climate. In the eighteenth century, cotton cultivation and processing were developed in the metropolitan province of Chihli and its
neighbour Shantung. Here, too, cotton was grown on the less water-
logged land, but in the isolated, endogamous and information-starved
villages of north China it produced a different society: more managerial, less cohesive, more class-divided. Whatever the sociology, however, cotton consumption continued to increase. It represented modest
affluence, greater warmth in the little ice age of early modernity, and,
because of washability, improved hygiene. By the eve of the Opium
War, the Chinese economic historian, Wu Ch'eng-ming, has calculated,
two-thirds of China's inland trade consisted in the exchange of cotton
cloth for grain. This figure reflected not only the importance of food
and dress in consumption but also China's character, emphasized by
François Sigaut, as a subtropical horticultural ecology applied in cool
temperate conditions. Cotton was something the Chinese ecology had
long wanted. Whether in padded jackets or as layers of garments, it
kept the farmer warm in a way no other fabric could. In the nineteenth
century, European textile exporters found China strangely impermeable
even in cottons. Except in providing fashionable exotics, Manchester
could not compete with a victorious system with its own statics and
dynamics.

Cotton Everywhere

Cotton's conquest of China was followed by its conquest via America
of Europe and via Europe of the rest of the world.

Cotton was unknown to European antiquity. Though it may have
been introduced to Egypt before the Muslims and certainly before the
'St Bartholomew' route of the *Periplus* was available for its convey-
ance from India, it was the Muslims who first made it big business, as
they did with sugar. Raw cotton began to figure in Venetian cargoes in

the thirteenth century in ships returning from Alexandria, Acre, Beirut, Tripoli, Latakia and Cyprus. By the first half of the fourteenth century, the import was sufficient for a twice a year galley convoy organized by the Venetian state to be designated the *muda del cotone*. In the case of round ships, salt was carried as ballast in the hold, bales of raw cotton, light but voluminous, between decks, and the compact and valuable spices in the officers' cabins. Some raw cotton was re-exported, more was spun in Venice and then sold for weaving elsewhere, especially in south Germany. Pure cotton cloth was uncommon: no doubt because the warp was not strong enough. Usually, cotton was used in combination with other fibres. While textile names are difficult to fix and changeable in denotation, fustian (from al-Fustat or Cairo) was probably a mix of cotton and linen or wool, while serge (ultimately from Chinese *ssu* = silk) and its derivative denim (from Nimes) was probably a mixture of cotton and silk originally. English sixteenth-century references show fustian as a material for blankets, servants' livery, and Elizabeth of York's white socks. Genoa traded in cotton, as well as in silk, though to a lesser extent than Venice. Christopher Columbus, however, was sufficiently interested to ask for, and get, examples of cotton plants in the West Indies: a discovery which must have confirmed him in the belief that he had reached East Asia.

Neither the Spaniards nor the Portuguese, however, did much initially to develop cotton in their intertropical New World dominions. The Spaniards were preoccupied with mining and ranching, the Portuguese with sugar and coffee. Nevertheless, particularly as France came to dominate European fashion with its taste for softer, less rigid fabrics, demand for cotton piece goods increased. It was met by muslins from the Levant and by calicoes from India. The calicoes were purchased by the European East India companies, for specie mainly, either at the western entrepôt of Surat or at Calcutta closer to the eastern centres of spinning and weaving. By the end of the eighteenth century, Europeans were exporting home about one-sixth of the total Bengal output of cotton piece goods. In addition, they took raw cotton from Bombay to Canton in the country trade, some of which subsequently returned to them in the form of high grade nankeens. Cotton piece goods were the foundation of the English East India Company's home trade. The import, however, was opposed in quotas and tariffs by mercantilists objecting to specie outflow and by domestic textile producers threatened in their sales. To circumvent the mercantilists, a domestic cotton industry was developed, supplied with raw cotton mainly from the Levant, but the high labour inputs required in ginning, cleaning, carding, spinning and weaving kept the products expensive, as they had in China back in the fourteenth century.

In China, this bottleneck, which turned the cheapest raw material into the most expensive fabric, was broken by organization: better management and more intelligent division of labour in the Yangtze delta. In Europe, as is well known, it was broken by technology: the Eli Whitney gin, powered spinning (by horse, water or steam), powered weaving, artificial soda (Leblanc, Solvay etc), aniline dyes. In both, however, the triumph of cotton was surcharged by three other supply-side factors which it gradually manifested: versatility, mimetic capacity and innovation. Cotton produced a wider range of fabrics than any other fibre: from flimsy cambric, muslin and lawn through to tough chintz, denim and gabardine. Many terms used in the cotton trade had started as denoting other fibres: poplin, for example, was originally a mixture of silk and linen produced or consumed in the papal city of Avignon, an early centre of European fashion. Other cottons, such as corduroy, velveteen and velours, imitated what had once been silk at Lyon. Cotton was a chameleon. But it also created new tastes, which required new, often oriental terms: chintz (Sanskrit *chitra*, variegated), dimity (Damietta), gingham (Malay, striped), seersucker (Persian *shir or shakha*, milk and sugar). It is not surprising that Say's law, that supply always produces demand, was originally formulated in the first age of cotton's conquests in Europe.

Versatility, mimesis and innovation, in combination with the removal of bottlenecks by technology, first in the West and then everywhere, generated an immense increase in the production of raw cotton. This took place not only in the New World, but also in the Old: notably, under both the Tsarist and Soviet regimes in Central Asia, Uzbekistan in particular. Marco Polo had been struck by the amount of cotton grown in Kashgar, Yarkand, Khotan and Keriya, but now the lead was taken by western Turkestan. In 1983, it is stated, 'Uzbekistan alone produced almost as much cotton as the entire United States': around 20 per cent of world supply.[31] In the early 1990s, China was the world's largest producer of raw cotton, the Soviet Union second, the United States third, and India, the original homeland of cotton, fourth. In thus conquering the world, cotton had democratized itself. It was no longer, *per se*, a fashionable fabric, only the obvious one. Indeed, in China under Chairman Mao, blue cotton cloth became a symbol of a uniform egalitarianism, while in the more pluralistic West a popular song declared: 'Everybody's wearing blue jeans, but everybody has their own dreams.' Uniformity itself could be fashionable.

ACCESSORIES: FUR IN CHINA, LINEN IN EUROPE

To basic wear, of whatever fibre, fabric or finish, the various functions of dress – thermoregulation, modesty, decoration, dignity, status and fashion – added overwear and underwear. This development may be illustrated by the two significant additions of the age of globalization: fur overwear in China and linen underwear in Europe. These aggregations also provide further evidence for the rise of cotton. For in China, the cycle of fur was brought to an end by padded or quilted cotton, and in Europe the 'linen' was increasingly made of cotton.[32]

Fur in China

To the Chinese, fur was part of a northern *limes* lifestyle. Under the T'ang, who were Turkish *qaghans* as well as Chinese emperors, fur had been briefly fashionable as overwear in the cold North China winter – then possibly colder than now – especially among military men. Fox, ermine and sable were all imported, especially from the Uighur allies of the dynasty, not yet sedentarized, but in touch with the *taiga* and already merchants. Whether Yang Kuei-fei ever imitated Hélène Fourment in Rubens' *Little Fur* we do not know, but, given what Po Chü-i says about her, it is not improbable. Under the Sung, civilians and definitely not *qaghans*, fur went out of fashion for both men and women. It did not revive under the Yüan, though Qubilai is portrayed by the court painter Liu Kuan-tao in a wonderful ermine coat with sable cuffs and collar. Some Ming emperors, such as Yung-lo or Chengte, who either consciously copied Qubilai or wished to present themselves as military bravos, wore fur, but the thrust of the dynasty was civilian. Middle Ming statesmen wanted to draw a clear line between Chinese and barbarians, so fur would have been both politically and ideologically incorrect. The *limes* lifestyle, however, returned with the Ch'ing. Unlike the Yüan who, although they had ceased to be steppe nomads, made little attempt to recruit the Chinese ruling class to their party machine, the Ch'ing came to power with the consent of the ruling elites in Peking. Even before the so-called conquest of 1644, they had recruited Chinese assistants from the frontiersmen and colonists of Fengtien and northern Chihli who, as bondservants, bannermen and bureaucrats easily adopted the styles of their masters and patrons. Fox, ermine and sable returned to fashion, and, lower down the scale, squirrel, weasel, wolf and dog entered it as the Chinese, along with the rest of the world, experienced the little ice age. Temperatures between 1645 and 1715 were the lowest since AD 1000. Court and climate combined to swell the demand for fur.

Part of the demand could be met from Manchuria: from the Ch'ang-pai shan range in Kirin and the Hsing-an hill country of Heilungkiang.[33] In the seventeenth century, quantities of sable were received as tribute by imperial officials at Ninguta, San-hsing, Deren and Tsitsihar from Tungusic and Mongol tribes not yet incorporated into the banner system. Japanese intelligence reports indicate that this disguised trade was still continuing in the early nineteenth century when it included the Sakhalin islands and the sea otter. Till 1860 Manchuria extended further north than it does today. Fur, indeed, was one reason why the Ch'ing negotiators at the treaty of Nerchinsk were careful to define its frontier along the Stanovoi mountains so as to include the whole Amur valley. Even a Greater Manchuria, however, was not enough to meet all China's needs, though Mukden remained a major fur market until the early twentieth century. Chinese demand, or more accurately Sino-Banner demand, had to draw on an ever-widening circle of supply in a genuine process of globalization.

First, the China market drew, via the Kiakhta trade established by the treaties of 1689 and 1727, on the supplies of eastern Siberia. It took in the animals of the middle forest, the taiga, and the tundra: squirrel, fox, sable and ermine. Collected by the Russians as tribute at their ostrogs or blockhouses from the Yakuts, Samoyeds and Tungus, these furs were conveyed along the Siberian rivers and porterages to Kiakhta, where they were exchanged for Chinese silks and, subsequently, tea. Second, particularly following the voyages of Vitus Bering in 1728–30 and 1740–1, the China market drew on the supplies of Pacific Russia: Kamchatka, the Kuriles, the Aleutians and eventually Alaska. It took in the animals of the coast, in particular the sea otter and the sea beaver. Most of these furs also went to Peking via Kiakhta, but in the early nineteenth century, the Russo-America Company tried, not very successfully, to trade at Canton as well. Third, with the coming of the first United States ship to Canton in 1784, the China market drew on the sea otter of the Oregon coast and the fur-bearing seals of the North Pacific. Dominance of these sources of fur enabled the Americans to trade at Canton without recourse either to silver or the complicated procedures of the country trade in Indian remittances, opium and tea. Finally, from 1782–3, the China market drew on the fur-bearing seals of the South Pacific in the waters of Tasmania, New Zealand and its sub-Antarctic islands: the Snares, Auckland, Campbell, Antipodes, Bounty and Macquarie. Here seals were hunted by an international community of British, Australians, Americans, French and Portuguese who sent the furs to the Canton market. Chinese demand for fur, therefore, for a time, put a number of new worlds under contribution: indeed in some cases it called them into existence.

That time, however, did not last. By 1867 and still more by 1905, fur had fallen to a low percentage of China's imports in both volume and value. Despite the continued activity of Mukden, there was little substitution of domestic for foreign product. The reasons for this contraction of a market which had once played a part in the global economy are not often sought, but are worth consideration.

First, it was not due to general impoverishment. The most recent assessments indicate that, with the stabilization of population around 1850, the stimulus to many economic sectors from foreign trade, better communications and greater urbanization, per capita living standards in China rose between 1800 and 1950 especially among the elite. Second, the shift away from fur may be associated with the end of the little ice age around 1850 in China as elsewhere. Indeed, in China, the climatic mutation may have been particularly sharp, as might be indicated by the disastrous series of drought famines which afflicted the northwest. Third, these were the years when cotton conquered the northeast, when Chihli and Honan decolonized themselves from the Yangtze delta, and Tientsin became a major textile centre. Padded cotton ceased to be elitist. One suit was essential for the winter, two were a sign of modest affluence, and it has been calculated that 20–25 per cent of all China's cotton crop went into this form of clothing. In effect, the Chinese pioneered the flying jacket and the ski suit long before these things acquired their names in the West. Vegetable could beat animal at its own game. Finally, as with the decline in furs in the West at the end of the Middle Ages, it is difficult not to postulate a shift in consumer preference. The prestige of the Ch'ing was in eclipse. The court itself had become highly sinicized and the empress-dowager took her style less from the *limes* than from the Chinese stage. It is significant that one of the few people we know of to have liked to present themselves still in fur was the arch-loyalist general Chang Hsün. Young China looked to other forms of chic: Sun Yat-sen's Chung-shan suits, Kuomintang long military greatcoats, Mao Tse-tung's baggy boiler suits, Chou En-lai's Savile Row outfits. Even the armies up on the Inner Asian frontier against the Soviet Union preferred New Zealand wool.

Linen in Europe

While fur as overwear progressed in China in the cold eighteenth century, in Europe with better thermoregulated housing, linen triumphed, not as a particular fabric, but in the sense of underwear: not just vest and pants, but shirts, blouses, stockings, handkerchiefs, collars. This original white-collar revolution, which like cotton in China had consequences for hygiene and health, has been brilliantly analysed by Daniel Roche in his study of French dress in the late *ancien régime*. His conclusions may be conveniently grouped under the headings of facts, implications and possible explanations.

The facts are indicated by wills and inventories. They show that between 1700 and 1789, expenditure on clothes more than doubled. Though as a percentage of total expenditure, that on clothes (as opposed to housing etc.) declined, within that category, linen showed a rising percentage of the whole. Linen was the leading sector in the dress boom. That boom was spread unevenly. It affected women more than men. By 1789 women's wardrobes were twice those of men in all classes, whereas in 1700 this had been true only of the noblesse and of domestic servants. It affected menials more than masters. Domestic servants, both male and female, quadrupled their expenditure on clothes in the course of the eighteenth century, surpassed only by female wage earners not in domestic service (shopgirls), who increased their expenditure six times. By 1789, linen amounted to 30 per cent of all expenditure on clothes, reaching 40–50 per cent in the case of domestic servants. It was Susanna and Figaro who made the white-collar revolution, not the Countess and still less Dr Bartolo. This was not a bourgeois revolution.

The implications of this expansion of wardrobes and of linen within them, Roche argues, were both concrete and evaluative. More clothes meant greater frequency of change of wear in the interest of hygiene, cleanliness and class. Water was not abundant in the eighteenth century. Cleanliness had to be achieved more by frequent change of blouses, shirts and stockings, than by greater washing of persons. Concomitantly, class, especially feminine class, was increasingly defined in terms of clean and dirty. With the cult of cleanliness, white became the colour of preference, because it would most obviously show the dirt in its absence. Thus the rise of linen represented an attack on invisible as well as visible dirt. Paris learnt to blow its nose, possession of handkerchiefs rose by 50 per cent, and spitting was discouraged, another major advance in hygiene. Concretely and evaluatively, the universalization of linen implied a significant social promotion of the less well-to-do: again, not so much the middle classes, the future makers of the French revolution, but its victims – domestics, shopkeepers, tradespeople, women generally.

Possible explanations may now be considered. First, the shift from outer to inner, from heavier to lighter, was not related to climate. The diaphanous *Directoire* styles were not worn for warmth, though they may have been worn for health and were certainly made bearable by warmer houses. Second, the new pattern of spending – copied from the aristocracy and practised by groups in contact with it such as domestics and upmarket shop people – has to be associated with the social structure of the late *ancien régime*. Daniel Dessert has cast new light on this.[34] In his analysis, the *noblesse*, both *épée* and *robe*, though defeated politically in the Fronde and the Regency, maintained, indeed under Louis XV extended, its domination of society. It did this through the fisco-financial system by which it monopolized bullion, liquidity and spending power to the disadvantage of the state and parallel social groups which were confined to credit, paper money or no money. An aristocratic culture of spending on dress therefore diffused itself through French society, particularly in groups in proximity to the *noblesse*. *Finance*, as Dessert calls it, was the distinctive feature of the French *ancien régime*, as open politics was of the English. But Paris was already so much the capital of fashion that its cult of unostentatious chic and high feminine expenditure on linen was quickly imitated in different social circumstances in the rest of Europe: especially in England where it converged with the more political preference for good taste and country informality, as for example in Gainsborough's *Mr and Mrs Andrews*.[35]

Third, on the supply side, Roche points to a diversification of institutions. Under Louis XIV, the rag trade in Paris had been dominated by the mercers: merchants of cloth, mainly male, who dealt direct with tailors or the public. Alteration, second hand, accessories and extras were all marginal organizationally. Under Louis XVI, the mercers and tailors were rivalled by largely female dressmakers, milliners and lingerists, who were not simply craftswomen but entrepreneurs and impresarios of fashion. Milliners – at that time novelty dealers, not confined to hats – had impressive establishments which, together with the lingerie shops, constituted a new feminine space. Second-hand business (*friperies*), again female more than male, extended its scope to include cleaning, repair, redyeing, embellishment, alteration, refurbishment, and, significant innovation, ready to wear new clothes. Frippery in its new sense both extended the vestamentary revolution socially and provided new links between home, shop and streets. In 1776 the tailors tried to neutralize the *fripeuses* by incorporation but this only produced a new group of unincorporated *revendeuses* who specialized in shirts, *linge* and handkerchiefs. By the end of the *ancien régime*, corporative closed shops had virtually collapsed. Other groups who achieved greater prominence were laundresses who worked on the banks of the Seine with salt, lye, soda, gravel and increasingly soap, and, more surprisingly, dry cleaners who used lemon juice, caustic soda and alum. Dress had become a complex service industry.

Fourth, on the interface between supply and demand, there was an increase in publicity: dress information as conveyed directly in shops, indirectly in fashion plates, dolls and magazines, or via the written word in novels. Whereas in the past tailors always came to the house, shopping was a recognized part of *ancien régime* urban life. Boutiques ceased to be mere stalls and became salons where husbands could sit and outside which carriages could be parked. Fashion plates were widely distributed to attract custom. Between 1600 and 1800, at least 143 books on clothes were published in French, 98 of them between 1750 and 1800. Many were profusely illustrated, showing what was being worn by the royal family, together with interesting exoticisms: Circassian dress, Chinese, even Australian! Between 1700 and 1793 Roche finds 20-odd fashion magazines, many edited by women, all precarious as publications, but a few establishing themselves long term. Like their modern descendants, these magazines dealt not only with what to wear, but also with what to read, what to see at the theatre, what to think about contemporary issues and current affairs. Roche calls this literature the specifically feminine component of the Enlightenment: a proclamation of *liberté* and *egalité* under the guise of *frivolité*. It set fashion within a wider context of socialization and liberation. If dress was brought into the public domain, choice of clothes now served to define the person rather than the personage, the Protean individual rather than the fixed social role. Fashion had already established its paradoxical quantum character of simultaneous outer wave and inner particle.

Finally, on the demand side, there were the new fashions themselves. Here Roche's account needs amplification in the light of the view of fashion as intransitive and structural outlined above. The central changes are not in dispute: from Baroque to Rococo or Neo-Classical; from heavier, concealing, *drap* to lighter, revealing *toile*; from wide equilateral triangle in silhouette to tapering isosceles triangle; from culture to nature. What is more open to question, or at least does not seem exhaustive, is the ascription of philosophical, social and political meanings, especially as presented as solidary with the French revolution, itself still seen as the logical outcome of the Enlightenment. No doubt these meanings could be attached to the new fashions, just as anti-Vietnam war sentiment attached itself to those of the 1960s. But in themselves they were simply changes of structure, polysemic, indeed pansemic, a new *langue* not new *paroles*. To ask why such changes occur by seeking localized philosophical, social or political explanations is to misconceive their dynamic, in the same way that Aristotelians before Newton misconceived the laws of physical motion. It was the nature of fashion to change in order to create space for novelty: redefinitions of chic and snobbery, an enigma code frequently changed to confuse cryptographers. In themselves, these changes carried no values. Revolutionary France and Loyalist Britain followed the same fashions. The space which fashion re-created was an unstable void, but one capable of providing endless new topologies for personal expression. For the empire of the ephemeral had ever to be reconquered from convention, protocol and sumptuarism, clothes had ever to be liberated from costume. Fashion was permanent revolution.

EXTRAS: TOP TO TOE – QUEUES, WIGS AND BOUND FEET

The distinctions between protocol and fashion, costume and clothes, fashion as code and outfits as message may also be illustrated from the field of extras additional to wear, overwear and underwear. Dress extras include hats, gloves, ties, scarves, jewellery and cosmetics. While it is tempting to investigate the different values given to various precious stones in East and West and the current globalization of diamonds, here the examples will be confined to two from hairstyle and one from foot style.

Queues

The most striking change in Chinese hairstyle between 1400 and 1800 was an act of protocol rather than fashion. This change was the imposition of Manchu hairstyle on all Chinese by edict of the Shun-chih emperor in July 1645. This hairstyle consisted of two parts: the shaved forehead in front, the braided queue or plait behind. Of the two, while it was the first which was initially most resented, it was the second which carried the stronger meaning. For, unlike fashion which is a code, protocol is a message. It is a message, however, which may be understood differently by the senders and the recipients. To the Ch'ing who issued the edict, the message was political, positive and triple. First, Manchus and Chinese should no longer be people of different states (*i-kuo chih jen*). Second, the Manchus were not barbarians. The Ch'ing had rites and music as much as the Ming, which the Chinese should adopt as a sign of unity and loyalty. Third, it should be no humiliation to do so, because the shaved forehead and braided queue were the style of a military elite well able to give new leadership after years of effete eunuch rule. To the Ch'ing, the edict of 1645 was a call for collaboration, a promise of partnership, and a programme for a Sino-Manchu empire.[36]

To the Chinese who received the edict, however, the message was cultural, negative and double. First, the adoption of the Manchu hairstyle was seen as a confusion of civilization and barbarism. It implied the removal of a demarcation which the recently built Great Wall had been designed to establish. Second, the shaved forehead was understood not as remilitarization but as emasculation: not a repudiation of the eunuchs, but a generalization of eunarchy, a ritual castration or circumcision. Initially, long hair, refusal to shave, and cutting off the queues of collaborators became hallmarks first of manifest Ming resistance and then of clandestine Ming loyalism. Subsequently, however, as the Ch'ing made good their promises and carried out their programme beyond anything which could have been imagined in 1645, the queue became an affirmation of loyalty to the dynasty and its achievements. Especially was this so from the mid-nineteenth century when the Christian Taipings, the long-haired rebels, rejected alike the Ch'ing, their hairstyle and Confucianism. Later again, the republicans repudiated the queue and tried to proscribe it, as Ataturk did the fez. When the loyalist general Chang Hsün was ridiculed for continuing to wear the queue under President Yüan Shih-k'ai, he replied: 'If anyone tries to deprive me of it, we shall die together.'[37] Chang had not a drop of Manchu blood. What he affirmed by his hairstyle, however, was not only Ch'ing loyalism, but also the Confucian and Chinese virtue of loyalty which could not serve more than one recipient of the mandate of heaven. A barbarian style had become a Chinese gesture.

Wigs

The most striking change in European hairstyle between 1400 and 1800 was an act of fashion rather than protocol. This change was the rise, floruit and fall of the periwig, the last major male fashion in the West.

The periwig indeed was opposed by what was often an upholder of protocol: the Church. In France, it was forbidden to the clergy, though the prohibition was more honoured in the breach than in the observance. In a book in 1736, the Abbé Thiers, a traditionalist Gallican, supported the ban. He did so precisely on the grounds that the wig was a fashion. The priest, as intermediary between God and man, should be above temporal mutations. Its use by the clergy was a conforming to the world, and a precursor of worse novelties in practice and belief.

As a fashion, the periwig is best understood, as fashions usually are, as a topological mutation: or set of mutations since wigs could be of various shapes and sizes. Initially, it was a synthesis, or superimposition of two previous, contrasting styles: Cavalier locks and Roundhead (not specifically English, of course, but derived from Holland) close shave. Above, Charles II was a Cavalier king, like his father 'with his long essenced hair', but below, to wear his wig, he must have a Roundhead crew cut. If fashion were interpreted semantically rather than structurally, it would be easy to argue that the periwig was the perfect expression of Restoration England: outwardly Cavalier, inwardly Roundhead. But in fact the fashion originated in France. It only came into England in 1663–4 when it was taken up by the Duke of York. On 15 February 1664, Pepys noted: 'To White Hall, to the Duke; where he first put on a periwig today; but methought his hair cut short thereto did look very pretty of itself before he put on his periwig.' The Duke was not aiming at any political effect, but simply at a modish, aesthetic one. Once established, the wig offered a gamut of possibilities: full-bottomed, campaign, travelling, Ramillies, bob, powdered or not. No doubt it was this potential for permutation, according to age, stage and circumstance, which ensured the fashion its longevity. Another element too was probably the fact that, for most of this period, women wore their hair high, so that men needed to increase their height too or risk looking ridiculous. Although male and female fashions seem to fly on separate beams, there is often a secret topological consonance between them.

Bound Feet

Foreigners, in particular, were struck by the end product of the painful process of juvenile binding. Lord Macartney was sufficiently interested to ask Chou, his diplomatic contact (probably Ch'iao Jen-chieh, a taotai at Tientsin) about its origins. He recorded:

Chou admitted that no very good reason could be given for it. Its being an ancient custom was the best he could assign, and he confessed that a religious adherence to ancient customs, without much investigation of their origin, was a principal feature in the Chinese character. He added, however, that it possibly might have taken its rise from oriental jealousy, which had always been ingenious in its contrivances for securing the ladies to their owners; and that certainly a good way of keeping them at home was to make it very troublesome and painful to gad abroad.[38]

Another informant added that 'in love affairs the glimpse of a tiny foot was to a Chinese a most powerful provocation'. Modern sinology has not gone much further.[39] Custom, misogyny, fetishism, conspicuous leisure and comparison with other mutilations remain the current stock in trade. Can a structuralist approach take us further?

Foot binding was fashion rather than protocol. It was sustained by society rather than imposed by the state. Indeed, under the Ch'ing, it was forbidden by a series of edicts, bound-feet women were excluded from the palace, and it was particularly discouraged for Manchu girls. Yet the practice continued, extended, was adopted by some Manchu families, even by the Chinese Jews in Honan. Food binding went back to the late eleventh century. Chang Pang-chi, writing in the early twelfth century, says it was infrequent before that. Chang put its origin in the court of the last Southern T'ang emperor Li Yü (961–75) when girls, or their mothers, wanted to imitate the tiny feet, special gait and alluring posture of a favourite ballerina and royal concubine. Such aetiologies are frequent in the history of dress, but as Yang-chou, a Southern T'ang capital, was later famous both for theatre and small feet, the ascription is not implausible. When the Southern T'ang were deported by the Northern Sung to Kaifeng, the fashion went with it. From Kaifeng the practice spread out over the northern provinces where it became and remained more widespread than in the south. To the south it returned, when the Sung had to transfer their capital to Hang-chou after the fall of Kaifeng to the Jurched in 1127, but slowly and to a limited extent. Marco Polo does not mention it, though only a decade or so later, Father Odoric does. Except in Yang-chou, foot binding never became fully established even among the upper classes. Li Hung-chang's mother, from one of the best Anhwei landlord families, had large feet, a fact of which the great viceroy was ashamed when he became permanently established in the north. In the late Ch'ing, foot binding was uncommon in the more rural parts of the Yangtze valley, but widespread in the even more rural provinces of Chihli, Honan, Shansi and Shensi. It was uncommon in Canton, near universal in Lanchow and Ta-t'ung.

If foot binding began as a fashion, it ended as an arrested fashion and its geography supplies clues to the mechanisms of its arrest. It was most prevalent in areas characterized by a high degree of so-called major, virilocal (often parentolocal) marriage, non-extended families and owner-occupier farming, and a low degree of inter-village solidarity, information flow and, until the rise of cotton cultivation, marketization. It was most prevalent, in other words, in Philip Huang's north China. Here it became entrenched as part of family strategy. Major marriage, the marrying in of *adult* daughters-in-law (as opposed to minor marriage, the marrying in of *child* daughters-in-law), was valued because of the stronger affinal ties it brought. In the anomie of the north China plain, such relationships were highly valued, particularly by widowed mothers struggling for their sons. If daughters-in-law were to be imported, as much as servants for the mothers as consorts for the sons, daughters must be exported to other families. Tiny feet might be an advantage here, not so much because they were erotic – Chinese families feared too-strong ties between husband and wife – but because they were a guarantee to those other families of a dutiful, housebound daughter-in-law. For in north China, female labour was not required in the fields or among the trays of cocoons as it was in the rice and mulberry lands of the south and west. Szechwan practised major marriage for its own reasons but, because of its paddy and silk, not foot binding.

Foot binding then was part of the north China variant of filial marriage: marriage where the advantage of the parents, and especially the mother, was paramount. It was not part of man's inhumanity to women. The eroticism was a consequence not a cause, male fetishism attaching to anything it is offered. Rather, it arose from that characteristically Chinese phenomenon: older women's inhumanity to girls in the interests of their sons, the force behind female infanticide. It was this powerful force which arrested what might have been a temporary fashion, a one-year issue, and turned it into an ongoing currency in the marriage market, or at any rate in some marriage markets. For the practice was never universal any more than major marriage was. In the nineteenth century, it faced increasing criticism, not only from Westernizers but from relative traditionalists as well, and disappeared rather quickly between 1890 and 1920. Silk, enlightenment, and new, conjugal, marriage patterns, particularly in towns, lifted the arrest.

Fashion was relatively weaker in China than in Europe. Yet cases of arrested fashion occurred in the West too. The conservatism of male dress may be one example. Military uniform, essentially an invention of the eighteenth century, might be another. In particular, male footwear has become much more conservative than it was in the early days of fashion in the fourteenth and fifteenth centuries. Then, the spikes or points at the toe of the *crackowes* or *poulaines*, introduced to the court of Richard II by gentlemen in the suite of Anne of Bohemia, daughter of Charles IV, might reach 18 inches or more. These fashions were eclipsed in the sixteenth century by the Spanish leather shoe or boot from Cordova, which has essentially held the field ever since.[40] China held no monopoly of conservatism any more than Europe did of fashion. But Europe grasped the possibilities of the empire of the ephemeral more eagerly than China. Perhaps, as Lipovetsky says: 'Protée at Prométhée sont de même souche.'[41]

4 Consumerism and Shelter

In the development of consumerism, shelter complemented dress. Both began in thermoregulation. As further values were required, however, shelter and dress diverged along different time scales of the permanent and the temporary. The divergence was sharper in Europe than in China. In China, shelter and dress remained part of a continuum. In Europe, they took opposite directions. Dress, under the command of annual fashions, entered the empire of the ephemeral. Shelter, under the command of cultural preferences, sought to be part of a kingdom of the perdurable. In both China and Europe, however, shelter, compared to dress, took longer views: the needs of children, the succession of generations, common ongoing history, the ageless unity of the human condition. Both dress and shelter, as they advanced from thermoregulation to consumerism in the age of globalization, were concerned with time, but where dress was ruled by the *événemental*, shelter was ruled by the *longue durée*. Each complemented the other. In China, the complementarity was convergent, while in Europe it was polarized.

The extent to which the provision of shelter dominates economies is often underestimated. In both traditional China and Europe, the building industry was the second largest activity after farming. Textiles did not surpass it in China until the cotton developments described in the last chapter, say around 1550, and in Europe until the industrial revolution of the nineteenth century, say around 1850. In nineteenth-century Hankow, 10 per cent of the workforce were employed in the construction industry. Even today construction carries clout. French business still believes that where building goes everything goes. At the end of the 1980s 85 per cent of domestic debt in England was attributable to domestic mortgages. House prices were the best index and a prime motor of economic activity. Shelter affects politics more than food or dress. A housing boom made the reputation of Harold Macmillan and dented that of Nigel Lawson. In Japan, until recently, the construction industry was widely regarded as the principal financial backer of the Liberal Democratic Party. In the developing world – whether in Teheran, Lagos, São Paulo, Mexico City or Istanbul – inadequate housing is a factor in the political volatility of its plethoric, shantytown-surrounded megapolises. Insufficient investment in housing helped to bring down the Communist regimes. In more advanced economies, shelter, more than food or dress, raises the question of positional values: the quest for recognition as well as acquisition. In principle, we may all eat caviar and be dressed by Christian Dior, but we cannot all live in Chelsea or the eighth *arrondissement*. Shelter goes beyond bricks and mortar. Like food and dress, in a consumerist world, it has its principles which then express themselves in essentials, accessories and extras.[1]

PRINCIPLES: SYSTEMIC OPTIONS, REASONS AND CONSEQUENCES

In a passage in *Tristes Tropiques*, Lévi-Strauss drew an analogy between certain kinds of shelter and dress. Looking back on a visit to a Burmese border village, he wrote of tree houses, 'not so much built as knotted together, plaited, woven, embroidered . . . The village rose round its occupants like a light flexible suit of armour closer to Western women's hats than to Western towns . . . when the natives slipped out of their huts, it was as if they were divesting themselves of giant ostrich-feather wraps.'[2] The analogy might be taken further. Like dress, shelter provides not only thermoregulation, but also concealment, display, social identity and personal idiosyncrasy. Like dress, shelter manifests itself in bewildering variety: the cave, the igloo, the yurt, the Roman villa, the Southeast Asian stilt house, the log cabin, the *yali*, the suburban bungalow, the terrace house, the high-rise apartment. At first glance, this variety has no more unity than that of all being roofs over ovens and bedrooms. A further look, however, indicates that, like dress, shelter has its structures of demand independent of what supply may offer. Yet there is a significant difference. Where the totality of wardrobes is the product of short-term individual choice, the existing stock of houses, what the French call the *parc immobilier*, is the product of long-term collective choice. These collective choices, with their ramifying implications, may be termed systemic options. It will be argued that significantly different options were made in Europe and China between 1400 and 1800.

Systemic Options

The substantial choice was between construction and maintenance, capital and income. Whatever the fabric, high initial outlay would be associated with low subsequent upkeep, and vice versa. Implied in this choice were differences of temporal orientation: over what period should debt be amortized, what value should be placed on liquidity, what length of cycle was appropriate to this particular commodity. It was because of these implications that the building industry had such wide-ranging consequences for the economy as a whole. More than food and dress, shelter involved the future.

In this option, China and Europe made different choices. China chose low initial outlay and high subsequent maintenance. Europe chose high initial outlay and low subsequent maintenance. The Chinese made a less radical distinction between dress and shelter than did the Europeans. One of the Seven Sages of the Bamboo Grove, those amiable antinomians of the third century AD, was reproached for receiving an important visitor when inadequately dressed. 'The whole world is my clothes,' he replied, 'what are you doing inside my trousers?' Chinese houses were not built to last: a few decades at most. Chi Ch'eng, a famous master builder and gardener of the seventeenth century, defended this on humanistic grounds: 'Even if one makes a thing so strong that it lasts for a thousand years, how can one know what man will be like a hundred years from now? One should be content to live a care-free life and live in one's house tranquilly.'[3] Consequently, Chinese cities contain few genuinely old dwellings and appear to be in a constant state of renovation. The European house, on the other hand, in particular what Chaunu called the heavy house, was built to last: as much as two or three centuries. The sturdy presbyteries built by the Catholic Reform in Normandy are only now beginning to fall into irretrievable disrepair. Consequently, European cities, if undisturbed by development, as in parts of London and places like Bath, contain an abundance of genuinely old dwellings. In Canton in the 1930s, a comfortable spinsterhouse for bachelor girls at work required an outlay of only £18 sterling. Already in the eighteenth century in Normandy, every parish was spending 20 times this on a simple house for the *curé*.[4]

How far back did this difference in systemic option go? In the case of Europe, it went back to the earliest days of reurbanization after the Dark Ages. A recent study of reconstruction at Rome between the tenth and thirteenth centuries indicates already a preference for sturdy buildings of permanent materials.[5] Masons, *muratori,* were differentiated from workers in wood, *carpentarii* or *magistri de lignamine*, with the former enjoying greater prestige. Tile increasingly replaced thatch. Buildings were intended to look well from the street. Staircases were prestigious, and by the twelfth century two-thirds of dwellings were double-storeyed. In title, as with land, the true realty, ground landlords were differentiated from long-lease holders and sitting tenants. Religious houses, especially nunneries, were built as much to institutionalize clients and parishioners as to produce rent. In Rome, the preference for capital over maintenance was already in place by 1300 and it was only extended and propagandized by Sixtus V's massive building programme in the sixteenth century. In the case of China, on the other hand, the preference for maintenance over capital came later, after 1300. Marco Polo was not struck by any essential difference between Chinese and European building. In Hang-chou, he said, 'The houses in general are very solidly built and richly decorated.'[6] In another passage, he indicates that the Southern Sung emperor actively encouraged the construction of multi-storeyed buildings. Such apartment blocks are referred to by Chinese, Muslim and other European sources. Yet subsequently they became uncharacteristic of China. By the early Ming, partly as a result of its crash rebuilding, things had changed. A work dating from this period, and recently edited by Klaas Ruitenbeck is the *Lu Pan Ching* or Classic of Carpentry. A summa of building lore and ideology, it was compiled by an official of the board of works, the *Kung-pu*, on the occasion of the building of Peking as the Yung-lo emperor's new capital. The title was significant. It asserted the leading position of the carpenters as against other building workers such as tilers, bricklayers and masons. Monumentality was de-emphasized and multi-storeyed buildings were not specifically considered. Although there was technological continuity between the *Lu Pan Ching* and earlier Sung works, in psychology and economics there had been a mutation.

The divergence between Chinese and European ideals of building was apparent to early Western travellers. Semedo wrote: 'The houses, where they inhabit, are not so sumptuous and lasting as ours...They build them not very high, esteeming them more convenient for being low, as well for habitation as for good accommodation.'[7] Jan Nieuhof, who accompanied the Dutch mission of Goyer and Kayser to Peking in 1655, thought Chinese buildings inferior to those of Europe, because they were built for one life only not for posterity. At the end of the seventeenth century, the Jesuit Louis Le Comte considered the Chinese less well housed than Europeans. Paris, he argued, was only a quarter of the area of Peking. Each house, however, had four storeys while those in China had only one, so the floor space available was equal. But whereas 10 people inhabited a building in Paris, 20 inhabited a building in Peking. In China a little after Le Comte, the Neapolitan layman Gemelli Careri admired the shops in Nan-ch'ang, but observed: 'it is vain to look for stately structures here, or in other parts of China;

for as the cities here are all built by one model, so all the houses are flat, low, and made of brick and mud, there being very few of stone'.[8] The concordance of the Western travellers is the more convincing in that some, Semedo for example, preferred the Chinese pattern and all agreed China was the richest country in the world. What was described was not a Third World, but an alternative First World.

Ideals of building do not stand alone. Before reasons are addressed for the divergence between China and Europe, three associated phenomena may be introduced which suggest that what is at issue is not something isolated, but forms part of a wider pattern of temporal orientation.

First, Chinese business generally, at least in the early modern period, preferred minimum use of capital, either fixed or floating, and aimed at rapid turnover. It was sophisticated and vast, but one hesitates to call it capitalism because of its preference for brokerage, commissions, and short-term bridging loans rather than risk capital. Desire to minimize turnover time was at the root of one of the most striking features of Chinese business: its extreme subdivision and the reluctance of businessmen to operate *wai-hang* outside their particular sphere of competence. Risk avoidance rather than risk management was the aim. Consequently, despite a lesser volume of trade, the insurance industry – risk on risk – was better developed in early modern Europe than China.[9] Even before the Great Discoveries and the formation of joint stock companies to exploit them, European business showed a greater propensity for capital intensivity than China, as in the massive papal alum works at Tolfa.[10] Turnover cycles were longer. Chaunu has argued that in the period 1500–1650 business activity was dominated by trades with the longest cycles such as the Carrera de las Indias or the Acapulco galleon, rather than by the Dutch trade to the Baltic or the Portuguese trade to Brazil. This was the opposite to China where the shortest cycles dominated, as in the cotton economy of the Yangtze delta.

Second, if one turns from equity to bonds, interest rates in China in the early modern period were consistently higher than in Europe, except in the case of short-term credit between business associates. In other words, liquidity was more highly valued in China and interest rates were often quoted by the month rather than the year. China does not support the Keynesian contention that long-term low interest rates are essential to growth. Chinese enterprise circumvented high liquidity preference by personalizing credit where it was necessary and by minimizing bonds as well as equity capital. It was a capitalism without capital.

Third, it should be observed that European attitudes to shelter were in counterpoint to their attitude to dress. From the fourteenth century, European dress was under the command of fashion: short-term cycles with built-in obsolescence, Lipovetsky's empire of the ephemeral. In China, on the other hand, durability was one of the achievements of the new cotton industry and a major reason why, even reinforced by powered machinery, Manchester could not compete with it in the nineteenth century. In clothes, the Chinese were interested not just in price but also in wear. Committed not to fashion but to standardization, they looked for a longer life cycle than Lancashire offered. The Europeans made a radical distinction between the life cycles of clothes and buildings. For the Chinese, they formed a continuum: longer for dress than the Europeans, shorter for shelter, but all of a piece. The Chinese had one dimension in their temporal orientation. The Europeans had two.

If this seems metaphysical, it may be replied that a considerable part of the *Lu Pan Ching* is metaphysical. It is concerned with geomancy and what Ruitenbeek calls chronomancy: correct siting and timing in accordance with definite principles to secure benefits and avoid misfortunes. In the past, scholarship tended to disregard such elements in Chinese literature. Currently, particularly in the work of Richard J. Smith, it is increasingly recognized that geomancy and chronomancy were significant background music to Chinese intellectual life, both high-cultural and low-cultural.[11] The set of assumptions about space and time they provided was an important unifying element in that life. The imperial almanac of lucky and unlucky days, put out annually by the astronomical bureau of the Board of Rites in an edition of over two million copies, may have been the most widely read book in the world. Foremost among the assumptions was that time was differentiated. It was not uniform, as in Newton's famous definition, but local: more like time in relativity physics. These ideas were not survivals. Though, as Needham and Nathan Sivin have shown, Chinese thought had a long record of interest in the physics of time, going back to *Wu-hsing* theory and the time-controlling substances of the alchemical side of Taoism, chronomancy experienced a revival in the late imperial period, of which the publication of the *Lu Pan Ching* under official auspices was an expression. In this revival, the construction industry held a privileged position because it necessarily involved time and space and because it was so widely diffused. For, unlike earlier manuals which dealt largely with palaces, the *Lu Pan Ching* dealt not only with local temples, ancestral halls and most private houses, but also with cow-sheds, sheep-pens, stables, pigsties and hen coops. As well as being a manual, the *Lu Pan Ching* was a tract and, to the illiterate, a talisman. If the Catholic counter-reformation under Sixtus V was relevant to the European option in shelter, so the Sinistic counter-reformation under Yung-lo was relevant to the Chinese option in shelter. Christianity juxtaposed the ephemeral and the perdurable. The Sinistic religion united a patchwork of times in the paradigms of the *I-ching*, the Classic of Change, the most commented on of all the classics in Ch'ing times.

Reasons

If the facts had metaphysical associations, it is tempting to look for metaphysical explanations. Lipovetsky connected the beginnings of fashion and the empire of the ephemeral with a widening Christian understanding of the Incarnation, prompted by the more visible ephemerality of life effected by the Black Death. Might not the double dimensionality of time latent in the European options regarding shelter and dress be a projection of the double nature of Christ, divine and human: houses founded upon a rock, clothes mutable as the lilies of the field? Similarly, Needham wrote of Chinese architecture: 'In no other field of expression have the Chinese so faithfully incarnated their great principles that Man cannot be thought of apart from Nature, and that man is not to be divided from social man.'[12] Might not the single dimensionality of time latent in Chinese options regarding shelter and dress be a projection of the four-fold but unified harmony concurred in by heaven, earth, man and the *wang*? Tempting as such explanations are, however, they prove too much. Not all Christendom went for the heavy house of stone. Orthodox Russia and Protestant Scandinavia preferred the light house of wood. Ongoing Chinese notions of harmony cannot explain multi-storeyed buildings before the Mongol invasion and single-storeyed buildings after. Beyond latent *Weltanschauungen*, more manifest reasons are called for.

First, ecological reasons. More than Europe, China is a land of disasters: earthquakes, typhoons and floods, which discourage capital outlay. Earthquakes followed a pattern: frequent but minor in Yunnan, common but medium in Shensi-Kansu, occasional but major in Shansi, Chihli and Shantung, infrequent in China south of the Yangtze except along the Taiwan strait.[13] As population returned to north China after the Mongol invasions, more earthquake-defensive styles of architecture were adopted. Light carpenters' buildings were safer than heavy masons' buildings. In the T'ang-shan earthquake of 1976, northeast of Peking, which killed 240 000 people, loss of life was heavier in heavy modern apartment blocks than in light traditional houses. In a strong earthquake, force eight and over, heavy loss of life could hardly be avoided. In 1556, the force eight Hua-hsien quake at the junction of Shensi and Shansi reputedly killed 830 000: probably because of the collapse of caves, a widespread form of housing in the northwest. In 1920, the better documented Ning-hsia quake certainly killed 200 000 people. But in a medium earthquake, or at some distance from the epicentre, design of building could make a considerable difference. In Lanchow in 1920, on the edge of the Ning-hsia quake, 30 per cent of the houses collapsed, but only 3000 people were killed out of a total population of 500 000. In 1730, there was a force 6.5 earthquake in Peking with its epicentre in the outer suburbs. There more than 20 000 people were killed, but within the walls, though 16 000 houses collapsed and many were initially buried, only 457 were killed.[14] European styles of building coped less well with earthquakes. In Lisbon in 1755, 12 000 dwellings were destroyed, but 30 000 people were killed. It was not until the twentieth century, with the new techniques so triumphantly demonstrated by Frank Lloyd Wright's Imperial Hotel in Tokyo in 1923, that European architects could offer more safety in earthquake zones than the Chinese.

Second, reasons of historical context. The European Middle Ages lived in the shadow of Rome and its monumentality in stone: a perception, not altogether well founded, that things had been better than they were. The successive fashions for the antique, from the Carolingians through the twelfth century to the Great Renaissance, therefore privileged capital in construction. It was from the south, especially from the *Terza Roma* of the Renaissance Papacy, that the taste for heavy building spread to the rest of Europe. As late as the mid-nineteenth century, slate roofs were more characteristic of southern France than the north where thatch was still widely prevalent, though the Midi had been the poorer of the two for centuries.[15] China, on the other hand, lived less in the shadow of the Han than Europe did of Rome. Its precedent was overlaid by the greater model of the T'ang. Neither, moreover, offered the monumentality in stone which Rome bequeathed to Europe. If the Sung in its hyper-urbanization manifested a shift to capital intensivity in building, the Ming consciously rejected Sung values as socially divisive and responsible for the barbarian conquests. Inspired by peasant sanctimonious poverty and the beggars' democracy of the routes, the early Ming were hostile to accumulation. Their capitals, Nanking and Peking, were imperial but jerry-built. Even the wealth acquired by the dynastic founders was dissipated in Hung-wu's purges of his own supporters. Eventually, the Ming revolution of the state was reversed by a consumerist counter-revolution of society, but its presuppositions about income and investment had entered deeply into conventional financial wisdom. When, in the mid-sixteenth century, Lu Chi wanted to defend extravagance against frugality as economically beneficial in the aggregate, it was to food, dress and services to which he pointed rather than shelter. It was only later when Western values had infiltrated through the treaty ports that what has been called the compradoric style of building was adopted by Chinese businessmen in Shanghai, Tientsin and Canton.

Third, consumer alternatives. Decisions about shelter must always be seen in the context of decisions about alternative forms of thermoregulation, notably dress. With the cotton revolution analysed in Chapter 3, China was better endowed than Europe in this respect. The option of putting on more layers of cotton garments as one went north was not open to Europeans. Cotton was still too marginally available and, till the eighteenth century, there were no pure cotton clothes because the warp was too weak. Silk and fur were too expensive to be layered and wool and coarse linen were too uncomfortable. The absence of alternatives was an incentive to deal with thermoregulation through heavy, weather-insulated houses, warm in winter and cool in summer. For the Chinese, clothing and housing formed a continuum. For Europeans, they formed a polarity, especially when fashion began to distinguish indoors and outdoors, wear and overwear. If textiles were a bigger rival to bricks and mortar in China than in Europe, so too was furniture. In the sixteenth century, European furniture was still comparatively primitive and cumbersome. In China, on the other hand, the period 1550 to 1735 has been described as the golden age of classical furniture.[16] Light and elegant, it made use of new, imported tropical hardwoods, notably the *huang-hua li*, *Dalburgia*, from Vietnam and Hainan. Craig Clunas, in his account of Chinese connoisseurship in this period, notes that, 'Fine clothes and fine furniture were an important part of the presentation of an upper-class persona to the world.'[17] Chinese furniture of this period anticipated not only Chippendale, Hepplewhite and Sheraton in its sophistication, but also Maples, Heals and Habitat in its functionalism. In China, furniture was an alternative to fabric. In Europe, the priority of masonry had been set before quality furniture appeared to rival it.

Fourth, urban organization. In the West, the Church began capital-intensive building, but it was quickly followed by the municipality. Against the fragility of urban life vulnerable to disease, fire, war, criminality and class conflict, the town hall, the exchange, the halls of city companies, bridges, walls and gates asserted the corporate perenniality of the city, and its component guilds and confraternities.[18] The period 1350 to 1500 saw a proliferation of such edifices, especially in northern Europe: the second London Guildhall (1411–39), the *stad huis* at Leuven (1448–59), to name only two. In China, on the other hand, because of the predominance of the bureaucratic state, corporate identities were slower to emerge. At Hankow, which has been studied by William T. Rowe, guild identities, as expressed in halls, appeared in the late seventeenth century, but city identity not till the nineteenth century.[19] In the late nineteenth century, as their power, both informal and formal, increased, guilds rebuilt their halls on more grandiose lines. Until then, the instinct of Chinese business was to take a low profile and to build for utility and today rather than for prestige and tomorrow.

Fifth, family reasons. This was the most important factor of all in shaping the different European and Chinese attitudes to initial outlay and subsequent maintenance in shelter. Behind the house was the household and households were differently structured in Europe and China. The most basic difference lay in what may be called the finality of marriage. In Europe, marriage, at any rate since the Dark Ages, was directed towards the couple marrying: it was conjugal. In China, marriage, at any rate since the Sung period, was directed towards the parent, especially the mother of the groom: it was filial. With this basic contrast of conjugality and filiality were associated three further distinctions, cumulatively significant for attitudes to shelter.

First, the unity of marriage. In Europe, since the sixth century AD, marriage was one. Justinian's codification and reform of Roman law did away with Antiquity's diversity of legal married statuses and established the principle that marriage was made by cohabitation. In the twelfth century, under the influence of Ivo of Chartres, this was modified to the more personalist principle that marriage was made by consent. Parents lost the right to dispose of their children in marriage, though this was hotly contested in France and some Protestant countries and was often more honoured in the breach than in the observance. Nevertheless, the principle, reaffirmed by the Council of Trent and reinforced by successive romanticisms, set a distance between parents and children in the matter of matrimony. However poor the material circumstances, marriage was a new beginning.

In China, on the other hand, marriage, at least as it came under observation in the nineteenth and twentieth centuries, was multiple. In *major* marriage, an adult girl, accompanied by a dowry only partly counterbalanced by bride price, went, with considerable pomp, to live in the household of her husband's parents, there to become a dutiful daughter-in-law to his mother. In *uxorilocal* marriage, a boy, unaccompanied by dowry though occasionally preceded by groom price, went with no pomp to live in the house of his wife's parents, there to become in effect a handyman to his father-in-law. In *minor* marriage, a non-adult girl, unaccompanied by dowry though occasionally preceded by bride price, went, with no pomp, to live in the household of her future husband's parents, there to be in effect a servant, generally to marry with no further formality when she was adult, but sometimes to be adopted as a daughter and subsequently to be married out in major marriage. Finally, in *delayed transfer marriage*, really part of an alternative and possibly pre-Chinese system particularly prevalent in the sericultural districts of the Canton delta, an adult girl would go through the forms of major marriage, but, instead of going to live in the household of her husband, would, for up to three years and sometimes more, return to her natolocal home, there to put her considerable earning power at the disposal of her parents. Characteristic of all these four forms of marriage (which were really only different strategies, however) was the paramountcy of an older generation. Marriage was not a new beginning, the foundation of a unit, but an addition to, or subtraction from, an existing unit.

Second, the age of marriage. In Europe, since the couple were primarily envisaged, marriage was relatively late: the mid- to late twenties for both bride and groom. In China, since the older generation was primarily envisaged, marriage was relatively early: late teens or early twenties for both genders, except in the case of minor marriage where the groom might not even be born when the child fiancée was brought into the household! These differences were related to the factors noted above. Since in Europe marriage was the constitution of a new unit, its creation required endowment: sufficient funds to support it, particularly as a separate establishment, were generally insisted on. In sixteenth-century Naples, for example, marriage often had to await the death of a parent, for only then would the necessary capital be available. Since in China marriage was the addition of a fresh term to an old series, it was initiated by parents at their most active, often against the resistance of their children. In Europe, marriage was a capital venture. It was a privilege, worked for, minoritarian probably, even when infantile mortality is taken into account. In China, marriage was for parents a hiring of services, for children a repayment of debt. Except in particular circumstances or unusual poverty, marriage was a universal obligation, especially for girls. It was less a capital venture than the payment of insurance premiums in a system of intergenerational mutuality.

Third, the locality of marriage. In Europe, the thrust of marriage, especially north of the Alps, was towards neolocality: a separate household for the new couple, whether in a different area or set within a kinship zone. This thrust, however, might be slowed or temporarily diverted by economic circumstance and by requirements of family solidarity. Thus Gérard Delille has shown that where Campania was a land of virilocality and Apulia a land of uxorilocality, in Naples itself, and many Mezzogiorno townships, an initial zone of uxorilocality was surrounded by a newer zone of virilocality as families once established brought to their compounds first male cousins and then wives for them, and beyond that, a newest zone of neolocality as numbers made compounds impossible and modernity encouraged couples to greater independence in suburbia.[20] A similar pattern was found by Étienne Hubert in Rome back in the Dark Ages. Chinese cities were not constituted like this. Before the twentieth century, they were primarily places of male work rather than household residence. Males outnumbered females, where the opposite was the case in Europe because of the number of life-cycle female domestics earning enough in service to be able to marry. Thus in 1917, Peking had 515 535 males (63.5 per cent) to 296 021 females (36.5 per cent), compared to Philadelphia: 760 463 males (49.1 per cent) and 788 545 females (50.9 per cent). Similarly, Tzu-liu-ching, the salt-producing centre in Szechwan, in 1909 had a population of 531 811 males and 366 545 females, compared to Pittsburgh's near equality of 273 589 males and 260 316 females.[21] It was a common pattern in China for a man to leave his wife with his parents and to reside for work purposes in an adjacent city. This might be continued until the parents died and the man divided the family property with his brothers. Such a pattern did not encourage capital outlay on housing. Urban housing was temporary, while rural housing, like property generally, was subject to partible inheritance. China, in general, knew neither primogeniture nor devisement by will. It was a land of Code Napoléon before Bonaparte. The family was ongoing but not the house. Heavy investment in its fabric would simply impede the inevitable periodic redistribution of assets. If anything were perdurable, it was not the house, but the tomb and the cemetery.

The unity, age and place of marriage thus concurred in leading Europeans to privilege initial outlay in housing, Chinese to privilege subsequent maintenance. For Europeans, a house was a capital expense, indeed the only capital investment most people would make. For Chinese, a house was an income expense, part of a continuum of such expenses which included other thermoregulatory spheres such as food and dress.

Consequences

If construction was the second economic activity after agriculture, in China until the sixteenth century, in Europe until the nineteenth century, it is only to be expected that the search for shelter in these two contrasting ways should carry consequences beyond itself, both positive and negative.

Chaunu in his introduction to the Bardet volume took a positive view of the European path. The Western option for heavy outlay and light maintenance pushed its economy in the direction of capital intensivity elsewhere: the substitution in manufacture of fixed capital for floating funds, plant for labour. It was a factor in the genesis of the industrial revolution. Moreover, the existence of a massive inherited *parc immobilier* meant that capital could be diverted to industrial investment and moderated the impact of the new economy on the old society. Nineteenth-century man still lived in a largely eighteenth-century habitat. Europe could have industrial revolution without political or social revolution. In the East, per contra, the Chinese option for low outlay and high maintenance pushed the economy in the direction of labour intensivity: the pattern of demographic revolution without industrial revolution. Moreover, when industrialization did come, it required essentially new cities and patterns of urban living, proving highly disruptive politically and socially. The trouble with these arguments is that, while the causality may indeed have run in these directions, it may not have been decisive, as can be seen from the example of Japan. Here a Chinese building pattern did not prevent European results.[22] Indeed, the personal discipline, social harmony and Confucian values it assumed, are now seen as ingredients in those results. What Fukuyama has called empires of deference present today a serious challenge to the economies of the West. Where Chaunu's argument goes wrong is the assumption that the industrial revolution was primarily a phenomenon of heavy investment, so an antecedent accumulation of capital or disposition to accumulate has to be explained. If the industrial revolution is understood more as a phenomenon of enterprise culture, information and associative creativity, as both Patrick Yerley and Michael Novak suggest, then this particular connection of construction options and modern business may be misplaced.

In contrast to Chaunu, who directed some of his arguments against him, Delumeau took a negative view of the European path, at least as regards southern Europe. In his book on Rome at the time of the Catholic reform, especially under the pontificate of Sixtus V, Delumeau argued that the decline of the papal state, and possibly of the Mediterranean generally, was due to excessive investment in unproductive prestige building. Construction crowded out more productive forms of invest-ment. Sixtus V, a Franciscan, may have wanted to encourage industry to relieve the poor. In fact, his urban renewal plus his thesaurization in the Castel Sant' Angelo inhibited it. Indeed, the taxes required to service the loans to finance these things crushed the economy outside Rome as well as inside. Any enterprise culture there may have been was buried beneath the weight of bricks and mortar. While this argu-ment may have some force in the particular case of papal Rome – never a good candidate for industrialization – its general application is questionable. If Bernini injured the economy of Rome by starving it of capital, why did Wren not do the same to London? Eighteenth-century Englishmen may have gone for country houses rather than Baroque churches, but the economic consequences of their vast piles – surely in aggregate heavier and more numerous than the Pope's – should have been the same. But clearly they were not. Britain was not crushed by Blenheim. Of course, it might be returned that the contexts were dif-ferent. Where a weak economy was crushed, a strong economy was stimulated. Alternatively, it might be argued that country houses were productive in some way that Baroque churches were not. However, on a Keynesian model at least, it is difficult to distinguish productive and unproductive investment. Where resources are underutilized – and this is probably the case in all traditional economies – the multiplier will always operate, whatever the character of the investment. Even if this condition is lifted, investment crowds in as well as crowds out, especially in conditions of the free movement of capital. Delumeau's negative assessment lacks theoretical foundations.

Delumeau's argument has recently been revived to explain, not the decline of the Mediterranean, but the supposed decline of Britain. The problem of recent economic history, it is argued, is why Britain, hav-ing invented the industrial revolution, has failed to pursue it. Thus posed, a number of solutions may be advanced: the absorption of the middle class into the aristocracy by way of the public schools; the dominance of classical culture over scientific training; restrictive prac-tices by trade unions; failure to be bombed out of existence during the Second World War; obsession with sterling in the post-war years. In an analysis of what he called the San Andreas fault in the British economy, Godfrey Barker argued the case for excessive investment in building: in particular in the national obsession, going far beyond most continentals, with home ownership.[23] What had been the folly of individual popes in the sixteenth and seventeenth centuries became the madness of a whole people in the nineteenth and twentieth centuries. Britain put the profits of the first industrial revolution, not into subsequent ones, but into suburban housing which engulfed villages, eroded green belts, proletarianized some areas, gentrified others, but always multiplied the *parc immobilier* to an extent greater than anywhere else in Europe. Because housing was a positional good as well as an interchangeable utility, there was no limit to the inflation of its market. Buying, improving and selling houses, rather than more productive investment, became the prime means of capital accumulation for most people. The vast stock of houses bequeathed to the twentieth century by the Victorians provided the basis for an indefinite expansion of mortgages. When a mortgage was raised, a portion of the funds was frequently diverted into consumer goods: durables for the most part, but sometimes clothes and holidays. It was this additional demand released from the housing market onto markets generally which was the prime cause of inflation. Inflation was a monetary phenomenon, but where the money came from was property. If property ceased to generate money, the result would be pause, downturn, recession and slump, as falling house prices and mortgage repossessions temporarily destroyed business confidence. The business cycle was basically a housing cycle – a fact the French had known for a long time – and in Britain a peculiarly uncreative one which secreted stagflation and inhibited enterprise culture.

Such arguments, like those of Delumeau, are only convincing at first sight. First, they assume a 'lump of capital', zero-sum theory so that what is invested in one object must automatically be taken away from another. In fact, enterprise largely creates its own capital. Second, they assume a closed economy, so that if the first assumption was correct, no appeal could be made from a capital deficient country to capital surplus countries. In fact, the Victorians achieved a high degree of freedom of capital movements. Third, although a distinction between productive and unproductive investment can be sustained, though not easily on Keynesian grounds, expenditure on housing need not fall into the unproductive category. A building produces services if not goods. That Britain provided herself with housing services to a greater extent than her continental co-Europeans is not evidence of misdirected investment, but only of choice and, as we shall argue, good choice. Barker's strictures on the property market and inflation, and in particular the role of its collapse in the recession of the late 1980s and early 1990s, may be better founded. But the fault lay less with the property market as such, or the consumerist values which underlay it, than with the miscalculation of risks by mortgage lenders and borrowers. Risk is of the essence of markets and its miscalculation may occur in any part of the economy: experiments to be meaningful must sometimes fail. Moreover, in itself, mortgage lending is no more inflationary than any other kind of lending: it is simply more widespread. There was therefore nothing inherently pathological about the figure Barker provides that in 1991, property assets in Britain, of which domestic residences comprised 75 per cent, were four times the value of factories and plant. It simply indicated a mature economy which was passing from goods to services, among which shelter rightly occupied an exceptional place.

It was in the services it provided that the Western heavy house made its greatest contribution to the growth first of its own and then of the world economy. Le Comte was struck by the greater space per person provided in Paris as compared to Peking. Cavils may be made to his arguments, but it is likely that in the early modern period, Europeans did give themselves more living space than Chinese, just as, even before the industrial revolution, they used more energy per capita. Living space here should be understood in a strong sense, as space for a variety of kinds of living: kitchens, smoking room, drawing rooms – masculine space, feminine space – rooms where children could do homework or practise musical instruments, rooms for books, large rooms, small rooms, tidy rooms, rooms for the exercise of personal idiosyncrasy in mess and disorder. Anthropologists have commented on the exhausting absence of privacy in primitive societies and the rare but welcome perception of the European need for it. Similarly, northern Europeans have contrasted their domesticity with the sociability of the south: life on the piazza or the agora in the Mediterranean, life on the street in many parts of Monsoon Asia. The European house contributed to recollection, interiority and what Teilhard de Chardin called the 'within' of things. By so doing, it encouraged the accumulation of information, again in a strong sense, which economists now see as the basic raw material and universal resource: more basic and universal than capital, labour or management in the usual sense. In a paper given at Leeds in 1874, which strikingly anticipates *Centesimus Annus* as expounded by Michael Novak, Cardinal Manning (who later sat on a royal commission on housing) sought to establish a hierarchy of economic values. Having quoted with approval another author to the effect that 'in the dim morning of society Labour was up and stirring before Capital was awake', he went on to affirm 'Mind must precede Labour.' He argued: 'I may say that not only in the "dim morning", but through the noontide of society, mind must be up and stirring before labour is awake.'[24] By mind here, Manning seems to have meant an intellectual morphogenetic field, superordinate to both labour and capital but in which both participated: a meaning akin to Julian Simon's notion of information as the ultimate resource. Domestic space was room for thinking.

The European option in shelter, like its option in dress for fashion rather than protocol, was fundamentally an option for mind in this sense. The space created by the European house was an intellectual space, or rather an assemblage of intellectual spaces. Its creation through a preference for outlay over upkeep, capital over labour was an expression of a deeper dichotomy in the appreciation and discounting of time. The Chinese continuum between dress and shelter was less noogenetic than the European contrast between them because it drew less clear distinctions and accepted more modest horizons. The Chinese, as so often, aimed at a harmonious middle. The Europeans went for the empire of the ephemeral in one direction and the kingdom of the perdurable in another. What the Chinese united, Europeans divided. Europeans sought to master both the fleeting moment by fashion and the ravages of time by stone. The Chinese sought to hold the middle ground from one generation to another, seeking neither to master the moment nor to achieve eternity.

ESSENTIALS: MATERIAL, DESIGN, LAYOUT

On the basis of their different systemic options, Europe and China erected characteristic stocks of housing which expressed those options in essentials, accessories and extras. Essentials may be defined here as the chief materials (stone, brick, wood, adobe), the groundplan and design, and the layout of actual rooms in the living space so provided and protected.

Material

Unlike stone and brick which seldom travelled long distances, wood, the material *par excellence*, definitely participated in the globalization process between 1400 and 1800. In traditional economies, wood was a universal raw material. Whatever the importance of copper, bronze, iron and steel, all ages before 1800 were wood ages. Wood was essential not only for house construction, but also for shipbuilding, fuel, domestic and industrial, and as raw material for furniture, tools, wagons and paper. Of these four primary destinations of wood, in both Europe and China, construction, domestic and otherwise, was the most important, but pre-eminently so in China. Wood was the material of predilection in China just as stone was in Europe. Joseph Needham asked with his usual insight: 'why was it that the Chinese throughout their history systematically built in wood and pile, bamboo and plaster, never making use of the stone which in other civilisations such as Greece, India and Egypt left such durable monuments behind? I have often felt that if a full answer to this question could be obtained, it would throw light on many wider aspects of cultural difference.'[25] The persistence of the Chinese preference for wood has been elucidated, it may be hoped, by the previous discussion of the systemic option for maintenance over capital outlay. However, the preference, very old in Chinese history, antedates the option, which can only be dated surely to the post-Mongol period. More, therefore, needs to be said about the origins of the preference as opposed to its persistence. Indeed, Needham's dissatisfaction with existing answers to the question he had posed, may have been due in part to their failure to distinguish between origin and persistence.

The origin needs to be set in a wider context: the fusions of northern and southern elements in traditional Chinese culture. Since Needham posed his question in 1971, archaeologists have become more aware of the composite nature of that culture, and in particular of the contribution of southern, coastal elements to the synthesis effected subsequently under northern, interior leadership. It is no longer supposed that Han civilization originated in a single, nuclear area in Shensi, Shansi and Honan. Many food plants, notably rice and soya beans, originated outside that area. François Sigaut has characterized Chinese food production as tropical horticulture transposed into temperate latitudes. Janice Stockard has suggested that the idiosyncratic marriage system of the Canton delta is of pre-Chinese, Southeast Asian origin. Timber was probably always more abundant south of the Yangtze than in the north China plain, which, though subsequently further denuded, in prehistory was more of a wetland than a wood. The preference for wood, not just in building but in other matters (in Chinese cosmogony wood was a fundamental element or process under which many other things were classified), may be regarded as part of a Southeast Asian, Yüeh/Viet complex in Chinese culture: a complex which included dragon boats, and the whole mythology of the dragon. Anthony Reid, in his search for the original, indigenous elements of Southeast Asian culture, points to the tree-like character of its stilt buildings constructed close to water. He emphasizes the fragility of its estuarial orchard cities such as Srivijaya or, one might add, Canton when it first became fully Chinese under the T'ang.[26]

If the preference for wood went back to prehistory, it will have been recharged by the temporary return of Chinese civilization to the south following the fall of Kaifeng to the Jurched in 1127. While high culture under the Southern Sung still looked to the north and saw its reconquest as a sacred duty, humbler strata of Chinese culture took on a renewed southern hue. The result was a contradiction at the heart of traditional China: a high demand for timber coexisted with a low, accessible supply. For while virgin forests existed in the eastern Himalayas and in the southern prolongations of the *taiga* in northern Manchuria, these long both lay beyond effective Chinese administration and lacked adequate transport. Though reafforestation within China was attempted under the Ming by the Hung-wu emperor, it was not very successful. It was easier to plant trees than to see they grew to maturity. In effect, China resolved its wood contradiction by a portfolio of expedients, two of which involved a measure of globalization.

First, they resolved it by a series of windfalls: the exploitation to destruction of accessible sources of supply. China shifted its catchment in a clockwise motion. In antiquity, it was southern Shensi, the upper valley of the Han, northern Szechwan, followed by Shansi and Shantung. Under the T'ang and the Sung, it was the forested hills of southern Anhwei exploited through the plantation zone of Hui-chou or the natural timber of western Fukien exploited through the port of Foochow. Under the Ming and early Ch'ing, the focus shifted to the other side of the Nan-shan: first to western Anhwei where Wu-hu became a major market in the Wan-li period; then to the timber port of Kiukiang in Kiangsi which drew on the forests round the P'o-yang lake; and finally to the prolongations of the Himalayas in southern Szechwan, Kweichow and western Hunan which were exploited from Hankow either across the Tung-ting lake at Ch'ang-te or via the Szechwan port of Fow-chou. In the early nineteenth century and the late Ch'ing, a last windfall was opened in eastern Manchuria and western Korea via the valley of the Yalu, which temporarily made the fortune of the port of An-tung. Timber was big business in late imperial China. The early Jesuits were impressed both by the huge timber rafts and the links of this trade with the predominant salt merchants. Both the Kweichow and Yalu windfalls, moreover, involved an extension of Chinese jurisdiction, trade accompanying the flag in a timber imperialism which turned non-China into China.[27] Windfalls, however, could not last forever.

Second, substitution. In the early modern period, China made increasing use of substitutes for wood both as fuel and raw material. As fuel, the substitutes were coal, natural gas, solar energy and *kao-liang* stalks. Coal and natural gas were the chief fuels in the expanding salt-boiling industry in Szechwan from the mid-eighteenth century. On the coast, natural evaporation by solar energy of marine brine, what the Chinese called *shai* salt, was substituted for artificial boiling with vegetable fuel. This happened in the north in the sixteenth century, in the south in the eighteenth century, and in the centre in the nineteenth and twentieth centuries, and was accompanied by greater sophistication in its use. *Kao-liang* stalks, hitherto often a waste product, were the fuel used by the great fortified distilleries of Kirin and Heilungkiang which processed the surplus millet of northern Manchuria. As building material, the chief substitute was earth, in one shape or another. Chinese construction, especially in the north had always made use of tamped earth: the American adobe or the New Zealand cob. As population re-expanded in the treeless north, its use was extended in the early modern period. In the northwest, caves were reactivated, hence the horrendous casualties in the earthquake of 1556. In the south, more use was made of brick and tile which, while they required firing, reduced the aggregate demand for wood. In Manchuria, the versatile *kao-liang* stalks figured as building materials. Yet tamped earth was unsatisfactory in the humid centre and south; transport costs set limits to the use of coal; natural gas was rare and with bamboo pipes could only be moved over a certain distance; solar energy was irregular and not easy to store; and even *kao-liang* had its limitations.

Third, reduction in demand. Faced with shortages of specific timbers and rising prices for any wood, some sectors of the economy opted to reduce demand. A major reason for the decline of the Chinese high seas fleet, which had dominated Southeast Asian waters and the Indian Ocean in the days of Cheng Ho, was shortage of suitable timber for the great masts it required. Unlike Britain which scoured the world for large timbers, China preferred to cut back on what the mandarins already regarded as a *Luxusflotte*. Private shippers followed suit and either had junks built overseas at Bangkok or chartered foreign vessels. Next, palace building, lavish under the Ming, showed cutbacks and stringencies under the Ch'ing. Magistrates in Szechwan reported that they could not find the timbers required by the court and the court was eager to avoid either oppressiveness to its subjects or corruption in its timber administration. Finally, if some living standards were retrenched, so too were standards of dying. Coffins, always a significant outlet for quality wood in China, became more modest, as well as more expensive, in the early modern period. Faced by an energy crisis in the seventeenth century, China, like the United States in the decade after 1973, reduced its demand, and did not suffer much from it.

Fourth, improvement in marketing. Until the nineteenth century, the history of wood in China is largely the history of particular timber ports: local demand, local supply, though the volume could be considerable. Then, from around 1850, there developed at Parrot Island, upriver from Hankow, what was certainly an interregional and possibly an all-China market for timber. The context of this market was, first, the Taiping war, then the post-rebellion reconstruction, and finally the building of China's late nineteenth-century urbanization. The market drew initially on the existing and still expanding timber port of Ch'ang-te in western Hunan, but it came to embrace supplies from most of western China. It was operated by a complex and sophisticated set of interlocking guilds, reminiscent of the Baltic exchange or Lloyds insurance, but for all kinds of wood. It brought producer and consumer closer together over a wide area to make better use of existing supplies. But, though a significant rationalization of a rare resource, it did not of itself increase those supplies.

Fifth, micro-privatization. Historians have long been puzzled by the comparative absence in China of large-scale afforestation, either public or private. The Hung-wu emperor certainly planted saplings, but he was recognized as being exceptional in this, and we are not told how many came to maturity. Except as regards mulberry for sericulture, Chinese treatises on gentry estate management show little interest in arboriculture. One reason may have been the attitude to investment, maintenance and time implied in the systemic option. Business in China liked quick turnover and forestry is not suited to this. But it is possible that this lack of interest was more apparent than real. Nicholas Menzies, who is writing the section on forestry in Needham's great work, has suggested that we may have been looking for afforestation in the wrong place. He writes: 'where we don't see large blocks of trees, we don't see forestry. In fact, I believe that a large proportion of domestic demand for wood products was met by small scale, intensive tree planting within the agricultural system – much along the lines of what is now termed "agroforestry".'[28] Interstitial microforestry went back a long way in Chinese history, but it increased in the early modern period as part of that involutionary development which Philip Huang deplores but which was effective in so many ways. Micro-privatization was highly successful in reducing local scarcities of wood. It bridged the gap between supply and demand at the village level, even in a dynamic area like the Yangtze delta mega-circuit. What is more open to question is whether agroforestry was adequate to the demands of mega-politicization, that is, the growth of super-cities.

Sixth, imports. Though Europe eventually overtook China in the distances over which it was prepared to procure wood, international trade in timber began in China, Europe's preference for stone and abundant forests making it for once more implosive. Fine wood timber – sanderswood, rosewood, camphor, sandal and ebony – was extensively imported from Southeast Asia under the T'ang: some of it was used in furnishing if not construction. In the twelfth century, more utilitarian woods began to be imported from Japan, while camphor and sandal continued to be obtained from Java. In the Ming period, imported hardwoods from Indo-China became fashionable for furniture. Hainan and Taiwan, both originally non-Chinese, were colonized as 'Madeiras', timber islands: the first for *Dalbergia*, the second for camphor. In the early seventeenth century, Ayudhya exported sapanwood to China in Japanese junks. Subsequently Chinese shippers used Siamese teak to build their own junks which continued to send sapanwood to Canton, along with the rice, sugar and pepper which predominated in the expanded trade after Bangkok became the Thai capital in 1769. Timber also figured in the list of imports from Vietnam to Canton in the early nineteenth century. Around 1850, Oregon pine began to be imported from the United States and in the twentieth century Australia and New Zealand joined the number of timber exporters to China. Timber then was a considerable factor both in China's internal territorial definition and in its external world relations.

In Europe too, the search for timber played a part in its spatial expansion, despite its greater resources and its preference for stone. Though stone might be used for foundations and walls, wood was still required for scaffolding, internal partitions, floors, ceilings, window frames and panelling, not to mention furniture. Northeastern Europe, Scandinavia and especially Russia with its tradition of the *isba*, were never conquered by the Mediterranean cult of stone. Nor was the new transatlantic Northwest with its tradition of the log cabin. It was from these two areas that in the twentieth century the reaction against the heavy house was to come. Even in Western Europe north of the Alps where stone established itself most firmly, there were cross-currents.[29] Improvements in carpentry in the late Middle Ages, notably the development of half-timbering, led to a revival of building in wood in fifteenth-century London, Paris and Rouen: a parallel in shelter to the efflorescence of fur in dress before the triumph of stone and silk in the Renaissance. Even then, aggregate demand for wood may have increased, despite the fashion for stone, if, as Le Comte believed, Europe housed itself more lavishly than China.

The first new area brought under contribution was the Baltic, Europe's proto-America, from which timber, along with wood products and naval stores (potash, spars, pitch, tar, hemp, and so on), was a staple. It was the dominance of the Baltic with its mixture of coniferous softwoods and temperate hardwoods which made Amsterdam the leading timber market of Europe in the seventeenth century and gave the Dutch fleet the edge in repair facilities, a major factor in seapower because of the encouragement it gave to aggressive strategy and tactics. Next, in the eighteenth century, though Britain now dominated the Baltic trade, and enjoyed the same maritime advantages, the Admiralty led the way into extra-European sources of timber. It brought New England and Canada under contribution, especially for red and white pine, while mahogany made the shipbuilding fortune of Havana for Spain. In the Revolutionary and Napoleonic wars, the Admiralty widened its scope again to include Bermuda cedar, Brazilian hardwoods, New Zealand kauri, and above all teak from India and Southeast Asia, the best of the tropical hardwoods.[30] Here, notably in the cultivated teak plantation of Java, European demand and supply overlapped with those of China to create a world market.

Design

Only at a high level of generalization is it possible to speak of *the* Chinese design, *the* European design. The advantage of taking this level is that it brings out a continuity of form in Europe while China shows a double disruption: a surprising reversal of the usual historical clichés.

Both Europe and China began at the same starting point: a rectangular dwelling of four walls with a triangular-shaped roof and a front door in the middle of one of the long sides. Innumerable buildings of this ground plan survive from the past and are still being built in Europe and China today. In Europe, indeed, this design was never abandoned. Greater space was obtained by adding another rectangle to make a square, by juxtaposing a half-rectangle to produce an L-shaped building, or by superimposing rectangles or squares to create a multi-storeyed structure. Though China made these moves, and in particular experimented with multi-storeyed apartment blocks under the Sung, in general its evolution followed a different path. First, from the T'ang through the Ming, the characteristic design was what the Chinese called the *kung-tzu hsing p'ien-mien*: the ground plan shaped like the character *kung* (works). Klaas Ruitenbeek calls this the H-plan, that is, an H set on one of its long sides.[31] It was this plan which was the presupposition of the *Lu Pan Ching*. It was arrived at less by addition as by multiplication: a second, and in some cases a third or fourth, rectangle being erected behind or in front of the first; the series being linked by what was essentially a covered way, the crosspiece of the H. Second, from the late Ming or early Ch'ing, the H-plan became rare, except in the case of imperial palaces where the pavilions of the Forbidden City to this day witness to its survival. For the H-plan was substituted the familiar courtyard house: a succession of quadrangles, like those of a Roman peristyle villa or an Oxbridge college. Unlike these Western analogues, however, the courtyard house was probably the product of the juxtaposition of two H-plans with their crosspieces removed to form a single space. If the process was repeated, a series of courtyards would be similarly formed.

What lay behind this double change from a rectangle to an H and from an H to a courtyard or series of courtyards? First, the permutations of the rectangular pavilion in China remind us of the permutations of the triangle in European female fashion. They may be seen, therefore, as an expression of the greater continuum between dress and shelter in China compared to Europe. In Europe, on the other hand, the simplicity of the characteristic four-square doll's house design contrasted with the growing complexity of dress under the rule of fashion. In design, where Europe added, China multiplied. Second, the Chinese house was related to marriage in China: multiple in form (major, minor, uxorilocal, delayed transfer and so on) but single in finality – filiality in an ongoing lineage. It was no accident that from the air a large Chinese house looked like a family tree. The H shape was rooted in two dualities: between masculine and feminine space, those at the front who went out and those at the back who did not; between older and younger generations, those who received filiality and those who gave it. The courtyard, simple or multiple, provided further refinements and ramifications of these dualities in a system where neolocality for a married couple was not even an ideal. The European house, with its more pedestrian system of combination of rectangles was well suited to that ideal and to a hierarchy of class rather than kin: upstairs/downstairs, reception and service, basement, main bedrooms and attics. Though its permanence might make it an heirloom, its finality was the couple: to get them off to a good start by freeing their income from rent and maintenance. The Chinese house, by contrast, was a piece of working equipment, the temporary instrument whereby generations were linked. Design reflected these differences.

Why was the European evolution different? The courtyard house, after all, was not completely absent. It is found in Roman villas and may underlie the ground plan of some English (and possibly French?) farm buildings. The villa was designed to relate the patron to his clients, the private life of the patrician to his public role. A recent study has indicated how changes in its design between the second and fourth centuries AD may be explained in terms of the changing function of the senatorial aristocracy in late Roman society: new definitions of domestic privacy and public action.[32] Similarly, subsequent social changes may explain the later move from the villa to the *casa*: the rectangular house of permanent materials. Particularly important here was the rise of smallholdings: the *casae coloniciae* detailed for Latium by Toubert.[33] Toubert insists that it was the *colonus*, the smallholder, 'qui in casa residet, qui casam regit cum uxore, filiis et filiabus', who laid the foundation for the European system of conjugal marriage: 'multiplication du nombre des hommes et surtout des unités d'exploitation adoptée à la famille conjugale'.[34] Marriage was an economic as well as social act, so its sacramentality had to be permanent. *Matrimonium* for the laity became the equivalent of major orders for the clergy: not capable of dissolution or removal. From the eighth and ninth centuries, Toubert argues, 'la famille conjugale comme la seule structure fondamentale' dominated society.[35] Even when farms were grouped together by *incastellamento* or families established precincts and compounds in the way Gérard Dellile has analysed, these units were assemblages of conjugalities, a company rather than a clan, rooted less in kinship than in property.

Layout

Here again there was a difference of emphasis between Europe and China. It might be assumed that a house is for living in. But this (ignoring for the moment the modern southern hemisphere) is a northern assumption of a particular time and place: a time when home and workplace coincided, a place where outside was rebarbative because of cold and wet; in other words the cities of northern Europe in the little ice age. The alternative assumption, more general, and prevalent both in the Mediterranean and China, was that a house was for living from: in the agora and piazza, the market and the street. The two assumptions, northern and general, led to different organizations of internal space, a different layout of rooms. The northern view emphasized the kitchen and subsequent differentiations from it: the parlour, the dining-room, the drawing-room and so on. It envisaged and embraced all the activities of the day. The general view emphasized the bedroom and had less tendency to differentiation. It confined itself to the lesser gamut of the activities of the night. At a high level of generalization, it may be said that Europe in the period 1400 to 1800 adhered to the northern view, while China remained loyal to the general view. Europe took its material from Ancient Rome, its design from Dark Age smallholders, but its layout from late-medieval burghers. Consequently, it came to ask for more space than the Chinese required, as Le Comte observed. The only significant exception to this in China were the silk and cotton districts where home and workplace were combined, this being particularly striking in sericulture.

The Chinese emphasis on the bedroom and night-time thermoregulation took two contrasting forms. In the north, with its bitter winters, it took the form of the *k'ang*, or fixed hypocaust sleeping unit. The *k'ang*, usually 8–10 ft by 6 ft, occupied a sizeable proportion of the conventional Chinese room or *chien* – the partitioned space between two roof trusses, usually standardized at 120 sq ft. In Peking in the 1920s, the average occupancy was 2.8, but as the capital was not a city of married couples and children, village occupancy would have been much higher. Though half the population had only two rooms or less available to them, the capital was probably better housed than its hinterland. In north China, a house was a roof over a *k'ang*. In the south, with its stifling summers, thermoregulation meant ventilation as much as heating. Chinese houses followed a layout more like that of the Indonesian houses described by Anthony Reid as designed to maximize coolness. Denys Lombard argues that the Indonesian term for a first-floor area destined exclusively for sleeping (*loteng*) is derived from Hokkien *lao-ding*, the equivalent of Mandarin *lou-ting*, which means precisely upper storey.[36] Though storeys went out of fashion in China from the Ming, the term is witness to the value which the Chinese continued to place on the sleeping area in the domestic context. *K'ang* and *lou-ting* were expressions of a single underlying attitude to room space in different climatic circumstances.

In Europe, the northern assumption that a house was a daylight place, a roof over a living area, only emerged gradually. In Dark Age Ravenna, though there were mentions of *salae*, *triclinia* and *coquinae*, most references were to *cubicula*. Similarly in Rome, when specific rooms began to be indicated in legal documents in the eleventh century, the most frequent references were to *cubicula*. Soon, however, *cubiculum* lost its specific reference to a sleeping area and came to denote any private room. In the twelfth century, Roman jurists began to distinguish one- and two-storeyed houses as *domus terrinea* and *domus solarata* or *cum solario*.[37] Here is the first mention of the solar, the private upper room into which the master and mistress of the house could withdraw, not to sleep but to live. In the thirteenth century, the better-off began to acquire in addition a *sala* or *aula* for general living. In northern Italy, references to *camminatae*, large living-rooms with fireplaces, go back to the seventh century. They had probably been introduced by the Lombards as the local version of that widespread Germanic institution, the hall. The accepted etymology of hall is from *holen* ('to cover'), but another possibility is *hal* ('salt'), from its association with the high cooking of the hall, as opposed to the insipid fare of the peasants. It was from the undifferentiated hall that the various rooms of the medieval manor house were developed: the solar, the kitchen, the chamber, the wardrobe. Even the houses of Le Roy Ladurie's peasants at Montaillou often boasted a *solier* as well as a *foganha* or kitchen and they were emphatically places of socialization. Similar peasant houses centred on the kitchen continued to exist in Hungary down to the mid-twentieth century.[38] Although the northern arrangement of space was widely diffused in Latin Christendom by one means or another, it was most fully expressed in the burgher houses of the Burgundian Low Countries. Surviving or replica examples are the older houses in the Rue Barre Saint Brice in Tournai or the houses of the Begijnhof in Leuven: the latter essentially superior seventeenth-century artisans' dwellings. Commerce, cloth and Erasmian piety made domestic living both possible and desirable. They reinforced the northern conception of comfort within and brought it to perfection in the Dutch interior.

ACCESSORIES: CERAMICS AND CARPETS

In the essentials of shelter, the effects of globalization were confined to the creation of a world timber market, Chinoiserie pagodas in Europe, and a few Sino-foreign buildings in China such as the Old Summer Palace. In the accessories, globalization went further, particularly in the case of ceramics and carpets. Here, too, there was an imbalance. While Chinese porcelain became universal in the West, the Persian carpet became naturalized in China only as an export, not a domestic, industry. Both nevertheless exhibited greater movement than materials, design and layout.

Ceramics

Porcelain, in the sense of a fully translucent and vitrified glaze, was a product of the T'ang. It represented, however, the culmination of a long period of Chinese ceramic achievement in the combination of materials and the control of kilns. Whereas the Western neolithic began with the domestication of plants and animals and went on to ceramics, in China ceramics preceded domestication. The reason for this was that while in the West, if Colin Renfrew's reconstruction be accepted, neolithic originated on the eastern Anatolian upland, or around its lakes, in a dispersed population, in China it originated on a number of coastal or riverine sites in a concentrated population. In both areas, neolithic came from the mobilization of information in late palaeolithic communities. In China, however, the concentrated character of those communities created greater need for storage and cooking and afforded more opportunities for experimentation with clay and fire. China's mastery of these ingredients, later transferred to a precocious metallurgy, was unchallenged by the West until the eighteenth century. If under the Ming, Ching-te-chen became the world's first industrial city, it had a long pedigree of ceramic industrial villages behind it.[39] It was on the basis of this pedigree that true porcelain was developed under the T'ang.

Exports began almost at once.[40] T'ang shards have been recovered from Siraf, Samarra, Fustat and Nishapur in the Abbasid empire, from Anuradhpura in Ceylon, and from the east African coast. The greatest quantity, however, went to Southeast Asia, where the earliest archaeological evidence comes from Takuapa, a ninth–tenth-century site at the western end of the Kra isthmus. Under the Sung maritime trade increased. As Chinese imports, especially of wood, grew, the Sung government actively encouraged the export of porcelain to reduce the outflow of copper cash. In 944, Liu Ts'ung-hsiao, city-state ruler of Ch'uan-chou, Marco Polo's Zayton, had established new kilns to the east of the city for the export market, which have recently been excavated. The Sung kilns at Te-hua, to the northwest of Ch'uan-chou, owed something to the export trades. So, too, did those of Kwangtung at Ch'ao-chou,

Hui-chou and Canton whose characteristic light green and pale grey shards have been found in Japan, Ceylon and Egypt. Lung-ch'uan green wares, exported through the port of Wen-chou in southern Chekiang, were a particular favourite in the Muslim world: in 1171, Saladin sent a 40-piece set to the ruler of Damascus. It was Islamic taste, too, which promoted blue and white wares, the cobalt for which came mainly from Persia. Till 1300 green wares ruled supreme both in trade and in China. Between 1300 and 1368, blue and white ran celadons equally. After 1368, blue and white triumphed both in trade and in China.

Chinese taste therefore followed that of Islam rather than led it. When Chiang Ch'i gave one of the first reports on Ching-te-chen in his *T'ao-ch'i lüeh* (Appendix to the Ceramic Records), its 300 kilns were mainly producing white wares, imitations no doubt of the famous *blanc de chine* porcelains from the northern Sung imperial kilns at Ting-chou in southern Chihli. However, when Tang Ying made his report as superintendent in 1743, blue and white predominated, though the kilns also produced the famous *sang de boeuf* and apple-green crackle developed by Lang T'ing-chi between 1705 and 1712. Blue and white became symbolic of China to the outside world: Ibn Battuta saw it at the court of Muhammed ibn Tughlug in 1334; Ma Huan tells us that it was popular in Java and Ceylon in the early fifteenth century; in 1495 Sultan Beyazit began the Ottoman collection at Topkapi; and in 1611 Shah Abbas made his magnificent bequest to the Ardebil shrine. Vietnamese potters copied blue and white and instances have been found at Topkapi and Ardebil, as well as in Mamluk Cairo. Both Vietnamese and Thai kilns benefited from the late Ming maritime embargoes and the disorders of the Ming-Ch'ing transition, both of which obstructed the trade of Ching-te-chen. With the permanent lifting of embargoes by the Ch'ing and their reorganization of Ching-te-chen in 1682, China resumed its lead on the Europeans. East India companies at Canton began regularly to include porcelain in their cargoes home. So massive did these exports become that soon the companies regarded them as simple ballast.

Serious European collection of Chinese porcelain had begun in the sixteenth century in imitation of the Ottomans. Philip II had 3000 pieces at the Escorial, Ferdinand of the Tyrol had 240 at Schloss Ambras, Rudolf II had 700 at the Hrdcin. In more provincial England, Henry VIII had at least one piece, but his daughter's minister William Cecil had more. Attempts to imitate porcelain, however, went back further: to the Hispanic-Moresque ware of late medieval Aragon which in turn inspired the semi-vitrified glaze of Italian *maiolica*. More direct Chinese influence is evident in the blue and white tiles produced in the

Ottoman kilns at Iznik. On the continent, the search continued and in 1672 in England John Dwight established the Fulham pottery to produce Continental-type salt-glazed wares. None of these, however, was true porcelain. This came only with Friedrich Böttger at Meissen in 1708, Jean Hellot at Sèvres in 1743, and William Cockworthy at Plymouth in 1768. Wedgwood's early wares were pottery rather than porcelain, but his Queen ware, named in 1765 from Queen Charlotte's patronage, was a close approximation. The Spodes, father and son, achieved mass production with their development of bone china. In the nineteenth century, the Doulton company at Lambeth advanced from pottery to porcelain to become Royal Doulton before, in 1956, withdrawing to make Stoke-on-Trent the centre of its operations. Meanwhile the fortune of Staffordshire and the Five Towns, in combination with the strange landscape of central Cornwall, had been made out of what was essentially a Sino-foreign product. For consumers, the universalization of high-grade ceramics meant that convenience, hygiene, aesthetics and manners could all take a leap forward. Ching-te-chen had transformed the quality of shelter everywhere.

Carpets

The earliest known pile carpet, in the Hermitage at St Petersburg, is from the tomb of a Saka chief at Pazyryk in the Altai dated to the fifth–fourth centuries BC. The carpet displays the characteristics of the later Persian carpet: central field with repeated medallions, multiple borders similarly patterned, outer piping and fringe.[41] It has been assumed, therefore, that the Pazyryk carpet was an import from Persia: perhaps a gift from the Shah to a vassal. Pazyryk, however, was some distance beyond the imperial frontier. The carpet may have come from the local nomads as did the felts also found in the tomb. The Turkmen, descendants of the Sakas, produce carpets to this day. A third possibility, perhaps the most likely, is that it came from the south: not so far as Fars, but from the future Uzbekistan, transitional between the steppe and the sown. This area, notably Ferghana, to defend itself against the light horsemen of the 'pointed cap' Sakas displayed on the Achaemenid tribute-procession relief at Persepolis, had pioneered the breeding of large horses to carry the cataphract, or armoured knight of Iran, against the forces of Turan. In the Pazyryk carpet, the widest of the borders certainly shows large horses and probably cataphracts riding them. It is this feature which makes Uzbekistan, or Sogdiana in a wide sense, the carpet's probable point of origin. Carpets are characteristically products of places where nomads and sedentarists interact: nomads to provide wool, sedentarists to provide looms. Sogdiana was such an area. True, Fars, to which carpet-making later migrated, had its own kind of interaction with the 'enclosed' nomads of the Zagros, but less outstandingly so than Sogdiana. So the Pazyryk carpet was probably a gift from the satrap of Sogdiana or Bactria, usually a royal kinsman enjoying latitude in foreign policy, to an ally or enemy beyond the frontier. It was only in Sassanid times that the production of carpets in Persia proper is certain. Central Asia was the home of the pile carpet.

China came into direct contact with Central Asia in the reign of Han Wu-ti (140–87 BC) through the diplomatic, not to say espionage, activities of his roving ambassador Chang Ch'ien. Chang's report preserved in the *Shih-chi* of Ssu-ma Ch'ien, distinguished carefully between Ta Hsia (Bactria), Ta Yüan (Ferghana) and the surrounding nomad territories. It was Ferghana whence came the famous blood-sweating heavenly horses and where Chinese overlordship was established a few years after Chang Ch'ien's death. Carpets are not mentioned among the goods China imported. However, it would be surprising if Han Wu-ti, unusual among emperors as a xenophile and exoticist, who acclimatized grapes and alfalfa on the palace estate and sent missions west of Ta Yüan specifically to find rare objects, did not receive some. Clearly they did not attract, and no remains have appeared in the archaeological record to date. It was not until the Sui period (581–618) that there is definite literary evidence of carpet imports from the West. Under the T'ang, carpets figured among the presents sent by the king of Bukhara to emperor Hsüan-tsung in 726 to solicit aid against the Arabs. In the flurry of diplomatic activity which preceded the ill-fated Chinese intervention which ended at the battle of the Talas river in 751, woollen rugs of deep pile, which the Chinese called dance mats, were included in the gifts of a number of Central Asian city-states. For a time, such carpets and rugs were fashionable in aristocratic households. There are references in the poems of Li Ho, the Persian word *taftan* (to spin, cp. taffeta) was acclimatized to describe them and decorative medallions were adapted in Chinese silk textiles. Yet the taste was confined to Hsüan-tsung's Iranophile court; there is little evidence of its continuation after the rebellion of An Lu-shan, and when links with Central Asia were curtailed, no sign of a Chinese carpet industry to provide import substitutes. Ch'en Ch'eng, Yung-lo's ambassador to Shah Rukh in 1415, noted rugs at Herat but did not suggest that China might have any use for them. The modern Chinese carpet industry, whose products rival those of Persia, is a recent development: essentially of the late nineteenth and early twentieth centuries at Tientsin. Moreover, the 200-odd carpet factories reported by the customs commissioner in 1921 were geared to an export rather than a domestic market. Essentially, China was offered the Persian carpet and refused it. There was no wool route to counterbalance the silk route.

It is worth asking why. First, at the level of thermoregulation, the wall-to-wall carpet went against the Chinese principle of punctiform rather than area heating which will be discussed in the next chapter. Second, the Chinese preference in building and furnishing was for the light rather than the heavy: rococo elegance rather than baroque luxury. Many Persian carpets did not conform to this preference (the magnificent Shah Abbas designs for example). It is noteworthy that when a Chinese carpet industry did develop, it was characterized precisely by pastel shades, flowing lines and flexible forms. Third, if as Patrice Fontaine has suggested, the Persian carpet reflects the complementarity of nomad and sedentarist in Iranian space and their integration in a garden of perpetual spring, such circumstances and ideals did not exist in China.[42] If China, like India, had been conquered by Tamerlane and the Mughals substituted for the Ming, then things might have been different. Carpets might have established themselves, as furs did under the Manchus, as nostalgia on the part of the conquerors and a sign of loyalty to the new regime on the part of the conquered. As it was, the carpet, like wool generally, indeed all products of the sheep, remained barbarian – its smell, texture and connotations unsympathetic to Chinese susceptibilities. Moreover, its key concept of the garden as culture in nature was structured on quite different lines from those favoured by the Chinese.

EXTRAS: GARDENS – DISPARATE FORMS, COMMON CONTENT

Like the choice of dress, work in a garden provides opportunities for consumerism in the sense of the imposition of mind on matter. It is a widely diffused form of consumerism and one which requires both long-term planning and constant renewal. In the early modern period, the garden took disparate forms in East and West, but its content was increasingly dominated by China.

Disparate Forms

Just as the Chinese made less of a distinction between dress and shelter than did the Europeans, so, within the category of shelter, they
distinguished less between house and garden. This worked in two ways.
First, a garden could be indoors like the room 'almost wholly occupied by a pile of rocks arranged to represent a wild and rugged mountain', in the Palace of Tranquil Old Age, *Ning-shou kung*, used by
Ch'ien-lung after his abdication.[43] Like rooms, gardens required to be
furnished: with dwarf trees, rockeries and pavilions, as in the Yü-hua
Yüan, the imperial garden at the northern end of the Forbidden City.
Second, if gardens were brought into houses, houses were taken to
gardens, as in the various summer palaces: the *Yüan-ming yüan* and *I-
ho yüan* outside Peking and the *Pi-shu shan-chuang* at Jehol. Here,
residences, pavilions and temples, often of a pastiche exotic character,
were arranged to 'house-scape' parklands. The summer palaces were
not retreats like Balmoral or Sandringham. They were more like Capri
under Tiberius. Ch'ien-lung spent half the year at Jehol and visitors
were assumed. They were similarly assumed by private garden makers
such as the salt merchants of Yang-chou, whose gardens, laid out in
the second half of the eighteenth century, were open to emperor and
general public alike. These gardens were not attached to the merchants'
town houses, which doubtless had their own interior gardens. They
were situated outside the walls in an exterior suburb which stretched
along a canal towards low hills to the northwest. The Yang-chou salt
merchants were, for the most part, non-natives, who came from She-
hsien in Hui-chou in southern Anhwei where many had started as timber
merchants. Their gardens therefore represented conciliatory philanthropy,
such as successful Chinese businessmen continue to practise in overseas communities round the world.

The comments of Lord Macartney reflected this dual character of
Chinese gardening without fully understanding it. In connection with
the road houses, or paradors, on the way to Jehol, he wrote: 'A Chinese gardener is the painter of nature and ... produces the happiest
effects by the management of or rather pencilling of distances ... by
relieving or keeping down the features of the scene, by contrasting
trees of a bright with those of a dusky foliage ... and by introducing
buildings of different dimensions, either heightened by strong colouring
or softened by simplicity and omissions of ornament.'[44] Subsequently
Macartney attempted to generalize:

There is certainly a great analogy between our gardening and the Chinese; but our excellence seems to be rather in improving nature, theirs to conquer her ... Though the sublime predominates in its proper station, you are insensibly led to contemplate it, not startled by its sudden intrusion; for in the plan, cheerfulness is the principal feature and lights up the face of the scene. To enliven it still more the aid of architecture is invited ... Proper edifices in proper places is the style they admire. The summer house, the pagoda have all their respective situations.[45]

At Jehol, Macartney had been impressed: but, reminded of Luton Hoo, Stowe, Woburn, Painshill and Lowther, he interpreted what he saw in terms of current controversies between Sir William Chambers and the supporters of Capability Brown and the fashionable dichotomy of the sublime and the beautiful, though aware that these might not be the proper categories. He enjoyed the effects of Chinese gardening, but one could not expect him to see its intellectual foundations. He did not see, for example, what Anne Chayet's study has brought out: the character of Jehol as a microcosm of the Ch'ing empire, variegated but unified. Where he saw nature as treated by Capability Brown, the Chinese saw a continuum of culture. At one time, Europeans might have brought different perspectives. Wilhelmina Jashemski's study of ancient Pompeii shows that the Romans would have understood the house in the garden and the garden in the house.[46] But, despite their avowed classicism, the men and women of the eighteenth century were a long way from that.

Common Content

Analogy, to use Macartney's term, lay not in the disparate forms of gardening, but in their increasingly common content. This unification was accomplished by the steady flow westward first of plants from Chinese gardens and then of wild flowers from the Chinese countryside. The removal of East Asian plants from Western gardens today would reduce them to a wilderness.

Jashemski's gardens in Pompeii were dark and monochrome. They were dominated by the laurel, myrtle, box, ivy and rosemary. Except for lemons, orchards were still un-Mediterranean: apples, pears, plums, cherries, quince as prevalent as grapes and figs. Peaches, from Persia but ultimately from China, had only just arrived, and apricots, from Armenia but ultimately from China, did not appear until the Antonines.

If the bitter orange existed at Pompeii, the pomelo was only introduced to Europe by the Arabs in the twelfth century, and the sweet orange by the Genoese in the fifteenth century. Both are reported in pre-imperial China as products of the kingdom of Ch'u. The earliest Chinese book devoted to oranges is the *Chü-lu* of Han Yen-chih, son of a famous river admiral, in 1178. Its European counterpart, the *Hesperides sive Malorum Aureorum cultura et usu* of the Sienese Jesuit J. B. Ferrari, had to wait till 1646. For the Chinese, the noblest flower was not the rose, but the peony, the *hua-wang*, the king of flowers, to which Po Chü-i devoted a poem in 810. It was closely followed in esteem by the chrysanthemum: the scholar flower because it blossomed best in the off-season when all else was decay. Three rows were planted by Magistrate T'ao Yuan-ming who resigned rather than show deference to an unworthy official of the eastern Chin. Under the T'ang, the two leading schools of Buddhist scholasticism, the T'ien-t'ai and the Hua-yen, were known as the orchid of the spring and the chrysanthemum of the autumn. Also, under the T'ang, the great Confucian minister Li Te-yü was the first devotee of the camellia known to us. He is credited, too, with the domestication of the azalea from the wild flora of the as yet only half-Chinese Sino-Tibetan borderlands which, under the eaves of the Himalayas, preserved so many plant species from the last ice age.[47]

It took time for these riches to reach Europe. Marco Polo was interested in many things but not, despite his description of Xanadu, in gardening. When European gardening revived in the Renaissance, it looked first to the Ottomans. Busbecq, Charles V's ambassador to Suleiman the Magnificent, brought back lilac and tulips to the Low Countries, where they did better than his other attempted acclimatization, the camel! Transfer of Chinese plants only began in the late seventeenth century. The chrysanthemum was introduced to Holland in 1688, but it died out and had to be reintroduced, to France, by the Marseille merchant Blanchard in 1787. Camellias may have been among the plants sent from the Philippines by the Czech Jesuit G. J. Kamel to John Ray and James Petiver in the early eighteenth century. They were certainly being cultivated by Lord Petre in 1739. Sir Joseph Banks, however, was the greatest acclimatizer of the eighteenth century. He introduced hydrangeas, peonies, magnolias, iris and tiger lilies to his garden at Spring Grove near Isleworth. He also participated in the reintroduction of the chrysanthemum and the hybridization of English and Chinese roses. In 1816, John Reeves, an executive of the East India Company, sent back a wisteria plant from the garden of the Co-hong merchant Consequa and it was soon doing well at Chiswick. Reeves was also instrumental in the despatch to China in 1843 of Robert Fortune on the first systematic plant-hunting expedition. More than anyone else, Fortune was responsible for the introduction of rhododendrons to Europe. He also virtually exhausted the repertoire of Chinese gardens, so that his successors turned to wild flora. Père David (1826–1900) is associated with cotoneaster, rhododendrons and clematis. Augustine Henry, customs official at Ichang from 1881, was the first to realize the huge potential of west China. E. H. Wilson followed this up, just before the First World War, introducing 60 new species of rhododendron as well as the Chinese gooseberry or kiwi fruit as it is now inaptly named.[48]

In adopting so many East Asian plants, for one cannot overlook the introduction of the Japanese flowering cherry, European gardens took on a Chinese colouring. Wisteria climbed up the verandah. The conservatory brought the garden into the house. Quantities of cut flowers were carried indoors. Gazebos looked out over artificial lakes surrounded by rhododendrons. Flowering cherries formed entrance drives. Humped bridges led visitors to banks of azaleas. Rockeries were heaped up. Even the herbaceous border, most characteristic of Victorian innovations, would contain peonies. Yet the basic differences remained. The European garden, like the European house, still sought permanence, whether in perennials or annuals. Unlike dress, it was not subject to fashion except in the long run. Capability Brown and his successors could envisage what their landscapes would look like in a hundred years time and the herbaceous border with its high mid-summer pomps was not envisaged as essentially different from year to year. The Chinese, on the other hand, rejected both the kingdom of the perdurable and the empire of the ephemeral in favour of a mean applicable to both dress and shelter: a timescale of successive generations rather than enduring realities or passing moments. Where the European mind in its imprint on matter ran to the infinitely large or the infinitely small, the Chinese mind stood in a *juste milieu*, a measure appropriate to a self-sufficient humanism.

5 Consumerism and Utilities

In the second half of this book, the focus shifts from structures, as they have been discovered in food, dress and shelter, to conjunctures: life as it was lived on the basis of these necessities. In this chapter, it shifts to utilities: activities involving heat, water and light in a mainly, but not exclusively, domestic situation, since the cut between street and home forms part of the background of such activities. Consumption is never without background in social context and intellectual antecedents, and consumerism is the intensification and extension of those antecedents. In particular, activities in Europe and China which involved utilities were inscribed in contrasting attitudes to the use of energy, the primordial utility. These contrasts developed in the period 1400 to 1800 and have continued to influence their societies down to the present. The first part of this chapter will therefore outline the history of energy in Europe and China. The succeeding parts continue the formula of essentials, accessories and extras, which here will be interpreted as heat, water and light.

ENERGY ATTITUDES

Consumerist societies are characterized by higher per capita inputs of energy than traditional societies and by more efficient use of this energy. It is often supposed that the higher per capita input of Europe as compared to China was the result of the industrial revolution. In fact, the European advantage existed well before the industrial revolution and should be seen as the cause as much as the effect of the subsequent technological developments.

In 1967, Braudel estimated total and per capita energy consumption in Europe around 1800.[1] There were, he says, around 14 million horses and 24 million cows. About 120 million tons of wood a year were used as fuel. Fifty million workers laboured with their hands and muscles. There were half a million watermills, so many windmills, three and a half million tons of sailing ships. Converting these different kinds of energy into a uniform equivalence, Braudel arrived at a figure of 25 million energy units for a population of 200 million, or roughly one unit for every 10 people. Similar estimates can be made for China:

less reliable because based on late nineteenth- or even twentieth-century evidence, but, none the less, convincing and suggestive.[2] In 1800, there were around 5 million horses and 23 million oxen and water buffaloes. About 10 million tons of wood a year were used as fuel. Seventy-five million workers laboured with their hands and muscles. There were half a million watermills, so many windmills, two and a half million tons of sailing ships. Converting these different kinds of energy into a uniform equivalence, one arrives at a figure of 13 million energy units for a population of 300 million, or roughly one unit for every 20 people. Even allowing considerable latitude for error, and in particular the estimate for Chinese wood may need revising upwards in the light of Menzies' theory of microforestry, these figures are striking. They mean that before the industrial revolution had made much progress in Europe, its consumption of energy, both total and per capita, was about double that of China.

It is hard to believe that this had been the case in Marco Polo's day. The Venetian regarded China as incomparably richer than Christendom. Almost certainly, this wealth was based on bigger inputs of energy, as well as on more efficient use of it. Europe and China shared the same traditional energy sources: human muscle, animal muscle, wood, wind and water. But China was already making industrial use of coal, natural gas and solar power to an extent unknown in Europe, and its machinery was more sophisticated. True, northern Europe operated a more symbiotic relationship with its forests than did northern China, but in the Sung period China was bringing the wooded hills of the Nan-shan under contribution, and there was no immediate shortage of timber. True, Chinese intensive arable agriculture had already opted for fewer animals than European mixed farming. Nevertheless, under the Yuan, China had partial access to Inner Asian horsepower. In the early Ming, the Yung-lo emperor was able to build up a cavalry reserve many times that of Christendom to confront Tamerlane. In the sixteenth century, Europeans were still surprised at the quantities of beef eaten in China. When the Christian powers of the West entered the globalization process in the Great Discoveries, they were still far behind China in the energy stakes.

Things began to change in the sixteenth century. Across Eurasia, in the courts of the Tudors, the Valois, the Habsburgs, the Ottomans, the Safavids, the Mughals and the Ming, the sixteenth century was a time of heightened consumption and therefore increased consumption of energy. Everywhere forests especially began to be put under strain and new sources had to be sought on the periphery of civilization in the

Baltic, in Siberia, in North America and in Southeast Asia. The evidence for strain is particularly striking for Szechwan whose forests were suppliers of last resort for as far away as Peking. The records of the *mu-cheng*, or imperial timber administration, in Szechwan show increasing difficulty in supplying masts for the imperial dockyard in Nanking and beams for the imperial palaces in Peking. Under the Ming, the Wan-li period (1573–1620) was notorious for its extravagance and fastuosity, as Mexican and Japanese silver surcharged its economy. Even in the first half of the sixteenth century, Confucian moralists had criticized the trend towards high consumption. This criticism prompted one of the earliest defences of consumptivity as good for the community if not for individuals: an essay by Lu Chi which ascribed wealth to extravagance and poverty to frugality in Southeast China.[3] Yet behind the debate, or lack of it since Lu Chi's view was in a small minority, there were signs that Chinese society was meeting the incipient energy crisis not by increasing supply, nor even by improving efficiency of use, but by reducing demand.

The clearest example of this was in the salt industry. In 1500, most salt in China was produced by the *chien* process of boiling brine, based on various kinds of vegetable energy: reeds, brushwood, timber. Only in the Sino-Mongolian borderlands was salt produced by spontaneous solar evaporation. Only in Szechwan were natural gas and coal added to vegetable fuels. Only in Ho-tung, Ch'ang-lu and Fukien, and there marginally, were forms of *shai*, planned solar evaporation, in operation. Everywhere else, and notably in the two flagship salt divisions of Liang-huai and Liang-che in the Yangtze delta, vegetable fuels ruled. From the sixteenth century, however, the pre-eminence of *chien* was challenged by the introduction of *shai* in its sophisticated, successive basin form. This took place first in Ch'ang-lu: certainly from 1522 and probably from at least a century earlier. Subsequently it happened in Huai-pei, the northern part of Liang-huai around 1550, Shantung in 1570, Fukien in 1575, Ho-tung in 1650. One of the advocates of the change was Hsü Kuang-ch'i, the Jesuits' convert, who wrote an essay in its favour.[4] He gave rising fuel costs as the principal reason and hoped thereby to reduce salt prices by two-thirds. His advocacy was not entirely successful, at least immediately. Chinese consumers regarded the larger salt crystals, *sheng-yen* or *ko'yen* produced by *shai*, as inferior to the smaller salt crystals, *huo-yen* or *mo-yen* produced by *chien*, despite their equal chemical purity, because of their unfamiliarity, less than white colour, and frequent lesser cleanliness. Nevertheless, over time the price factor was decisive. Thanks to *shai*, the energy crisis was circumvented. Between 1500 and 1800, salt production tripled. Yet the per capita figure was only maintained and quality declined. Not only did *shai* provide what many Chinese regarded as an inferior product, but to compete the *chien* section of the industry was forced to adulterate. By the early twentieth century, Chinese complained that much of what they were sold as salt was sand.

The shift from *chien* to *shai* was a substitution of one form of energy for another in what could be seen as technological advance. In other areas, such as shipbuilding and in some industrial processes involving water power, there is reason to believe in an actual reduction in energy use, or at least in the substitution of human labour for other energy forms. What most signified for consumption, however, was the attitude adopted in the face of the energy crisis: ideological suspicion of consumerism, a preference for low energy solutions, and a too-easy acceptance of zero growth. Semedo, who shared some of these assumptions, noted that the Chinese used everything and wasted nothing. Though sometimes extolling China's affluence in the tradition of earlier European discoverers, his considered judgement was different: 'They are not so rich there as in Europe; nor so many which can properly deserve that name; nor are the poor here so many, nor so poor, as those there. The people is infinite, nor can they have a capital, or stock, sufficient for so many; or money to fill so many purses. Hence it comes to pass, that the partition among them is such, that much comes to few, a mediocrity to not many, and a little to almost infinity.'[5] In the seventeenth century, the Chinese utopia was dissolving into a dystopia.

Meanwhile in Europe, a different option was being made: in the face of shortages of energy, not to reduce demand, but to increase supply. New sources of timber were sought out worldwide. Fossil fuels, notably coal, were first extensively conscripted for both domestic and industrial uses. Horses were improved in size and multiplied, not only in the studs and home farms of old Europe, but on the prairies, pampas and plains of the new Europes in North America, the Argentine and Cossack Russia. Soon, for the first time in its history, Europe had more horsepower than Inner Asia. Similarly, water power was extended to drive not only millstones for flour, but fulling rollers for wool, saws for timber, ore crushers and bellows in metallurgy, and eventually throwing machines for silk. Wind power, too, was more fully utilized for a wider variety of purposes. In China, the only major use of windmills was in raising marine brine to the successive basin solar evaporation salines of Ch'ang-lu salt division outside Tientsin. In Europe, windmills served most of the purposes of water mills in grinding, rolling, crushing, pumping and sawing. Nowhere, of course, except perhaps in the Greek islands, were windmills in greater use than in Holland.

Poorly endowed with traditional energy sources, its forests sparse and its rivers slow, Holland was the greatest example of the European option for high energy. As Schama has shown, Holland rested on a created resource base. It was conscious of itself as a diluvian society. The Dutch were the first to understand that resources are not finite, but infinite, because creatable by intelligence. They appreciated, too, that consumption and investment are only contraries in a short-term perspective. In a medium-term perspective, both may increase, either *pari passu* or in alternation, over a period of time. Schama argues that in the Golden Age Dutch consumption rose steadily in absolute terms, while it fell as a percentage of gross national product.[6] The consumerism of Amsterdam, unlike those of Valladolid and Rome, did not crush its economy or precipitate it into recession. The Dutch attributed this to their Christian moderation and avoidance of *overvloed* (excess), but a truer reason was their greater reliance on the market than in the Catholic bureaucratic monarchies. Not that state power was inactive in Holland. In a dynamic situation public and private functions will grow together in the same way as consumption and investment. But its activity took architectonic rather than managerial forms, rules more than regulation, provision rather than prescription. In the south, it was the combination of consumerism and bureaucracy which was deadly, which impeded the flow of funds and information and inhibited capital formation. Holland was able to avoid this combination because its princely state had been destroyed in the course of its war of independence from Spain. When that state had partially to be revived, as a result of the war of the Spanish succession and the acquisition of territorial power in the east, Holland began to experience some of the difficulties of other societies and the Golden Age was over. By that time, however, Amsterdam's once unique combination of consumerism and capitalization had begun to be imitated: the consumerism emphasized in Paris, the capitalization emphasized in London, but in both sufficiently combined to generate the long eighteenth century of growth based on increasing inputs of energy.

Why did China, so antecedently rich and incipiently consumerist, make a different choice from Holland in particular and Europe in general? In this case, it is not so easy to blame bureaucracy and an over-regulatory state. Precisely in the Wan-li era, the reforming minister Chang Chü-cheng and his successors made serious efforts to reduce the budget, to raise essential revenues by less frictionful means, to simplify government monopolies and to privatize state functions, particularly in the field of hydraulics. These principles of less mass and more organization were continued after 1644 by the reforming Ch'ing dynasty. In 1712, the K'ang-hsi emperor issued the law of *yung pu-chia fu*, perpetual non-increase of the land tax, which froze rates of assessment for ever: in its assumptions of no inflation or rise in expenditure, one of the most remarkable acts of any government. The Chinese might conceptualize the market less fully than the Europeans, but in many ways they practised it better. In 1787, the Ch'ien-lung emperor rejected a proposal to requisition shipping on the Upper Yangtze to transport grain to Fukien where it was needed to supply an army on Taiwan, on the grounds that it would upset private trade and inflate rice prices in the Yangtze delta.[7] In general, the Ch'ing bureaucracy, unlike that of Counter-Reformation Europe, was not heavy, expensive and inhibitory, but light, cheap and neglectful. Like all bureaucracies, it ran to red tape, but over a limited sphere which left much freedom for private and corporate action, for example in the development outside state channels of systems of binding arbitration and self-enforcing legal instruments. If Chinese society refused the high energy option taken by northern Europe, it was not because of capital asphyxiation by a tentacular state.

Other more convincing reasons suggest themselves. First, China, compared to Europe, received a double dose of anti-consumerist puritanism. At the same time as Europe was redefining itself in the fourteenth century in the extravagant, febrile courts which initiated the fashion revolution in dress, China was being reborn after the Mongol invasions in the provincialist Ming revolution. For its first three-quarters of a century, the Ming dynasty, inspired by a Manichaean dualism superimposed upon a Buddhist eschatology, was consciously anti-consumerist, egalitarian and anti-capitalist. Originating in tax protest and salt smuggling in central Anhwei, the movement found its supporters among the *yu-min*, the floating population of the routes: lesser merchants, coolies, itinerant tradespeople, entertainers, martial arts teachers, students and boat people. Its leader, Chu Yuan-chang – ex-monk, mendicant, soldier and bandit – was the most plebeian dynastic founder between Liu Pang and Mao Tse-tung. Though Chu was aware of the need for sufficient support from the Confucian scholar gentry if he was to construct a viable state, his movement remained provincial. Chu was hostile to the metropolitan ruling class which had collaborated with the Mongols and supported rivals to himself. He was particularly hostile to Soochow and Hang-chou, the heart of Marco Polo's China. He intended originally to place his capital in an obscure provincial town in central Anhwei and only settled on Nanking, then a dockyard rather than a city and only on the periphery of the Yangtze delta, as a compromise. Chu's suspicion of elites continued throughout his long reign 1368–1398. Though attenuated by more relaxed emperors in the fifteenth century, it resurfaced from time to time in the eunuch dictatorships which were a feature of the Middle Ming period.

A separate wave of anti-consumerist puritanism developed in the early sixteenth century with the rise within Confucianism of the *hsin-hsüeh*: the school of the heart or intuition, founded by Wang Yang-ming (1473–1529). The *hsin-hsüeh* was a kind of Protestant reformation: provincial, but cultivated and intellectual; subjectivist in cognition and interiorist in piety, but active and fervent in practice. Wang was a general. He taught that action preceded and followed knowledge and was superior to it. The *hsin-hsüeh* never became orthodoxy. It never captured an emperor's patronage. It loathed one prime minister (Yen Sung) and rejected the overtures of another (Chang Chü-cheng). Like the Protestant reformation, it could be described in Le Roy Ladurie's phrase, as an unsuccessful heart transplant. Yet for two or three generations, it was the predominant inspiration in gentry society. It reoriented provincial Confucians away from the court and the bureaucratic rat-race to local concerns: peer group approbation, philanthropy and community leadership. Though the movement later divided into ethicist and antinomian wings, the second of which served to discredit it, its predominant influence was didactic and moralistic. Moreover, a puritanism of the left called into being a countervailing puritanism of the right. The rival *li-hsüeh*, school of reason, became as moralistic, anti-court and critical of extravagance as the *hsin-hsüeh*, particularly in the insufferable Tung-lin academy which ran a campaign against corruption in the early seventeeth century. So where in Europe, puritanism, whether Protestant or Catholic, was a matter of single, threatened or embattled, generations, in China it was a matter of successive generations, the rule in values rather than the exception. Consumerism, the partner of capitalization, was thereby impaired. Max Weber's equation will not stand. It was the defeat or absorption of puritanism which paved the way for capitalists, capital and capitalism in Europe. Jacques Gernet's equation of Buddhist extravagance and the spirit of capitalism is more convincing, but this kind of Buddhism had been defeated in China in the ninth century. Without sufficient consumerism, even uninhibited by bureaucracy, an enterprise culture will not become dominant. The intelligence of the entrepreneur needs to be stimulated by the intelligence of the consumer.

Next, behind the different frequencies of puritanism in Europe and China, were structural differences. European society in the late Middle Ages and early modernity was top-heavy. Whether one takes Gregory King's ancient impressions for England or Daniel Dessert's newer analysis for France, European society was aristocratic, highly stratified and inegalitarian. Even in its poorer sections, such as the large class of domestic servants, it spent its money in accordance with upper-class values. This was why notions such as fashion in dress and permanence in shelter – what we have called the empire of the ephemeral and the kingdom of the perdurable – became so diffused so quickly. People became consumerist before they could consume. It was the groups most in touch with the aristocracy – servants, upmarket shopkeepers, design specialists – who led the way, rather than the bourgeoisie who often had an ethos of their own. Thus, by a trickle-down effect, Europeans became, whenever they could be, big spenders and high consumers of energy. Chinese society in the late Middle Ages and early modernity, on the other hand, was base-heavy. Because taxation was light, hereditary aristocracy only marginal, inheritance partible, labour highly productive and new land widely available for the taking, more wealth was retained at the base in farms and workshops. Chinese society in the early Ming and middle Ch'ing was more egalitarian, less highly stratified and, compared to Europe, relatively democratic. Even in its richer sections, among the lower gentry, it spent its money in accordance with lower-class values: what Leon Stover called the sanctimonious poverty of the Chinese peasant.[8] This folk culture, effectively endorsed by the *sheng-yu* or sacred edict, a moralizing Confucian encyclical issued by the Yung-cheng emperor in 1724, permeated the higher levels of society like a rising damp. Thus, by a trickle-up effect, Chinese became, even when they did not have to be, small spenders and low consumers of energy.

Finally, a mechanism, present in northwest Europe, was relatively absent in China. Successful societies must simultaneously spend and save. For this to occur, there must be a mechanism to ensure that, at a given moment, there are those that spend and those that save. One such mechanism would be a static system whereby a class of spenders coexisted with a class of savers: aristocracy and bourgeoisie, cities and countryside, landowners and peasants. Such a system, however, would be unstable. The spenders would run out of funds, the savers would not accumulate and the result would be a downward spiral of over-consumption, disinvestment, and general impoverishment. Something like this may have happened in the Mediterranean in the seventeenth century, if Delumeau's picture of Rome and Bennassar's picture of Valladolid are correct. A more sustainable mechanism would be a dynamic system whereby groups and individuals alternated as spenders and savers, so that in the aggregate equilibrium was maintained. A model of this kind for later times has been provided by P. Modigliani in his life-cycle theory of consumption and investment. Something similar may have been operative in northwest Europe in the seventeenth century. Thus Peter Laslett has emphasized the importance in England, but relative absence elsewhere, of the life-cycle servant as opposed to the perpetual servant: the person, male or female, who lives part of their life in domestic service, with a view to acquiring sufficient capital to establish a separate household or place themselves in another trade or profession. Such people, once established, might then save again to pay off a mortgage or finance their children's schooling. The alternation mechanism might lack perfect synchronism and so contribute to an undulation of booms and slumps. But its presence would co-ordinate consumerism and capitalization in the long term, just as its absence would lead either to a culture of honourable extravagance and under-investment, as in the Mediterranean, or to a culture of sanctimonious poverty and under-consumption, as in China.

Alternation required the existence of socially approved and economically attainable forms of expenditure in food, dress and shelter which legitimized and motivated non-consumption, saving and investment. In Europe, such forms existed in fashion in dress and permanence in shelter: the mania for new clothes and enduring housing, the latter reinforced by the demand for neolocality after marriage and by the preference for the home over the family. Consumerism thus fulfilled its antecedent conditions and a high energy economy got under way before the industrial revolution pushed it higher. In China, where the modish never conquered the durable and the external in stone was less sought after, peasant preferences for low energy solutions overall prevailed. Material goods, whether in dress or shelter, exerted less finality. The family was preferred to the home, networks to frameworks, the ancestors to posterity. Because of this contrast, the cycle of consumerism and capitalization moved faster in Europe than in China and Europe established its pre-industrial lead in the production and consumption of energy.

HEAT: COAL – RISE, RULE AND RETREAT

In the history of energy in early modernity, coal holds a privileged place. Coal was for a long time the most important of the new energy sources which were progressively added to the traditional big five: human muscle, animal muscle, wood, wind and water. It was the fuel *par excellence* of the first industrial revolution: the revolution in cotton, iron, steel and railways. In this section, the primary focus must be on coal as a domestic fuel in warming rooms and powering kitchen stoves, but its development in the home needs to be seen in relation to the wider uses of coal. Here there was a difference between Europe and China. In Europe, as led by England, the use of coal on any scale began as urban and domestic, and only became industrial subsequently and derivatively. Its rise was the result of consumerism in heat: the desire for continuous, widely diffused heat within the thermoregulatory space of the European heavy house. In China, on the other hand, the use of coal was rural and industrial rather than urban and domestic. Even in areas, such as north China or Manchuria, where climatic and supply conditions were favourable, domestic consumption remained spotty. For the Chinese, a house was a place to be lived out of rather than lived in. Thermoregulation meant putting on more layers of clothing. Where interior space had to be warmed, the preference was for concentrated rather than diffused heat: heat in the kitchen stove and under the *k'ang* or hypocaust bed, rather than open fires in drawing-rooms, dining-rooms and even bedrooms as in the West. The Chinese pattern anticipated that of subsequent modernity where industrial use greatly outweighed domestic, but within a non-consumerist context. In the West, it was the domestic consumer who pioneered what became the world-wide coal revolution. Coal provides one of the clearest cases of the leading role of consumerism in economic growth.

In China, too, the use of coal is first described by a European in a distinctly, if transitory, consumerist context.[9] Marco Polo begins as if he is describing a north China singularity: 'It is a fact that throughout the province of Cathay there is a sort of black stone, which is dug out of veins in the hillsides and burns like logs. These stones keep a fire going better than wood.' After some explanation, he continues: 'And you must know that these stones are burnt throughout the province of Cathay. It is true that they also have plenty of firewood. But the population is so enormous and there are so many bath-houses and baths continually being heated that the wood could not possibly suffice, since there is no one who does not go to a bath-house at least three times a week and take a bath, and in winter everyday, if he can manage it.' Finally, Polo notes: 'And every man of rank or means has his own bathroom in his house, where he takes a bath. So it is clear that there could never be enough wood to maintain such a conflagration. So these stones, being very plentiful and very cheap, effect a great saving of wood.'

Polo's passage is remarkable. First, from the European end, it is striking that Polo, or Rustichello da Pisa, his ghost writer, assumes total ignorance of coal on the part of his readers. But the assumption was only true in the Mediterranean. In northern Europe, coal was in widespread, if sporadic, use for industrial purposes in the Meuse valley round Liège, in parts of northern England, and in areas of central France. Edward I of England, a contemporary of Polo's, found it necessary to forbid its use in London as a fire hazard and a pollutant. Polo's assumption reflected a dichotomy between north and south which was to grow with the centuries. Second, from the Chinese end, the situation described is anomalous. In the Peking of the 1920s, public bathhouses were a widespread and well-frequented institution, but not to the extent described by Polo. Elsewhere, Polo describes the 3000 public baths of Hang-chou, but it is not clear that these provided *hot* water, except for foreigners used to Turkish baths: Turkish in their use rather than origin because they probably derived from the *calidarium* of antiquity. The early court of Khubilai was under strong Muslim and Turkish influence as a result of its origins as a sub-khanate in Chinghai and Yunnan, a fact Polo was not keen to advertise because he hoped to effect an alliance between the Great Khanate and the Papacy. The situation described in Peking and possibly Hang-chou was therefore a transient one: a temporary high point of Turkification rather than a settled state of Chinese consumerism. Among Chinese-speaking Muslims, the Tungans of the northwest, bath-houses continued to be a major social institution, as witness the famous quarrel in one at Kan-chou of the rival warlords, Ma Chung-ying and Ma Pu-fang, in 1930. Polo caught China in its Islamic moment.

Among the mines whose products Polo saw were those of Ment'ou-kou in the Western Hills outside Peking. Their development has been studied by the modern Chinese historian Teng T'o, though more from an organizational and production point of view than from that of consumption.[10] These mines, already in existence in the Yuan period, revived under the Ming and underwent rapid development first in the Wan-li period of late Ming and then, more particularly, under the Ch'ing in the Ch'ien-lung period. State involvement was reduced, more private capital was admitted, and production rose. Coal was carried to the capital by camel and still figured in domestic fuel in the 1920s, but its role was not predominant. Dr Gillan, the scientific attaché to the Macartney mission noted that: 'The Chinese prefer charcoal of wood for fuel, but in some of the northern provinces where wood is scarce and very dear they used coked pit-coal, prepared in the same way as we do in England.' He added that: 'This coked coal, as far as I could learn, is only used for culinary purposes, for baking of bricks and burning of lime.'[11] The lime kiln together with the forge were the main outlets too for coal mined in England before the sixteenth century, according to J. U. Nef.[12]

In his geological travels between 1870 and 1872, Richthofen attempted systematically to investigate China's coal reserves and to describe their current use. His *Letters* therefore provide a good picture of the pre-modern Chinese coal industry. What is striking in his portrayal is the high percentage of coal applied to industrial rather than domestic purposes. Coal *was* used as a domestic fuel: in Peking, as we have seen, and in eastern Szechwan, where it was supplied by the coalfield of K'uei-chou in the Yangtze gorges, which also supplied a local salt industry. Here Richthofen wrote: 'All kinds of coal, not excluding the worst, are used for domestic purposes: the fuel is within reach of the majority of the people, at low prices, and the necessity of using firewood, and therefore of planting trees for that special purpose, much restricted.'[13] Eastern Szechwan, however, was exceptional: the product of land shortage and coal primarily for salt. In general, Richthofen's observations referred to industrial use. In Hunan, with regard to its low grade coal, Richthofen mentions iron foundries, lime kilns and smithies; in Honan, iron works again, though some domestic purposes; in Shansi again, predominantly furnaces, foundries and forges: 'The mining of coal, the manufacturing of iron, and the conveying of both to market employ a large number of men and animals.'[14] Domestic consumption, where it existed, was a by-product of industry. More coal was produced and of lower quality than could be absorbed by the iron industry, so it could compete locally with timber which had to come any distance. Iron was the prime mover of coal. This was because of its precocity in China. The Chinese could cast iron 1500 years before the Europeans and coal was used alike in furnace, foundry, forge and smithy long before Europe did so in the eighteenth century.[15] Yet it is significant that industrial demand alone was not sufficient to generate an industrial revolution in the sense of a widespread shift to coal as a source of energy.

It was different in England. In his pioneering studies of the British coal industry, J. U. Nef was concerned to show that there had been a minor industrial revolution in the late Tudor and early Stuart period, which laid the foundations for the major industrial revolution at the end of the eighteenth century. What he really showed was that in London, there had been a consumerist revolution in domestic heating. Before 1550, in England, as in China and on the Continent, most coal was applied to industrial purposes, notably the lime kiln and the smithy. The quantities were not large. Nef estimated total English production of coal in 1560 at around 200 000 tons: a figure comparable to Richthofen's guess of 200 000 to 300 000 tons for Honan or the 180 000 tons estimated by him for a leading mining area in Hunan. By 1770, however, according to Nef, English production had risen to 3 000 000 tons. Two-thirds of this was used domestically: 'It was undoubtedly the rapid spread of the use of coal in warming rooms, in cooking food and in all other common services requisite in housekeeping, that occasioned the chief demand for it, and that relieved in greatest measure the drain on the timber supplies of Britain during the seventeenth century.'[16] The rise in domestic consumption of coal, though spurred by an increase in the price of wood from 1540, was due primarily to a greater desire for heat, not merely at isolated points, the cooking stove or in China the *k'ang*, but throughout continuous space. It was the expression of a consumerism which manifested itself in the demand for more space as such which lay behind the great rebuilding of Jacobean England. The house was for living in, not just living out of: a perception most likely to have been promoted more by women than by men. Coal had its inconveniences, but its advantages became clear if it were not available. Nef liked to quote a parliamentarian pamphlet of 1644. Before the royalist blockade: 'some fine Nosed City Dames used to tell their husbands: O Husband, we shall never be well, we nor our children, whilst we live in the smell of this Cities Seacoale smoke; Pray a Country house for our health that we may get out of this stinking Seacoale smell.' Now, however, with the blockade: 'how many of these fine Nosed Dames now cry, Would to God we had Seacoale, O the want of Fire underneath us! O the Sweet Seacoale fire we used to have, how we want them now, no fire to your Seacoale!'[17]

In England, the opposite to China, domestic supply stimulated industrial. The prime example here was the Durham salt-boiling industry at South Shields and Sunderland, which, on the basis of coal fuel, became the largest saline in the world. Tyneside was the principal source of supply for London. In addition to the large coal required for that market, it produced, as a by-product, quantities of small coal which could not be sold there. The coalmasters were therefore happy to dispose of it at knock-down prices to the salt masters who, despite their weak marine brine, were able to undercut their strong brine competitors in Cheshire and Worcestershire, who did not enjoy the advantage of cheap fuel. Nef reckoned that in 1700 salt makers consumed 300 000 tons of coal: a tenth of total production. A second example was bricks. As domestic coal fires became more popular, better chimneys were required. Good chimneys had previously been made of iron. This was expensive, so a cheaper substitute was sought in high-grade brick, which now became possible thanks to by-product coal. A third industry which shifted to coal in Nef's period was glass. This, too, may be associated with consumerism: in this case, the demand not for heat but for light, just as a fourth case, soap boiling, was related to cleanliness and the demand for water. A fifth customer of Newcastle coal was linked to consumerism in dress. This was the North Riding alum industry, which, added to those of Tolfa and Foca, loosened a key supplyside bottleneck for the European textile industry. Other new openings for coal were sugar refining, part of consumerism in food, brewing, perhaps a matter of consumption rather than consumerism, and saltpetre manufacture for use both in peace and war. The greater part of the new demand for coal in the seventeenth century came from consumerist-related demand rather than from industry. Metallurgy, which predominated in China, only became a major factor at the end of the eighteenth century. Subsequently, of course, in the nineteenth century, industrial demand came to outweigh greatly domestic demand, but this fact should not obscure the initial primacy of the domestic customer in London.

London's predilection for coal fires was copied first in Amsterdam, which imported from Newcastle and the Firth of Forth as well as Liège and early mines in the Ruhr. Paris was not far behind and the nineteenth century everywhere saw an increased use of coal, though in the United States its consumption did not overtake that of wood until the 1880s. It was in Britain, however, that the coal fire had its widest and deepest implications. Economically, as Nef saw, it gave Britain a headstart in the first industrial revolution, though it was an ambiguous advantage and in the long run perhaps not an advantage at all. More far-reaching were the social and political implications, some of which only became conspicuous as coal began to retreat in the home before gas and electricity.

First, within the home, coal fires encouraged the upstairs–downstairs society: the massive use of domestic service which was a feature of English society down to the Second World War. A large part of domestic service revolved round coal. Grates required to be cleaned, laid and lit, scuttles had to be filled and ashes disposed of, bins must be kept at a certain level. Coal inevitably generated dirt and dust. Domestic service, particularly in its temporary, life-cycle form, which was especially prevalent in London, was a major factor in the diffusion of consumerism. Whatever its stratifications, its intimacy brought cultural contact, even when it was formally rejected as familiarity unwanted by all concerned. Mass consumerism trickled down less from the suburban villa than from Mayfair and Belgravia. It has been estimated that, thanks to domestic service, one person in six in England spent some time in London in the eighteenth century, a figure much higher than would have been the case with, say, Naples and its hinterland.

Second, if coal promoted cultural intimacy at one level, it highlighted cultural distance at another. More than other consumerist commodities, coal presented a contrast between the conditions of production and the circumstances of consumption. The coalmine was a world apart from the drawing-room, the library or the boudoir. A visit to a mine was more disquieting than a visit to a mill. Coal generated class and bad conscience about class. With their isolated communities and distinctive lifestyle, miners were labour to a superlative, even though other workers, farmhands for example, might be objectively worse off. Mining disasters attracted sympathy to a greater degree than ordinary industrial accidents. H. G. Wells put the Morlocks, like miners, underground. Yet from another perspective, the miners were an aristocracy themselves: the Old Guard of the labour movement, whose retreat in 1985 spelled the end of an age. Consumerism eventually dissolved the Victorian dichotomy of the classes and the masses in a common culture, but it had one of its roots in a particularly glaring case of class division.

Third, coal shaped social structure. If Germany had its alliance of rye and iron, England had its alliance of coal and acres, as exemplified in the Lambtons in County Durham and the marquises of Bute in South Wales. A number of great houses were built out of coal: Woollaton, Seaton Delaval, Wentworth Woodhouse. Coal led aristocrats to improve rivers and build canals. An example of the first was the canalization of the River Weaver which combined coal and salt interests and embraced most of the county families of Cheshire. Of the second, the best example was the Duke of Bridgewater whose first canal in 1761 was designed to convey coal to Manchester from his mines at Worsley. The solidarity of land and commerce in coal made the idea of a necessary conflict between 'feudalism' and the bourgeoisie even more implausible in England than elsewhere. Eventually it gave rise to a secondary aristocracy. William Thomas Lewis, agent to the

Marquis of Bute, became Lord Merthyr; Henry Austin Bruce, a coal and iron entrepreneur, became Lord Aberdare; while another, David Alfred Thomas, became Lord Rhondda. Nationalization only made honours bureaucratic: Lord Robens, Sir Derek Ezra, Sir Ian MacGregor, to name only three chairmen of the Coal Board. As in Germany, this unity of elites helped produce a certain social stability during a period of great economic change. It was not without a sense of history that Harold Macmillan, ex-MP for Stockton and exponent of One Nation conservatism, opposed the determination of the Conservative government to defeat Mr Scargill's insurrection in 1984–5.

Finally, coal was an equilibrating factor in politics: between north and south, provinces and metropolis, Celtic fringe and English heartland. English politics are rooted in these dichotomies which divide in debatable land along the Fosse. When coal was primarily a domestic fuel, it united north and south, Newcastle and London. When, in the nineteenth century, coal became primarily an industrial fuel, its new consumers too tended to follow the metropolitan interest. Manchester has a long record of adherence to the Conservative Party. Birmingham was brought over to the Conservative cause in 1886 by Joseph Chamberlain. These extensions to the party beyond its homelands were essential to the success first of Disraeli and then of Salisbury. It was where coal was consumed in iron industries on its own doorstep, as in South Wales and South Yorkshire, that Conservatism found it difficult to establish itself. It was not only the modernity of the Nottinghamshire mines, but also their integration into a wider market, which led to their support of the government in 1984–5. Similarly, South Wales, in a partly deindustrialized context through the decline of iron and steel into rustbowl, gave only lukewarm support to Scargill's rebellion. Coal brought down the Heath government and Margaret Thatcher told Ian MacGregor that the fate of her government was in his hands. With the retreat of coal to being only an alternative energy source for the electricity industry and a reserve of chemical raw materials, it is unlikely that any British government will find itself in this position again. The long cycle of coal, set off by the consumerism of London in the sixteenth century, appeared to be at an end. But it had been a dramatic and glorious cycle, significant for the world as well as for England. It justified the prescient enthusiasm of the poet Nef liked to quote:[18]

> England's a perfect World! has Indies too!
> Correct your Maps! New-castle is Peru!

WATER: ABOVE AND BELOW, WHOLESALE AND RETAIL

If heat was the essential of domestic utilities, water was the number one accessory. Consumerism implied more domestic water for drinking, cooking, washing and waste removal. If the demand for more heat in Europe was related to consumerism in shelter, the demand for more water was related to consumerism in dress. As London led the first, so Paris led the second. It was the fashion for cleaner, whiter, less soiled, more sophisticated clothes, which led first Parisians, and then other Europeans, to catch up and surpass China in the consumption of water. For, except in a few favoured, pioneering places such as Rome, the seventeenth century in Europe was still an era of rare water. Its very scarcity indeed put a high value on its products and promoted the cult of cleanliness, the high use of laundry facilities, the precocious development of dry cleaning, the new emphasis on personal hygiene, which Daniel Roche analyses as elements of the Parisian *révolution vestimentaire*.[19] Yet the European conquest of water, as Jean-Pierre Goubert calls it, was, from one perspective, only the occupation of territory long held by the Chinese on the basis of a different hydraulic tradition.[20]

Both Europeans and Chinese valued water. For Europeans, until Lavoisier, it was one of the four elements. For Chinese, until the coming of Western science, it was one of the five *hsing* or fundamental processes. Both took it as a symbol of purity. Europeans associated the waters of the biblical Flood, the Red Sea and the baptismal font. In China, when the Manchus wished to proclaim their opposition to eunuch corruption, they took the dynastic style of Ch'ing, the character for which has a water radical. If a county wished to honour a magistrate, it would present him on departure with a single cup of pure water: so you have dealt with us and now we return the gift to you. A Chinese proverb advised, 'when you drink water think of the source'. Yet Europeans and Chinese saw water differently. For Europeans water was *yang*, super-terrestrial. It came from above. Rain was its most obvious source. For Chinese, as for the Aztecs, water was *yin*, sub-terrestrial.[21] It came from below. Rivers were its most obvious source. From these different perceptions came different hydraulic strategies and schemes of operation. Strategically, Europe emphasized wholesale: the reservoir, the aqueduct, the fountain; China emphasized retail: the water carrier, the nightsoil collector, localized pipes. For Europeans, water was an overhead. Like the house, it was a piece of capital investment to be amortized long-term. For Chinese, water was a current expense.

Like the house–clothes continuum, it was a piece of maintenance to be met out of income account. Moreover, not only was water perceived differently, its control took place in different environments. In China, water was commonly either in excess or default. It was part of a disordered nature which required constant regulation by culture. In Europe, flood and drought were uncommon. Water was part of an ordered providence which only intermittently or locally required regulation by culture. These contrasts in perception and environment produced different hydraulic agendas and schemes of operation.

Above and Below

The Chinese hydraulic tradition began from below. Its agenda was flood prevention and irrigation promotion and its schemes of operation envisaged rivers and earthworks. Here, as in other specialized branches of management, there was a range of options. Sinologues have never been convinced by Wittfogel's simple equation of despotic state, macrohydraulic agriculture, and major government works as the link between them.[22] Each term in the equation is too open to question or qualification to make it acceptable as a general theory. By the early modern period, there were at least four major traditions of hydraulic engineering active: two in the state and two in society.

Needham calls the two state traditions the channel expansion and the channel contraction methods.[23] For both, the problem was the volume of silt carried by the Yellow river. As the current slowed on the north China plain, silt was deposited on the riverbed, raising its level in relation to the surrounding country. When the next strong freshet came down, the river might flood, burst its banks, or change its course altogether, threatening the plain with reversion to its original state of extended wetland. Over history, the mouth of the Yellow river had oscillated between just south of Peking to just north of the Yangtze. The channel expansion method did not seek to prevent movement by the river altogether. It aimed only to moderate it by widely spaced dykes and the provision of overflow basins, where the deposits of valuable, fertilising silt could eventually be taken advantage of by the farmer. For the river was seen as an opportunity as well as a threat, its problems sociological as well as simply hydraulic. The channel contraction method, however, did seek to prevent movement by the river. By narrowly spaced dykes, it aimed to constrict the current, increase its speed and scour power, so that silt would not be deposited, but carried out to sea to create new land on the coasts of Chihli and Kiangsu. Flood prevention by ever higher dykes became the only agenda and wider problems of silt utilization were excluded as too complex for government adjudication. In the Ming-Ch'ing period, the majority of hydraulic engineers belonged to the channel contraction tradition. This limitation of state action left a wide field for hydraulic activity on the part of society.

Private hydraulic engineering was most evident in the Yangtze valley. Here, in the interior delta below the gorges and in the actual delta in Kiang-nan, it has been studied by Pierre-Étienne Will and Philip Huang.[24] Compared to the Yellow river, the Yangtze was, until recent times, a well-behaved river which did not require macrohydraulic action on the part of the imperial authorities. It began with a lower silt content, created its own overflow lakes, and had its current sustained by powerful tributaries. Nevertheless, in Hupei and Kiangsu, it threatened, like the Yellow river, to produce wetlands. In both areas, hydraulics were left essentially to private enterprise: not the microhydraulics of a peasantry, but the medio-hydraulics of local elites. In Hupei, hydraulics took the form of *yu* or *yuan*, embankments. These protected individual units of land, rather like the *terpen* or *buttes* of ancient Frisia, from inundation and sought to hustle water downstream. It was a defensive strategy, implicitly at the expense of those downriver, a local channel contraction method. In Hupei, it was successful in producing the cotton and rice landscape of Han-yang county south of the Han. In Kiangsu, on the other hand, hydraulics took the form of *wei*, enclosures. These reclaimed land from lakes or the sea, rather like the *polders* of modern Holland. It was an offensive strategy, implicitly at the expense of those upstream, whose drainage to the sea was impeded, thus creating a kind of sump, the T'ai-hu, in the middle of the delta. Since water was prevented from reaching the sea and encouraged to settle in an artificial overflow lake, this strategy produced results similar to the channel expansion method. In Kiangsu, it was successful in producing the patchwork of rice, mulberry, cotton, irrigation, communication and conurbanization so characteristic of the delta.

The European hydraulic tradition began from above. Its agenda was urban supply or protection, and its schemes of operation envisaged either springs in hills or tidal surge by the wind. In Europe, there were no super-rivers like the Huang-ho and the Yangtze. Macrohydraulics of the kind envisaged by Wittfogel, and sometimes effected in China, were unnecessary. Hydraulic problems were simpler and less critical. Where rivers flooded, the problem was often interpreted as one of storm water, either from the sea or from rain at the source. In the sixteenth century, Rome was prone to serious flooding by the Tiber in the months of December and January, when the river could rise 10 metres or more. The floods were commonly attributed to high tides preventing the egress of water, land reclamation at Rieti which increased its flow, or heavy rain up at Lake Trasimene. Less attention was paid to the river itself or to sources of flooding much closer to the city. Sixtus V considered a defluent canal or spillway from the Milvian bridge to below Trastevere to carry off excess water and a canalization of the Tiber from Ripa Grande to the sea to facilitate flow, but these plans, reminiscent of the Chinese channel contraction method, found no favour and were not carried out. Until the nineteenth century, no attempt was made to embank the Tiber or provide its affluents with winter overflow basins, as a Chinese engineer would have done. Similarly, in the Pontine marshes, where Sixtus V undertook the most ambitious scheme of drainage before Mussolini, his engineer Ascanio Fenizi concentrated too much on the top and bottom of the drainage canal to the neglect of the middle. Consequently, the canal was overwhelmed by the winter inundations of 1589–90 and the Pope was dead before works were recommenced.[25] In China, in the rather similar problem of the Chihli marshes south of Peking, Chinese engineers achieved a better degree of success through the stabilization between 1690 and 1840 of the middle course of the Yung-ting Ho by a mixture of expansion and contraction methods.

In some cases, of course, the European approach did give good results, notably in Holland where the problem really was the sea, tides, rain and storm. Here the *polder*, the Chinese *wei*, was used even more effectively than in China. In other cases, European methods were not unlike those of the Chinese. Even Needham allowed the comparability of the work of the Milanese engineers on the Ticino and the Adda in the plain of Lombardy with those of Li Ping on the Min in the plain of Chengtu. Here the Europeans fixed on the middle as much as the Chinese. But this was not their usual focus, and in domestic supply their tradition led them to concentrate on wholesale, just as the Chinese tradition led them to concentrate on retail.

Wholesale

Here provision long led from removal. Whatever the precedents of the palace at Knossos, the *Cloaca Maxima* and a few medieval religious houses such as Kirkham, closets, connecting sewers and mains drainage were an invention essentially of the nineteenth century: invented in response to the great cholera scare. Cholera, diffused to both Europe and China from Bengal by the *haj* traffic stimulated by the dervish orders, was a new disease outside its home territories. The simplest of the great epidemics in aetiology and the most readily diffused by water, cholera provided a motive for the removal of waste products beyond consumerist aesthetics. Sixtus V, forward-looking in many aspects of consumerism, had taken little interest in mains drainage. Londoners contented themselves with taking water from one tributary of the Thames, while putting it into another. Paris, the centre of the dress revolution, was better than London: it had 10 000 metres of drains in 1663 and 23 000 in 1806. Amsterdam was best of all. Dutch cleanliness was famous, even notoriously obsessive. It extended from the doorstep to the street to the canal, enforced as much by public sentiment as by municipal regulation, rather in the manner of Singapore today. Yet none of these places approached the drainage introduced to London by Sir Joseph Bazalgette between 1858 and 1876. This provided for interceptor main drains built into his Thames embankments which carried sewage, fed into it by subsidiary drains attached to domestic sewers, to disposal stations beyond the metropolitan limits at Barking in Essex for the north bank and Crossness in Kent for the south bank. Between 1858 and 1869, Paris also received a new drainage system from Baron Haussmann and his engineer Eugene Belgrand, but its principles, a central collecting point under the Place de la Concorde, *a cloaca maxima*, and eventual deposit in the Seine albeit well below Paris, were less radical than those of London. Berlin, by contrast, did not receive proper drains till after 1873, and Naples, notoriously one of the most insanitary of European cities, not till the ministry of Depretis in 1884–7.[26]

Wholesale provision was more ancient. In the Graeco-Roman world, there were the aqueducts, baths, cisterns and fountains; in the Iranian world, the famous *kariz* or *qanats*, the underground water channels which in desert climates avoided surface evaporation. The two traditions came together in Ottoman Constantinople. New Rome, like the old, had been provided with aqueducts by its emperors. The principal was that of Valens, reconditioned by that great but unfortunate civilian emperor, but initiated by Hadrian, reactivated by Constantine and subsequently enlarged by Justinian I and Justin II. It brought the waters of the Ali Bey Suyu, which Westerners later called the Sweet Waters of Europe, to the city, in particular to Justinian's underground cistern, Yerebatan serai, which had a capacity of 78 000 m^3. Other major cisterns were those of Aetius, Aspar and Anastasius. The combined capacity of covered and open cisterns at the end of the sixth century was around 1 000 000 m^3 at a time when the city's consumption has been reckoned at 10 000 m³ a day. Subsequently additions and enlargements were made by the Comnenians. In the sixteenth century, the whole system was restored and extended by Suleyman through his engineer-architect Sinan. From the Kagithane Suyu, more of the Sweet Waters of Europe were brought to the swollen populations of Stambul, Pera and Galata, Taksim being one of the internal distribution points. Suleyman was acting as a Byzantine emperor, but he was also influenced by the Persian delight in pools and gardens introduced by his Iranophile father Selim and by the Islamic institution of the *haman*, the warm-water bath-house attached to many mosques for ritual ablutions. In 1800, the Seraglio contained not only *hamans* for the Sultan, the Valide Sultan, the harem and the palace hospital, but also a hot and cold swimming pool, a boating pool and garden fountains. It was closer in spirit to a Roman villa than anything being built in Western Europe, while also containing elements of a Sassanian palace.

In Western Europe, the Roman bath fell into abeyance in the Dark Ages when the clientele for its particular kind of sociability disappeared. The aqueducts, which in most cases supplied them, were revived in the Renaissance, most conspicuously in Rome itself. Here the popes undertook three major works. First, there was the *Acqua Vergine*. Built originally by Agrippa to bring water from Salona to the Pantheon, this aqueduct was repaired in 1453 by Nicholas V who built the first Trevi fountain to receive it. Further repairs under Sixtus IV and Leo X proving unsatisfactory, Paul III and Pius IV devised a general reconstruction, which was put into effect by Pius V and completed in 1572. This aqueduct carried a capacity of 65 000 m³ a day. Next, there was the *Acqua Felice* which was completed by Sixtus V in 1586. It followed the line of an ancient aqueduct of Claudius from Subiaco. It brought 20 000 m³ a day to the area round Santa Maria Maggiore which, long neglected, the pope was trying to reurbanize. Finally, there was the *Acqua Paola* from Lake Bracciano to Trastevere, on the lines of canalization initiated by Trajan, which was completed by Paul V in 1612. It had a carrying capacity of 94 000 m³ a day. By the early seventeenth century, Rome was being supplied with 180 000 m³ of water a day, or 1700 litres for each of its 100 000 population. A few comparisons indicate the magnitude of the papal achievement. London consumed 250 000 m³ in 1848, Paris 112 000 m³ in 1852, but both were much larger than Rome. At the end of the nineteenth century, 100–120 litres a day per capita were reckoned sufficient for a major city. In 1950 large European cities averaged 250 litres a day, large American cities up to 1000. Papal Rome, indeed, had a superfluity of water. Much was not used in washing, sanitation or industry, but ran to waste in ornamental fountains, of which 35 were built between 1575 and 1600. In no area other than hydraulics was the Renaissance in Rome so genuinely a rebirth, rather than a reinterpretation. Yet papal prestige euergetism painted the way for more pragmatic cultures.

If in Rome improvements in water provision were the work of the popes and the state, in London they were the work of water companies and society. In the Middle Ages, London, like most cities which could do so, drew its water from its river. The first London water company, the London Bridge of 1581, took its supplies at that location by means of undershot water wheels. When steam pumps were introduced in 1712 by the York Buildings company of 1691, it was still from the Thames that the water was raised. With increased population, however, and the use of tributaries such as the Walbrook, the Fleet, the Effra and the Wandle as drains, the Thames in London became seriously polluted, as the incidence of cholera revealed. Three solutions were attempted. First, water was drawn from unpolluted tributaries of the Thames. This was done by the New River company of 1613 from a mixture of its own 'New River', in effect an aqueduct canal from springs near Hertford, and of the River Lea which ran parallel to it. In this way, the company provided 20 000 m³ day, the same as the *Acqua Felice*. Second, water might be taken from the Thames upstream of the metropolis. Thus the Grand Junction of 1811 moved its supply from Chelsea to Kew and the Southwark and Vauxhall of 1845 moved theirs from Battersea to Hampton Court. Third, water could be obtained from springs or ponds on London's surrounding rim of hills. This was done by the Corporation itself in Tudor times from the Hampstead ponds and from 1682 more systematically by the private Hampstead company. It was done too by the Lambeth company of 1785, which, having abandoned the Thames near the Festival Hall, took water from Streatham Hill, before moving its source to Surbiton. Compared to papal activity in Rome, company activity might appear haphazard, but by the mid-nineteenth century most houses were provided with cisterns which were filled at stated times. Wholesale provision at least was adequate.

Retail

In China, aqueducts played only a limited part in water provision, just as mains drains played only a limited part in waste product removal. Where sewers existed, as in Peking, constructed under the Ming, their purpose was storm-water control rather than sanitation. Instead, Chinese domestic hydraulics focused on retail. Needham gives an explanation: 'The near absence of aqueducts in China must certainly be redated to the abundance of waterways, surrounding and penetrating most of the principal cities – fortunately the Chinese early learnt to boil their drinking-water, hence the apotheosis of tea. Bamboo pipelines were prominent, however.'[27] What Needham says here is true, but not the whole truth. The basic factor was the greater use of human nightsoil as agricultural fertilizer in China as compared to Europe. The Chinese had earlier and greater understanding that agriculture was applied biochemistry. European cities exploited their countrysides. Chinese cities lived in symbiosis with theirs. It used to be said that, flying out of a Chinese city, one passed over successive bands of dark green, light green, yellow-green and yellow as the price of nightsoil rose and its availability fell. Nightsoil collectors, ordure stations and *fu-fu* boats were characteristic of Chinese cities. So lucrative was the trade, that in pre-war Shanghai, contractors paid the municipality for the privilege of undertaking it on a local monopoly basis. As a result, rivers, though no doubt polluted by modern standards, were less so than in traditional London, Paris or Rome. Consequently, their water could be used for washing, and, if boiled, for cooking and drinking too. The water carrier was the counterpart of the nightsoil collector. Because of the activities of his colleague, he was under less pressure to seek more distant, less polluted waters: those on his doorstep would do. Both water provision and water removal came to be seen in essentially local, retail terms. Thanks to the nightsoil collector too, cholera had a lesser impact in China than Europe.

A second factor which told against aqueducts was Chinese proficiency in well-sinking. The supreme examples here were the brine and gas borehole wells of Szechwan, one of which in 1835 reached a depth of a kilometre.[28] But in parts of China with a higher water table, shallow shaft wells sufficed for irrigation and domestic purposes. In Chihli, for example, Philip Huang contrasts the massive imperial dykes needed for flood prevention with the small private wells, 7–10 metres deep, adequate for water provision.[29] In Peking in the 1920s, most water came from surface wells from which it was brought to individual houses by water carriers. Hankow, on the other hand, relied on a mixture of wells and water from the relatively unpolluted Han river. Similarly, in Shanghai, water was obtained from wells, from the Soochow creek, or from the Whangpoo, either above the city where fed by underground streams or below where cleansed by the purer waters of the Yangtze.

Where wells had to be drilled, and not merely dug, China for long enjoyed the advantage of more and better steel than Europe for the purpose of drill heads. Where Europeans looked up for water – to rain, hill springs or upper valleys – Chinese looked down.

Finally, if the Chinese preferred the retail pipeline to the wholesale aqueduct, it was partly because of the availability in China of Nature's piping, the bamboo. Bamboo pipeline had long been in use in the Szechwan salt industry to move both brine and natural gas. It was applied first to short-distance water supply, from the West lake to the city in Hang-chou, by the Szechwanese minister and poet Su Tung-po in 1089. Subsequently it was used, in suitable circumstances, in a number of Chinese cities, for example, Canton.[30] When the London water companies began to enter the retail business in the eighteenth century and to replace open conduits to public cisterns with closed pipes to private houses, they were, unknowingly, following the path of an earlier, oriental consumerism.

LIGHT: NATURAL AND ARTIFICIAL

If heat and water were grounded in consumerisms of shelter and dress, light looks forward to consumerism of information, which will be the subject of the next chapter. Without light, books would not be read, homework would not be done, letters might remain unwritten, confidences unexchanged and news not disseminated. Without more light, the European revolution in literacy, which transformed relations between China and the West, would not have been possible.

The problem of light posed itself differently in Europe and China. Without artificial illumination, *annual* light and darkness are everywhere the same and equal. But, according to latitude, there are large *diurnal* and seasonal variations in the distribution of this quantum. These are minimal at the equator and maximal at the poles. That the sun rises every day is often cited as an inductive truth, but, as Popper remarked, its falsity has been known since Pytheas of Massilia in the fourth century BC! The problem of light is different in the lower and higher latitudes. If what is wanted is a supply of light constant throughout the year, then more recourse must be had to artificial light in the higher than in the lower latitudes. Though both Europe and China belong to the temperate zone, average latitudes were higher in Europe than in China. This was especially significant in periods, like the early modern, when European life was moving north while Chinese life was moving south. As a result, Europe came to be a greater provider of light, both natural and artificial, than China, Europeans more consumerist in their demands for it than Chinese.

Natural Light

In both Europe and China, the way to bring natural light indoors was the window. In both, however, because of rain and cold, the window had to be covered. Where Europe and China differed was in the material used for the covering. In Europe, by the eighteenth century, it was glass, though shutters remained predominant in many rural cottages. In China, it was paper, as it had been for many centuries and would continue to be in modern times. When fully developed, glass gave more light and better protection than paper, but in the early days, when glass was cloudy, mullioned and fragile and where paper was perfected in transparency and strength, there was not much to choose between them. Why then the different choice, since China made good glass in the fourth century AD, while Europe learnt to make paper from the Muslims, ultimately from the Chinese, in the twelfth century AD? True, glass was something in which Europe excelled, paper something in which China excelled, but these facts themselves are not self-explanatory. In both cases, the positive fact was linked to a negative fact, the hypertrophy of one commodity may be associated with the absence of another.

In the case of Europe and glass, the absentee was porcelain. As noted above, in the coastal neolithic of China, ceramics preceded agriculture. In the inland neolithic of the Levant, it was the other way round. Though Graeco-Roman pottery achieved considerable technical mastery and great beauty in its decoration, it remained pottery. No vitrified ceramics could be produced without much higher temperatures than Western antiquity was capable of. Consequently, there was a need for high grade, translucent tableware. That this need was met by glass – a silicate of sodium or potassium, produced by the fusion of sand, limestone and an alkali – no doubt owed something to its occasional, accidental occurrence on the edge of the Syrian and Egyptian deserts. But its subsequent development was due to Syrian artisans and Greek entrepreneurs in Ptolemaic Alexandria responding to particular Hellenistic tastes. Thanks to its *pharos* and its library, Alexandria was already the city of light. The development of the glass industry gave it a new dimension in consumerism. With the fall of the Ptolemies, Alexandria lost some of its local, elite clientele, but it remained the centre of the glass industry in the Roman world. Its products were exported east as well as west. They reached China by both the central land route and by the southern sea route, as well as by the Afghan interlink which joined the two, if the indications of the Begram treasure are correct.

Within the Roman world, the principal use of glass was tableware: vases, jugs, bowls, beakers, dishes and so on. In something like the Portland vase, however, glass became, so to speak, the supreme ceramic, perfect and incomparable. It was also used as window covering, less for its translucency than for its heat conserving qualities. Thus it was used, not so much in private houses where textiles or horn sufficed, as in the *calidaria* of Roman baths. It was probably from such public buildings that glass entered ecclesiastical architecture. Benedict Biscop brought Roman glassmakers to Monkwearmouth and Jarrow at the end of the seventh century and some surviving fragments are coloured. From the eleventh century, stained glass began to be used widely in church windows. Soon it became almost an end in itself. Cathedrals became greenhouses, Beauvais being the extreme example. It was not, however, until the sixteenth century that window glass began to be widely used in secular, domestic architecture. As part of Renaissance enlightenment, descastellation and civilianizing, it too became an end in itself, the extreme example being Hardwick Hall, 'more glass than wall', the lay counterpart of Beauvais, completed in 1597. Nevertheless, window glass continued to be expensive and to require mullions until the development of plate glass casting. This occurred first in France from 1688 on the basis of wood fuel at Saint Gobain in Picardy, and then, more massively in England from 1776 on the basis of coal fuel at St Helens in Lancashire. With the expansion of St Helens, which could draw on alkali produced by the Leblanc process from brine supplied by the Cheshire 'wiches', the age of mass consumerism in glass had arrived.

In the case of China and paper, the absentee was papyrus. In papyrus, the Graeco-Roman world, since at least the time of Herodotus who regarded its use as commonplace, had had a writing material that was effective, cheap and convenient. Egyptian only in origin, it met the rising demand of increasing literacy in the Greek cities, the Hellenistic kingdoms and the Roman empire. Unlike paper, however, papyrus was neither durable nor translucent, so it was never a candidate for window covering. Egyptian papyrus had no equivalent in China. The earliest extant Chinese writing, under the Shang and the early Chou, was on bone: the famous oracle bones – tortoise carapace and ox scapula. Under the later Chou, the Chin and the early Han, its place was taken by silk, wood and bamboo. The Etzingol strips, which give such a vivid picture of frontier life under the Han, are the counterpart of the Vindolanda strips from Hadrian's wall. Paper was invented in the reign of Han Wu-ti (140–87), but less as a writing material than as an absorbent felt, used mainly for wrapping. Its potential for writing, however, was soon apparent, especially when its raw materials were changed from silk and hemp rags to fresh mulberry bark. This invention is credited to the later Han court eunuch Ts'ai Lun in 105 AD, when he forged the fateful alliance of paper and bureaucracy.

Improved paper, subsequently made to a variety of specifications, soon drove out other writing materials. Greater quantities met the rising demands of increasing literacy in the San-kuo, Six dynasties and Sui-T'ang periods. Paper became more widely available for non-writing purposes: fans, umbrellas, toiletry, clothes, ceremonial replicas and, in durable and translucent specification, window covering. Here it replaced an earlier use of gauze. In the Ming period, a superior paper 7 ft x 4 ft was manufactured for window purposes at Kuang-hsing in Kiangsi. Its protective adequacy and the soft light it provided made the development of window glass unnecessary, just as the existence of papyrus in the West made early experimentation with paper unnecessary. In the long run, of course, glazing admitted more natural light than papering, especially in the higher latitudes. Europe secured an advantage over China. When the K'ang-hsi emperor was renewing the paper in the Forbidden City, Louis XIV was installing glass at Versailles.

Artificial Light

The rising demand of increasing literacy for information could never be contented by even the maximal use of natural light. A *Punch* cartoon, commemorating the introduction of daylight saving in 1916, suggested: 'the best of all ways to lengthen our days is to borrow an hour from the night'.[31] Apart from William Willett's simple invention, this could only mean artificial light. Here there was another contrast between Europe and China in the early modern period. In Europe, the wax candle predominated over the oil lamp. In China, the oil lamp predominated over the wax candle. Moreover, the sources of wax and oil were different.

In the Graeco-Roman world, oil lamps are one of the artefacts most frequently recovered from archaeological sites. There was a time, however, when they were infrequent. Homer has only one reference to lamps. Their widespread use came only with the sociability of the city-state and the growth of the olive economy to supply fuel. Bee-keeping, however, was widely diffused, as the source of sweetening. Homer mentions both wild bees and domestic and hives would have produced the standard one part of wax to ten parts of honey. Wax was employed in writing tablets, seals, dolls, in the *cire perdue* technique of bronze casting, and candles. Wax candles, however, were not a common form of illumination in either Greece or Rome. In Rome, their most explicit use was in the law courts, where judges were accompanied by lights from a mixture of practical and prestige reasons. From the Roman law courts, lights passed to the Christian liturgy which borrowed more from the basilica than the temple. When the liturgy was decentralized from Constantine's basilicas to parish *tituli*, so too were wax candles. As Christianity popularized the book, as opposed to the scroll, so it popularized the means of reading. Bees, wax and candles acquired Christian symbolism in the writings of Origen, Athanasius and Ambrose and in the ceremonies of Candlemas and the Easter Vigil. Christ was both light and word. Ambrose is one of the first people known to have read silently, instead of out aloud which Augustine regarded as normal. Candles in the West brought a new interiority of reading and a further separation from speaking. For in China, the written text, like our numerals independent of sound, was not designed to be read aloud, but silently in the privacy of a study.

The primacy of the candle over the lamp initiated by Christianity was carried further by the decline in the north of olive oil imports from the Mediterranean during the Dark Ages. It was boosted again by one of the earliest forms of European expansion: the establishment of the Baltic trade. In the eleventh century, Gotland traders reopened the Viking route to Novgorod. The Rus consumed their own honey, but were happy to export wood, pitch, ash, furs and wax. Wax, indeed, figured in the trade of the Teutonic knights before they went in for either amber or fur. In the classic age of the Hanseatic cousinages, wax was the number two commodity after fur. Unlike fur, which came to be obtainable from a number of points, Novgorod remained the principal outlet for wax. The English were particularly big buyers, an anticipation perhaps of their later role in the literacy revolution. Wax amounted to a quarter by value of their imports from the Hanseatics. This was the period, especially in northern Europe, of the proliferation of religious confraternities (male, female and mixed), one of whose principal activities was the provision of candles for altars and side chapels. Lights, lay piety and literacy went together. It is not surprising that the imagery of bees, honey and wax came so readily to Bishop

Foxe when he founded Corpus in 1516 as a centre of the new learning, or that another devotee of that learning, Latimer, invoked the candle to Ridley before they both suffered for it in 1555.

If oil and lamps continued in use after 1600, the form they took was less vegetable than animal or mineral. The animal was the whale, or its lesser relatives, the porpoise and dolphin. Cetaceans served consumerism in a number of ways. First, sperm oil, a form of liquid wax from the tropical sperm whale, was used for top quality candles. Indeed, the candle power unit of lighting was originally defined in terms of a standardized spermaceti candle. Second, whale oil proper or train oil, produced in a tryworks from the blubber of polar *Mystacoceti* whales ('right', great blue, fin and humpback), was used for lamp oil and in soap-making. This was another industry being swelled by the consumerist demand for whiter clothes and cleaner persons. Third, often more valuable than their oil, the *Mystacoceti* whales provided baleen or whalebone, whose tough flexibility was essential in Victorian fashions. Illumination, however, was the number one function down to 1800.

The history of whaling in the West was one of shifting locations and widening horizons. All coastal peoples are familiar with the occasional stranding of whales when their sonar becomes confused in shallow water. The next step is to produce this phenomenon artificially, shepherding the whales inshore by boats. This was done in the eleventh and twelfth centuries by Basques on both sides of the French–Spanish frontier, where the ocean and its denizens penetrate most deeply into the continent. Whaling may be regarded as the greatest Basque contribution to civilization. They took the final step of actively pursuing whales on the high seas with spears, lances, harpoons and similar precursors of the modern Svend Foyn harpoon cannon. It was the Basques who after 1500 extended the catchment area from off-shore to far-shore in the waters of Newfoundland and Labrador, Brazil, Norway, Spitzbergen and Greenland. In the seventeenth century, the Basques, already rivalled by the French and English, lost their dominance to the Dutch who extended the catchment to the Bering and Davis straits. In 1721 when they reached their apogee, the Dutch whaleries operated 250 ships and employed 14 000 men. Thereafter, the Dutch lost ground to the English and the Americans. Where the English focused on Greenland, Whitby being the outstanding port, the Americans, especially from Nantucket, were more adventurous. It was they who opened up the whaleries of the South Pacific. In 1839, of 200 whaling ships operating in New Zealand waters, 150 were American and perhaps a higher percentage of the skilled crews. By the end of the nineteenth century, however, the Americans too were losing ground. Their place was taken by Scandinavians, Norwegians especially, who, from South Georgia, the South Orkneys and South Shetlands, led the industry into the waters of Antarctica, the last refuge of major whale populations. Here they were joined by the Japanese, who, unlike most of East Asia, had their own independent tradition of whaling.

The mineral source of illumination which was coming on to the horizon in both London and Paris at the end of the eighteenth century, was coal gas. Here light was a by-product of heat: the conversion of coal into coke for industry. An inflammable gas was first deliberately produced from coal by John Clayton, rector of Crofton near Wakefield, around 1684, but his report was not published till 1739. Around 1760, George Dixon, a colliery owner near Newcastle, was the first to use coal gas for illumination, but an explosion convinced him it was too dangerous for common use. In 1784, Jean-Pierre Minkalers, professor of natural philosophy at Louvain, is said to have lighted his classroom with gas, though he was more interested in it for ballooning than illumination. In 1801, Philippe Lebon successfully demonstrated illumination by gas from wood in Paris, but he was assassinated in 1804 and the idea got no further on the Continent. In England, however, Lebon's scheme was taken up on the basis of coal rather than wood, by William Murdock of Boulton and Watt, Samuel Clegg the elder and by the enthusiastic, if eccentric, Hanoverian, Frederic Albert Winsor. Murdock and Clegg established gas plants at individual cotton mills, but it was Winsor who promoted the idea of a central generating station with pipelines to consumers, though his company was not a success till Clegg joined it as a technical expert. In 1814, St Margaret's Westminster abandoned oil lamps in favour of gas, and by the end of 1815 there were over 25 miles of gas mains in London. By 1825, consumers of gas included churches, banks, clubs, East India House, *The Times* printing office and Drury Lane theatre.

The development of gas light was not a purely intra-European story. The Chinese had been using *natural* gas from hydrocarbons for centuries in illuminating the round-the-clock saltworks in Szechwan as well as in boiling the brine. Moreover, with deeper drilling and the sinking of new fire wells at Tzu-kung, more gas was being used more conspicuously. Though the first European known to have visited and reported on Tzu-kung was Father Imbert in 1827, there was a flourishing branch of the Missions Étrangères in Szechwan for most of the period of the prehistory of the gas industry in Europe.[32] Its members went on leave and it is possible that one of them communicated information about what Szechwanese regarded as a wonder of their province. Gas wells, fewer in number than brine wells, often served a number of the second by bamboo pipeline. A description of Tzu-kung would therefore contain the notion of gas mains. If so, the development of gas light in Europe, with its immense consequences for productivity, street safety and information diffusion, may have had an extra-European dimension.

In China, artificial light followed different paths. Carl Crow, an archetypal Old China Hand, argued that there was a prejudice against it in China. In his account of the success of the Standard Oil Company of New York in selling lamps and oil to the Chinese, he wrote:

> The sun has always provided the Chinese with all the illumination they found necessary. From high to low the general mode of life was to get up at daylight and to go to bed with the birds. Even in the Imperial Palace court audiences were held at daybreak . . . The use of any kind of artificial illumination was associated in the Chinese mind with a certain amount of moral turpitude because only gamblers, prostitutes and drunkards habitually stayed up at night. The prejudice against interference with the routine of nature persisted for years.[33]

Crow's remarks should not be dismissed as a stereotype but they do require serious modifications as to times and places.

As regards demand, four observations may be made. First, lamps indeed are less characteristic of Shang, Chou and Han archaeology than they are of comparable sites in the West. Those that occur, such as the beautiful Chang-hsin palace lamp from the Man-ch'eng tomb in Chihli of the Western Han prince Liu Sheng and his wife Tou Wan, are works of art rather than common utensils.[34] Nocturnal illumination, it may be inferred, was part of a luxury lifestyle. Second, lamps on archaeological sites increase over time. There are more in the Han than in the Chan-kuo, more in the Eastern than in the Western Han. Materials became more diversified. In the Eastern Han, iron lamps were as popular as bronze or pottery. Any prejudice against borrowing an hour from the night was dissipated, it would appear, in the transition from the austere, meritocratic Early Han to the refined, aristocratic Later Han. Third, in medieval China, *public* illumination is frequently reported: in T'ang Yang-chou and Chengtu, in the night markets of Sung Kaifeng and Hang-chou. Chinese houses were places to be lived from rather than lived in. Domestic darkness might be compensated by social light in restaurants, theatres, shopping areas and places of amusement. If illumination subsequently acquired a bad name, it may have been because of its association with the Sung *wa-tzu* or pleasure quarters. Fourth, Marco Polo's account of Hang-chou contains no suggestion of illuminated night life. On the contrary, he implies that a strict curfew was enforced by the Mongol authorities. Was this practice continued by the puritan early Ming emperors, who were more hostile to elite consumerism than to Mongol austerity, and did the underlying attitude pass into the provincialist, born-again Confucian reformation of Wang Yang-ming in the sixteenth century? Crow's mistake was to suppose Chinese tradition monolithic and unchanging. It may be that what Socony was doing was less creating a demand than calling one out of abeyance.

On the supply side, China cultivated a wider range of oil-yielding plants than Europe. In 1904, Consul-General Hosie noted among the vegetable oils of Szechwan: rape, wood-oil, ground nuts, poppy, cotton seed, camellia, castor and flax. Rape, he observed, was the great lighting oil: 'The small lamp with its tiny flame which vainly tries in the public interest to pierce the darkness of night in the streets of Ch'engtu, the round copper lamp with its three flaming spouts on the street stall or in the shop, and the foreign looking glass tumbler of Chinese manufacture suspended in the guest hall of a Chinese inn . . . all burn rape oil.' With such abundance, resort to wax was unnecessary. Candles could be made with suitably treated rape oil.[35] Such wax as was required for candle-making and paper-glazing was obtained, not from bees, but from the famous white wax insect raised in Chiating prefecture and points west. China lacked a strong tradition of apiculture. Hosie noted:

> So far as my observation has extended, bee culture is not an absorbing hobby nor a favourite industry in China. True, over a farmhouse door one may frequently see one or even a couple of hives made out of parts of the hollowed-out trunks of trees . . . but one misses the collection of hives so commonly met with in the old-world gardens of English farmhouses . . . the fact that honey is not an article of diet, or even a food relish, is sufficient reason for the absence of any serious attempt at bee culture.[36]

Beeswax never enjoyed the place in artificial lighting it did in Europe. China went straight from the age of vegetable oil to the age of hydrocarbons.

In the last resort, Hosie shared Crow's view that the Chinese were different. He wrote: 'It has always been a puzzle to me how it is that the Oriental can find his way about in the darkest of nights. True, he usually carries a paper lantern which is more for show than for use, and the solution would appear to be that he has never had eyes dazzled by electricity, gas or kerosene, and that, being accustomed to light little removed from actual darkness, he has learned to penetrate darkness itself.'[37] Hosie's mind was concrete. His explanations tended to be positivistic and perhaps circular. What is lacking in his many precise accounts of technology is a sense of wider consumer context. For what lay behind the demand for artificial light in both Europe and China, or rather in front of it, was the consumerism of information. Heat looked to thermoregulation and the past, water looked to fashion and the present, but light looked to knowledge and the future.

6 Consumerism and Information

When consumerism reached information, it began, as Teilhard de Chardin would have said, to involute upon itself. Food, dress, shelter and utilities were all external to the mind, territories for its conquest, but information was the homeland of the mind itself. Yet information was not isolated from commodities and the productive processes which lay behind them. Indeed, a series of recent developments have highlighted the role of information in the modern economic and social worlds.

First, the oil crisis of 1973, subsequent perceived energy shortages, and Green emphasis on the finiteness of planet Earth's physical resources, led to a re-evaluation of information. Julian Simon pointed out that resources were relative to information, that technology created resources as well as exhausting them, and that raw materials no longer held the place they had in the nineteenth century. Information itself was the ultimate resource. Moreover, since Earth was not a closed system and there was in principle no limit to knowledge and only very remote limits to its storage and transmission, there was no need to believe Green prognostications. Second, as the notion of information became fashionable, the computer revolution of the 1980s, the sudden evolution of peering persons drew attention to the new forms information was assuming in hardware, software, cyberspace and the internet community. No doubt the consequences of the computer will be as hotly debated as those of print, but already it has transformed the conditions of business, scholarship and medicine. Third, as the 1980s ended, the collapse of the Soviet Union dramatized the consequences to a society of deliberate isolation from international information networks. Fourth, as boom turned to depression in the early 1990s, sociology woke up to the fact that access to information was a major determinant of class. In 1991, in *Centesimus Annus*, the Pope referred to those without such access as constituting an internal Fourth World corresponding to the external Third World. He noted that 'whereas at one time the decisive factor of production was the land and later capital ... today the decisive factor is man himself, that is, his knowledge, especially his scientific knowledge, his capacity for interrelated and compact organization, as well as his ability to perceive the needs

172

of others and to satisfy them'.[1] Finally, a number of intellectual currents have underlined the importance of information in the construction of humankind. One thinks of Teilhard de Chardin's noosphere and its convergence; Hayek's defence of the market as more informationally inclusive than any plan; Popper's World 3 and his distinction between logical and information content in theories; Wheeler, Barrow and Tipler's cosmic anthropic principles, weak, strong, participatory and final, which suggest that the universe itself runs on information. Even if none of these currents should stand the test of time, they have lent our species more justification for its name of *homo sapiens* than many others in the twentieth century.

If the present and future importance of information is accepted, it is reasonable to enquire about its significance in the past. In particular, it may be rewarding to ask about its role in the rise of consumerism, first in isolated, discontinuous patches in Chinese cities and European courts, and then increasingly as a global overlay. Indeed, the technology of information, which consumerism uses, has always been closely related to globalization. Speech is a universal human characteristic, bilingualism must always have occurred, and translation can never have been impossible. Script, apparently, was invented independently in the Near East and China, though attempts have been made to show mutual influence. Paper and print, certainly, were of Chinese origin. Both had been involved in the earlier phase of consumerism in China before becoming the vehicle of even profounder changes in Europe. The first step in understanding must be a fuller examination of the notion of information and of the ways in which information is related to consumerism.

INFORMATION AND CONSUMERISM

Consumption does not take place in isolation. Always there are structures, habits and presuppositions, articulated or unarticulated, which shape the decision to consume. Still less can consumerism, the materialization of mentality in commodities, be isolated from its intellectual antecedents. Indeed, the phase transition from consumption to consumerism may be defined in terms of, on the one hand, the degree of choice, and, on the other hand, of the level of information applied to the act of consumption. Such level may be gauged both individually and collectively, the person and the society.

Information

In traditional societies, information may be divided into potential and actual. Potential information is what is going on: what is being thought, said and done, which could become matter for communication by the available media. Like its physical counterpart, the number of events over a given stretch of time, potential information without further specification, is an indefinite, unquantifiable manifold. It may be supposed, however, to be a function of number and concentration. A more populous area will contain more potential information than a less populous, a city than a countryside, a countryside than a wilderness. Potential information has a spatial aspect. Thus prehistorians, seeking to understand the origins of agriculture in East Asia, have hypothesized an increase in potential information about plants and their behaviours as a result of concentration of coastal populations when sea levels rose at the end of the last ice age.[2] Contrariwise, if Colin Renfrew is to be believed that Western neolithic originated in eastern Anatolia, it will have been against a background of more dispersed population and a lesser degree of potential information.

Actual information, on the other hand, is that part of potential information which is actually conveyed through the available media. Unlike potential information, actual information is not an indefinite, unquantifiable manifold. Computer engineers have no difficulty in quantifying in terms of bytes and megabytes the amount of information their machines can carry. Estimates can be made of the storage capacity of the human brain and even of the universe and its magic figure of 10^{79}.[3] For most historical purposes, however, quantification is unnecessary. It is enough to estimate the content communicated through the three basic technologies of information: speech, script and print. Such estimates will be sufficient to assess the level of information, that is, the degree of informated-ness, in particular persons and societies. Here again, number and concentration are important. Thus Western Eurasia has always had the advantage over East Asia in point of numbers. But in the period 500 to 1000, maybe to 1500, China, reinforced by paper, print and a higher level of urbanization, had the advantage in point of concentration, certainly over Christendom and probably over Islamdom and non-Muslim India. Hence the generally westward flow of information in the Middle Ages and the role of China in the making of Europe which has been detailed by Needham.

Consumerism

Actual information, as conveyed by speech, script and print, enters into consumerism in one of two ways. First, it enters it as a means for both buyers and suppliers. For consumption and still more for consumerism, a would-be buyer has to have a minimum of information about what is available at what price. At the audio-visual level of communication, such information will be acquired through visiting a market, looking at shops, talking to a broker, listening in *tavernas*, pubs, coffee shops or teahouses, attending to television commercials. At the manuscript level of communication, information will be acquired through written signs, logos, hand-copied offers of goods and services, chalked-up price lists, private correspondence. At the print level of communication, information is acquired through books, catalogues, duplicated handbills, newspaper advertisements, specialist brochures and so on. All this information is acquired, at least ostensibly, not for itself, but with a view to a purchase, though in fact the brochure may be more enjoyable than the holiday, browsing more profitable than buying, so that what starts as a means may finish as an end. Cookbooks are sometimes better than meals.

For the supplier, information is even more vital than for the buyer. An ill-informed buyer will end dissatisfied and out of pocket. An ill-informed supplier, unless subsidized, will end out of business. It is often asked what a business person is paid for: why the entrepreneur is not a mere middleman, parasite or exploiter. Entrepreneurship is primarily rewarded or penalized in accordance with its success or failure at risk taking. Risk taking, however, falls into two kinds – speculation and management – a distinction apparently ignored by Lloyds insurance in recent years. What distinguishes risk management from risk speculation is, precisely, information. The speculator relies on the mathematics: on the improbability of several parts of the spiral collapsing simultaneously. The manager relies on the facts: or rather, on the synthesis of a variety of disparate, but potentially interconnected facts. Mathematical probability is not the same as commercial risk. To suppose so, is to confuse the ideal with the real. What actually happens is always highly improbable, but its choice of improbabilities may be circumscribed by attention to information.

Michael Novak is particularly convincing in his account of the information synthesizing activities of the business person. Markets must be targeted, products designed, skills enlisted or trained, raw materials secured, competition identified, costs and benefits monitored, outlets arranged, customer feedback assessed, tax planned for and the financial environment borne in mind. Even for a simple product, such factors may stretch over several continents and involve a host of other independent variables. Business people will differ in individual motivations, but among them, delight in risk management for its own sake is common if not always avowed. Profit is secondary. It is only a speedometer, an indication that the business has been properly conducted over a period of time. To say that a business person seeks profit is no more illuminating than to say that he or she seeks to avoid loss. Both belong to the realm of *sine qua non*. As an example of the synthesis of information required in business, Novak takes the example of pencil manufacture. He writes:

> It does not ordinarily occur to theologians, but it is a matter of everyday experience to businessmen, that even so simple an object as a pencil is made up of elements of graphite, wood, metal, rubber, and lacquer (to mention only the most visible, and to leave aside others that only specialists knew about) which come from vastly separated parts of this earth. The knowledge and skills needed to prepare each one of these separate elements for the precise role they will play in the pencil represent a huge body of scientific and practical knowledge, which is almost certainly not present in the mind of any one individual, but is widely dispersed among researchers, managers, and workers in factories and work places in different parts of the world. All these factors of production – materials, knowledge, and skilled workers – must be brought together before anyone has a pencil in his hands.[4]

Information is the universal resource.

The second way in which information entered into consumerism was as end. What for most buyers and suppliers most of the time was a means to desirable commodities, for others, or even all part of the time, was a desirable commodity in itself. Information as consumerist end may be found at each of the levels constituted by the three primary means of communication: speech, script and print. At the level of speech, gossip, scandal and news might be enjoyed for their own sake at the gymnasium, the ancient baths, the symposium; at the pilgrims' hostel, the alehouse, the barber's, the geisha house; at the club or the hairdresser's; in the salon, the lobby, the common room, the vestry, the waiting room. Richard Rorty was not the first to discover conversation as an end in itself. At the level of script, information might be acquired for more than practical purposes in a variety of manuscript collections: in the libraries of Alexandria and Pergamum, in monastic scriptoria, princely *kitabhane*, clerical *madrasa*, or in the libraries open to the public in Yang-chou, Chinkiang and Hang-chou where the Ch'ien-lung emperor placed copies of his *Ssu-k'u ch'uan-shu*. In all literate societies, private correspondence has been enjoyed for its own sake: as witness papyri from Graeco-Roman Egypt, wood and paper from fourth-century Lou-lan. Marshall McCluhan was not the first to discover that the medium was the message. At the level of print, which lifted the limitation of manuscript copying, there could emerge the full panoply of *incunabula*, pamphlets, handbills, newsletters, court circulars, law reports, official gazettes, condensations of memorials, almanacs of lucky and unlucky days, newspapers, journals, company reports, political manifestos, religious tracts, which might be read as much for curiosity as utility. The library was more than a record office. Whether in the Vatican, the Bodleian, the Ambrosian, the Hanlin academy or the *shu-yüan* of the Lower Yangtze or Canton, the library was a window on a wider world and not just an extended set of yellow pages. Elizabeth Eisenstein was not the first to discover that print was more than mechanization.

Unlike information as a means, whose reasons for acquisition were almost endless, information acquired as end may be classified under four broad categories. First, it was acquired as religious message, whether in speech, script or print. Not all religions, however, had messages to deliver. Some, or large parts of some, were unthematized religions primarily of cult, in which explanations in terms of myth, history or philosophy were secondary and optional. Such were many of the temple cults of classical antiquity. Much of Indian religion was like this, as was the widely diffused cult of places and occasions in China which is sometimes called Sinism on the analogy with Hinduism. Even unthematized religion, however, might produce information desired as end rather than means, in the shape of amulets, almanacs and guides to various mantic practices. It has been calculated, for example, that the publication in China of the annual imperial almanac was the largest, regular, single printing operation of the eighteenth century: over two million copies, not to speak of authorized private and pirated editions.[5] Among thematized religions with a message to deliver, there were significant differences in its length and complexity which affected the character of their consumption. In early medieval China, following the invention of print, Buddhist scholasticisms, such as T'ien-t'ai and Hua-yen, with their huge patrologies and critical metaphysics, lost out, either to simpler or less textual forms of Buddhism such as Ching-t'u, Chen-yen or Ch'an, or to a revived Confucianism with its shorter but now more accessible Canon. Contrariwise, it may have been the very simplicity of the message of Islam, rather than any reluctance to translate the Koran, which led the Muslim world to neglect for so long the opportunities afforded by print. Where Mahayana Buddhism had too much theology, Islam, despite the elaborations of *kalam*, had too little. Within Christendom too, distinctions might be drawn between complex Catholicism and simple Protestantism, Hellenized eastern Orthodoxy and unlettered oriental Dissent. Here, Protestantism initially had the advantage in print, as Elizabeth Eisenstein shows, but its long-term tendency to bifurcate into modernism and fundamentalism, neither with a rich message, put it eventually at a disadvantage.[6]

Second, information as end was acquired as culture in the sense of the classical *paideia* or what the Chinese called *wen*. The Confucian classics were always read more for vocabulary, style and mind-set than for content whether exegetical or hermeneutic. They were absorbed as cultural patina, especially after the establishment of the imperial examinations by the Sui and their reinvigoration by Empress Wu. Oral repetition and memorization formed an essential part of the Chinese primary school, as they did in the Koranic *mekteb* or in pre-Petrine Russian education where learning to read meant memorizing one book, then another. In the early days of the examination system, the increased demand for texts was met, as in the medieval university in the West, by more manuscript. From the ninth century, we have the name of a famous female copyist T'ang Ts'ai-lun, who produced books for civil service candidates.[7] In 932, during the Five Dynasties period and following the temporary conquest by the north of Szechwan where xylography had been developed under Buddhist auspices, a set of Confucian classics was printed at Kaifeng with the support of the imperial ministers Feng Tao and Li Yü.[8] A further edition followed in Szechwan itself in 944, to be followed by innumerable later ones, as, from the Sung period, the Confucian classics became the criterion not merely for civil service entry, but for membership of the *shih*, the scholar gentry. It was not so different in the West with humanism. The little renaissances, Carolingian and twelfth-century, made use of monastic scriptoria to republish texts valued as concomitants of political and intellectual revival. The Great Renaissance, the systematic replacement of the specialist literature of antiquity by its generalist literature, made use of Gutenberg's invention (or rather borrowing from the Chinese) which had been developed primarily to serve the needs of late medieval religion, the *pietas literata* of the Rhineland with its psalters, books of devotion and indulgences. Like the Confucian classics, *literae humaniores* were both means and end. How Chinese is Dean Gaisford's commendation of Greek as 'serving to elevate above the vulgar herd, and not infrequently leading to positions of considerable emolument'! His near contemporary Ch'ien Ta-hsin, another good college man, would have enjoyed that.

Third, information was acquired for scientific ends. It was acquired as a result of what Bernard Lonergan called the *eros* of *logos*, the unrestricted desire to know. Science has always been an end in itself quite apart from its utility, which is often small. Since its character is inherently intellectual, it is a fit subject for consumerism. As such it has always been sought by its connoisseurs by any means of communication available. Popper showed that early Greek cosmology was best understood as an ongoing debate, often conducted in actual discourse and dialogue. The same was true of early Buddhist scholasticism. In Christian scholasticism, the disputation remained central to assessment till the Jesuits introduced the written examination from China in the seventeenth century. In medieval Paris, *quaestiones disputatae* made good copy but the dialogue, as used by Eriugena and Anselm (as later by Berkeley), became a literary convention subordinate to script. Anselm, indeed, in the *Cur Deus Homo*, complained of the pressure he was under from the copyists who were threatening to put out incomplete, and therefore misleading, versions of his work. When print came to Europe, scholastic science, for example Mertonian mechanics, fared less well, though it was one of the currents which flowed into Galileo, but its successors were not immediate publishing successes either. Of the 352 books printed at Valladolid between 1481 and 1600, only 23 can be classified as science, most of them medicine. Yet Pedro Enrique, professor of philosophy at the university and a true universal man, who died in 1584, had a library of 852 books. Medicine embraced 234 titles, metals and alchemy 14 and mathematics 14, while the authors included Vesalius, Fallopius and Agricola. Enrique was a person of insatiable curiosity. It was the same in China. Medicine was the branch of science which sold best. Li Shih-chen's pharmaceutical treatise, the *Pen-ts'ao kang-mu* was first published in 1596. It was twice republished under the Ming and went through 15 editions under the Ch'ing. It was a philosophy of medicine as well as a pharmacopeia, and it was bought by scholars who had no intention of being clinicians. Innovative science has to create its own market. The *Traümdeutung* initially sold only a few hundred copies and made little impression. Yet the desire to know is widespread, as witness the publishing success of Stephen Hawking's *A Brief History of Time*.

Fourth, information was acquired as an element in dignity: in what Francis Fukuyama calls *thymia*, whether the *megalothymia* of the aristocrat or the *isothymia* of the democrat. Knowledge and the right to convey it have always been an element in status. In pre-literate Maori society, ability to speak well on the *marae* was an acknowledged source of prestige. Lévi-Strauss has one Matto Grosso chief asserting his leadership by pretending to literacy, another by acting as the rhapsode of an improvised epic. Similarly, Jack Goody has argued that 'where writing is, "class" cannot be far away'.[9] In China, texts such as the *Lu Pan Ching* were ritual as well as technological. Constantly reprinted, it served to assert the dignity of the carpenters' craft within the world of literacy, specifically within the tradition of *wu-hsing* or five processes, going back to the philosopher Tsou Yen. Again, Chinese medical literature sought to distinguish between scholar doctors (*Ju-i*), common physicians (*yung-i*) and itinerant healers (*ling-i*).[10] Similarly, in the medieval West, the 'mastery' of crafts easily got transmuted into the 'mystery' of guilds and a pretension to dignity via arcana: a tradition still alive in some branches of trade unionism. Megalothymia, indeed, is no stranger in the university. No police on campus, liberty of expression and protest, entitlement to expose official secrets, a duty to comment on public affairs: all these are aristocratic demands for informational privilege which would have been familiar to a medieval baronage. Isothymias too in their assertion of equality have an informational component. The Virago Press did much for feminism. The emergence of the special category of children's books helped free the young from being regarded simply as inferior adults. A literature of *négritude* is part of the black awakening. The massive literature of the Holocaust serves more than historical curiosity, just as the movie *Philadelphia* was not just concerned with an employment tort. Victims seek redress in information, just as the privileged seek address.

Levels of Information

Potential information, actual information used as means and ends in consumption and consumerism, add up to the level of information of individuals and societies. Since the level of information as a factor in historical development is commonly underrated, before looking at it in Europe and China it will be useful to illustrate the notion with reference to a third area in between: the world of Islam and, specifically, the Ottoman empire in the early modern period.

Islamdom long enjoyed a privileged position in information. It occupied the crossroads of three continents. It formed a larger free trade area than China. It actively promoted the growth of cities. It both conserved classical learning and created more of its own. It had its own script, two international languages in Arabic and Persian, and introduced Chinese paper to replace Egyptian papyrus. Yet, as Ibn Khaldun observed, moments of Islamic enlightenment were brief compared to those of the Franks and the Cathayans. Over time, the handicaps of Islam's position reasserted themselves: diverse legacies to accommodate, multiple challenges to respond to, overextension and under-intensification. Muslim attitudes to birth control, especially in the 'bad times' so widely perceived as prevalent in the period following the Mongol invasions, did not encourage a strong demography. Islamdom, unlike Christendom, did not fight back against plague with quarantine.[11] Islam itself, a religion without a theology, did not communicate sufficiently. Paper was absorbed but not print except among the Hui within the print culture of China.[12] Muslim cities might remain splendid, but, like their classical antecedents, they had become parasitic on their countrysides. By 1400, Islamdom suffered from both a population and an information problem. It drew less benefit than Europe or China from the new basic information circuit set up by the Mongolian explosion. Where Marco Polo became a bestseller, Ibn Battuta remained in an archive.

The Ottoman empire promised solutions. Born on the Anatolian frontier, its liberal dervish orders, the Bektashiyya and the Mevleviyya offered, if not a theology, then a gnosis and a mysticism. The *Mesnevi* of Celaleddin Rumi did not need print to become a bestseller. Transplanted to the Rumelian frontier between Latin and Greek Christendom, the new Ottoman system of privileged slavery, as grounded in the *devsirme* or compulsory recruitment from the Christian population, supplied the answer to both the population and information problems. Christendom should be conquered by its own Slav manpower, its own German artillery technology which it had recently borrowed from the Chinese or the Mamluks. Alternatively, power could be carried from Rumelia to Anatolia and the Arabic and Persian worlds beyond, and, who knew, to China itself, as suggested by Ali Ekber to Selim I. In the sixteenth century, compulsory recruitment was extended by slave trading and slave raiding. Trade, conducted through the khanate of Crimea and the sultanate of Bornu, brought brawn and beauty: black slaves and eunuchs, Ukrainian heavies and Circassian concubines. But raid, conducted through the Barbary pirates, provided the crucial brains: Italian, Spanish, Portuguese, French, English and Flemish, as has been extensively documented by Bartolomé and Lucile Bennassar. It was these people, who amounted to as many Europeans who went to America in its first century, who brought European expertise to the Ottoman empire at only minimum cost to itself. The golden age of the Ottoman empire, and of the Islamic world under its leadership, was thus founded on privileged slavery and the induced brain-drain of renegation. Constantinople was dependent on Algiers, the centre on the periphery.

Yet, in the longer run, the Ottoman promise could not be kept, and largely because of failure of information. Externally, as the Christian defence improved, costs at Algiers rose and profits fell. The Turkish leadership there began to invest in the land rather than the sea, the army rather than the navy. Much renegation had been voluntary, but now, better instructed by the Reformations, Christians were more reluctant to convert, more likely to try to escape. Christendom was richer, possibly more meritocratic. Algiers no longer beckoned as Eldorado or Utopia. Internally, as power shifted from the sultans and the seraglio to an oligarchy of *evkaf* beneficiaries and trustees, the Ottoman empire ceased to be an opportunity state. When the Janissaries could marry and their sons succeed, the *devsirme* crumbled because no new slaves were needed. Moreover, the open, meritocratic mafias of Serbs, Croats and Italians were replaced in the days of the Koprulus by a closed, hereditary mafia of Albanians. If the empire needed information, it had to turn either to foreign advisers, French or Austrian, for whom renegation became increasingly a formality, or to its own non-Muslim subjects in the Orthodox, Armenian and Jewish *millets*.

Thus the Ottoman system gradually unravelled. Even in its heyday, its information circuits had been unsatisfactory. Between 1513 and 1675 only half a dozen works relating to the Great Discoveries had been published and then only in short runs.[13] Print, abortively and temporarily introduced for Greek type in 1627 by Cyril Lucaris, was finally provided for Ottoman Turkish in Arabic script in the relatively liberal Tulip period of Ahmet III, 1703–30, through the activities of a Hungarian renegade, ex-Calvinist or Unitarian, but only non-religious works were published and not many of them. Ottoman printing compared badly to that of their co-religionists in China. It was not until the nineteenth century and the publications in Ottoman Turkish pushed forward by the interpreters' office, the Phanariot community, and even some Albanian intellectuals, that the level of information began to rise significantly. Till then, the Sick Man of Europe had been starved of knowledge more than material goods. Information was at the heart of the long cycle of Ottoman history, as it was in the histories of Europe and China in the same period.

ESSENTIALS: SPEECH AND THE SPOKEN WORD

That, in the period 1400–1800, speech was the essential means of communication, is far from self-evident. True, palaeontologists claim that speech is the only specific human attribute and constitutive of humanity. Man makes the word and the word makes man. Speech and enlarged vocal chords came before enlarged brain size. Evidence for speech long antedates evidence for script and print. Three million years ago, its existence may be inferred from the complexity of tools whose making must have required explanation as well as imitation. Similarly, the palaeolithic juxtaposition of hunting, gathering and fishing seem to demand verbal pre-planning and words of command in execution. All the more, neolithic agriculture and pastoralism would have been impossible without highly developed linguistic skills. One does not have to go all the way with Lévi-Strauss's argument that humanity only built big at the beginning to acknowledge the primordiality of speech in this sense. Moreover, it could be argued that speech was the essential and only possible basis for script and print. Even Chinese characters, partially independent of sound like our number system, presuppose speech. For the most part, they are logographs not ideographs. Supporters of sign, like Oliver Sacks, claim that it is as subtle and sophisticated as speech, and we have all known people whose shrug or hand movement was more eloquent than words. But if all human beings had been born deaf and dumb, script, in order to represent sign, would have taken different paths, perhaps closer to mathematical notation. It might have been longer in coming and found more difficulty in standardization. Modern sign, of course, has overcome these problems, but only through the aid of conventional script and print based on spoken languages. Speech was fundamental to communication and remains so today. Nevertheless, it must be accepted that the primacy of speech has been profoundly affected by script and print, as both Derrida and Jack Goody have argued, and as was always recognized by the Confucian tradition of the primacy of the written language.[14]

First, wherever literacy existed, language and words based on it became divided, sometimes sharply, between spoken and written. In the case of Chinese, the distinction between *pai-hua* (vernacular) and *wen-yen* (the literary language) was within a single language, though *wen-yen* had its own vocabulary, grammar and syntax. In early Roman Egypt, Latin and Greek were both spoken and written, but, between the decline of Demotic script and the rise of Coptic in the third century AD, Egyptian was only spoken.[15] Similarly, in the early West European Middle Ages, the clerical technostructure spoke and wrote Latin, while, with exceptions in Anglo-Saxon England, the Romance and Germanic vernaculars were only spoken. Again, in the fourteenth century, the chancery language of the grand duchy of Lithuania was Church Slavonic. Later, following the union of Krevo, it became first Latin and then Polish. Lithuanian itself was only written in the sixteenth century as a result of the Reformation. Subsequently, as the Lithuanian aristocracy plumped for Catholicism and Polonization, it went into abeyance and had to be reinvented as a literary language by intellectuals in the romantic period. Similar reinventions were required for Estonian, Latvian, Belarus and Ukrainian. Script and print created inequalities among languages. Languages not written or printed tended to decay and become incapable of conveying the full panoply of modern information. Speech without script, as in the case of some kinds of inner city Black English, becomes potentially an ignorance and poverty trap.

Second, script, especially as reinforced by print, has altered speech by changing the notion of information. Goody argues that Homer may have been written down before the traditional date of 750 BC, because the current text is not purely oral in character. It shows signs of circumambient literacy. Similarly, the Serbo-Croat rhapsodes, whose performances Parry and Lord saw as latter-day prototypes for Homeric composition, were, though illiterate themselves, part of a world where literacy was known. Literacy altered orality by introducing into information the notions of documentary reference, exact reproducibility and comparison, together with allied notions such as storage, incrementality, selection, condensation, etc. Involved were an ascendancy of the visual over the aural in communication and a shift from the temporal to the spatial in what was communicated. For speech, the medium of communication was performance, which involved duration. The response to it was a collective 'hear, hear'. For script, the medium of communication was presentation, which might be instantaneous. The response to it was an individual 'I see'. For script, reality was out there and to know was to replicate. Against speech's diachronic, quantum interplay of subject and object, script insisted on a synchronic, classical separation of the two. Speech must tell it as it is, or be content to remain silent. Wittgenstein's dictum falls into a long tradition of the intimidation of speech by script. Neither Schrödinger's riposte 'but that's when the discussion gets interesting', nor Rorty's insistence that the job of philosophy is to keep the conversation going, have restored speech's self-esteem.

Third, as a result, speech itself became partially scripted. Exact repetition was demanded of witnesses. Dramatic performance should be by the book and not ad-libbed. Recollection must photocopy and not reinterpret. Often pronunciation meekly followed spelling as when Pomfret turned into Pontefract or Parnell was given a different stress. Script gave speech an inferiority complex. Put it in writing, watch the fine print, an unwritten agreement is not worth the paper it is not written on: verbal indications of the constraints which script and print have imposed on speech. As the Chinese, the least oral of people, say: 'The strongest memory is weaker than the palest ink', and, as historians, we can only agree.

If a case is to be made for the ongoing primacy of speech, it must be from within a wider or deeper perspective. First, whatever the subordination to script and print, speech has remained the most widely used form of communication. The spoken word retains the lead in quantity, not least with regard to the consumerism of food and dress. A high percentage of information is conveyed by conversation.

Second, as regards quality too, speech was crucial to information, both at the beginning and at the end. At the beginning, reality was effectively speech-constituted. Gadamer contended in an interview: 'Language is a centre where I and the world come together.'[16] Elsewhere he wrote: 'Language is not just one of man's possessions in the world, but on it depends the fact that man has a world at all ... this world is linguistic in nature.'[17] Speech turns private thought into public assertion. Unlike script and print which do the same, it is open to immediate contradiction, interpretation and qualification in interlocution. As Gadamer wrote: 'Language is the middle ground in which understanding and agreement concerning the object takes place between two people.'[18] If speech was at the beginning in the initial enunciation, it was also at the end in the final refinement. Speech is the hermeneuticist of last resort. Script and print address the past and privilege exegesis: original meaning in author, text or audience. Speech addresses the present and privileges hermeneutics: current meaning between persons, the contemporary now which can never be wholly taken out of knowledge. Theologians may argue, diatribes be exchanged, pamphlets be thrown at one another, but finally the Council of Trent must meet, even if its authority is no greater than that of the Pope by himself. Similarly, diplomats can prepare, position papers be put out, and drafts circulated, but only the summit can decide, whether at Tilsit or Reykjavik.

Finally, speech remained primary in information because of its laicity. The spoken word was the enemy of jargon, professional arcana and closed clericalism, all sometimes befriended by script and print. It stood for limpidity, open discourse and the need for laicization, if the flow of information was not to be interrupted. Technical language must exist, obscurity cannot always be avoided, especially when new intellectual ground is being broken, but vernacular should not be lost sight of, and the spoken word, the need to communicate face-to-face, keeps it in view. Moreover, if communication is to be universal, it must be to the pre-literate in childhood and the post-literate in age. Speech has not been made redundant by script and print. Its ongoing services to information in scale, initiation, completion and universalization are rooted in the character of cognition. Knowledge may expand to infinity, but it will always end in an interface of persons and speech. Speech is the essential means of communication because of its perpetual circumambience. It may no longer be the centre, but it is the eternal periphery.

Enquiry may now be made about the role of oral communication in consumerism in Europe and China in the early modern period. Here one finds both a similarity and two differences.

A development common to Europe and China, which underlines the continuing role of the spoken word even in expanding print culture, was the raised profile of drama. The role of the theatre and the opera house in the constitution of public space has already been touched on in relation to dress and the rise of fashion in the West. Here their role in the diffusion of information generally needs to be brought into focus. For the West, those who stress the revolutionary effects of print often neglect drama. They overlook the fact that of the bestsellers of the sixteenth and seventeenth centuries, those which remain steady sellers refer to the spoken word. Luther's pamphlets no longer trip off the presses, the Tridentine catechism has been superseded, the Authorized Version ends its shelf life, and Copernicus has joined Ptolemy, but new editions of Shakespeare, Marlowe, Lope de Vega, Corneille, Racine and Molière continue to fill publishers' lists. Contemporaries may have felt the same. Pepys, civil servant, intellectual, man about town, expends as many lines on the plays he saw as on the books he read. It was the same in China where Peking opera, a synthesis of metropolitan and provincial music drama, reached its classic form in the Ch'ing period.

In China, where the stage was less literized, it was actors rather than authors who took the lead in the expansion of drama. Drama, however, was probably more widely diffused than it was in Europe. It was not only urban but rural as well. Where religion and drama in Europe had been at odds since the days of St Augustine and, except in Jesuit schools and some Latin American evangelization, became further dissociated in the early modern period, in China they were closely associated. Temple festivals were accompanied by theatrical performance. James Hayes, in his account of the 'kaifongs' (*chieh-fang*) or neighbourhood associations of the Hong Kong area, says: 'they were required to make all the arrangements for the opera and puppet performances that were a prime requirement of major religious rituals, whether at the community, clan branch or rich family level'. On Pengchou island, with its mixed Hoklo, Tanka, Hakka and Cantonese population, the opera season at the T'ien-hou temple lasted five weeks during a lull in the fishing calendar. Similarly, at Cheung Sha Wan on the mainland: 'The temples provided village people with a traditional and very welcome break with daily routine through the opera shows that were held there at different festival times of the year. At the San T'ai Tzu opera performances were held for the traditional four nights and five days at the time of the god's birthday in the third moon.' Hayes noted that, 'At such times the temple environs and the adjoining beaches were packed with people from the surrounding area.' In conclusion, he remarked: 'Love of the theatre linked different classes which were otherwise poles apart. The Dowager Empress in her palace, the judge or magistrate in his Yamen, the soldiers in the adjoining barracks, shared this common passion.'[19] Indeed, for the empress-dowager, the theatre was more than a passion. Theatre parties were a means of faction-building and theatricality an instrument of government.

In both Europe and China, the expansion of drama represented a counterattack by speech against script and print. In Tudor England, many playwrights and theatre groups were associated with crypto-Catholic patrons, Catholicism then being a religion of less radical literacy than Protestantism, strongest in backward areas such as Lancashire and among groups with a higher than average illiteracy such as women.[20] On the Continent, the nearest equivalent to Chinese popular music drama was local opera and puppet shows in Italy: the world of *Pagliacci* and *Cavalleria Rusticana*. These were often associated, especially in the Mezzogiorno, with areas of high illiteracy, but strong oral culture, as for example in the emotional preaching of the early Redemptorist fathers. What was different was the context. In Europe, literacy, newly reinforced by print, was expanding. To assert itself, drama had to adopt literary forms: emphasize authors rather than actors, take humanist subjects (especially in France), and go into folio as soon as possible.

In China, literacy depotentiated by shifts in population, was contracting. To gain an audience, drama had only to appeal to a lower level of literacy by taking subjects from folkloric history and presenting characters from traditional street story-telling. In Europe, orality was fighting a rear-guard action, until relieved by the movie and the video. In China, orality was on the offensive, until checked by *pai-hua* novelettes and, less enduring, the fundamentalism of the Little Red Book.

Because of this difference, the theatre was more ideological in China than in Europe. It is difficult to find ideology in Shakespeare, even in the *Histories*. The connections of the Elizabethan stage with crypto-Catholicism and opposition to Cecil are tenuous. Sheridan was a Whig, but one would not have known it from the plays. When Shaw packaged socialism in wit, Edwardian audiences accepted the medium, but filtered out the messages as idiosyncrasy. Not only must the theatre entertain, it could not be allowed to do anything else. In China, however, popular drama could give rise to political movements. Joseph Esherick has shown that the Boxer movement of 1900 was closely related to operas performed at local temples in western Shantung, especially in its characteristic practice of spirit possession. He writes: 'the gods by which the Boxers were possessed were all borrowed from these operas'.[21] The Spirit Boxers were not sectarians, martial arts people, or would-be militia. They began as stage-struck teenagers, then became amateur performers, and finally, professionals. They ended as a loose movement, with minimal, if hydra-headed, leadership by charisma, which was susceptible of takeover by officials, imperial princes and eventually the empress-dowager herself, who were accustomed to theatrical patronage. The Boxer message, like that of the popular dramas, was patriotic, historical, anti-foreign, and especially anti-Christianity: the religion of the book and the school. Boxerdom produced a political movement because as Esherick says, 'There is no strict functional division between religion and theatre in Chinese society', and because in China orality was on the attack.[22] In the West, the nearest equivalent to Spirit Boxerdom has been the Afro-Brazilian *candomblé* and *umbanda*, which figure so dramatically in Umberto Eco's *Foucault's Pendulum*. These, however, have not yet given rise to such a movement.

One major development of European speech culture in the early modern period, however, had no parallel in China. This was the rise of vernacular languages so that they could become the vehicle of literature. The requisite standardization and refinement are often attributed to script in general and print in particular, but the counter-example of China suggests that these were not the only factors involved. For in China, script and print did not produce a refined spoken language, nor, till the twentieth century, much vernacular literature. True, there were reasons. Characters being, like our numbers, independent of sound, produce a wider gap between spoken and written than does an alphabet. The spoken language tended to become what Achilles Fang called baby talk. Consequently, China had no tradition of oratory and rhetoric. Moreover, since the unity of the empire depended on its single but unvocalized language, there was little political incentive for the development of vernaculars. Nevertheless, vernacular literature existed in medicine and the theatre. Philosophy had a tradition of *ch'ing-t'ao* or written repartee. Ch'an Buddhism combined the literary and the oral in its records of sayings, dialogue and performance. All these might have given rise to a *pai-hua* movement. In neither China nor Europe do the purely technological explanations convince. In Europe, the rise of vernaculars was due not only to print, but also to purely oral social institutions: dinner parties, salons, sermons, parliamentary debate, symposia, coffee-house chatter, talk in hairdressers' and barbers' shops. Here, one of the big differences from China was the greater presence and participation of women. Women, it may be suggested, are better conversationalists than men. The eighteenth-century feminization of so many speech occasions was a major reason for the refinement of vernacular languages. Moreover, many of the occasions, the salon and the dinner party especially, were opportunities in particular for the consumerism of information as means and end. For once one is past health and the weather, food, dress and houses are natural topics of conversation, while exchange of news, scandal and gossip is an end in itself. The sociability permitted to women in Europe united orality and literacy, while its absence in China, until the twentieth century, kept them apart.

A second development in Europe, this time in the audio-aural sphere, which had no parallel in China, was the rise of polyphony and the perfection of new musical instruments. Historians, with the exception of Charles Morazé, have commonly underestimated the significance of music in the creation of meaning and hence as a factor in consumerism.[23] Anthropologists and philosophers have done better. Lévi-Strauss argued that music was the modern mythology, but endowed with greater interiority and universality. He wrote, 'music has its being in me, and I listen to myself through it'. It is, he continued, 'a language with some meaning at least for the immense majority of mankind . . . the only language with the contradictory attributes of being at once intelligible and untranslatable'.[24] Popper drew a parallel between polyphony and scientific method: 'Thus musical and scientific creation seem to have this much in common: the use of dogma or myth as a man-made path along which we move into the unknown, exploring the world, both creating regularities or rules and probing for existing regularities.'[25] Plainsong represented the initial dogma, counterpoint the subsequent alternative. The difference was that where music sought harmony between different voices, science sought to resolve their contradiction by appeal to the evidence. Both, however, dealt in contingent alternatives. If polyphony anticipated theory, the perfection of instruments anticipated practice in industrial technology. Similarly the multiplicity of sounds produced by a full orchestra prefigured the multiplicity of goods produced by an advanced economy. Music may be intransitive, that is, refer only to itself, and be untranslatable, as Lévi-Strauss says, but a relationship to consumerism is not thereby excluded. Many shops and restaurants, especially those catering for the young, find it worthwhile to provide music, presumably to increase sales, as acoustic excitement incites the thrill of purchase. Music mimics consumerism in two further ways: its capacity for indefinite expansion and variation, and its combination of enduring classics and perpetual innovation, often through exoticism. In the T'ang period, China had borrowed both instruments and scores from Central Asia, but from the Sung to the Republic, China entered a period of musical self-sufficiency. Moreover, though polyphony may have been less unique to the West and Chinese music less traditional than Popper imagined, Chinese musicologists have not yet come up with a change on the scale of the West. In 1596, the Ming prince Chu Tsai-yü formulated the mathematics of equal temperament, but no Bach followed and no revolution in the quality and quantity of the musical component of essential aural/oral culture.

ACCESSORIES: SCRIPT AND THE WRITTEN WORD

In drama, vernacular refinement and music, Europe and China showed divergences, but, it could be argued, minor ones. In the culture of the written word, however, there was a more major divergence. In 1400, perhaps in 1600, China was ahead of Europe in both male and female literacy. In 1800, perhaps in 1700, Europe was ahead of China, particularly in the matter of female literacy. In this great leap forward, the introduction of print to Europe was no doubt significant, but its long presence in China without comparable effects suggests that other factors were involved. In particular, one may wonder whether changes in manuscript culture may not have been at least as important: notably, increased writing of letters. Manuscript did not disappear with print any more than orality disappeared with literacy. In addition to letters, private and public, there were written examinations, tax returns, school exercises, ledgers, ballot papers, and all the multifarious uses of the signature, today more important than ever in the world of the credit card and the cashless society. Moreover, script, unlike print, demands active writing as well as passive reading. The prose is a better test of linguistic mastery than the unseen. The present section, therefore, considers manuscript culture: its conditions and consequences.

Conditions

An active script culture needed more than a writing system. It needed writing materials, writing implements and some degree of orthography, punctuation, and calligraphy. Script culture is an assemblage. In Europe and China they were assembled somewhat differently.

First, the writing systems themselves. In 1400, both the Western alphabet and the Chinese characters were old: over 4000 years in the case of the alphabet, at least 3000 years in that of the characters. Yet neither was immobile. The Romans had not possessed a musical notation. Indian numerals, unlike Chinese, lacked a zero. In the West, *scriptura continua*, which encouraged slow vocalization rather than rapid silent reading, was only regularly replaced by the separation of words in the Dark Ages by Irish and Anglo-Saxon scribes less familiar with Latin.[26] Punctuation in Europe did not become anything like standardized till Aldus Manutius. It was only fully adopted by the Chinese under Western influence in the twentieth century. By 1400, however, the two writing systems were fixed in the basic difference of their principles: phonetic in the one case, logographic in the other. Moreover, their situation had long been different. Disregarding minor derivates such as Tangut and Khitan, moribund if not dead, the characters were one throughout China and had been exported to Korea, Japan and Vietnam. Alphabets, however, were many. Christendom was divided between Latin, Greek and Cyrillic, not to mention Syriac, Coptic, Georgian, Armenian and Arabic. As Braudel liked to say, one-half of the Mediterranean wrote from left to right, the other half from right to left. In 1400, Arabic script, used not only for itself but for Persian, Turkish and Malay, looked to have a more hopeful future than the Latin alphabet, but Chinese characters were even more widely written, as students crowded into the Ming examination halls.

It is sometimes supposed that the Chinese characters inhibited mass literacy. Early European travellers certainly did not think so. Mendoza noted that in China, 'there is none, although he be never so poor, but doth learn to write and read, because amongst them he is accounted infamous who cannot do both'. Semedo thought high literacy was one of the most admirable qualities of China. Having compared the 50 000 characters to European numbers, he continued, 'almost all have some skill in them, at least as much as is sufficient for the exercise of their trades'. Father Magellan thought that literacy was 'universal', at least in the south. Modern research suggests that it only takes Chinese children a little longer to read and write than Western children. Once learnt, moreover, a non-phonetic script encourages fast and silent reading more than does an alphabetical script. Further, in the absence of an index, characters, especially the more complicated, are easier to locate on a page than alphabetically written words. Where characters do have disadvantages are in the transcription of foreign words and in the formation of neologisms, but neither prevented the Chinese from absorbing Sanskrit terminology from Buddhism, or from producing a new scientific vocabulary in the modern age. In compensation, the characters' relative independence of sound carried, what seemed to the Chinese, two considerable advantages: preservation of the unity of China and openness to the literature of antiquity, whatever the changes in the spoken language. It is not clear that for these advantages China had to pay a price in lower literacy.

Second, writing materials. Here China had already made an immense contribution by the invention of paper. According to tradition, the technology of paper was transmitted to the West by the Chinese prisoners taken by the Abbasid caliphate when Ziyad ben Salih defeated Kao Hsien-chih at the battle of the Talas river in western Turkestan in 751. Too much should not be derived from this single episode. Sogdian had been written on paper since the fourth century, paper was produced in Turfan in the fifth century and in the seventh century the Koran mentions paper, using a word of Chinese origin. The transfer reflected a wider pattern of intra-Eurasian exchange at that time, which included unwanted items such as the first plague pandemic and the diffusion of smallpox. But the results ascribed to the Talas river were considerable. Papyrus went into decline. Paper mills appeared all over Islamdom: at Samarkand not long after the battle, at Baghdad in 794, at Cairo by the tenth century. From Islamdom, paper spread to Europe. It was used in Spain in 950, in Sicily, Europe's first bureaucratic monarchy, in 1102. Paper was manufactured in 1150 at Jativa, then still Moorish, between Valencia and Alicante, then at Fabriano, between Perugia and Ancona, where Appenine water power was employed in the early stages of the process. Paper-making became a Europe-wide industry: Bologna, the lawyers' capital, in 1293, Basle 1423, Crakow 1491. Yet China long retained a primacy. Before most Europeans had seen a piece of paper, Chinese in the late Yüan had experienced the horrors of hyperinflation of a paper currency. Ricci thought paper was more widely used in China than anywhere else, while Semedo said that its production exceeded that of the rest of the world. Early European paper, like early Chinese, was made from rags, though in its case, from linen or cotton rather than silk or hemp. Fresh plant fibre, one of Ts'ai Lun's innovations in the second century and a major facilitator of mass supply, only began to be used in Europe at the beginning of the eighteenth century. Wood pulp, suggested by Réaumur, did not become dominant till the early nineteenth century. In China, because of shortage of timber, wood pulp was never substituted for bamboo and paper mulberry. Unlike China again, paper in Europe was intended from the beginning for writing. From 1630, however, a factory in Rouen began making the Chinese-style wallpaper which became so popular in eighteenth-century Europe as an ingredient in Rococo. Other consumerist applications, as in packaging and hygiene, followed soon after. By 1800, Europe, like China, was a paper-dependent civilization.

Paper was crucial in the circulation of information by script and by print. In Europe, printers preferred it to parchment because of its greater flexibility and its availability encouraged publishers to switch from manuscript to print. Mechanization of paper production at the end of the eighteenth century lowered the cost of books. In 1740 paper was 20 per cent of book production. In 1910, it had fallen to 7 per cent. Mechanization and wood pulp were not the only factors involved. In the early nineteenth century, the greater availability of chlorine bleach, a by-product of the Leblanc process for soda manufacture and of developments in the textile industries, allowed printed rags to be used as raw materials as well as unprinted. None of these factors was paralleled in China at that time. Paper remained a handicraft, a mainly rural sideline industry. In his survey of Szechwan in 1904, Hosie described five raw materials in use: rice straw, a kind of reed, bamboo, the paper mulberry, and a *fatsia* used particularly in so-called rice paper. Manufacture was widely diffused as it was in next-door Kweichow. Though this lack of development may have saved China the ecological problems associated with modern paper mills elsewhere, it meant that, when rising literacy increased demand, it had to be met by imports. By then, immense disparities had opened up between China and the outside world in a key indicator of the supply and demand for information. In the mid-twentieth century, per capita consumption of paper in China was 2 lb a year compared to Japan's 100 lb and the United States' 300 lb. Though not all paper in advanced economies is used as a means of communication, most communication, outside the oral sphere, requires paper as its medium. China had invented paper, but had not made full use of it, and therefore, as both cause and effect, suffered from information deficiency.

Third, writing implements. Here the most significant development, between the perfection of the quill and the brush and the invention of the ball point, was not the patrician fountain pen, but the plebeian pencil.[27] This was Europe's particular contribution to early modern script culture, though East Asia also played a part.

The pencil – mineral enclosed in vegetable for the purpose of writing – was an assemblage. Its epicentre, however, was Protestant Germany and in particular the Nuremberg of the printer Anton Koberger and the poet Hans Sachs, both humanist artisans. It was first described by Konrad Gesner of Zürich, bibliographer, naturalist and polymath, in a work published in 1565. Even at this stage the pencil had an international aspect. Gesner described the mineral as a kind of lead, which some called English antimony. Here Gesner was wrong. The lead pencil had at its heart, not *plumbum*, but *plumbago*: graphite from Borrowdale in Cumberland, where Keswick subsequently became a centre of pencil production. Till the late seventeenth century, however, most English graphite was exported to Nuremberg, where firms like Staedtler and Faber had become among the earliest international brand names. In the literate eighteenth century, raw materials began to run dry. In 1794, under pressure of wartime shortages and heightened revolutionary demands, Nicholas-Jacques Condé, in Paris, developed a process of graphite reconstitution which both relieved the situation and gave an improved product. Condé's process was adopted in Nuremberg once the Protestant city's conservatism had been reopened by its inclusion by Napoleon in 1806 in the Catholic kingdom of Bavaria. Minerals remained a problem till in 1847 a new source of graphite was discovered on the border between Siberia and Mongolia by Jean Pierre Alibert and brought on stream at Nuremberg in 1856. Wood was the next bottleneck until, by the end of the century, this was solved by the use of the incense cedar from southern Oregon and northern California. By 1900, half the world's pencils were made of American cedar, over a quarter of them in the United States. In 1912, the United States produced yearly eight pencils per capita of its population. The pencil thus successively involved German craft ingenuity, early English mines, French polytechnic improvisation, Mongolian graphite and Oregon pine. In this way a new edge was added to script culture. In 1987 world production of pencils amounted to 14 billion or about three per capita.

Consequences

Improved script, abundant paper and the pencil created a new situation as surely as did the printing press. Pencils extended the frontiers of script in three key areas. First, until the advent of the fountain pen, which did not become widely available until the 1880s, the pencil was the most mobile of writing instruments. Stuffed into a pocket or combined with a notebook, it could go places where pen and ink could not. It was ideal for sketching, design or calculation outside. It was the engineer's and artisan's implement, though the scholar might be grateful to it in archives where ink was excluded. Second, the pencil was more numerate than the pen. Elegant mathematics could be done in ink, but for rapid application of unitary method, cancellings out, dropping of perpendiculars, drawing of graphs and so on, the erasable pencil was best, especially for poor mathematicians. In China, low-grade mathematics used the abacus, but its advantage of speed was offset by the disadvantage of the elimination of the steps of the calculation. It gained time but lost space: an inversion of the advantage Goody sees in the shift from speech to script. Third, the pencil was better for children, because it was cleaner than the pen. In an age when cleanliness was next to godliness, it did not soil their clothes or stain their hands. It promoted earlier literacy, just as among adults it encouraged more thorough numeracy. Coloured pencils provided wider range than coloured inks and were a controllable precursor to the painting box. Active use of colour brought opportunities for expression which were not merely psychological or aesthetic. As Lévi-Strauss has shown, colours, like animals, are good to think with. The pencil brought the rainbow into the classroom. It was the sharp point of manuscript in the age of print.

The capacity of manuscript to generate books is often underestimated. The library of Alexandria is credited with 700 000 volumes, that at Pergamum which Antony gave to Cleopatra with 200 000, and the Souda mentions a private library of 30 000. Significant collections existed at Qumran and Nag Hammadi. Bede was able to obtain copies of papal documents relating to the conversion of England. In the Middle

Ages, the library catalogue of Whitby abbey, by no means a major centre of learning, show it in 1180 in possession of 87 volumes, 60 theological, 27 secular.[28] Together they provided a cross-section of Christian and Classical information just prior to the explosion produced by scholasticism and the recovery of Aristotle. In the Renaissance many of the private libraries at Valladolid analysed by Bennassar contained manuscript as well as printed books. It was the same in China. In 1771, the Ch'ien-lung emperor, solicited by the scholarly community, decided to produce a set of the finest works in Chinese literature. The commission established for this, *Ssu-k'u ch'üan-shu* (complete library of the four treasuries) as it was called, looked at over 10 000 titles, of which it selected 3500-odd for inclusion and 7000 for cataloguing only. A considerable number of the works examined were still in manuscript despite the long invention of print in China. The *Ssu-k'u ch'üan-shu* itself did not see print till the twentieth century. Though the annotated catalogue was printed and has remained an indispensable tool of bibliography to this day, it was decided that seven manuscript copies sufficed: one in each of the four imperial palaces and three in the scholar cities of Hang-chou, Chinkiang and Yang-chou. In India, printed books only became common in the nineteenth century, yet it was not a land of ignorance. In the Islamic world, a famed intellectual centre such as Bokhara could in 1833 supply the libraries of its 60-odd colleges on the basis of manuscript alone.

Though manuscript continued to contribute to book production longer than one might have expected, its real contribution to information in the early modern period was in private or public correspondence. Letters, business and personal, were a major factor in the expanding frontier of literacy. Unlike printed books which had only to be read, letters had to be written. Letters, of course, were not new. A high percentage of papyrus fragments from Graeco-Roman Egypt consists of correspondence, mostly about taxation. Private correspondence passed into publication, as with Cicero's letters, St Paul's epistles, or St Basil's correspondence which he used to circumvent the censorship of Arian emperors. In the Middle Ages, St Bernard's letters, some of them written with a view to publication, were collected and issued as a manifesto of monastic reform. Yet the volume and variety of letter writing increased markedly in Europe after 1400. In England, there were the Paston letters in the fifteenth century, the Lisle letters in the sixteenth century, not all of them exclusively concerned with business. On the Continent, Erasmus was an indefatigable letter writer, while Loyola ruled the Society of Jesus through his correspondence, and Protestant reformers under Elizabeth wrote to Zürich for advice. After 1650, letters personalized and secularized, as in Madame de Sevigné and Lord Chesterfield. In the nineteenth century, correspondence of all kinds was multiplied by government post offices: a characteristic instance of the facilitative rather than regulative state action favoured by classical liberal theory. Beatrix Potter's illustration in *Samuel Whiskers* to her line 'when I was going to the post late in the afternoon' conjured up what had become a familiar routine across a wide spectrum of society. It was a scene with profound implications both for the flow of information and its role in consumerism. Letters were written to acquire objects, to tell friends about objects acquired, to express thanks for presents, to issue invitations, to describe menus for meals, designs for clothes, plans for buildings, to make suggestions about heat, light and water, to exchange ideas, or to communicate for its own sake. How much poorer we should be without the Freud–Jung correspondence or the letters of Asquith to Venetia Stanley.

In China too, correspondence was significant at both the top and the bottom. In government, the basic mechanism was the memorial from the provinces prompting an imperial response from the centre. Until the appearance of the telegraph in the late nineteenth century, both were originally manuscript productions, though, subsequently, edicts might be printed and published in the Peking or provincial gazettes, while the collected memorials of retired high officials were a recognized literary genre. Much of the business of the Chinese state, however, remained in manuscript. When a memorial arrived on the emperor's desk, he did one of four things. He endorsed it (*p'i*): noted, do as you suggest, relevant board to advise please. He wrote a rescript (*chih*) on the original again: a few lines of specific comment, query or warning. He gave oral instructions to the Grand Councillors to write a court letter (*t'ing-chi*) to the correspondent dealing with the points raised, which they then issued on their own authority. Finally, he might order the Grand Councillors to get their secretaries to draft a formal edict (*yü*) in the technical language appropriate, which he would then sanction at the next dawn audience. Only the last was likely to leave the realm of manuscript. In the village too, correspondence formed part of the normal circuits of information. James Hayes describes a village handbook, itself in manuscript and dating probably from the reign of the T'ung-chih emperor (1862–74), which provides models for the wide range of literary activities in which rural communities were involved: notices, contracts, agreements, marriage arrangements, and especially invitations to weddings, funerals, and other extended family events.

Even if the villagers were themselves unable to write, teachers or other literate persons were expected to follow the models free of charge.[29] Hayes's example is not unique and forms part of a body of evidence indicative of growing circulation of correspondence in the late imperial period, especially as postal facilities improved.

Government by correspondence presupposes a post. Down to the late nineteenth century, China possessed two postal services: the public *i-chan*, or courier service organized through the board of war, for official mail, and the private letter hongs for mail from anyone willing to pay for it. H. B. Morse described the letter hongs as, 'usually established by a remittance bank or a merchant's firm having its own business connections with certain other places, and having its own correspondence to forward undertaking for a consideration to forward the letters of other people, and gradually extending their postal operations to other places to which their ordinary business does not extend'. Morse commented: 'On the whole the system has suited admirably the public which it serves, but it has the fatal defect, from a national point of view, that it does not encourage postal development on lines not immediately profitable, the funds for this purpose, derived from the more profitable routes, being diverted to private pockets.'[30] In 1896, therefore, at the instance of Hart who had been urging it since the 1860s, an imperial post was established, first under the auspices of the Maritime Customs and then, from May 1911, as a separate institution headed by Théophile Piry. Although intended for revenue as well as communications purposes, it did not initially enjoy a monopoly, but it absorbed the *i-chan* in July 1912 and the letter hongs were gradually forced into association.

The results were striking. In 1910, 100 million pieces of mail were posted; in 1920, 400 million; in 1925, over 500 million; in 1929, over 700 million. Although newspapers and printed matter, which in 1910 amounted to 40 per cent of mail matter, expanded, they expanded less fast than other items and in 1920 amounted to 20 per cent. Parcels, too, expanded, but it is clear that the main increase was in private correspondence. By the early 1920s, the Post Office reckoned that it was handling one letter per head per annum of the Chinese population. Fairbank was much struck by these figures and argued that from them alone one could have predicted a massive upheaval in China. No doubt in Chinese terms the mobilization of information was explosive and the Post Office may have been the most revolutionary of the synarchic institutions. Yet proportion must be kept. In Britain, over 300 million mail items were posted in 1850, 3000 million by 1900, and over 8000 million in 1950. Even with the new postal facilities, manuscript culture was spread thin in China. Moreover, it was not spread evenly: thick in the conurbations of the Yangtze delta and the coastal fringe, thin in the inward-looking villages of north China. Nevertheless, manuscript was probably expanding faster than print. In village Kiangsi in the 1920s, where literacy reached 22 per cent, keeping accounts and reading and writing letters were given as the two main reasons for its acquisition. As in most early modern societies, the written word was an accessory where the printed word was only an extra.

EXTRAS: PRINT AND THE PRINTED WORD

It now remains to examine the contribution of print in the early modern period to the diffusion of information and in particular to the information used by consumerism via books, newspapers, magazines and catalogues.

The case for a profound effect of print on information flow in Europe has been strongly made by Elizabeth Eisenstein in a classic book which describes it as the unacknowledged revolution. In particular, she emphasized the effect on what she took to be two key concepts of early modern European culture, scripture and nature, and on the overall level of literacy in Europe. The unique leap upwards in literacy in turn underlay the industrial revolution and the rise of democracy. By this focus on print, Eisenstein brought a new technological dimension to an essentially Whiggish view of the rise of Europe through the Renaissance, Reformations and the emergence of science. Despite this enrichment, however, the view itself remained simplistic and parochial, and Eisenstein's hypothesis a special rather than a general theory of print. Some criticisms were quickly made: that she was more at home in modern than medieval history, that within modern history she was Protestant rather than Catholic or Orthodox, and that what was attributed to print should really be attributed to script and placed earlier. Others emerged gradually. Insufficient attention was paid, it was argued, to Islamdom which did not adopt print yet achieved a high level of scripturalism, and to China which had long possessed print yet did not draw the benefits ascribed to it in Europe. In particular, a comparison with China suggests that Eisenstein inverted the order of causality. It was not print that produced a culture, but a culture which took up print. The real unacknowledged revolution lay in three interrelated features of European culture, not found in China to the same extent, at least in the early modern period: revealed religion, consumerism itself and a particular family structure.

In China, the origins of print in the T'ang period were associated with these same three factors. The earliest surviving printed materials are a miscellany of Buddhist sutras, magical charms and 'beware of the dog' notices. They came from a hard-riding yet raffinate aristocratic society which enjoyed the niceties of Buddhist scholasticism as well as the latest dance groups from Central Asia. It was a society inspired by the ideals of lavish expenditure which Gernet has shown were implicit in Mahayama as perceived in China.[31] It was a society in whose family structures women were playing a more active role. At the top and in politics, the transition from magnates to mandarins provided temporary opportunities for a madamate: leadership by imperial women, conspicuous under Empress Wu but not confined to her reign. At the bottom and in the economy, larger farms and more sericulture boosted female status, income, independence and literacy. This particular conjuncture of religion, consumerism and feminism, however, did not last. After 800 Buddhism turned to less intellectual forms and lost its ascendancy. The print it left slack, though, was more than taken up by the needs of the Confucian examination system which in the Sung period became dominant in bureaucratic recruitment and elite structuration. It was then that Chu Hsi, the Aquinas of Neo-Confucianism, declared that the enjoyment of books was the only pleasure without satiety. The golden age of the scholar ministers, the *shih ta-fu*, saw the rebirth of consumerism in the imperial capitals of Kaifeng and Hang-chou, not least in the consumerism of information via print. From this culture, Patricia Ebrey has recently shown, women were less excluded than was at one time thought. Subsequently, despite the puritanisms of the Ming revolution and the Wang Yang-ming reformation, consumerism resurfaced in the late Ming in the Wan-li period. It tried to distinguish itself from mere consumption in the literature of connoisseurship analysed by Craig Clunas. One of the messages of the erotic novel *Chin-ping mei*, published in 1617, was to separate the empty hedonism of its *nouveau riche* hero from the discriminating spending of the true literatus on *objets d'art*, antiques, books and a few exotica. Print culture certainly existed in China.

The initial form of the press in China was woodblock. Movable type was a development of the Sung. Shen Kua, the Confucian polymath, tells us that it was an invention of a certain Pi Sheng (990–1051). He used earthenware for his type and also wood. Subsequently, copper was employed, especially by private printers in Kiangnan towards the end of the fifteenth century. Moveable type, however, remained minoritarian. The earliest surviving example is several hundred pieces in the Uighur script of around 1300 recovered from Tun-huang at the beginning of the twentieth century. A little earlier, but also under the Mongols, Wang Shu had used movable wooden type for his great agricultural treatise, the *Nung-shu* of 1297–8. The Ch'ing, perhaps influenced by Mongol precedent, also used it in official publications: 250 000 bronze characters were cast for the K'ang-hsi encyclopaedia *T'u-shu chi-sheng* completed in 1725, and some of the *Ssu-k'u ch'uan-shu* reprints were done with moveable wooden type. In general, however, woodblock prevailed until the twentieth century.

T. H. Tsien has explored the reasons for this prevalence.[32] First, the nature of Chinese script meant a font of between 200 000 and 400 000 pieces, compared to the 100 or so pieces required in an alphabetical script. Second, type-setting was laborious and not worthwhile for the short runs which were characteristic of Chinese publishing. In 1574, 100 was considered a relatively long run. Third, woodblocks were easy to store and could be re-used indefinitely. Chinese publishers envisaged a succession of short runs over a long period. Woodblocks did not require the large initial investment of moveable type. Their continued availability and frequent use avoided capital being tied up in books. Publishers, like other Chinese business people, sought to minimize fixed investment and maximize rapid turnover. Fourth, moveable type, the Chinese felt, took ink less well, was more prone to error, while its calligraphy was less artistic and its page less aligned (because less rigid) than woodblock. The Chinese therefore invented moveable type, but only made restricted use of it. Better suited to an alphabetical script and different publishing conditions, it was transmitted to the West, probably as a result of the Franciscan mission in the Mongol period, who would have used it in religious propaganda, not least in the conversion of the Christian Alans from Orthodoxy or Nestorianism to Catholicism. When printing arrived in Europe, at least half a century before Gutenberg, as Christopher de Hamel has shown, it was used initially for the kind of literature promoted by the Franciscans: bibles, books of hours, aids to devotion, indulgences.

The partial rejection of moveable type did not prevent Chinese publishing from being on a massive scale in the early modern period. It is likely that down to 1700 more was printed in characters than in any other script and that the greatest percentage of the world's reading public was Chinese. Under the Ch'ing, publishing fell into two sections, public and private, and served three markets: official, elite and popular.

First, there were imperial printeries. In Peking, the Imperial Printing Office was established in 1673 on Ming precedents in the Wu-ying throne hall in the southwest of the Forbidden City. Here, it was under the auspices of the *Nei-wu fu*, the powerful imperial household department, and headed by a household minister or even an imperial prince. The Wu-ying *tien* printed both books and serials. It published the scholarly books commissioned by imperial patronage and the military campaign outlines, *fang-lüeh*, put out by the history office. It produced the court circulars of palace activities, condensed memorials and imperial responses, which foreigners called the *Peking Gazette* and was in fact a group of official and semi-official periodical publications with no particular promulgatory status. As well as imperially approved scholarship for the elite and red books and white papers for officials, the Wu-ying *tien* supplied two million almanacs a year to the popular market, where again it was tolerant of supplementary editions by the private sector. In addition to the Imperial Printing Office in Peking, there were secondary public printing offices in regional capitals, which relayed applicable metropolitan material and added the local administrative orders of viceroys, governors, salt commissioners and so on. Chinese government was not secretive. As the Tao-kuang emperor said in 1836: 'in directing the government of the people, we do nothing which we are not willing to declare openly to all our servants and subjects', though this was qualified by the addition, 'but when secret investigations are necessary they are not to be known beyond those directly concerned'.[33] The imperial printeries combined the functions of a stationery office and a state publishing house.

Second, there were the private printeries in the major cities of the empire. These were ongoing businesses with collections of woodblocks and moveable type, but on a small scale, working to order and seldom envisaging runs of more than a hundred. They provided versions of the Peking gazettes for the official market. They published the texts and commentaries required for the examinations for the elite market. They produced innumerable less elevated publications for the popular markets: almanacs, genealogies, guides to geomancy and cheiromancy, horoscopes, physiognomies and dream interpretations, craft manuals such as the *Lu Pan Ching* (first published in Peking by the palace *c*.1420, then taken up in countless editions by the private sector), rule books for guilds and secret societies, contract forms, handbooks to official procedure and for writing letters, scriptural texts for the new sectarian Buddhisms of the late imperial period. James Hayes and Richard Smith have shown that print penetrated deep into Chinese society, at least in the coastal provinces and those served by water. Moreover, there was no radical distinction between the official, elite and popular markets. All involved the press and the emperor, who was chief executive, protector of scholarship, head of the Chinese religion, and living divinity of certain kinds of Buddhism and Taoism. In this sense, China was as much a print culture as early modern Europe. What it was not, however, was a publishers' culture. Benjamin Elman speaks of the scholar printers of Kiang-nan and compares them to Aldus Manutius, Frobenius and Plantin. Yet the differences are more striking than the similarities. The Renaissance printers were indeed the ancestors of the enlightened modern publisher: actively encouraging and seeking out authors, intellectually abreast of the latest currents, willing to risk his own judgement. Their Chinese counterparts were less promotive, more artisan, and less wide-ranging. It was not until the 1920s when Wang Yün-wu and Chang Yuan-chi energized the Shanghai Commercial Press founded in 1901 that China possessed a modern publishing house.[34] This relative absence of publishers' culture was a major factor in levels of literacy and the degree of information.

What levels of literacy were achieved in early modern China? Evelyn Rawski, after a detailed investigation, comes down in favour of an optimistic assessment: males 30–45 per cent, females 2–10 per cent, both together 16–28 per cent, the mean 22 per cent.[35] These are high percentages for a traditional society. Chaunu's figures for Normandy in 1700, an advanced part of France, itself an advanced part of Europe, indicate an average of 10 per cent only: 12 per cent males, 8 per cent females. Europe as a whole in 1700 probably had a mean literacy of only 7 per cent. No wonder then that early European travellers, observing from a mainly urban standpoint, thought China enjoyed near universal literacy. Yet in the eighteenth century, Europe caught up fast. By 1800, Normandy averaged 70 per cent (80 per cent males, 60 per cent females), France 50 per cent, Europe as a whole 33 per cent. In the same period, China changed little: maybe up, maybe down, most likely with contrasts between coast and interior, south and north, but with nothing equivalent to Europe's cerebral revolution of early modernity.

Literacy, hard to define, is harder to explain. The obvious answer, the number and quality of schools, is a half-truth. Wise parents teach their children to read before sending them to school and children can go through school without acquiring effective literacy. What a school imparts depends on circumambient culture, as much as vice versa. Much literacy is acquired outside school, especially at work, as much as is needed to do the job, particularly in an urban environment. Historically, cities have probably done as much for literacy as schools. Family structure too affects the acquisition of literacy: the number of children, their life expectancy and hence investment-worth, the availability of adults for teaching, the need for child labour in and around the home. So, too, does what the printed word has to offer: the urgency of publishers' culture in providing information in books, serials and advertisement.

Rawski shows that early modern China was not ill-equipped with schools. The Confucian tradition, especially as reinterpreted by the Wang Yang-ming reformation which believed everyone a sage, valued education. Many failed examination candidates (and at best only 10 per cent passed) found their way into the teaching profession. Yet schools and teachers were often in the wrong place: in towns rather than on the agricultural frontier where population was growing. Though there were more towns in China in the eighteenth century than ever before, it is arguable that the level of urbanization was falling because of the growth in farm population. If so, it is not surprising that literacy levels were static or even falling. Chinese family structure too was not conducive to investment in education: early marriage, high natality, high child mortality, low female celibacy. Except for scholarly families seeking to place daughters on a marriage market where educated mothers for sons were at a premium, female literacy in particular was neglected. Finally, Confucianism, Buddhism and Taoism, not to mention the indigenous Chinese religion which does not have a name, lacked the urgency of European publishers' culture. In Europe, the drive to literacy came primarily from the Reformation, the Catholic Reform and the Enlightenment: movements with a message, dogmas to proclaim. Confucianism basically had no message. It was a mind style rather than a metaphysic, with only a literary paradigm to propagate. Though not without missionary imperatives, especially in frontier provinces such as Kweichow, it lacked the evangelical zeal of the European movements, since it was a set of categories rather than a creed. Buddhism and Taoism had more message, since both had begun as revealed religions, but Buddhism had deintellectualized itself, while Taoism had turned esoteric as the secrets of an alternative medicine. As for the indigenous religion, it was a matter of cult rather than belief. None of these ways of thinking surcharged literacy.

Revealed religion was one factor in Europe's cerebral revolution, consumerism itself was another. Consumerism requires information as both means and end. Increasingly, information comes in printed form.

Consumerism therefore evokes literacy to read that print. If China was less consumerist than Europe in so many ways in 1800 (in dress, shelter, energy), it was also likely to be less literate. The Bible will teach to read, but the Sears Roebuck catalogue will teach to both read and write. Madison Avenue was another kind of evangelism: marketing was mission. High-pressure salesmanship was not read into the Gospel. It was read out of it.

Finally, two further aspects of family structure in China are relevant to literacy and information. First, as Jack Goody has argued, marriage in China was less exogamous than in Europe.[36] Thanks to the Church's insistence on its tables of kindred and affinity, which Goody sees as less motivated by horror of incest than by considerations of testamentary freedom, Europe, alone among civilizations, was led into a structure which favoured exogamy, while everywhere else 'oriental systems' favouring endogamy prevailed. Among other things, marriage is a device for the circulation of information, just as it is a device for the conservation of family property. It is not difficult to show that, while endogamy favours the conservation of property, exogamy is better for the inclusion of information: a fact of which the Church fathers may not have been unaware. While Chinese marriage systems did contain prohibitions, especially between same-name families (a serious matter given the relatively few surnames in China), they were consistently more tolerant of endogamy than European systems. Endogamy sacrifices information to solidarity. Conversely, exogamy brings not just new blood – genetic information – but new ideas. Second, associated but separate, marriage in China was filial rather than conjugal. It sought the optimum of the parents rather than the couple. 'Pillow ghosts', undue intimacy between husband and wife, was felt to be actively injurious to family solidarity. This feeling was one reason for the system which Wolf and Huang call minor marriage and have shown to be more prevalent than was at one time thought.[37] This system, in which an infant girl was taken into the family for subsequent marriage to the son, was tantamount to artificial incest. By weakening conjugal affection, it sought to give a servant to the mother-in-law rather than a partner to the son. Such a system did not promote female literacy. Moreover, under it, affinal ties were kept to a minimum, so that the flow of information was further impeded. Further, Wolf and Huang argue that minor marriage only expressed more clearly what was the thrust of all Chinese marriage. Despite the high value Confucianism placed on education, Confucian family structure limited literacy, impeded the circulation of information and failed to mobilize the key element of the consumerism of the West: female intelligence. Directly or indirectly, these inhibitions applied to all three means of communication, speech, script and print, as the means or ends of consumerism. Madame Butterfly had not yet joined the internet where Mimi Pinson had already done so.

7 Consumerism and Symbolism

The previous chapters have explored the notion of consumerism as mind mattering. Consumerism was more than consumption. It was not only the acquisition of more, but also the discrimination of better. It was the application of those mental structures in food, dress, shelter, utilities and information, which have been analysed above. The present chapter is concerned with the inverse phenomenon: matter minding. Here, commodities, used as symbols, shaped thought in a reversal of the previous order of causality. Lévi-Strauss declared that for primitives, animals were not just good to eat, but also good to think.[1] The same principle of symbolism applied to the other natural and cultural objects in which they found structures variously encoded. During the period of globalization 1400–1800, as consumerism stretched out its hands to the planet, the number of such objects multiplied, not only for Europeans, but also for Chinese. The effect of this multiplication on thought is what is discussed below. Though concrete mythological thinking had long been marginalized, in the early modern period, philosophy, science, politics, art theory and religious devotion did not disdain the reinforcement afforded by the new commodities. This chapter, like its predecessors, consists of two unequal parts. First, it will examine the ways in which commodities enter thought as symbols. Second, it will delineate the role of commodities in three branches of early modern thought which may be regarded as essential, accessory and extra, because they can be related to four systems of order, which, following and extending Hayek, will be called taxic, intertaxic, ataxic and antitaxic.[2]

COMMODITIES AND SYMBOLISM

At its simplest, the notion of symbol is of one thing standing for, or pointing towards, another thing. The word *symbolon* originally meant part of a broken object: the torn postcard of the Le Carré world, used as a means of identification. It was a counterpart, though how the two bits were related was not always the same. Symbols are frequently distinguished from signs. A sign, it is said, is monovalent or arithmetic. It refers uniquely to a known object. It is a coding capable of only one translation. It is purely replicative. Thus, for Freud, the manifest elements of a dream, though scrambled by the dream work, referred directly to the latent contents of the repressed. A symbol, on the other hand, is polyvalent or algebraic. It refers obliquely to an object not fully known. It is a coding capable of more than one translation. It is amplificatory as well as replicative. Thus, for Jung, the manifest dream might suggest new aspects of the underlying archetype. For while the sign was an ambassador bound by instructions, the symbol was a plenipotentiary. Yet, as F. H. Bradley pointed out, the difference was not absolute.[3] Signs went beyond themselves. At the entrance to a path, a picture of a black horse with a line across does not exclude merely animals of this colour. Nor do we suppose that riders of cows or camels will be tolerated. Symbols were conventional. Only the context will determine whether a red rose signifies love, Labour or Lancaster. What sign and symbol have in common is that neither *are* the objects they refer to. In addition to their own existence and content, they have been endowed with meaning. Commodities, as a sub-class of symbols, were particularly convenient, because they came already freighted with a range of consumer significance. They could therefore be used variously as myth, metaphor, paradigm and prototype.

Myth

The fullest account here is that of Lévi-Strauss in the second volume of the *Mythologiques* which is devoted to a set of myths involving honey and tobacco. Lévi-Strauss distinguishes between the myth – the simple story, the code (culinary, acoustic, sexual, astronomical, zoological etc) – and the underlying logic. At first sight, much is reminiscent of depth psychology. However, as against Freud, the sexual code is no more fundamental than any of the others and, as against Jung, what is latent is not irrational unconscious archetypes, but conscious, if unarticulated, rational structures, mostly of a binary character. For Lévi-Strauss, as for Rousseau, savages were rational, almost Cartesian. For him too, unlike Freud and Jung, there were no natural symbols, only cultural. It is unlikely that Lévi-Strauss read Bradley, but his view of symbolism is closer to that avowed enemy of psychologism than it is to the founders of depth psychology. Bradley distinguished the existence, content and meaning of symbols. He concluded: 'meaning consists of a part of the content (original or acquired), cut off, fixed by the mind, and considered apart from the existence'.[4] Similarly, in the *Mythologiques*, Lévi-Strauss shows that it is often unexpected or unusual characteristics of objects which are fixed on in myths to encode binary oppositions. Thus honey stands for culture in nature because it *begins* in a tree trunk, while tobacco stands for nature in culture because it *ends* in ash. If similar commodities appear in myths from widely separated parts of the Americas, it is not to be explained by a pre-Columbian collective unconscious. Rather, it is better comprehended on the analogy of different members of a language family which may never have been in touch with each other: a Middle Ages without a Rome as Lévi-Strauss puts it. Myth therefore is not dream, even collective dream. What leads to their confusion is their common lack of self-explanation, their just-so character. What is characteristic of myth as a form of symbolism is the absence of distance between itself and what it stands for. Myth is immediate. It is not figurative. Consequently, while it can be endlessly permutated across the four massive volumes of the *Mythologiques*, it cannot be translated. Signifier and signified are inseparable, and in the end the colours vanish into darkness.

Metaphor

By this is understood any of a number of rhetorical figures of speech. The fullest account of this kind of symbolism is contained in Bernard Cottret's analysis of Reformation controversies regarding the Eucharist.[5] Cottret stresses the philological dimension. The basic problem was the relation of the bread and wine to the body and blood of Christ: that is, the reference of two commodity signs or symbols to something symbolized. It is customary to characterize the Catholic and Protestant positions by saying that the Catholics believed in a real presence, while the Protestants believed in a symbolic presence. While this characterization may be adequate for some purposes, it is not altogether exact. What was at issue was also the nature of symbolism. Authors of high if not unimpeachable orthodoxy from the Catholic point of view, such as Origen and William of St Thierry, used the term symbolic of the Eucharist without any denial of the real presence.[6] What Protestants argued, claiming Origen as one of their number, was that symbolism could only be figurative: it could not be real. The counterfoil was not part and parcel of the document. Hence, as Cranmer argued, transubstantiation overthrew the nature of a sacrament, which demanded the continued existence of a separate substance. Philologically, the signifier could not *be* the signified. Cranmer thought rhetorically and pastorally.

As he put it: 'Christ ordained the sacrament to move and stir all men.'[7] The gospel was not about the sacraments, but the sacraments were about the gospel: figurative devices for its proclamation. As to what figures were involved, however, Protestants differed: synecdoche in Luther's consubstantiation, metaphor in Zwingli's real absence, metonymy in Calvin's more positive position, a stronger form of metaphor, *signum exhibitivum* rather than *signum representivum*, in Cranmer's true presence. Where all the figures differed from myth was in the distance they placed between signifier and signified, *signum* and *res*. Myth did not explain itself. Metaphor did. It explained itself by philology.

Paradigm

The term paradigm occurs frequently in Lévi-Strauss: generally as an adjective and in contrast to syntagmatic.[8] Both terms are used to describe the permutation in myths of the underlying *mythologiques*. Although Lévi-Strauss associated paradigm with metaphor and syntagm with metonymy, the new dichotomy went beyond rhetorical figures. For where figures referred to externals of similarity or continuity, paradigm and syntagm referred to comparability of inner structure. Hence, Lévi-Strauss speaks of chains of sytagms and systems of paradigms. Like metaphor, paradigm involved similarity, but in its case the similarity was not merely physiognomic and superficial but physiological and profound. Consequently, paradigm referred to processes rather than facts, becoming more than being. An example here would be the Chinese system of five elements, *wu-hsing*, as contrasted with the Greek system of four elements. Both were examples of what Needham called correlative thinking, but what was correlated was different. For Empedocles, earth, air, fire and water were facts, *rhizomata*, acted on by the two forces of attraction and repulsion, *philia* and *neikos*. So, too, in Galen were their organic counterparts: the four humours of blood, choler, bile yellow or black, acted on by three kinds of *pneuma*. The relationship between the two quaternities, physical and organic, was therefore one of similitude or metaphor. For Tsou Yen, Tung Chung-shu and the exponents of the *wu-hsing* tradition, what was elemental was not facts but processes. *Hsing* denoted action: walking, doing, conduct, business and so on, and its character was said to depict a crossroads. The five *hsing* – wood, fire, earth, metal and water – were actions rather than things. They and their microcosmic correlatives were linked, not statically, but dynamically in a variety of enumeration orders: cosmogonic, mutual production, mutual conquest or so-called modern. The correlations were in terms of arrangement rather than appearance. Another instance of paradigmatic symbolism in Chinese thought was the image of *hsün-hsi*, perfuming or fumigation, in Vijnanavada Buddhism, to model the action of various levels of consciousness or the collective unconscious. In Europe, paradigm was less common than in China until the appearance of alchemical medicine, itself of Chinese origin, but there are instances in religious imagery. For example, mustard seed, which in the Gospels was metaphor, through elaboration of crushing, grinding, inflammation, became, in a monastic writer such as Isaac of Gaza, a paradigm of asceticism. Ginger, too, had a dual character: as colour, metaphor; as action, paradigm.

Prototype

Here the advance of paradigm over metaphor was carried a stage further. Metaphor drew an analogy. Paradigm suggested a similarity of action. Prototype claimed structural identity. It was, however, a different identity from that of myth, because based on full intelligibility in both directions. Prototype is reductionist. It asserts, first, that the signified may be understood fully in terms of the signifier, and second, that the signifier itself is fully intelligible. Prototype was rare before modernity because so little was fully intelligible except geometry and that did not seem applicable to the real world. It was in modernity that the heart was understood as a pump, the earth as a magnet, prices as feedback, the brain as a computer. The application of geometry to the real world, which was the hallmark of seventeenth-century science, could only follow the abstraction and quantification of the primary qualities of objects. This procedure of isolation was the counterpart in reality of that cutting off and mental fixing which Bradley saw as the essence of symbolism. It allowed a new conjuncture of thought and reality which enriched both and at once marginalized primitive myth, ancient metaphor and medieval paradigm. Other symbolisms could be replaced by mathematical notation. Leibniz could hope for a universal characteristic through which all problems would be resolved by calculation. Prototype was higher-level myth in that it supposed that there was nothing non-algorithmic.

Salt

As an illustration of the use of commodities in these four kinds of symbolism, we may take the example of salt.[9] Distinctive in flavour, properties and methods of acquisition, salt has struck imagination since its discovery by palaeolithic man in following game to saline deposits. Writers on salt, however, have been insufficiently attentive to the diversity of this imagery and have fallen prey to the idea of a timeless symbolism of salt. The categories of myth, metaphor, paradigm and prototype may help redress the balance.

First, salt as myth. In the more than 800 myths of the *Mythologiques*, salt makes only a few significant appearances in either Amazonia or Greater Oregon. One reason for this relative infrequency was that salt was not a universal object of diet in pre-Columbian America. It was acquired either from natural deposits and outcrops or by boiling brine, natural or reinforced by saline ash. In neither form was it very pure and it made less impact than honey or tobacco.

In Lévi-Strauss's view, there is nothing accidental in myth. Every reference to salt in any story is meaningful. It is part of a code in which the underlying *mythologiques*, the primary polarities, are expressed. In the system described by Lévi-Strauss, salt featured in three codes. First, it featured in a condimentary code, along with honey on one axis, and tobacco and pimento on the other. In this code, salt and honey were sometimes contrasted, sometimes assimilated. Moreover, both condiments, salt inedible by itself and honey sometimes toxic, could be placed on the interface between aliment and excrement: food and the uneatable. Thus Lévi-Strauss writes: 'Une analyse de la mythologie du sel dans les deux Ameriques permettrait aisement de montrer que le sel, substance minérale et pourtant coméstible, se situe, pour la pensée indigène, à l'intersection de l'aliment et d'excrément.'[10] Second, salt featured in an acoustic code. Here, the basic dichotomy of silence and sound gave rise to secondary contrasts: sound continuous and discontinuous, noise and music, secular instruments, sacred instruments. Salt had a place in this code because of its property of crackling when thrown into a fire. It was a proto-explosive. Thus a Guarani myth speaks of 'le crépitement des graines éclatant' and their 'force explosive', while a Zuni myth from North America recounts a recovery of game 'grâce à l'éclatement bruyant d'une poignée du sel jetée au feu'.[11] Finally, salt featured in a vestimentary code. In the concluding volume of the *Mythologiques*, Lévi-Strauss recapitulates his themes in their Oregon context, and in particular in the Yana myth of Dame Diver or the Loon Woman, a bird whose weird cries have always attracted attention. Here he notes the occurrence of honey and salt, natural objects but, like feathers, ready for human use, in myths about the beginning of dress. He writes: 'Chaque fois aussi, le condiment salé ou sucré fait fonction d'antécédent ou de moyen des parures pour les mythes qui se rapportent à leur origine.'[12]

Second, salt as metaphor. This has been studied most thoroughly in the case of the Gospel passages: 'Ye are the salt of the earth' (Matthew, 5: 13); 'Have salt in yourselves and have peace one with another' (Mark, 9: 50); 'Salt is good, but if the salt have lost his savour, wherewith shall it be seasoned?' (Luke, 14: 34). Latham elucidates by a method of amplification. He examines the Old Testament texts which led into them and the liturgical and Patristic texts which led out of them. His search is for a common range of meaning, which, at least for this family of texts, will provide a definitive symbolism of salt. Whether this search is realistic or not, it is fruitful. In the Old Testament, Latham finds salt, as sprinkled, associated with sacrifice. Sacrifice in turn was associated with covenant and remembrance. In Leviticus, 2: 13 reference was made to 'the salt of the covenant' and in II Chronicles, 13: 5, to 'a covenant of salt'. Sacrifice was memorial. It was a reminder to God (*azharah* or *zikkaron*) of the covenant. Similarly, the remembrance of the Eucharist was not primarily a commemoration of Christ who might otherwise be forgotten, but the proclamation to the Father of a sacrifice about to be accomplished, a covenant about to be sealed. In this way, salt acquired the meaning of permanence. A covenant of salt was an irrevocable contract which, once joined, could not be put asunder. Consequently, in his survey of liturgical and patristic texts, Latham finds that the predominant theme is that of preservation or incorruptibility: 'by far the most universal throughout the history of salt symbolism'.[13] This predominance was due not simply to the contemporary use of salt as a preservative in meat and fish, but to the whole system of literary resonances set up by the biblical texts.

If salt was a signifier, what in the last resort was the signified? Latham is again suggestive. In the Sermon on the Mount, Christ proclaimed the people of God the salt of the earth and the light of the world. In this imagery, the fact that in Palestine salt frequently appeared spontaneously as a white excrescence, particularly striking in sunlight, will have played a part. Subsequently, in John, 8: 12, Christ declared himself to be the light of the world. But he never declared himself to be the salt of the earth, as the notion of a *communicatio idiomatum* between himself and his church might have suggested, because that permanence of his presence was the office of the Spirit. That salt is fundamentally the Spirit is further suggested by a turn of phrase in the Acts of the Apostles.[14] In the Authorized Version, the passage Acts 1: 4 reads: 'And, being assembled together with them, [he] commanded them that they should not depart from Jerusalem, but wait for the promise of the Father', that is, the gift of the Spirit soon to take place irrevocably at Pentecost. The word translated 'assembled together with them' is *synalizomenos*, which in one pronunciation could mean to take salt in common, while in another only to bring together. Consult or consalt: that is the issue. If the second is preferred, then it would indicate a marker by St Luke in the direction of the coming of the Spirit he was about to describe. A similar association of salt, baptism, Christ, the Spirit and the Church is found in a passage of St Chromatius of Aquileia on Christ's words quoted by Latham.[15] Here the Church was compared to the salt produced from the sea, = baptism by the action of the sun, = Christ and the wind, = the Spirit. From these associations, Chromatius derived other metaphorical meanings of salt as preservative, demonofuge, Wisdom, Word and remedy, but the prime signified was the divine action itself: its permanence and sacrificial character. Salt was the sacrament of the Spirit.

Third, salt as paradigm. In the early modern period, paradigm became the principal way in which commodities were used in symbolism. On the one hand, paradigm was a halfway house between speculation and theory. By focusing on structural and not just surface similarities, it made enquiry more exact, quantifiable and testable. On the other hand, the flood of new commodities brought by the age of discovery provided mint-fresh signifiers not worn thin by overuse in metaphor or myth. Salt was not a new commodity, but it was being produced in new ways which renewed its symbolic potential. When St Chromatius wrote, he was probably thinking of a spontaneous, natural process. Even if he did have in mind a planned scheme of salt production, that scheme would have been the simple kind known as single basin solar evaporation such as was described in the fifth century by Rutilius Namatianus in his poem *De Reditu Suo*. But between antiquity and the Renaissance, the more complex process known as successive basin solar evaporation had been invented in China, transmitted westward by the Islamic world, and adopted in Christendom as its principal technique of salt production. The new technique, with its series of basins performing distinct functions, required greater chemical understanding and skill than the earlier schemes. In particular, along with the virtually new industries of sugar and alum boiling, the new technique fostered awareness of the phenomenon of crystallization. Salt became the end product of a process, rather than a substance. It was in this sense that salt, along with sulphur and mercury, figured in Paracelsian medicine. They were elements in the Chinese rather than the Greek sense. This, indeed, is one reason for suspecting a Chinese influence in the prehistory of Paracelsianism. Thanks to these paradigms, the Aristotelian image of the organism ruled by final causes could be replaced by the alchemical image of the world as a workshop ruled by material causes. From being a unique substance, salt expanded to become one of a category of precipitates: Glauber's salt (sodium sulphate), Epsom salts (magnesium sulphate), saltpetre (potassium nitrate), sal volatile (ammonium carbonate), sal ammoniac (ammonium chloride); crystalline, soluble, noninflammable and defined in relation to acids and alkalis, the end products of the concurrent processes of sulphur and mercury.

As Lord Dacre has shown, the Paracelsian movement was a mixture of empiric practice, materialist theosophy and political messianism.[16] Paradigm was its preferred form of symbolism. Jung, who studied its literature in the belief that it represented an anticipation of his own version of depth psychology, found at least eight different meanings for salt in the alchemical texts.[17] Salt was the arcane substance to be transmuted. It was the active part of the sea which turned red in the evaporation basins. Salt was bitterness, *amaritudo*, ash, corrosive, deadening, the end of evaporation. On the other hand, salt was *polyophthalmia*: meaning in mere fact, its shining crystals corresponding to the multiple luminosities of the unconscious. Salt was the mysterious earthly fourth which had to be united to the heavenly three. In the system of Michael Maier, it corresponded to the new dark continent of Africa. Salt signified ascent and descent, fission and fusion, the *solve et coagula* of the spagyric art, as Paracelsus termed his method. Salt represented *albedo*, the whitening of unstable dirt on its way to permanent gold. Finally, as ash, salt was residue: matter freed from decomposition, the wisdom of the alchemist who completed the work in nature and in himself. Salt, like sulphur and mercury, was there at the beginning and at the end. Some alchemists combined the Paracelsian trinity with the Empedoclean quaternity. Thus for the Pole Sendivogius, fire acted on air to produce sulphur, air acted on water to produce mercury, water acted on earth to produce salt. Sulphur was active, salt was passive, mercury was ambivalent. From their interaction, everything else was produced. For another alchemist, Khunrath, salt was the oldest of mysteries.[18] Athanasius Kircher, the semi-Paracelsian Jesuit, who stuck to the old doctrines almost in the age of science, declared that salt was the semen of the earth, that all nutriment was steeped in sulphur, mercury and salt, and that all diseases were related to the same three processes.[19] Yet by this time, there had already appeared Boyle's *Sceptical Chemist* which finally quashed the 'experiements whereby vulgar Spagyrists are wont to endeavour to evince their Salt, Sulphur and Mercury to be the true Principles of Things'.[20]

Fourth, salt as prototype. When salt ceased to be a principle or an element, it was freed to become a compound: indeed, a prototype of the vast array of compounds discovered by physics and chemistry. Salt was identified as a compound of sodium and chlorine by Sir Humphrey Davy in 1810. From much earlier, however, it had played a part in chemical analysis. Boyle had upgraded the notion of compound. First, he insisted that many of the substances which the Spagyrists claimed were permutations of elements were in fact compounds: 'I shall hereafter make it evident that the Substances of which Chymists are wont to call the Salts and Sulphures and Mercuries of Bodies, are not so pure and elementary as their hypothesis requires.' Second, he argued that compounds were more diverse than the Spagyrists had supposed: 'Nor does it appear more congruous to that variety that so much conduceth to the perfection of the Universe, that all elemented bodies be compounded of the same number of Elements, than it would be for a language, that all its words should consist of the same number of Letters.'[21] Third, Boyle, by his denial of the existence of the Spagyrists' Alkahest or universal solvent, opened the way to a longer and more varied programme of analysis. In the course of the eighteenth century many of the calcium and magnesium compounds associated with common salt in seawater began to be correctly classified, along with the other salts of the Paracelsian system. All this work found its way into Lavoisier's *Traité Élémentaire de Chimie* of 1789.

The major factor, however, in the redefinition of salt as a compound was soda manufacture on the basis of the process discovered by Nicholas Leblanc in 1791. Synthetic soda was the first large-scale product of the modern chemical industry.[22] Soda, sodium carbonate, was a raw material in the textile, glass and soap industries, key components in the consumerist revolution in dress, shelter and utilities. In the course of the eighteenth century, supplies of natural soda from Egypt and Syria began to run short. Although another alkali, potash, potassium carbonate, mainly from the Baltic, had long been used as a substitute, and artificial soda was made from saline plants, kelp in Scotland and barilla in Spain, neither of these expedients proved adequate to rising demand. Alkali shortage was becoming a serious bottleneck. Paracelsians had believed that soda was a form of salt and were aware of its affinity with potash. But their doctrine of only three fundamental processes in nature stood in the way of further enquiry, just as their search for a universal solvent, the alkahest, inhibited the use of mineral acids in chemical investigation. Boyle's argument that there were many solvents, many kinds of compound, opened new perspectives. What was now lacking in the shift from paradigm to prototype was quantification. This was what was added by Lavoisier with his insistence on the conservation of matter, the use of scales, and the measurement of volume, weights and temperature in the course of an experiment. Enquiry initiated research, quantification completed it. On this basis, first air, and then water, were analysed as compounds of gases. The new understanding of combustion gained *en route* eliminated phlogiston and removed fire too from the list of elements from which earth had long since been dropped. Both the Greek and the Chinese notions of elements were now dead.

It was against this background that in 1791 Leblanc perfected a process for manufacturing sodium carbonate by the application of sulphuric acid to common salt. The application gave rise on the one hand to hydrochloric acid and on the other to saltcake (sodium sulphate) which, when treated with lime (calcium carbonate) and charcoal (carbon), became the desired soda. The Leblanc alkali industry, as it developed in Glasgow and on Tyneside, with its sulphurous fumes and hydrochloric waste, was a particularly noxious piece of early industrialization. It had, however, considerable scientific spin-off. First, it demonstrated that salt was indeed a compound. It therefore became only a question of time and the application of Lavoisier's quantitative techniques before its character as sodium chloride was established by Davy. Second, ordinary soda was soon distinguished from caustic soda (sodium hydroxide) and from its cousins in the potash family. Shortly a kali industry would join that of soda. Third, the quantities of chlorine produced by the Leblanc process and unwanted save in limited quantities for bleach, prompted the investigation and identification of the vast range of chlorinated hydrocarbons. At the time, little use was found for these, but in the twentieth century they became the basis of a new branch of the chemical industry. Once salt was understood as a compound and as the prototype for other, more complex compounds of solids and gases, the Spagyrist dream of creating new substances by fission and fusion could become reality in successive chemical revolutions. A failure as a paradigm in physics, salt was a success as a prototype in chemistry. As a result of that success, salt ceased to be mainly a commodity for direct human consumption and became primarily an industrial raw material, valued more for its chlorine than for its sodium. As this happened, and as salines ceased to be conspicuous industrial enterprises, salt largely dropped out of symbolism of whatever kind. Its place was taken by other commodities which more struck the public imagination. Some of these had already found a use as paradigms in the early modern period.

ESSENTIALS: CLOCKS AND GUNPOWDER IN THE SYMBOLISM OF *TAXIS*

Two commodities in particular, both with roots at least outside Europe, were used extensively as paradigmatic symbols in a major current of European thought in the early modern period. The commodities were clocks and gunpowder and the current of thought may, following Hayek, be called *taxis*: a belief in order in the sense of a single system of causality, at least within a particular field, based on a universal principle of sufficient reason. Taxic, as applied to bodies of thought, may be regarded as equivalent to the 'prima facie deterministic character' which Popper ascribed to classical physics.[23] The taxic current in European thought was one in its common assumption of undivided causality, complete determinism, and total predictability, given sufficient knowledge of initial conditions and of the appropriate laws of nature. But it was also dual because of its involvement in an ancient and basic dichotomy of wide scope. In the *School of Athens*, Raphael grouped the philosophers of antiquity round the two central figures of Plato and Aristotle, the first, the idealist, pointing upwards, the second, the empiricist, pointing downwards. It is not difficult to classify minds as Platonist or Aristotelian, but for bodies of thought, an older antithesis, that between Heraclitus and Parmenides, may provide a more appropriate classification. Heraclitus, as is well known, believed that everything changes, whereas Parmenides believed that nothing changes. Parmenides therefore saw reality in terms of space, or at least a space–time continuum, whereas Heraclitus saw reality in terms of time, or at least a time/space duality. Within this antithesis, the clock, a reduction of time to spatial movement, was an appropriate paradigm for Parmenidean thinking, just as gunpowder, an explosion of space in temporal sequence, was an appropriate paradigm for Heraclitean thinking. Together the two commodities formed an apt binary system for the expression of the polarities of classic taxic physics as they developed in early modernity from world clock to big bang.

Mechanical clocks and gunpowder were twins from the beginning. They first appeared in Europe towards the end of the thirteenth century and became conspicuous elements in their respective spheres of consumption in the course of the fourteenth century. Joseph Needham argued for the Chinese origin of both, but whereas in the case of gunpowder his argument has generally been accepted, in the case of mechanical clocks, it has been rejected by David Landes and other students of the subject.[24] Landes's alternative account of the purely European origins of the mechanical clock in Europe, however, still leaves something to be explained: in particular, its rather sudden appearance. Here, the context, the new relations with China and the simultaneous reception of gunpowder, are relevant. Landes's arguments may suffice for the material structure of the clock, but they are less adequate for its intellectual conjuncture. Continuity and homogeneity in the one do not exclude discontinuity and heterogeneity in the other. Needham was right.

Needham's argument was based on his reconstruction of the massive astronomical timepiece erected at Kaifeng in 1094 by the statesman, engineer and pharmacologist Su Sung: a reconstruction derived from Su Sung's account of it in his long neglected *Hsin I-Hsing Fa Yao*. The timepiece was water-driven. It was a super clepsydra. It embodied, however, the component known as an escapement: a device which interrupted the turning of a wheel, intervened between the motive power of the machine and the time regulator, and 'divided the flow of water into countable units and allowed relatively fine adjustment of the rate'.[25] The escapement is the brain of any clock. It allows for the adjustment of a terrestrial machine to correspond with the apparent celestial movements of the earth, sun and stars, by running it faster or slower. The escapement turns an egg timer into a chronometer. Through a number of literary sources, Needham traced the escapement back to a similar astronomical tower built in the reign of the second Sung emperor T'ai-tsung, though powered by a mercury rather than a water flow. Behind the Sung, however, were the T'ang clockmakers: notably the Tantric monk I-hsing who constructed an astronomical clock for Emperor Hsüan-tsung in 725, perhaps inspired by the late Han seismologist Chang Heng. Needham regarded what I-hsing built as 'the first of all escapement clocks'.[26] From the presence of an escapement tradition in China and its absence in Europe until the thirteenth century, Needham hypothesized a stimulus diffusion from China to Europe during the contact period of the Mongol empire, when a large packet of techniques moved from East to West.

Against Needham, Landes advanced four arguments. First, he argued that, on Needham's own evidence, the escapement tradition in China was not strong, and that Su Sung's clock was a magnificent dead-end. After the fall of Kaifeng to the Jurched in 1126, the Northern Chin, who took the timepiece to Yen-ching could not maintain it. Conversely, the Southern Sung, who migrated to Hang-chou could not duplicate it, despite the support of the Su family, the interest of Chu Hsi, and the availability from 1172 of Su Sung's account. Yet dead-end is too strong. The escapement featured in the astronomical timepiece constructed for the Mongols in 1276 by Kuo Shou-ching, parts of which survived to be seen by the early Jesuits, and in the palace clock realized by the last Yüan emperor Toghon Temur himself in 1254. It was only when the Ming rejected high technology in the name of anti-consumerism and Confucian astronomy in the name of Manichaeism, that the escapement disappeared temporarily. In the appropriate period, the tradition was sufficiently strong to transmit, particularly as amplified by the Yüan court.

Second, Landes argued that the two escapements, Chinese and European, were so different as to have only the name in common. The Chinese used a weighbridge and linkwork escapement to interrupt a unidirectional flow of water into discrete units. The Europeans used a verge and foliot escapement to interrupt a wheel powered by weights to produce a bidirectional oscillatory movement of discrete units. Between the two devices, Landes insists, there was a radical, mechanical, discontinuity, which cannot be papered over by any stimulus diffusion. Nevertheless, it might be said that both devices rested on the antecedent and not self-evident notion of the measurement of time through the creation of artificial units. Both presupposed the reduction of continuous temporal flow to discontinuous spatial movement, duration to time to use Bergson's terminology, quality to quantity. If these ideas were more strongly implanted in China than in Europe, then a stimulus diffusion from the one to the other might have produced a not utterly different effect.

Third, Landes argued that Needham produced no evidence for even this level of transmission. Here it might be replied that it is not clear what kind of evidence is being demanded. In the late thirteenth century, there were a number of information circuits crossing Eurasia which could have carried the message. From the west, there was the Franciscan mission which placed an archbishop in Peking. From the east, there was the Nestorian mission which sent ambassadors to the Pope and the kings of France and England. There was the Persian scientific mission which linked the observatories of Tabriz and Peking. There was the Armenian diaspora which joined Tabriz to Latin Christendom. There was the Alan heavy cavalry connection which, rooted in the north

Caucasus, supplied the Great Khan's army and sent ambassadors to the Pope at Avignon. There was the Italian mercantile network which made a trip to Hang-chou commonplace in fourteenth-century Venice. Any of these might have transmitted a spark and medievals were more attuned than we are to making maximum use of a minimum of information. Much was transmitted by these circuits at this time: gunpowder, blast furnaces, paper currency, moveable type, official postal services.[27] A notion of the spatialization of time does not seem beyond their carrying capacity, even if it was decoded differently by the recipients from what was encoded by the senders.

Finally, Landes argued that the appearance of the verge and foliot escapement could be sufficiently explained by intra-European developments without need for extra-European stimuli. If endogeneity was enough, why appeal to exogeneity? Landes pointed to the long-term interest of Benedictine monasticism, especially the Cluniacs, in accurate time measurement for the horarium. He pointed to the newer concern of employers and employees for their fair share of the working day. He pointed to civic routine, bureaucratic punctuality, regularity in business. These things demanded temporal precision: 'The clock did not create an interest in time measurement; the interest in time measurement led to the invention of the clock.'[28] Landes found a prehistory of the escapement in European campanology: 'time keeping machines began as automated bells'.[29] The validity of these explanations need not be gainsaid. Indeed, other endogenous factors, such as the discussions of time in Aquinas and Scotus, might be added. What might be questioned, however, is their sufficiency to account for the sudden appearance of monumental clocks all over Europe in the late thirteenth century and steadily on into the fourteenth century. This appearance had the character of a fashion as much as a technological revolution. Everyone wanted a clock just as in the 1980s everyone wanted a computer. It was not a slow progression but a rapid explosion. This suggests that a new, outside factor had been injected on the supply side.

That factor may have been, as Needham supposed, a stimulus diffusion in the form of a broad notion of an escapement. But there may have been two further factors, one abstract, one concrete. First, the principle of the European verge and foliot escapement was the oscillating, to and fro, positive and negative motion of its balance, produced by the contact of the toothed wheel with the pallets of the verge. The idea of oscillating motion was not one which came easily out of Aristotelian physics. It was familiar, indeed basic, as *yang* and *yin*, to the Confucian repository of concepts known as the *I-ching*. True, the

Chinese had not used the idea in the construction of their escapement, but then the basic design had been done by a Tantric monk at a time when Confucianism was at a low ebb. The Yüan dynasty, too, was not entirely Confucian, but several schools of divination were patronized, one of which, in Marco Polo's account, sounds like the *I-ching* tradition. From Chinese sources, we know that the Ch'an monk Liu Ping-chung, who was a leading adviser to Khubilai between 1249 and 1274, was regarded as a second Shao Yung, the greatest expert on the *I-ching*.[30] Indeed, it was he who selected the dynastic name of Yüan, 'origin', because of its *I-ching* resonances. Moreover, he was the patron of Kuo Shou-ching, the designer of the new astronomical clock of 1276. In the next generation, Wu Ch'eng, the dynasty's leading Confucian scholar, wrote a commentary on the *I-Ching*. That its basic idea of progression through oscillation was current in Peking is therefore certain. Moreover, divination, being less orthodox in Christendom, was always an object of interest to Christian visitors.

Second, if *I-ching* divination gave the abstract idea of alternation of forces, gunpowder provided a concrete instance of countdown, all or nothing firing, and accelerated or retarded action. The earliest investigations of a compound of saltpetre, sulphur and charcoal were in the context of the Taoist notion of time control: retardation or acceleration, through the instability of the maximum state of variables in an alternation of *yang*, *yin* and *yang*, and achieved in the case of gunpowder by variations in the saltpetre component. The most widespread use of gunpowder in thirteenth-century China, whether in arms or crackers, was as rocket propellent: fuel to impel an object forward by the recoil or reaction to the initial backward action of the explosive. The inspiration for the oscillatory motion of the verge and foliot escapement may, therefore, have come from outside the horological field altogether. The network most likely to have synthesized these elements would have been the Franciscans. John of Plano Carpini witnessed the enthronement of the Great Khan Güyug in 1246 and could have witnessed *I-ching* divination. Roger Bacon, who described Chinese firecrackers to Clement IV in 1267, knew William of Rubruck who had visited the Great Khan Möngke in 1255. John of Montecorvino was active as a missionary in Peking from 1295 to 1332. In Europe, the Franciscans were the evangelists of cities: builders of churches for prolonged sermons, promoters of attendance at the canonical hours by the laity, itinerants who encouraged the telling of time as well as the telling of beads. The time revolution was part of the Franciscan revolution, Europe's first great leap outwards.

The history of gunpowder was more straightforward. A text in the Taoist patrology, composed around 850, warned against the combination of saltpetre, sulphur and charcoal. The term *huo-yao*, fire drug, which commonly refers to gunpowder, occurs in an account of a naval battle between two Chinese states during the Wu-tai interregnum. In 1044, the military compendium *Wu-ching tsung-yao* gave a formula for a low-nitrate *huo-yao* in an account of weapons called *huo-ch'iang* or fire lances. These flame throwers were used extensively by both the Sung and the Chin against their northern neighbours. The next major Chinese military compendium, the *Huo-lung ching* of 1412, referred to *huo-chien*, fire arrows: originally incendiary devices, but by the thirteenth century, rockets propelled by gunpowder, deployed by the Southern Sung against the Mongols. Around 1250–80, from a cave temple at Ta-tsu in Szechwan comes the first iconographic evidence for a hand gun, probably powered by a high-nitrate gunpowder. Gunpowder was used both as retroactive and forward propellant in rockets and guns, and as explosive in crackers, bombs, grenades, land and sea mines, and rock blasting. The Mongols themselves did not use gunpowder before 1300, but intelligence about weapons travels fast. Roger Bacon had heard about gunpowder by 1265. A low-nitrate gunpowder is mentioned in the *Liber Ignium* of c.1250, perhaps from Muslim Spain, and the Syrian Hasan al-Rammah at the same time refers to a high-nitrate version. A common Arabic term for saltpetre was 'Chinese snow'. Mamluk Syria, notably the circle round Sultan Baybars al-Bunduqdari, which sought to counter the Mongol threat by copying Chinese institutions such as the state horse post and imperial stud farms, was probably the key liaison area for gunpowder technology. From there, the intelligence would have passed to the last Crusader states which Sultan Baybars was preparing to extinguish.

Gunpowder and clockwork, reborn together in the West, began to be used as symbols in the fourteenth century. John Dumbleton, one of the four celebrated Mertonians who founded the kinematic school of mechanics which led ultimately to Galileo and Newton, displayed a new interest in the mathematics of projectiles. In his fellow Mertonian, Thomas Bradwardine, axiomatization became determinism, with God, in the last resort, the only cause. In his *De Causa Dei*, he advanced an all or nothing logic. Between grace and sin there was no half-way position: the absence of the one implied the presence of the other in a system of oscillation. Similarly, John Buridan, if the ass paradox is rightly attributed to him, was describing a deterministic system of alternatives immobilized by its own presuppositions, a kind of rundown clock.

It was Buridan's pupil, Nicholas Oresme, scientific popularizer, adviser to Charles V of France and eventually bishop of Lisieux, who first compared the physical universe to a clock. In his *Livre du Ciel et du Monde* of *c.*1375, he wrote: 'the situation is much like that of a man making a clock [*horloge*] and letting it run and continue its own motion by itself. In this manner did God allow the heavens to be moved continually according to the proportion of the motive powers to the resistances and according to the established order of regularity.'[31] However, unlike a real timepiece, Oresme's world clock was a perpetual motion machine, untouched by a second law of thermodynamics. It was, therefore, on the cosmic scale, an atemporal Parmenidean universe. Its only temporality was the sublunary span of Christian revelation: a high cultural version of what Le Roy Ladurie, in the context of Montaillou, called an island of time suspended between the earthly paradise and the second coming.[32] In his book, Oresme discussed five theories of time: the Aristotelian world without beginning or end; the Platonic world of a beginning but no end; the Judaeo-Christian and Muslim world of one beginning and one end; the world of Heraclitus and Empedocles of many beginnings and many ends; and a fifth view of a world with no beginning but an end, which he says nobody holds. Oresme did not come down decisively in favour of any one of these views. His penchant, however, was towards the Platonic position, which he defended against its Aristotelian critics and which was most in accordance with his view of the outer cosmos at least as a perpetual motion machine. Oresme wanted to extend the realm of natural causality and limit the sphere of the miraculous. In his *De Causis Mirabilium* he wrote: 'There is no reason to take recourse to the heavens, the last refuge of the weak, or demons, or to our glorious God, as if he would produce these effects directly, more so than these effects whose causes we believe are well known to us.'[33] Though avoiding any assertion of the ubiquity of natural causes, Oresme was pushed by his clock paradigm to look further for them. Similarly, the projectile paradigm drove the Mertonians and Buridan in the direction of a concept of physics as, as Stanley Jaki puts it, 'the quantitive study of the quantitative aspect of things in motion'.[34] Through the two paradigms, a determinist *taxis* was articulated as a heuristic programme for the first time. Mechanism, measurement and motion might not be the whole of reality, but they were the parts proportionate to human reason.

Scholastic science was very nearly abortive, like Hellenistic, Muslim and Neo-Confucian science before it. The trail from the Mertonians to Galileo is hard to follow and uncertain, and while Leibniz may have admired Richard Swineshead, another Mertonian, it is not clear how much he really used his work. Oresme's incipient rationalism as well as his vernacular *haute vulgarisation* were continued in the fifteenth century by Reginald Pecock, bishop of Chichester, but following his condemnation, as much for anti-Yorkist politics as for unorthodoxy, that stream went underground, or was submerged by one or other of the fashionable pietisms. Scholastic science, in an age of humanism, was not helped by its style. It bred no diplomatic courtiers and after Charles V found no princely patrons. Though Platonic in inspiration, its mathematical Platonism was very different from the mystical Platonism of Marsilio Ficino or the playful Platonism of Erasmus. When science revived in the seventeenth century, it had to be on a different basis, with only minimum debts to its medieval predecessor.

The sixteenth century saw the further naturalization of guns and clocks. Shakespeare was familiar with both. In *Hamlet*, Marcellus, in speaking of evident preparations for war, refers to 'such daily cast of brazen cannon'. In *Macbeth*, the bleeding sergeant described to the king his victorious generals 'as cannons overcharged with double cracks'. In *Henry IV* part one, Harry Hotspur was enraged by the court lord who spoke of 'guns and drums and wounds', 'villanous saltpetre', and 'these vile guns'. Clocks were just as familiar. Leontes in *The Winter's Tale* accuses his wife of 'wishing clocks more swift, hours minutes, noon midnight' and the poet himself opens one of the sonnets with the line 'when I do count the clock that tells the time'. Time, indeed, and its irreversibility, are seldom absent from Shakespeare. In science, Niccolo Tartaglia wrote the first systematic treatise on gunnery in his *Nuova Scienzia* of 1537 which was translated into English by Cyprian Lucar in 1588. J. U. Nef, although not sympathetic to any positive role for war, noted that: 'A study of artillery was one source of Galileo's formulation of the laws of the interdependence of motion and force. By watching the flash and hearing the report from cannon, he was able to prove that the movement of sound took time.'[35] Aristotle believed that light was propagated instantaneously, that is, with an infinite velocity, but if sound had a finite speed, so might light. This was first suggested and assessed by Ole Roemer in 1675. In the long run, the speed of light was to play havoc with the notions of time and space for which projectile and clock stood as symbols in the seventeenth century, but immediately its measurement was a notable triumph of the orderly Newtonian cosmology.

Newton's cosmos was not a piece of clockwork, but he wished it was. His wish was due to the lingering prestige of Descartes. For, in

Cartesian science, clockwork was more than a paradigm: it was a hypothesis. By his definition of matter as *res extensa*, a truth known intuitively and a priori, Descartes opened the way to an essentialist ontology based on the mechanics of push. As Popper explained: 'The Cartesian physical universe was a moving clockwork of vortices in which each "body", or part of matter, pushed its neighbouring part along, and was pushed along by its neighbour on the other side.'[36] Newton rejected the essentialism: extension was an attribute of matter not its definition. He rejected, too, the plenum and the vortices. Celestial and terrestrial movements were to be explained, not in terms of push, but in terms of pull: that is, by the attractive force of gravity. Gravity, however, was not an ultimate explanation in Descartes' sense. Newton was worried by this, but he rejected the possibility of a reduction of pull to push by the kind of cosmic particle bombardment later strongly supported by the Swiss savant G. L. Le Sage. But equally, he rejected the suggestion of his Cambridge colleague Roger Cotes that gravitational attraction be regarded as an essential property of matter, in the same way as extension had been for Descartes. Newton's cosmos was thus left without ultimate physical explanation. The best he could do was to postulate absolute space and time as the *sensoria* of God: omnipresent, omniscient and capable of acting omnipotently with infinite velocity. Initially, Newton's justaposition of theology and science was admired and felt to be superior to Descartes' parallel but different justaposition. Subsequently, it was criticized, from different standpoints by Bishop Berkeley and the Oxford Hutchinsonians, as involving either a materialization of the Divinity or a divinization of matter.[37] It is sometimes suggested that Newton borrowed the notion of the *sensoria* from the Cambridge Platonists, notably Henry Cudworth. It is more likely that it arose from within his own system by an absolutization of the paradigms of the clock and the projectile. Space and time were essentially reifications of relationships, as Leibniz was soon to point out.

If Newton was haunted by the clock paradigm, which in Descartes and Spinoza had been a hypothesis, Leibniz, who criticized all three, did not escape its influence, despite his rejection of push as ultimate. First, in his criticisms of Newton, expressed in his correspondence with Samuel Clarke, what he initially objected to was that the English doctrines made God an incompetent watchmaker: 'Mr Newton and his followers have also an extremely odd opinion of the work of God. According to them God has to wind up his watch from time to time. Otherwise it would cease to go. He lacked sufficient foresight to make it a perpetual motion.'[38] Similarly, the English notion of gravity was insufficiently mechanical: 'For a free body naturally departs from a curve along a tangent. It is in this sense that I maintain that the attraction of bodies, properly so called, is a miraculous thing, since it cannot be explained by their nature.'[39] In effect, Descartes was preferable to Newton: 'A body is never moved naturally except by another body which impacts it by touching it; and after this it goes on until it is hindered by another body touching it. Any other operation on bodies is either miraculous or imaginary.'[40] Leibniz thinks it *is* imaginary, not in the sense of not happening, but in the sense of having a better explanation. Second, in his own explanation, which he opposed to French materialism and to English mathematics, Leibniz still used the clock paradigm if only to make contrasts. Superficially, matter was a simple collection: 'This can only be regarded as like an army or a flock, or like a pond full of fish, or a watch made up of springs and wheels.'[41] More profoundly, every monad had an integrative principle: 'Yet if there were no true *substantial unities*, there would be nothing real or substantial in the collection.'[42] The paradigm appears again in Leibniz's account of the relations of soul and body in a monad, which he compared to two clocks or watches keeping perfect time with each other. The synchronization was explicable in one of three ways: natural interdependence, occasional adjustment by a watchmaker, or, as Leibniz argued, by pre-established harmony.

Finally, within his own, non-mechanical system, the ongoing influence of the clock paradigm drove Leibniz in the direction of making space more real than time. In Leibniz's system, space and time were not things, vast empty containers as they were in Newton. They were systems of relationships: space the order of compossibles, time the order of non-compossibles. Compossibility is logical content: what is affirmed. Non-compossibility is what Popper called information content: what is denied. Information content is richer than logical content. This is why falsifiability is a better criterion of scientific status than verifiability. Leibniz might, therefore, have given preference to time over space. Yet, in his exposition to Clarke, preference is nearly always given to space, with time only added as a second best. This was more than a matter of presentation. In the last resort, Leibniz believed in a bloc, Parmenidean, universe without spontaneity or innovation. He wrote: 'true reasoning depends on necessary or eternal truths (like the truths of logic, numbers and geometry) which make the connection of ideas indubitable and the sequences inevitable'.[43] Hence Leibniz's desire to reduce the principle of sufficient reason to the principle of contradiction, and to move from 'all analytic statements are true' to 'all true statements are analytic'. The arrow of time was buried in the debris of space. Entropy made no difference: 'There is here no loss of forces, but the same thing happens as takes place when big money is turned into small change.'[44] The converse operation was equally possible. Though Leibniz discarded mechanical clockwork, whether of push or pull, his cosmos remained paradigmatically a clock.

That the clock so long retained its predominance was partly due to the weakness of the other paradigm, gunpowder. That today the Big Bang seems more convincing than the world clock may be attributed to a reversal of that situation. Indeed, physicists have some difficulty in communicating the new Parmenidean notion that the Big Bang may be imaginary in Leibniz's sense: a mere illusion of the cosmic anthropic principle or the story of only one among a multiplicity of universes. If before 1800, the Big Bang did not have more appeal, except as inspiration for artists as in Haydn's *fiat lux*, it was not only because of the short horizons afforded by geology and pre-evolutionary biology. Early artillery divided the explosion from the projectile, the gunpowder from the cannonball. Science focused on the projectile whose trajectory could be assimilated to physics by ballistics. The explosion itself was less open to investigation. It afforded no model of intelligibility and so was less used as a paradigm by philosophers until the time of Bergson. In a well-known passage, he wrote that evolution 'proceeds rather like a shell, which suddenly bursts into fragments, which fragments, being themselves shells, burst in their turn into fragments destined to burst again, and so on for a time immeasurably long'.[45] Yet Bergson was notoriously unscientific, taken seriously only by mavericks like Teilhard de Chardin or literary people like Shaw and Proust. It was not until the work of Prigogine, in the wake of Big Bang theory, the rediscovery of Boltzmann, and doubts about the status of the second law of thermodynamics, that his distinction between duration and time and his emphasis on irreversibility began to be of scientific interest.[46] In 1990, Roger Penrose wrote: 'It is my opinion that our present picture of physical reality, particularly in relation to the nature of *time*, is due for a grand shake-up – even greater, perhaps, than that which has already been provided by present-day relativity and quantum mechanics.'[47] It may be that the long dominance of Parmenides over Heraclitus is coming to an end in a resolution of the rivalry between the clock and the explosion as symbols of taxic order.

ACCESSORIES: NEW DRUGS IN THE SYMBOLISM OF *INTERTAXIS*

At the end of his controversy with Clarke, Leibniz reiterated a distinction between two kinds of substance: 'The natural forces of bodies are all subject to *mechanical laws*; and the natural forces of minds are all subject to *moral laws*. The former follow the order of *efficient causes*; and the latter follow the order of *final causes*. The former operate without liberty, like a watch; and the latter are exercised with liberty, although they agree exactly with that kind of watch which another, superior, free cause has set beforehand to fit in with them.'[48] Finality, liberty, pre-established harmony: in this passage, Leibniz opened the way to a kind of order other than taxis. It may be termed *intertaxis* because it is established unwittingly and without intention by free agents acting according to their own finalities. Intertaxic order is found most frequently in economics and biology, the two being linked by Darwin, who read market competition into the survival of the fittest.

In the early modern period, both in Europe and in China, paradigmatic symbols of intertaxis were often chosen from the new medicinal drugs which became available as a result of globalization. A search for drugs frequently accompanied the spread of civilization beyond their home territories. In 1220 Chinggis Khan summoned the Taoist macrobioticist Ch'ang Ch'un to Samarkand to find out whether he really had the secret of immortality. On one of Cheng Ho's voyages, there were 180 medical officers, some known by name, who sound more like a research team than ship's doctors. Ma Huan recorded a drug – Momordica Cochinensis – as one of the commodities obtained by the fleet in Dhufar. Columbus claimed, falsely, to have found medicinal rhubarb and cinnamon in the West Indies on his first voyage. Captain Cook kept a look out for useful resins among the eucalypts of Botany Bay in 1770. From East to West went China root, borax, camphor, ginger, star anise, galingale, ginseng and medicinal rhubarb. From West to East went mastic, myrrh and opium. From America to the Old World went various resins, cocaine, sarsaparilla, guiac and quinine. Of these drugs, the three most significant in symbolism were tar-water, rhubarb and opium.

Tar-water

Bishop Berkeley's *Siris* in praise of tar-water has always been a puzzle.[49] Berkeley, of course, lends himself to multiple interpretations: solipsist in popular philosophy, pantheist in religious romanticism, phenomenalist in post-war linguistic analysis, instrumentalist and precursor of Mach in Popper's philosophy of science, anticipator of the participatory anthropic principle in one school of cosmology. The problem is not with what Berkeley said but with which element in his thought is to be regarded as most central. With the *Siris*, this problem is compounded by its immersion in the obscure, post-Paracelsian medical world of the early eighteenth century. Sense and nonsense seem inextricably confused in a bog of hypochondria and quackery. Yet confusion was hardly characteristic of Berkeley's mind. In the most convincing interpretation to date, J. O. Wisdom argued that the *Siris* was an internal parallel to the external world described by the philosophical works.[50] Without disputing this, it may be suggested that another dimension of the *Siris* was the intention of extending into biology the kind of reconstruction (or deconstruction) Berkeley had achieved in physics. Berkeley no doubt believed in the virtues of tar-water, ultimately for the Kleinian reasons Wisdom analysed. But besides being a medicine, tar-water was a paradigm for the intertaxic order which would be found to prevail in the biological sciences. In his other works, Berkeley was providing a heuristic structure for a post-Newtonian physics in which God should not be materialized nor matter divinized. In the *Siris*, Berkeley was providing a heuristic structure for a post-Paracelsian medicine. That Berkeley's intention has been unperceived and the book put down to eccentricity is due to the fact that, while Newton was the foundation for subsequent physics, Paracelsus was simply bulldozed away by subsequent medicine.

Tar-water was not a new commodity. Resinous tar had long been a component of the Baltic trade and its medicinal properties were not unappreciated in either Galenic or Paracelsian medicine. Berkeley, however, only became interested during his stay in America between 1728 and 1731. The context was his Utopian plan to found a theological college in Bermuda to train missionaries for the evangelization of the Red Indians. This was part of another of Berkeley's post-structuralisms: rationalization of Fifth Monarchy millenarianism into colonial initiative, as expressed in the line 'Westward the course of empire takes its way.' Back in Ireland and bishop of Cloyne in 1734, Berkeley used tar-water in a famine in 1739, recommended it against dysentery in 1741 and finally supported its efficacy in relation to smallpox, giving rise to the controversy which prompted the *Siris* in 1744. The Greek meant cord, chain or system. It was also, Berkeley believed, an Egyptian name for the Nile. What he was concerned with was a con-

necting principle or universal biochemical process of which tar-water
was the expression.

Berkeley made high claims. As he wrote to the Dublin philanthro-
pist Thomas Prior: 'I freely own that I suspect tar-water is a panacea.
I may be mistaken but it is worth trial.'[51] It would cure, not necessarily all individuals, but all kinds of disease. It must contain the ingredients of guiac, the other American wonder drug, so highly regarded
against syphilis. It must be similar to myrrh: 'It is an apothegm of the
chemists, derived from Helmont, that whoever can make myrrh soluble by the human body has the secret of prolonging his days.'[52] Another
parallel was ginseng. Tar-water was mild: 'In which it emulates the
virtues of that famous plant Gen Seng, so much valued in China as the
only cordial that raiseth the spirits without depressing them.'[53] The
existence of panaceas, and Berkeley insisted that tar-water was superior to soap, opium or mercury, presumed the existence of a universal
cause of disease. J. O. Wisdom suggested that this cause was blockage, a kind of abstract and generalized costivity, a view he related to
Berkeley's childhood experiences. But this leaves open the question
how blockage should be understood and how tar-water remedied it.

In physics, Berkeley's principle was *esse est percipi*. God was the
universal observer. Errors resulted when perceptions were reified, theories
separated from their evidence, and notions such as space and time were
hardened into realities. In the *Siris*, Berkeley reaffirmed this principle:
'We have no proof, either from experiement or reason, of any other
agent or efficient cause than mind or spirit.'[54] How would this translate in biology? Berkeley rejected matter, but he did not reject energy.
His conception of the biosphere was of a photosynthetic process of
fire, light and heat, centred on the sun as a kind of sublunary god.
Energy originated in the sun: 'There is no effect in nature great, marvellous or terrible but proceeds from fire.'[55] Fire was diffused as aether
and light and became *calidum innatum* in man and resin in plants:
'fixed in the vissid juices of old firs and pines'.[56] Hence the power of
tar-water. 'A plant or tree', noted Berkeley, 'is a very nice and complicated machine', a laboratory of solar emanations, whose products
could be used to loosen human rigidities.[57] Tar-water was a paradigm
of a range of photosynthetic substances which could be used to restart
a cosmic process which had locally stalled.

Berkeley was a radical Anglican in the sceptical line of Erasmus.
Like his predecessor, he admired Plato, but rejected Platonism. His
enthusiasm for fire indicates that he also owed something to Heraclitus.
Consequently, he was less hostile to time than he was to space. In a

letter to the American Samuel Johnson, the president of King's College, New York, he wrote in March 1730: 'We are confounded and perplexed about Time (1) Supposing a succession in God (2) Conceiving that we have an abstract idea of Time (3) Supposing that the Time in one mind is to be measured by the succession of ideas in another.'[58] Berkeley here indicated three errors about time: its attribution to God, its existence without regard to events, and its simultaneity as between different individuals. What was left after this deconstruction was duration: the order of succession in a mind, psychological time, processual time. Of that time, tar-water was a positive, re-energizing distillation. It could be used to counteract the blocked, fixated negative time of the human organism. It was a paradigm of relations in an intertaxic energy system of plants, bodies and souls.

Rhubarb

In *An Inquiry Concerning Human Understanding*, published in 1748, David Hume used two drugs as a paradigm for inconstant effects. He wrote: 'Fire has always burned, and water suffocated, every human creature. The production of motion by impulse and gravity is a universal law which has hitherto admitted of no exception. But there are other causes which have been found more irregular and uncertain, nor has rhubarb always proved a purge, or opium a soporific, to everyone who has taken these medicines.'[59] Earlier, Hume had demonstrated that cause and effect were not a logical relationship except with respect to an antecedent general law. He had cast doubt, however, on any principle of induction by which such laws might be derived. Here, having established that custom and habitual expectation were the only basis of law, Hume extended his theory to inconstant effects in what amounted to a frequency interpretation of probability. Why, however, did he choose rhubarb and opium as his illustrations? Both were conspicuous parts of the synthesis of Galenism and Paracelsianism which dominated contemporary medicine. Opium was old in the West.[60] The poppy was cultivated in Switzerland around 3000 BC, though possibly more for its oil than its medicinal properties. The Sumerian Nippur tablets, the first pharmacopeia, may refer to it, and Galen described it as the strongest of drugs. Its main centres of commercial production were probably where they are today in Anatolia and Iran and this would account for its partial eclipse in Latin Christendom after the fall of antiquity. It was revived by the Paracelsians who, though they generally preferred mineral drugs, such as mercury, arsenic and antimony, to vegetable, promoted its use as laudanum.

Rhubarb, however, was a relative newcomer.[61] The rhubarb which Ramusio reported to be in universal use in Venice in the middle of the sixteenth century was *Rheum palmatum* var. *tanguticum*, from the Chinghai borderlands of northwest China and northeast Tibet, where it grew or was cultivated in high country between 7500 and 12 000 feet. Another, less efficacious rhubarb, *rhaponticum*, a product of the Black Sea region, had been known to the ancients, Dioscorides in particular. There is no reason to think Chinghai rhubarb reached the Roman empire and *rhaponticum* was not widely available or prescribed. It was the Muslim pharmacists who introduced what they called Chinese rhubarb to the West, carefully distinguishing it from their own inferior Persian product. Marco Polo correctly placed the source of rhubarb in what he called the major province of Tangut: 'In all the mountains of this region, rhubarb grows in great abundance; it is brought here [Suchou in the Kansu panhandle] by merchants, who export it far and wide.'[62] Although correct, Polo's information was not believed until it was confirmed by the Russian explorer Prejevalsky in the late nineteenth century. In the meantime, rhubarb was exported to the West by Muslim merchants, Turkish or Chinese-speaking, based on Sining. It was exported by all available routes, but particularly by land as rhubarb sent to Canton did not travel well by sea. From the fifteenth century, two factors boosted the rhubarb trade. First, more temporarily, the protection afforded to the central land route by the Timurids and their successors the Uzbeks. Second, more permanently, greater clinical demand as medical requirements changed.

The characteristic of preparations made from rhubarb root, which attracted physicians and patients and prompted Hume, was its principle, either successive or alternative, of double effect. As Hume said, rhubarb was a purgative, but an unusual one. It was an initial laxative and a subsequent astringent. Moreover, in both respects, its action was mild, the same quality that Berkeley attributed to tar-water. Consequently, it was the ideal weapon, and at that time almost the only effective weapon, against the largest component in the premodern death rate: infantile dysentery. It was also tried at least against the other flail of nurseries, against which Berkeley had promoted tar-water: smallpox, the red death of children, which affected eight children out of ten, and killed 10 per cent of those affected. Rhubarb was part of the child revolution. As children were more prized, planned, invested in and cherished, high infantile and child mortality or disfigurement were increasingly unacceptable. Parents welcomed rhubarb even if its consequences were uncertain, just as they later gave variolation and vaccination a remarkably rapid acceptance, even though the desired effects were not always produced. As Bishop Butler argued, probability was the guide of life. Similarly, rhubarb was embraced by doctors, especially those of a non-Paracelsian persuasion, who preferred vegetable to mineral remedies. Rhubarb was part of the Galenic counterattack. No wonder Hume was interested.

The conclusions he drew from this paradigm, however, were too limited by his psychologistic and phenomenalist presuppositions. This drove him, as in his political theory too, into a kind of fideism without faith.[63] The reduction of causality to habituality in the case of constant effects and to frequency in the case of inconstant effects, does not do justice to the scientific search for laws whether deterministic or probabilistic. In the case of medicines of irregular effect, Hume should have paid more attention to the circumstances of the patient in the spirit of Claude Bernard's remark that 'the microbe is nothing, the terrain is everything'. He might then have arrived at a more satisfactory theory of probability as objective propensity. Similarly, in his political theory, which also involved an intertaxic system, Hume was right to reject the Whig theory of the invariable action of a few simple institutions as sufficient to create a free society. But he failed to see that what was required was not less institutional analysis but more. Consequently, his own doctrines of habit, consensus and enlightened Toryism, as the middle ground between divine-right legitimism and ahistorical contractarianism, remained ill-grounded, and in the next generation became entangled in the romantic obfuscations of Burke. Hume was at once the apogee and nemesis of British empiricism. After him, the only way forward was that of Kant with his synthetic a prioris which provided a new solution to the problems of space, time and causality.

Opium

As rhubarb flowed West, opium flowed East, similarly as both import and transplant. There it became not only a commodity, but also a paradigmatic symbol of a policy debate about the role of government in society: that is, the place of taxic action in an intertaxic system. Like rhubarb in the West, opium had been known to the Chinese before it became the object of significant consumption.[64] In the middle T'ang, the opium poppy was described by Ch'en Ts'ang-chi in his supplementary pharmacopeia, *Pen-ts'ao shih-i*. At that time, it may have been only an exotic, but by the end of the dynasty it was being grown in Szechwan. In the Sung, the medicinal properties of the seeds were known to the pharmacopeia issued by Emperor T'ai-tsu, the two famous literati Su Shih and Su Ch'e experimented with poppy preparations for pleasure and poetry, and opium also figured in the *Pen-ts'ao t'u-ching*, the illustrated pharmacopeia of Su Sung, whom we have already met as the designer of the Kaifeng astronomical clock. It was not until the late sixteenth century, however, in the famous *Pen-ts'ao kang-mu* of Li Shih-chen, that opium, described as a new drug, was given its alternative Chinese names of *a-fu-yung* in the interior and *ya-pien* on the coast: both forms of *afyun*, the Arabic version of the Greek *opion*. This greater presence was probably the result of the revival of the central land route by the Timurids, but opium was soon coming by the southern sea route as well, a pharmacopeia of 1801 describing it as an import from Luzon and Java. By this time, the Europeans and Americans were selling opium from Bengal, Malwa, Persia and Turkey in ever-increasing quantities at Canton and along the China coast. Persian opium, however, continued to be imported along the central land route in the trade with Kokand and it was Persian opium which was first successfully acclimatized in China in Yunnan in the early nineteenth century. Opium in China originated on the Islamic frontier.

The consumption of opium in China is usually attributed to foreign promotion. Demand, however, was as important as supply. In particular, as with rhubarb, the medical situation needs to be taken into account. For the use of opium generally began in sickness, or the anticipation of it, and was then continued in health for psychological or social reasons. This was the conclusion of the most thorough investigation of opium in China, that of the British Royal Commission of 1894–5. In Szechwan, which produced most of the opium raised in China and consumed much of it itself, opium was both prophylactic and therapy. Here General W. Mesny noted that 'opium smoking is regarded in western China as the best possible and sure shield against malaria', while Archibald Little noted that: 'Many are led to smoke opium as a cure for diarrhoea, rheumatism, chills and fever – all of which are very prevalent in this damp warm province.'[65] Many of the population in Szechwan were immigrants, or the children of immigrants, and hence vulnerable to a new disease structure of which malaria and dysentery were major components. In towns, where more opium was consumed than in the country, tuberculosis was prevalent because of low investment in housing, and smoking was taken up to relieve the symptoms. On the coast, where foreign opium was most consumed, cholera was a new threat in the nineteenth century and opium was recommended as a preventive. Part of a medical conjuncture initially, opium passed into a social conjuncture. On the one hand, it became an expression of conspicuous leisure, a modest consumerist luxury. On the other hand, it became a way of survival, a practical, physiological necessity for groups with a hard but irregular lifestyle, such as itinerant tea coolies or shiftworkers in salt. Opium was never epidemic in China: 12 million regular users would be a reasonable estimate. But in understanding it, to use Bernard's language, the terrain was as important as the microbe, the Chinese consumer as significant as the foreign pusher, whether Central Asian Muslim or European.

Chinese law distinguished the medical and addictive uses of opium, the first being legal, the second illegal. Although opium originally entered China on the landward side from the drug-tolerant cultures of Islamdom, its addictive use was more conspicuous on the seaward frontiers where opium as an additive to tobacco was introduced from the Dutch maritime area linking Java and Taiwan. Taiwan became part of the Ch'ing empire in 1683 and in 1729 the Yung-cheng emperor issued an edict against addictive opium which imposed penalties for its sale or the operation of dens. Medicinal opium, however, remained legal and, of course, at the point of entry, it was impossible to distinguish the two destinations. Demand continued strong and supply provided resources with which to purchase Chinese tea. The annual import at Canton rose from 200 chests in 1729, to 1000 in 1767, and 4000 in 1790. In 1796 all import was forbidden and in 1800 the edict was repeated. The English East India Company then ceased to take part in the trade, except to the extent of selling opium from its monopoly in Bengal to private traders. Opium was now contraband at Canton, but it still found a ready market there and up the coast at Swatow. It was landed at Macao or, when that was sealed off in 1820, at Lintin island in the Pearl River estuary, or at Namoa island outside Swatow. From these places it was smuggled inland by a well-paid and ill-concealed underground run with the connivance of the authorities. By 1830 the import had increased to 18 000 chests, and by 1838 to over 20 000. At this point, the Chinese authorities, in the person of the imperial commissioner Lin Tse-hsü, began to take stronger measures, which were also applied, though less vigorously, to opium imported to Kashgar and Yarkand by merchants from Kokand, Badakhshan and Kashmir.

This action had been preceded by considerable debate at the highest level of Chinese government. It was conducted, as was usual, not always by the grand councillors and governors-general themselves as by their political advisers, underlings and stalking horses. It continued after the imperial decision and Commissioner Lin's measures led to a disastrous war. The debate was prompted by the belief, maybe mistaken, that the inflow of opium was leading to an outflow of silver which, by making bullion scarcer, was altering the exchange rate between silver, the currency of large transaction, and copper, the currency of everyday use. The monetary issue was important, but enveloping it was a series of not always avowed issues, which were of greater significance to Ch'ing officials. It might be expected that one of these issues would be *laissez-faire* versus state interference, the market versus management. In fact, until much later, Chinese official thinking found it hard to conceptualize the market, even though Chinese practice, as relayed through the Jesuits, had provided the Physiocrats with examples of it. Deregulation was one thing, the market was another, but the Chinese debate was structured along different lines.

First, there was the polarity between, to use Frederic Wakeman's terminology, the Moralizers who insisted that the law must be enforced, and the Legalizers who feared a reign of terror and argued that the bullion issue could be addressed more conveniently through import by barter under a state monopoly.[66] Next, behind this polarity, was an issue of political correctness: the dichotomy which went back to the Eastern Han between the Pure Stream and the Turbid Stream, whose definition, demarcation and designation were not matters of fact, but of value, power and control of the appropriate media. Chinese politics were biased in favour of self-proclaimed virtue. Third, though no one said so, the proclaimed dichotomy was often identical with the line between Chinese and Manchus, or more accurately Banner people whether Manchu, Mongol or Chinese. The Bannermen were loyal primarily to the leadership, to the dynasty. In its defence, they were prepared to be pragmatic, to switch from one means to another, to try out alternatives. The Chinese elite was loyal primarily to the system, to Confucian values. In its defence, they were not prepared to sacrifice principle to expediency, to treat ends as means, to veer from the only way. Concretely these divisions were embodied at the court of the Tao-kuang emperor in the great patronage machines of Mu-chang-a and Ts'ao Chen-yung. What was at issue was not only policy but who should implement it. Fourth, the debate had an ideological dimension. In Confucianism, the *k'ao-cheng hsüeh*, the school of empirical research, which had shifted the focus of study from philosophy to philology, textual exegesis and pure scholarship, was losing ground to the *hsin-wen chia*, the new text school, which mixed practice and prophecy, pursued hermeneutics for today rather than the exegesis of yesterday, and urged applied scholarship.[67] The *k'ao-cheng hsüeh* had been the chief recipient of imperial patronage in the days of the Ch'ien-lung emperor, but to a new generation those days looked less golden and it was easy to blame its inactive, cloistered philosophy.

Finally, implicit in the debate was the growing antithesis of Continental China and Maritime China. This was particularly well understood by one of the participants, Wei Yüan, political adviser to Lin Tse-hsü and New Text scholar, who wrote a book on the subject, the *Hai-kuo t'u-chih*.[68] Continental China was homogeneous, bureaucratic, law-abiding and stable. Maritime China was heterogeneous, plutocratic, lawless and unstable. Opium was a symbol of its unacceptable face: half-foreign, profit-seeking, selfish and corrupting. For both sides, the Opium War was a misnomer. What the British were demanding was diplomatic equality and the European system of international relations. What the Chinese were attacking was not the foreigner or opium *per se*, but the Canton interest: its business ethos, its multiculturalism, its links with Maritime Asia, its ability to corrupt any official sent to govern it. They were attacking it both for what it was and for what it might become. When Lin Tse-hsü had those chests of opium destroyed, he was making implicitly a bonfire of all the vanities. In attacking the Canton of the present, he was also attacking the Shanghai and Hong Kong of the future. He was attacking consumerism itself as an intertaxic system not susceptible of taxic control. What could not be controlled must be destroyed.

EXTRAS: FLOWERS IN THE SYMBOLISM OF *ATAXIS* AND *ANTITAXIS*

The early modern period saw a considerable globalization of flowers and floral practice.[69] Because of its richer, post-glacial resources, the flow of flowers was mainly from China to the West: azalea, camellia, forsythia, gardenia, peony, rhododendron, some roses, wisteria, to name only the principal transplants. But there were transplants in the other direction: dahlia, jasmine, some roses, tulips, water lilies and, in the treaty ports, a greater interest in cut flowers and the floral celebration of Western festivals, such as St Valentine's day. What was striking in both areas, however, was the conservatism of flower use, whether in festivals, funerals, decoration, iconography or imagery. It was the old flowers which were preferred rather than the new, though Monet's devotion to wisteria and the funerary use of chrysanthemums in continental Europe were exceptions. This preference was marked where flowers were employed as paradigmatic symbols in bodies of thought. Flowers were nostalgic in their appeal to the conservative sense of smell. They were also spontaneous, ephemeral, responsive to water and sunlight, and brilliantly coloured in relation to the rest of nature. Consequently they were employed especially in two kinds of system: ataxic, where causality appears absent (chaotic in the modern sense, whether deterministic or indeterministic), and antitaxic, where the ordinary or expected course of causality is inverted or reversed. These uses may be illustrated from the water lily and the lotus in Western art and Chinese religion, and from floral imagery more generally in Buddhist piety and Marial devotion.

Water Lilies

The most famous representations of water lilies are surely those of Monet painted from the garden at Giverny, which he once described as his greatest works of art. They were therefore art on art, a statement of theory as well as creative practice. As with Hume in empiricism, Monet's water lilies were the apogee and *ne plus ultra* of Impressionism. Locke, Berkeley and Hume sought to reduce concepts and judgements to sense data: *esse est percipi*. Similarly, Impressionism, with its aversion to conventions of subject and presentation and its demand to paint what is seen and not what is known to be there, was a kind of phenomenalism. Objects were reduced to patches of colour, epiphenomena of light and shade, puckers in space/time one might almost say in Eddington's phrase. Water lilies, so close to their background, wisteria hanging down from a bridge, hardly separable from its reflection, were an ideal vehicle by which to present a vision of reality as a supra-dimensional whole of water, land and light. The British empiricists had cast doubt on causality. Monet went beyond this. His water lily paintings expressed not disorder, but an order orderless, acausal spontaneity of conjuncture akin to Jung's connecting principle of synchronicity. Monet was strongly aware of the role of time in the constitution of reality. Hence his experiments, more than any other artist, with serial paining, whether of the gardens of Giverny or in the series on haystacks. Monet's series were not attempts to get a single picture right, as was the case with Renoir's different versions of the two girls at the piano, but an enunciation that only a series with shifts of time and perspective can fully portray the reality. Reality so conceived, was Heraclitean rather than Parmenidean: the evening star was not the morning star, and *le facteur temps* was constitutive. If Elstir is Monet, Proust was right to put him into a novel about time and to make him the point of conjunction between the hero and his multiple anima, the *Jeunes filles en fleur*. For the meeting with Albertine at Elstir's studio was chance only in appearance. It emerged from a complex background of ataxic order, a historian's realm of insufficient reason.

The Lotus

Bradley argued that there are no natural symbols: that symbolism always involved the isolation by culture of some characteristic of an object, so that it could stand for another object. If the characteristic of the Western water lily, *Nymphaea*, which attracted Monet was its closeness to its background, the characteristic of the Eastern lotus, *Nelumbo nucifera*, which attracted Buddhists, was the opposite: its escape from its muddy roots under the influence of the sun. In Christianity, nature was good because it was made by God, had not sinned and could be the source of sacraments. In Buddhism, nature was more problematical. In Hinayana, it was part of *samsara*, an illusion created, not by God, but by its own *pratityasamutpada*, the infernal interdependent origination of cause and effect due to nescience. Salvation was escape from self-creating nature through knowledge. Knowledge saved and absolute knowledge saved absolutely. In Mahayana, however, the dichotomy of illusion and salvation, *samsara* and *nirvana*, was attenuated. There was no absolute knowledge outside the world, only absolute charity, *mahakaruna*, within it. In the last resort, *samsara* and *nirvana* were identical. The only liberation was from liberation itself. Yet the insights of this second Buddhism did not cancel the insights of the first. They simply gave rise, particularly in China, to what has been called Multiple Buddhism, with different layers of truth.[70] In all the layers, the lotus retained its vitality as the symbol of whatever saving knowledge was appropriate at that level.

The most famous Buddhist text to use the name lotus was the *Saddharmapundarikasutra*; in Kumarajiva's Chinese version *Miao-fa lien-hua ching*, *lien* being the Chinese for lotus or water lily; and in English, The Lotus of the Wonderful Law *sutra*.[71] Lotus signified climax of finality and the Wonderful Law was Buddhism. The text purports to be Buddha's last sermon, though he is portrayed as a divinity rather than a sage. It probably dates from the first century, as a gnosticized version of the parable of the prodigal son suggests that it may have been subject to Christian influence. In China, it became the basis of the T'ien-t'ai sect, known as the orchid of the spring and dominant in the Sui period, and it has remained the most widely read of the Mahayana scriptures.

The Lotus sutra was used by T'ien-t'ai to propound a less agnostic and more theistic form of Buddhism than its predecessors, Madhyamika and Vijnanavada. Madhyamika had taught that nothing could be known because thought was inherently disjoined from reality. Vijnanavada reversed this counterposition by pointing out that at least this disjunction was known and that thought must be real. T'ien-t'ai went beyond idealism to phenomenology. Thought is intentional, is always partly outside itself, and co-affirms the universe and God as horizon. Within this horizon, the Cosmic Buddha, the Tathagata, operates. The central doctrine of the Lotus sutra is of the Buddha's possession of *upayakausalya*: infinite skill in means. By this was meant, not just omnipotence or providence, Calvin's predestination or Berkeley's synergism, but an omnimodality, an ability to use any situation to the end of salvation. 'I reveal the law in its multifariousness with regard to the inclinations and dispositions of creatures. I use different means to rouse each according to his own character. Such is the might of my knowledge.'[72] In any situation, the Buddha gave his message, the Dharmaparyaya: 'In that respect any word that the Tathagata speaks is true, not false. But in order to produce the roots of goodness in creatures, who follow different pursuits and behave according to different notions, he reveals various Dharmaparyayas with various fundamental principles. The Tathagata, young men of good family, does what he has to do.'[73] In this way, the taxic or intertaxic causality of *pratitya samutpada* was set aside by an ataxic system where, thanks to the Buddha's skill, any cause could provide the desired effect. In Christian soteriology, the nearest equivalent would be the 'salvation by dodges' teaching of the Occamist theologians of the later Middle Ages, whereby the means of grace set up by God's *potestas ordinata* could be set aside by God's *potestas absoluta*.

Flowers in General

A second Buddhist text to carry a flower name was the *Avatamsakasutra*; in Chinese *Hua-yen ching*; and in English, the Flower Garland or Ornament Sutra.[74] The appeal to many kinds of flowers rather than one may not be accidental. For while the Lotus sutra stressed the single, central activity of the Cosmic Buddha, the unity of absolute and relative (*li-shih wu-ai*) in all circumstances, the *Avatamsaka* stressed the unity of the relatives between themselves (*shih-shih wu-ai*) and their multiple, peripheral action in the formation of the ultimate centre, the tower of Maitreya. The *Avatamsaka* purported to be Buddha's first sermon, which, not being fully understood, was first simplified and only gradually revived by the crescendo of Mahayana sutras. The text is dated to the first or second centuries AD, later than the Lotus sutra, because it shows signs of being a response to that earlier work. In China, the *Avatamsaka* was first used in the T'ang period by the Hua-yen sect, predominant under Empress Wu and known as the chrysanthemum of the autumn, to propound a form of Buddhism more philosophical than T'ien-t'ai semi-theism. Subsequently, though eclipsed by the anti-intellectualism which followed the persecution of 845, it became at the end of the sixteenth century the intellectual basis of the reformation which dominated Chinese Buddhism until the twentieth century.[75] Where T'ien-t'ai emphasized the intention of universal mind, its *Vorgriff*, Hua-yen emphasized its performance, its *Vollzug*: the structure less of knowing than of any known.

A structure presupposes an order. In the *Avatamsaka* that order may be described as antitaxic because it inverts the expected direction of causality. In Buddhist scholasticism, a distinction was made between *shih* and *li*: phenomena and noumenon, relatives and absolute, effects and cause. The normal direction of causality, as set out in T'ien-t'ai philosophy, was from absolute to relative. In Hua-yen philosophy, however, in addition to the stress on relative to relative intercausality, there was also the implication that the absolute itself was constituted by this intercausality. There was a counterflow from relative to absolute, so that while the Buddha was the divine substance, the infinity of the enlightened were his divine persons. He was a collegial absolute like that of McTaggart. In depicting this vision of cosmic order, the *Avatamsaka* makes use of four kinds of imagery: flowers, jewels, mirrors and palaces, all mutually identified. All stand for the enlightenment which changes the universe from the slavery of *pratityasamutpada* to the freedom of the Cosmic Buddha who was re-created by his creatures. One name for this freedom was the flower bank world. Here, 'beautiful flower ornaments circulate throughout the universe reaching everywhere'; 'It is webbed with beautiful precious stones, which reflect the states of all the Buddhas like the net of Indra'; 'What the Supreme knower did in days gone by is all seen within their jewels.'[76] God was passive to creatures, like Indra with his harem of 92 trillion goddesses: 'causing each to think to herself that the king is amusing her alone, as he responds to all the goddess' bodies', while at the same time providing 'the heaven of access to others' enjoyment'.[77] The final image of cosmic order, presented when the pilgrim Sudhana reached his destination and achieved enlightenment, was that of the tower of Maitreya, the Buddha of the future, the omega point of the cosmic drama. 'He saw the tower immensely vast and wide, hundreds of thousands of leagues wide . . . Also, inside the great tower he saw hundreds of thousands of other towers similarly arrayed . . . yet those towers were not mixed up with one another, being each mutually distinct, while appearing reflected in each and every object of all the other towers.'[78]

In Christianity, the nearest equivalent to the *Avatamsaka* inversion of absolute and relative was the high Marial devotion, to which Luther objected precisely because it made God less than God. He objected in particular to notions of the Virgin as *Spes omnium*, *mediatrix ad Mediatorem*, *advocatus peccatorum*, as found in Gabriel Biel.[79] Floral imagery was an important vehicle of this devotion. Mary was associated especially with the rose, but also with the lily, the violet and the marigold. Goody lists 23 wild flowers whose common names before the Reformation included reference to Our Lady, the Madonna, the Virgin and so on.[80] This is significant because, in Goody's view, the use of flowers, whether in imagery or fact, is based on the notion of mediation, one of the most controverted issues in Mariology. St Alphonsus de Liguori, the apostle of Naples, who defended Mary's position as mediatrix of all grace, recourse to whom was a quasi-necessity for salvation, made vigorous use of floral hyperbole in his Acclamations in Praise of Mary: 'The white lilies and ruby roses stole their colors from thy lovely lips . . . The scented jasmine and fragrant Damasc rose stole their perfume from thy breath. The loftiest cedar and the most erect, the fairest cypress, were happy when they beheld their image in thy erect and lofty neck. The palm-tree, emulous and jealous likened itself to thy noble stature. In fine, O Lady, every created beauty is a shadow and trace of thy beauty.'[81] Alphonsus de Liguori followed the principle of *de Maria nunquam nimis*. Though he avoided Biel's excesses and seldom cites him, he had no hesitation in following Gerson's opinion: 'The kingdom of God consists in power and mercy: reserving power to himself, he, in some way, yielded the empire of mercy to his Mother', while Mary herself, in a sense, 'owed all to sinners'.[82] It was this antitaxic reversal of right order to which Luther and later Protestants objected, accusing Catholics of making Mary a fourth person of the Trinity. Liguori, of course, would have replied that by giving glory to creation, he was giving glory to the Creator, and the debate continues to divide Christendom.

In 1451 Stefan Lochner painted his *Virgin in the Rose Garden*, and the late fifteenth century saw Marial devotion rise to new heights. The flamboyant Burgundian age which commissioned these fashionably dressed madonnas, with their books of devotion, their floral bowers, and attendant donors and devotees, was a key period for the rise of consumerism in the West. It was a time when royal households expanded into bureaucratic courts, when residences became capitals, when city companies, guilds and confraternities adumbrated public space,[83] when the north began to appreciate the south, when, within the north, the Netherlands began to exercise its fascination, when Europe discovered wider worlds in the Ottoman empire, Black Africa, America and ultimately China. Clocks, gunpowder, new drugs and therapies, new fauna and flora, formed part of this wider world. Utilized by thought in symbolism, they enriched it and strengthened its drive to incarnate itself in commodities and thus create the world of consumerism. At one time, a school of history, over-impressed by the fact that it was in the north, which rejected some parts of that flamboyant Rhenish civilization, that consumerism first triumphed, ascribed the triumph to the rejection: Weber's famous thesis of the connection between Puritanism and capitalism. A better view would be that it was not what was rejected, but what was retained that laid the foundations of consumerisms in the West. By reason of a particular intellectual conjuncture, an iconic culture was succeeded by an aniconic. But the habit of mediating thoughts and values in commodities, whether in food, dress, shelter, utilities or information has continued to the present, not only in Europe, but increasingly as a benign global overlay. It is an overlay, or world institution, which promotes economic growth, social solidarity and the intellectual creativity on which both depend.

Notes

1 MATERIAL CULTURE

1. Fernand Braudel, *Capitalism and Material Life*, London: Fontana/Collins, 1974, p. 445.
2. Karl Rahner, *Spirit in the World*, London and Sydney: Sheed and Ward, 1968.
3. H. R. Trevor-Roper, *Historical Essays*, London: Macmillan, 1957, p. 129.
4. J. L. Simon, *The Ultimate Resource*, Princeton: Princeton University Press, 1981.
5. Sidney W. Mintz, *Sweetness and Power: The Place of Sugar in Modern History*, New York: Viking, 1985.
6. Mintz, *Sweetness and Power*, p. 200.
7. Marie-Clare Amouretti, 'L'attelage dans l'Antiquité, Le Prestige d'une erreur scientifique', *Annales, Économies, Sociétés, Civilisations*, 46(1), January–February 1991, pp. 219–32.
8. Arthur Waldron, *The Great Wall of China: From History to Myth*, Cambridge: Cambridge University Press, 1990.
9. Patricia Crone and Michael Cook, *Hagarism: The Making of the Islamic World*, Cambridge: Cambridge University Press, 1977.
10. Thomas J. Barfield, *The Perilous Frontier: Nomadic Empires and China, 221 BC to AD 1757*, Oxford: Blackwell, 1992.
11. Patrick Verley, 'La révolution industrielle anglaise: une révision', *Annales, Économies, Sociétés, Civilisations*, 46(3), May–June 1991, pp. 735–55.
12. Jean Delumeau, *Vie Économique et Sociale de Rome dans la seconde moitié du XVIe siècle*, 2 vols, Paris: Boccard, 1957–9; Bartolomé Bennassar, *Valladolid au Siécle d'Or*, Paris: Mouton, 1967.
13. Robert Darrah Jenks, *The Miao Rebellion, 1854–1872*, Harvard dissertation, University Microfilms, 1988.
14. Michel Cartier, 'Aux Origines de l'Agriculture intensive du Bas Yangzi', *Annales, Économies, Sociétés, Civilisations*, 46(5), September–October 1991, pp. 1009–19.
15. Robert Delort, *Le Commerce des Fourrures en Occident à la fin du Moyen Age*, 2 vols, Rome: École Française de Rome, 1978.
16. Laurier Turgeon, 'Le temps des pêches lointaines', in Michel Mollat (ed.), *Histoire des Pêches Maritimes en France*, Paris: Privat, 1987, pp. 133–81.
17. Denys Lombard, *Le Carrefour Javanais, Essai d'histoire globale*, 3 vols, Paris: École des Hautes Études en Sciences Sociales, 1990.
18. Bartolomé Bennassar and Lucile Bennassar, *Les Chrétiens d'Allah. L'histoire extraordinaire des renégats, XVIe – XVIIe siècles*, Paris: Perrin, 1989.
19. Francis Fukuyama, *The End of History and the Last Man*, London: Hamish Hamilton, 1992.
20. Bennassar, *Valladolid*, p. 573.
21. John-Paul II, *Centesimus Annus*, London: Catholic Truth Society, 1991, pp. 27, 16, 29.

22. Hilary J. Beattie, *Land and Lineage in China. A Study of T'ung-ch'eng county, Anhwei, in the Ming and Ch'ing dynasties*, Cambridge: Cambridge University Press, 1979.
23. Daniel Roche, *La Culture des Apparences, une histoire du vêtement, XVIIe – XVIIIe siècles*, Paris: Fayard, 1989.
24. Gilles Lipovetsky, *L'Empire de l'Éphémère, la mode et son destin dans les sociétés modernes*, Paris: Gallimard, 1987.
25. Joel Mokyr, *Industrialization in the Low Countries 1795–1850*, New Haven and London: Yale University Press, 1976.

2 CONSUMERISM AND FOOD

1. J. Ruffié and J. C. Sournia, *Les Épidémies dans l'Histoire de l'Homme*, Paris: Flammarion, 1984, pp. 8–10.
2. Claude Lévi-Strauss, *Mythologiques IV: L'Homme Nu*, Paris: Plon, 1971, pp. 556–8.
3. Etienne Balazs, *Chinese Civilization and Bureaucracy*, New Haven: Yale University Press, 1964, pp. 94, 98.
4. Marco Polo, *Travels*, ed. Ronald Latham, Harmondsworth: Penguin, 1958, p. 190.
5. Pierre Hurtubise, 'La Table d'un Cardinal de la Renaissance: Aspects de la Cuisine et de l'Hospitalité à Rome au milieu du XVIe siècle', *Mélanges de L'École Française de Rome*, Tome 92, 1980, 1, pp. 249–282.
6. Marco Polo, *Travels*, pp. 189–90.
7. Jacques Gernet, *Daily Life in China on the Eve of the Mongol Invasion 1250–1276*, London: Allen and Unwin, 1962, p. 137.
8. Balazs, *Chinese Civilization*, pp. 93–4.
9. F. Alvarez Semedo, *The History of That Great and Renowned Monarchy of China*, London: John Great, 1655, pp. 14, 63.
10. Antonia Finane, 'Prosperity and Decline under the Ching: Yangzhou and its Hinterland, 1644–1810', Ph.D. thesis, Australian National University, Canberra, 1985, pp. 292–5.
11. Alain Huetz de Lemps and Jean-Robert Pitte (eds), *Les Restaurants dans le monde et à travers les âges*, Grenoble: Editions Glénat, 1990; Jean-Robert Pitte, *Gastronomie Française, Histoire et Géographie d'une Passion*, Paris: Fayard, 1991; Peter Clark, *The English Alehouse, A Social History 1200–1850*, London: Longman, 1983.
12. Françoise Sabban, 'Le Système des Cuissons dans la Tradition Culinaire Chinoise', *Annales, Économies, Sociétés, Civilisations*, 38(2), March–April 1985, pp. 341–68; E. N. Anderson, *The Food of China*, New Haven: Yale University Press, 1988.
13. Claude Lévi-Strauss, *Mythologiques III: L'Origine des Manières de Table*, Paris: Plon, 1968, p. 406.
14. A. C. Graham, *Two Chinese Philosophers*, London: Lund Humphries, 1958, p. 99.
15. E. J. Kahn, Jr., *The Staffs of Life*, Boston: Little Brown, 1985, p. 299.
16. H. Dogget, *Sorghum*, Harlow, Essex: Longman, 1988.
17. Paul J. Smith, *Taxing Heaven's Storehouse*, Cambridge, Mass.: Harvard University Press, 1991.

18. Philip C. C. Huang, *The Peasant Economy and Social Change in North China*, Stanford: Stanford University Press, 1985, pp. 62–4, 72–3, 108, 116; Pierre-Étienne Will, *Bureaucratie et Famine en Chine au 18ᵉ siècle*, Paris: Mouton, 1980, pp. 121, 164, 166.
19. Peter Fleming, *One's Company*, London: Cape, 1940, p. 142.
20. Steven I. Levine, *Anvil of Victory, The Communist Revolution in Manchuria, 1945–1948*, New York: Columbia University Press, 1987, pp. 123–72.
21. Michel Cartier, 'Aux Origines de l'Agriculture intensive du Bas Yangzi', *Annales, Économies, Sociétés, Civilisations*, 46(5), September–October 1991, pp. 1009–19; David N. Keightley (ed.), *The Origins of Chinese Civilization*, Berkeley: University of California Press, 1983; D. H. Grist, *Rice*, Harlow, Essex: Longman, 1986; Akira Hayami and Yoshihiro Tsubouchi (eds), *Économic and Demographic Development in Rice Producing Societies*, Leuven: Leuven University Press, 1990.
22. E. W. Lane, *Manners and Customs of the Modern Egyptians*, London: Dent, 1954, p. 198; E. Ashtor, 'Essai sur l'alimentation des diverses classes sociales dans l'Orient médiéval', *Annales, Économies, Sociétés, Civilisations*, 25(5), September–October 1968, pp. 1017–53; Bennassar, *Chrétiens d'Allah*, pp. 414–26.
23. Ogier Griselin de Busbecq, *The Turkish Letters*, Oxford: Clarendon Press, 1968, p. 108.
24. Mark Wise, *The Common Fisheries Policy of the European Community*, London: Methuen, 1984; Japan Fisheries Association, *Fisheries of Japan*, Tokyo, 1987.
25. Laurier Turgeon, 'Le temps de pêches lointaines', in Michel Mollat (ed.), *Histoire des Pêches Maritimes en France*, Paris: Privat, 1987, pp. 134, 168.
26. R. E. F. Smith and David Christian, *Bread and Salt, A Social and Economic History of Food and Drink in Russia*, Cambridge: Cambridge University Press, 1984.
27. China, Industrial Handbooks, *Chekiang*, Shanghai: Ministry of Industry, 1935, pp. 357–70.
28. K. C. Chang (ed.), *Food in Chinese Culture*, New Haven and London: Yale University Press, 1977, p. 13.
29. China, Imperial Maritime Customs, *Salt: Production and Taxation*, Shanghai, 1906, p. 2.
30. Will, *Bureaucratie et Famine*, pp. 190–1.
31. Kahn, *The Staffs of Life*, p. 269.
32. Basil Williams, *The Life of William Pitt, Earl of Chatham*, London: Longman, 1915, p. 53.
33. H. B. Morse, *The Chronicles of the East India Company trading to China 1635–1834*, 5 vols, Oxford, 1926–1929, Vol. I, pp. 125, 158.
34. Louis Dermigny, *La Chine et L'Occident: Le Commerce à Canton au XVIIIᵉ siècle 1719–1833*, 4 vols, Paris: S.E.V.P.E.N., 1962–4.
35. Frédéric Mauro, *Histoire du Café*, Paris: Éditions Desjonquères, 1991; Claudia Roden, *Coffee*, Harmondsworth: Penguin, 1981.
36. Michael Winter, *Society and Religion in Early Ottoman Egypt*, New Brunswick, New Jersey: Transaction Books, 1982, p. 190.
37. Lane, *Manners and Customs*, pp. 340, 140–1; Mauro, *Histoire du Café*, p. 226.

38. Hugh Trevor-Roper, *From Counter-Reformation to Glorious Revolution*, London: Secker and Warburg, 1992, p. 94.

3 CONSUMERISM AND DRESS

1. Gilles Lipovetsky, *L'Empire de L'Éphémère*, Paris: Gallimard, 1987, p. 35.
2. *Ibid.*, p. 154.
3. J. C. Flügel, *The Psychology of Clothes*, London: Hogarth, 1930, p. 20.
4. Robert Delort, *Le Commerce des Fourrures*, pp. 489, 513, 515, 522, 524.
5. Alison Lurie, *The Language of Clothes*, New York: Random House, 1981.
6. Lipovetsky, *L'Empire de L'Éphémère*, p. 337.
7. Zhongshu Wang, *Han Civilization*, New Haven: Yale University Press, 1982, pp. 181–2; Michael Loewe, *Everyday Life in Early Imperial China*, London: Batsford, 1968, pp. 185–6.
8. Edward H. Schafer, *The Golden Peaches of Samarkand. A Study of T'ang Exotics*, Berkeley and Los Angeles: University of California Press, 1963.
9. Bernard Faure, *Chan Insights and Oversights*, Princeton, New Jersey: Princeton University Press, 1993.
10. Lipovetsky, *L'Empire de l'Éphémère*, p. 79.
11. Jean Delumeau, *Reassurer et Protéger, Le Sentiment de Securité dans l'Occident d'autrefois*, Paris: Fayard, 1989, pp. 261–89.
12. Craig Clunas, *Superfluous Things: Material Culture and Social Status in Early Modern China*, Cambridge: Polity Press, 1991, pp. 38–9; Colin P. M. Mackeras, *The Rise of the Peking Opera: Social Aspects of the Theatre in Manchu China*, Oxford: Clarendon Press, 1972, pp. 16–48.
13. Jane Austen, *Northanger Abbey*, London: Macdonald, 1961, pp. 8, 11.
14. Baron F. von Richthofen, *Letters 1870–1872*, Shanghai: North China Herald, 1903, p. 179.
15. Flügel, *Psychology of Clothes*, p. 160.
16. Peter Gay, *Freud, A Life for Our Time*, London: Dent, 1988, pp. 501–22.
17. Flügel, *Psychology of Clothes*, p. 139.
18. Lurie, *Language of Clothes*, p. 5.
19. Rupert Sheldrake, *A New Science of Life*, London: Paladin, 1984.
20. Lévi-Strauss, *Mythologiques IV*, p. 604.
21. *Ibid.*, pp. 603, 604.
22. Michael Novak, 'Two Moral Ideals for Business', IEA Second Annual Hayek Memorial Lecture, 22 June 1993.
23. Robert Musil, *The Man Without Qualities*, 3 vols, London: Pan, 1979, Vol. I, p. 155.
24. Robert H. S. Robertson, *Fuller's Earth. A History of Calcium Montmorillonite*, Hythe, Kent: Volturna, 1986.
25. Michel Balard, *La Romanie Genoise (XIIᵉ – début du XVᵉ siècles)*, 2 vols, Rome: École Française de Rome, 1978, pp. 723–33.
26. Richard Gascon, *Grand Commerce et Vie Urbaine au XVIᵉ siècle, Lyon et ses marchands (environ de 1520–environ de 1580)*, 2 vols, Paris: Mouton, 1971; Maurice Garden, *Lyon et les Lyonnais au XVIIIᵉ siècle*, Paris: Belles Lettres, 1970.
27. Carlo Poni, 'Archéologie de la Fabrique: la diffusion des moulins à soie

"*alla bolognese*" dans les états venetiens au XVIe au XVIIIe siècles', *Annales, Économies, Sociétés, Civilisations*, 27(6), November–December 1972, pp. 1475–96; Alain Dewerpe, *L'Industrie aux Champs*, Rome: C.E.F.R., 1985.

28. C. Stella Davies (ed.), *A History of Macclesfield*, Manchester: Manchester University Press, 1961.
29. Hosea Ballou Morse, *The Trade and Administration of the Chinese Empire*, London: Longman, 1908, p. 296.
30. Philip C. C. Huang, *The Peasant Family and Rural Development in the Yangzi Delta, 1350–1988*, Stanford: Stanford University Press, 1990, p. 44.
31. Boris Z. Rumer, *Soviet Central Asia: 'A Tragic Experiment'*, Boston: Unwin Hyman, 1990, p. 62.
32. Mark Mancall, 'The Kiakhta Trade', in C. D. Cowan (ed.), *The Economic Develop-ment of China and Japan*, London: Allen and Unwin, 1964, p. 19–48; Mark Mancall, *Russia and China: Their Diplomatic Relations to 1728*, Cambridge, Mass.: Harvard University Press, 1971; Richard A. Kraus, *Cotton and Cotton Goods in China, 1918–1936*, New York: Garland, 1980.
33. Robert H. G. Lee, *The Manchurian Frontier in Ch'ing History*, Cambridge, Mass.: Harvard University Press, 1970.
34. Daniel Dessert, *Argent, Pouvoir et Société au Grand Siècle*, Paris: Fayard, 1984.
35. Janet Wolf, *The Social Production of Art*, London: Macmillan, 1981, pp. 55–6.
36. Philip A. Kuhn, *Soul Stealers: The Chinese Sorcery Scare of 1768*, Cambridge, Mass.: Harvard University Press, 1990, pp. 53–72.
37. Reginald F. Johnston, *Twilight in the Forbidden City*, London: Gollancz, 1934, p. 157.
38. J. L. Cranmer-Byng (ed.), *An Embassy to China*, London: Longman, 1962, pp. 228–9.
39. Howard S. Levy, *The Lotus Lovers: The Complete History of the Curious Erotic Custom of Footbinding in China*, Buffalo: Prometheus, 1966.
40. James Laver, *Costume and Fashion: A Concise History*, London: Thames and Hudson, 1988, pp. 71–2, 102.
41. Lipovetsky, *L'Empire de l'Éphémère*, p. 38.

4   CONSUMERISM AND SHELTER

1. J. P. Bardet et al., *Le Bâtiment: Énquête d'Histoire Économique 14e–19e siècles*, Tome I, *Maisons rurales et urbaines dans la France traditionnelle*, Paris: Mouton, 1971.
2. Claude Lévi-Strauss, *Tristes Tropiques*, Harmondsworth: Penguin, 1976, pp. 278–9.
3. Klaas Ruitenbeek, *Carpentry and Building in Late Imperial China*, Leiden: Brill, 1993, p. 8.
4. Janice E. Stockard, *Daughters of the Canton Delta, Marriage Patterns and Economic Strategies in South China, 1860–1930*, Stanford: California University Press, 1989, p. 87; Bardet, *Le Bâtiment*, p. 141.
5. Étienne Hubert, *Espace Urbain et Habitat à Rome du Xe siècle à la fin du XIIIe siècle*, Rome: École Française de Rome, 1990.

6. Marco Polo, *Travels*, Harmondsworth: Penguin, 1958, p. 191.
7. F. A. Semedo, *The History of That Great and Renowned Monarchy of China*, London: John Great, 1655, p. 3.
8. John Francis Gemelli Careri, *A Voyage round the World*, London, 1745, p. 288.
9. Delumeau, *Reassurer et Protéger*, pp. 524–34.
10. Jean Delumeau, *L'Alum de Rome XVe–XIXe siècle*, Paris: S.E.V.P.E.N., 1962.
11. Richard J. Smith, *Fortune Tellers and Philosophers. Divination in Traditional Chinese Society*, Boulder: Westview, 1991.
12. Joseph Needham, *Science and Civilisation in China*, vol. IV, *Physics and Physical Technology*, Part III: *Civil Engineering and Nautics*, Cambridge: Cambridge University Press, 1971, p. 60.
13. Gu Gongxu et al., *Catalogue of Chinese Earthquakes (1831 BC – 1969 AD)*, Beijing: Science Press, 1989; Chen Yung et al., *The Great Tangshan Earthquake of 1976*, Oxford: Pergamon, 1988.
14. Antoine Gaubil, *Correspondence de Pékin 1722–1759*, Geneva: Droz, 1970, pp. 265–268; Gu, *Catalogue*, p. 132.
15. Bardet, *Le Bâtiment*, p. 43.
16. Wang Shixiang, *Classical Chinese Furniture*, USA: China Books and Periodicals, Inc., 1986.
17. Clunas, *Superfluous Things*, Cambridge: Polity Press, 1991, p. 63.
18. Jonathan Barry, 'Identité Urbaine et Classes Moyennes dans L'Angleterre Moderne', *Annales, Économies, Sociétés, Civilisations*, 48(4), July–August 1993, pp. 853–83.
19. William T. Rowe, *Hankow: Commerce and Society in a Chinese City 1796–1889*, Stanford: Stanford University Press, 1984, pp. 232–340.
20. Gérard Delille, *Famille et Propriété dans Le Royaume de Naples (XV–XIX siècles)*, Rome: École Française de Rome, 1985.
21. Sydney D. Gamble, *Peking, A Social Survey*, New York: Doran, 1921, pp. 412–15; *Fu-shun hsien-chih*, 1931 edition, Taipei, 1967, pp. 457–8.
22. Jacques Pezeu-Massabuau, 'La maison Japonaise: standardisation de l'espace habité et harmonie sociale', *Annales, Économies, Sociétés, Civilisations*, 32 (4), July–August 1977, pp. 670–701.
23. Godfrey Barker, 'Wealth, Unhealthy and Unwise', *Spectator*, 10 April 1993, pp. 21–3.
24. Henry Edward Manning, *Miscellanies*, 2 vols, London: Burns and Oates, 1877, Vol. II, pp. 70, 74.
25. Needham, *Science and Civilisation*, Vol. IV, part III, p. 90.
26. François Sigaut, 'La Chine, L'Europe et les techniques agricoles', *Annales, Economies, Sociétés, Civilisations*, 44(1), January–February, 1989, pp. 207–16; Anthony Reid, *Southeast Asia in the Age of Commerce 1450–1680*, Vol. I, *The Lands Below the Winds*, New Haven: Yale University Press, 1988, pp. 51–2, 62–6, 69–72; John N. Micksie, 'Traditional Sumatran Trade', *Bulletin de l'École Française d'Extrême Orient*, 74, 1985, pp. 423–69.
27. Claudine Lombard-Salmon, *Un Exemple d'Acculturation Chinoise: La Province de Gui Zhou au XVIIIe siècle*, Paris: École Française d'Extrême Orient, 1972, pp. 202–3, 288–91, Map 6.
28. Letter to the author, 24 November 1986; Nicholas Kaye Menzies, 'Trees,

Fields and People: The Forests of China from the Seventeenth to the Nineteenth Centuries', Ph.D. thesis, Berkeley: University of California, 1988.

29. J-L Biget, J. Boissière, and J.-C. Hervé (eds), *Le Bois et La Ville du Moyen Age au XXe siècle*, Saint-Cloud: École Normale Supérieure de Fontenay, 1991.
30. Robert Greenhalgh Albion, *Forests and Seapower. The Timber Problem of the Royal Navy 1652–1862*, Cambridge, Mass.: Harvard University Press, 1926.
31. Ruitenbeek, *Carpentry and Building*, pp. 51–3.
32. Jenny May, 'The Late Roman Villa: The Relationship between Architectural Form and Social Structure', unpublished paper, Department of Classics, University of Canterbury, 1993.
33. Pierre Toubert, *Les Structures du Latium Médiéval*, 2 vols, Rome: École Française de Rome, 1973, p. 455.
34. *Ibid.*, pp. 480, 487, 736–61.
35. *Ibid.*, p. 711.
36. Lombard, *Le Carrefour Javanais*, Vol. II, p. 267.
37. Hubert, *Espace Urbain*, pp. 172–3, 200–3, 205–6.
38. Emmanuel Le Roy Ladurie, *Montaillou, Village Occitan de 1294 à 1324*, Paris: Gallimard, 1975, pp. 69–71; Margit Gari, *Le Vinaigre et le Fiel*, Paris: Plon, 1983, pp. 378–81.
39. Robert Tichane, *Ching-te-chen*, New York: New York State Institute of Glaze Research, 1983.
40. John S. Guy, *Oriental Trade Ceramics in South-East Asia: Ninth to Sixteenth Centuries*, Singapore: Oxford University Press, 1986; Hugh R. Clark, 'Quanzhou (Fujian) during the Tang-Song Interregnum, 879–978', *T'oung Pao*, 68, (1–3) (1982), pp. 132–49; Peter Y. K. Lam, *A Ceramic Legacy of Asia's Maritime Trade*, Singapore: Oxford University Press, 1985.
41. Patrice Fontaine, *Le Tapis Persan ou Le Jardin de l'éternel Printemps*, Paris: Editions Recherche sur les Civilisations, 1990.
42. *Ibid.*, pp. 99–102.
43. Johnston, *Twilight*, pp. 172, 26–27.
44. Cranmer-Byng, *An Embassy to China*, pp. 116–17.
45. *Ibid.*, pp. 271–2; Anne Chayet, *Les Temples de Jehol et Leurs Modèles Tibetains*, Paris: Editions Recherche sur les Civilisations, 1985.
46. Wilhelmina F. Jashemski, *The Gardens of Pompeii, Herculaneum and the Villas destroyed by Vesuvius*, New York: Caratzos, 1979.
47. Joseph Needham, *Science and Civilisation in China*, Vol. VI, *Biology and Biological Technology*, Part I, *Botany*, Cambridge: Cambridge University Press, 1986, especially pp. 363–439.
48. E. H. M. Cox, *Plant-Hunting in China*, London: Collins, 1945; E. H. Wilson, *A Naturalist in Western China*, London: Cadogan, 1986.

5 CONSUMERISM AND UTILITIES

1. Fernand Braudel, *Civilisation matérielle et capitalisme, destins du monde XVe–XVIIIe siècles*, Paris: Armand Colin, 1967.

2. S. A. M. Adshead, 'An Energy Crisis in Early Modern China', *Ch'ing-shih wen-t'i*, 3(2), December 1974, pp. 20–8.

3. Lien-sheng Yang, 'Economic Justification for Spending – An Uncommon Idea in Traditional China', *Studies in Chinese Institutional History*, Cambridge, Mass.: Harvard University Press, 1961, pp. 58–74.

4. Hsü Kuang-ch'i, 'T'un-t'ien su-kao', *Tseng-ting Hsü wen-ting kung-chi*, Taipei, 1962, *Chuan* 2.

5. Semedo, *The History of That Great and Renowned Monarchy of China*, p. 7.

6. Simon Schama, *The Embarrassment of Riches: An Interpretation of Dutch Culture in the Golden Age*, London: Fortuna, 1991, pp. 322–3.

7. Will, *Bureaucratie et Famine*, p. 250.

8. Leon E. Stover, *The Cultural Ecology of Chinese Civilization*, New York: Mentor, 1974, pp. 133–140.

9. Marco Polo, *Travels*, p. 127.

10. Teng T'o, 'Les mines de charbon de Men-t'ou kou', *Annales, Économies, Sociétés, Civilisation*, 22(1), January–February 1967, pp. 50–87.

11. Cranmer-Byng, *An Embassy to China*, p. 297.

12. J. U. Nef, *The Rise of the British Coal Industry*, 2 vols, London: Routledge, 1932, Vol. I, p. 201.

13. Richthofen, *Letters*, pp. 173–4.

14. *Ibid.*, pp. 10, 34–38, 46.

15. Donald E. Wagner, *Dabieshan, Traditional Chinese Iron-production Techniques practised in Southern Henan in the Twentieth Century*, London and Malmö: Curzon, 1985.

16. Nef, *Coal*, Vol. I, p. 196.

17. *Ibid.*, p. 198.

18. John U. Nef, *War and Human Progress: An Essay on the Rise of Industrial Civilization*, London: Routledge and Kegan Paul, 1950, p. 10.

19. Roche, *La Culture des Apparences*, pp. 163, 175, 366, 377.

20. Jean-Pierre Goubert, *La Conquête de l'Eau*, Paris: Lafont, 1986.

21. Alain Musset, 'De Tlaloc à Hippocrate: L'Eau et L'Organisation de L' Espace dans le Bassin de Mexico (XVIᵉ – XVIIIᵉ siècles)'. *Annales, Économies, Sociétés, Civilisations*, 46(2) March–April 1991, pp. 261–98.

22. Karl A. Wittfogel, *Oriental Despotism, A Comparative Study of Total Power*, New Haven: Yale University Press, 1957.

23. Needham, *Science and Civilisation*, Vol. 4, Part III, pp. 229–31, 234–7.

24. Pierre-Etienne Will, 'Un Cycle Hydraulique en Chine: La Province du Hupei du XVIᵉ au XIXᵉ siecles', *Bulletin de L'École Française d'Extrême Orient*, 68, 1980, pp. 261–98; Philip C. C. Huang, *The Peasant Family*, pp. 21–43.

25. Delumeau, *Vie Économique et Sociale de Rome*, pp. 346–53, 578–83.

26. J. H. and Brian Chapman, *The Life and Times of Baron Haussmann*, London: Weidenfeld and Nicolson, 1957, pp. 111–13; Gerhard Mansur, *Imperial Berlin*, London: Routledge and Kegan Paul, 1971, p. 68.

27. Needham, *Science and Civilisation*, Vol. IV, Part III, p. 376.

28. Hans Ulrich Vogel, 'The Great Well of China', *Scientific American*, June 1993, pp. 86–91.

29. Huang, *The Peasant Economy*, pp. 55–7.

30. Joseph Needham, *Science and Civilisation in China*, Vol. IV, *Physics and Physical Technology*, Part II, *Mechanical Engineering*, Cambridge: Cambridge University Press, 1964, pp. 127–134.
31. *Mr Punch's Cavalcade, A Revue of Thirty Years*, London: The Educational Book Company Ltd, 1930, pp. 160–2.
32. *Cahiers des Annales de la Propagande de la Foi*, Tome III, 16, pp. 369–381; Tome IV, 22, pp. 414–417, Letters of Father Imbert, September 1826, September 1827, September 1829.
33. Carl Crow, *Foreign Devils in the Flowery Kingdom*, London: Hamish Hamilton, 1941, p. 48.
34. Wang Zhongshu, *Han Civilization*, New Haven and London: Yale University Press, 1982, p. 101, Plate 120.
35. Alexander Hosie, *Report by Consul-General Hosie on the Province of Ssuch'uan*, British Parliamentary Papers, China No. 5 (1904), p. 32.
36. *Ibid.*, p. 78.
37. *Ibid.*, p. 32.

6 CONSUMERISM AND INFORMATION

1. *Centesimus Annus*, pp. 24–25.
2. William Meacham, 'Origins and Development of Yüeh Coastal Neolithic: A Microcosm of Cultural Change on the Mainland of East Asia', in David Keightley (ed.), *The Origins of Chinese Civilization*, Berkeley: University of California Press, 1983, pp. 147–175.
3. John D. Barrow and Frank J. Tipler, *The Anthropic Cosmological Principle*, Oxford: Oxford University Press, 1986, pp. 136, 659–662.
4. Novak, 'Two Moral Ideals', pp. 14–15; Henry Petroski, *The Pencil: A History of Design and Circumstance*, London: Faber, 1990.
5. Richard J. Smith, *Fortune-Tellers and Philosophers: Divination in Traditional Chinese Society*, Boulder: Westview Press, 1991, pp. 74–83.
6. Elizabeth L. Eisenstein, *The Printing Press as an Agent of Change: Communications and Cultural Transformations in Early Modern Europe*, 2 vols, Cambridge: Cambridge University Press, 1979, pp. 303–450.
7. Joseph Needham, *Science and Civilisation in China*, Vol. V, *Chemistry and Chemical Technology*, Part I, *Paper and Printing*, by Ts'en Tsuenhsuin, Cambridge: Cambridge University Press, 1983, p. 135.
8. Wang Gung-wu, 'Feng Tao: An Essay in Confucian Loyalty', in Arthur F. Wright and Denis Twitchett (eds), *Confucian Personalities*, Stanford: Stanford University Press, 1962, pp. 122–145, p. 135.
9. Lévi-Strauss, *Tristes Tropiques*, pp. 388, 471; Jack Goody, *The Interface between the Written and the Oral*, Cambridge: Cambridge University Press, 1987, p. xv.
10. Paul U. Unschuld, *Medical Ethics in Imperial China. A Study in Historical Anthropology*, Berkeley: University of California Press, 1979, pp. 15–115.
11. B. F. Musallam, *Sex and Society in Islam*, Cambridge: Cambridge University Press, 1983; Daniel Panzac, *La Peste dans L'Empire Ottoman 1700–1850*, Louvain: Peeters, 1985.

12. Françoise Aubin, 'Chinese Islam: In Pursuit of its Sources', *Central Asian Survey*, 5(2), 1986, pp. 73–80.
13. Thomas D. Goodrich, *The Ottoman Turks and the New World*, Wiesbaden: Harrasowitz, 1990.
14. Goody, *The Interface between the Written and the Oral*.
15. Roger S. Bagnall, *Egypt in Late Antiquity*, Princeton: Princeton University Press, 1993, pp. 235–241.
16. *Kultur Chronik*, no. 4, 1986, p. 36.
17. Hans-Georg Gadamer, *Truth and Method*, New York: Seabury, 1975, p. 401.
18. *Ibid.*, pp. 345–6.
19. James Hayes, *The Rural Communities of Hong Kong*, Hong Kong: Oxford University Press, 1983, pp. 8, 36, 97, 235.
20. Charles Nicholl, *The Reckoning: The Murder of Christopher Marlowe*, London: Picador, 1993.
21. Joseph W. Esherick, *The Origins of the Boxer Uprising*, Berkeley: University of California Press, 1987, pp. 64–65.
22. *Ibid.*, p. 330.
23. Charles Morazé, *Essai sur la Civilisation d'Occident: L'Homme*, Paris: Armand Colin, 1950, pp. 192–202.
24. Claude Lévi-Strauss, *The Raw and the Cooked*, London: Jonathan Cape, 1970, pp. 17, 18.
25. Karl Popper, *Unended Quest: An Intellectual Biography*, Glasgow: Fontana/Collins, 1976, p. 58.
26. Paul Saenger, 'Physiologie de la lecture et séparation des mots', *Annales, Économies, Sociétés, Civilisations*, 44(4), July–August 1989, pp. 939–52.
27. Petroski, *The Pencil*.
28. George Young, *A History of Whitby and Streoneshalh Abbey*, 2 vols, Whitby: Clark and Mudd, 1817, pp. 918–20.
29. Hayes, *The Rural Communities of Hong Kong*, pp. 195–6, 231.
30. Hosea Ballou Morse, *The Trade and Administration of the Chinese Empire*, London: Longman, 1908, pp. 379–80.
31. Jacques Gernet, *Les Aspects Économiques du Boudhisme dans la Société Chinoise du Vᵉ au Xᵉ siècle*, Saigon: École Française d'Extrême Orient, 1956.
32. Needham, *Science and Civilisation*, Vol. V, part I, pp. 220–2.
33. Roswell S. Britton, *The Chinese Periodical Press 1800–1912*, Shanghai: Kelly and Walsh, 1933, p. 11.
34. Manying Ip, *The Life and Times of Zhang Yuanji 1867–1959*, Peking: The Commercial Press, 1985.
35. Evelyn Sakakida Rawski, *Education and Popular Literacy in Ch'ing China*, Ann Arbor: University of Michigan Press, 1979, p. 23.
36. Jack Goody, *The Development of the Family and Marriage in Europe*, Cambridge: Cambridge University Press, 1983.
37. Arthur P. Wolf and Chieh-shan Huang, *Marriage and Adoption in China 1845–1945*, Stanford: Stanford University Press, 1980

7 CONSUMERISM AND SYMBOLISM

1. Claude Lévi-Strauss, *Totemism*, Harmondsworth, Middlesex: Penguin, 1969, p. 162.
2. F. A. Hayek, *Law, Legislation and Liberty*, Vol. I, *Rules and Order*, London: Routledge and Kegan Paul, 1973, pp. 35–54.
3. F. H. Bradley, *The Principles of Logic*, 2 vols, London: Oxford University Press, 1992, pp. 1–7.
4. *Ibid.*, p. 4.
5. Bernard Cottret, 'Pour une Sémiotique de la Réforme: Le Consensus Tigurinus (1549) et *La Brève Resolution* (1555) de Calvin', *Annales, Économies, Sociétés, Civilisations*, 39(2), March–April 1984, pp. 265–85.
6. Louis Bouyer, *The Cistercian Heritage*, London: Mowbray, 1958, pp. 107–10.
7. J. I. Packer and G. E. Duffield (eds), *The Works of Thomas Cranmer*, Appleford, Berkshire: Sutton Courtney, 1965, pp. 65, 149–50, 163, 208.
8. Lévi-Strauss, *Mythologiques*, Vol. IV, pp. 302, 607.
9. James E. Latham, *The Religious Symbolism of Salt*, Paris: Beauchesne, 1982; Jean-François Bergier, *Une Histoire du Sel*, Fribourg: Presses Universitaires de France, 1982; Robert P. Multhauf, *Neptune's Gift: A History of Common Salt*, Baltimore: Johns Hopkins University Press, 1978; S. C. Aggarwal, *The Salt Industry in India*, New Delhi: Government of India, 1976, pp. 1–20; Michel Mollat (ed.), *Le Rôle du Sel dans L'Histoire*, Paris: Presses Universitaires de France, 1968, pp. 277–303.
10. Lévi-Strauss, *Mythologiques II: Du Miel aux Cendres*, Paris: Plon, 1966, p. 242.
11. Lévi-Strauss, *Mythologiques, II*, p. 321.
12. Lévi-Strauss, *Mythologiques, IV*, p. 125.
13. Latham, *Religious Symbolism*, p. 161.
14. *Ibid.*, pp. 57–63.
15. *Ibid.*, p. 116.
16. Hugh Trevor-Roper, *Renaissance Essays*, London: Secker and Warburg, 1985, pp. 149–199, p. 158.
17. C. G. Jung, *Mysterium Conjunctionis*, London: Routledge and Kegan Paul, 1963, pp. 183–256, 459–60.
18. C. G. Jung, *The Practice of Psychotherapy*, London: Routledge and Kegan Paul, 1954, p. 306.
19. Athanasius Kircher, *Mundus Subterraneus*, Amsterdam, 1665, Vol. I, p. 345, Vol. II, pp. 134–5.
20. Robert Boyle, *The Sceptical Chemist*, 1661, facsimile, London: Dawsons, 1965, pp. 34–5.
21. *Ibid.*, pp. 75, 345–6.
22. Kenneth Warren, *Chemical Foundations: The Alkali Industry in Britain to 1926*, Oxford: Clarendon Press, 1980.
23. Karl R. Popper, *The Open Universe, An Argument for Indeterminism*, London: Hutchinson, 1982, pp. 5–8, 23–32.
24. Joseph Needham et al. *Heavenly Clockwork*, Cambridge: Cambridge University Press, 1960; David S. Landes, *Revolution in Time: Clocks and the Making of the Modern World*, Cambridge, Mass.: Harvard University Press, 1983, p. 83.

25. Landes, *Revolution in Time*, p. 18.
26. Joseph Needham, *Science and Civilisation in China*, Vol. IV, *Physics and Physical Technology*, Part II, *Mechanical Engineering*, p. 474.
27. Didier Gazagnadou, *La Poste à Relais: Le Diffusion d'une technique de pouvoir à travers L' Eurasie*, Paris: Editions Kimé, 1994.
28. Landes, *Revolution in Time*, p. 58.
29. *Ibid.*, p. 68.
30. Chan Hok-lam, 'Liu Ping-chung (1216–74), A Buddhist-Taoist statesman at the court of Khubilai Khan', *T'oung Pao*, 53(1–3), 1967, pp. 98–146.
31. Nicole Oresme, *Le Livre du Ciel et du Monde*, ed. Albert D. Menut and Alexander J. Denomy CSB, Madison: University of Wisconsin Press, 1968, p. 289.
32. Le Roy Ladurie, *Montaillou*, p. 430.
33. Bert Hanson, *Nicole Oresme and the Marvels of Nature*, Toronto: Pontifical Institute of Medieval Studies, 1985, p. 137.
34. Stanley Jaki, Rochester Lecture, University of Canterbury, New Zealand, 23 July 1992.
35. John U. Nef, *War and Human Progress, An Essay on the Rise of Industrial Civilization*, London: Routledge and Kegan Paul, 1950, p. 54.
36. Popper, *The Open Universe*, p. 135.
37. C. B. Wilde, 'Matter and Spirit as Natural Symbols in Eighteenth Century British Natural Philosophy', *British Journal for the History of Science*, 15, 1982, pp. 99–131; 'Hutchinsonianism, Natural Philosophy and Religious Controversy in Eighteenth Century England', *History of Science*, 18, 1980, pp. 1–24; Albert J. Kuhn, 'Glory or Gravity: Hutchinson vs Newton', *Journal of the History of Ideas*, 22, 1961, pp. 303–22.
38. G. W. Leibniz, *Philosophical Writings*, London: Dent, 1951, p. 192.
39. *Ibid.*, p. 203.
40. *Ibid.*, p. 218.
41. *Ibid.*, p. 103.
42. *Ibid.*
43. *Ibid.*, p. 224.
44. *Ibid.*, p. 227.
45. Henri Bergson, *Creative Evolution*, trans. Arthur Mitchell, London: Macmillan, 1912, p. 103.
46. Ilya Prigogine and Isabelle Stengers, *Entre Le Temps et L'Eternité*, Paris: Fayard, 1988, pp. 11, 19, 31–2.
47. Roger Penrose, *The Emperor's New Mind*, London: Vintage, 1990, p. 480.
48. Leibniz, *Philosophical Writings*, p. 229.
49. George Berkeley, *The Works of George Berkeley, Bishop of Cloyne*, ed. A. A. Luce and T. E. Jessup, Vol. V, *Siris, A Chain of Philosophical Reflections and Inquiries concerning the virtues of Tar-water and diverse other Subjects connected together and arising One from Another*, London: Nelson, 1953, pp. 25–164.
50. John Oulton Wisdom, *The Unconscious Origins of Berkeley's Philosophy*, London: Hogarth, 1953.
51. Berkeley, *Siris*, p. 175.
52. *Ibid.*, p. 47.
53. *Ibid.*, p. 53.

54. *Ibid.*, p. 83.
55. *Ibid.*, p. 84.
56. *Ibid.*, p. 177.
57. *Ibid.*, p. 43.
58. Berkeley, *Works*, Vol. II, p. 293.
59. David Hume, *An Inquiry Concerning Human Understanding*, Indianapolis: Bobbs-Merill, 1955, pp. 70–1.
60. Mark David Merlin, *On the Trail of the Ancient Opium Poppy*, London and Toronto: Fairleigh, 1984.
61. Clifford M. Foust, *Rhubarb: The Wondrous Drug*, Princeton: Princeton University Press, 1992.
62. Marco Polo, *Travels*, p. 60.
63. H. R. Trevor-Roper, 'Review: *David Hume: Politico e Storica* by Giuseppe Giarizzo, Einaudi, Turin, 1962', *History and Theory*, 3(2), 1964, pp. 381–9.
64. Paul U. Unschuld, *Medicine in China: A History of Pharmaceutics*, Berkeley: University of California Press, 1986, pp. 158–67.
65. Royal Commission on Opium 1894–95, Vol. V, Appendix XXVI, pp. 247, 342.
66. Frederic Wakeman, Jr. 'The Canton Trade and the Opium War', in John K. Fairbank (ed.), *The Cambridge History of China*, Vol. X, *Late Ch'ing, 1800–1911, Part I*, Cambridge: Cambridge University Press, 1978, pp. 163–212, esp. pp. 178–81; Hsin-pao Chang, *Commissioner Lin and the Opium War*, Cambridge, Mass.: Harvard University Press, 1964.
67. Benjamin A. Elman, *From Philosophy to Philology: Intellectual and Social Aspects of Change in Late Imperial China*, Cambridge, Mass.: Harvard University Press, 1984; *Classicism, Politics and Kinship: The Ch'ang-chou School of New Text Confucianism in Late Imperial China*, Berkeley: University of California, 1990.
68. Jane Kate Leonard, *Wei Yüan and China's Rediscovery of the Maritime World*, Cambridge, Mass.: Harvard University Press, 1984.
69. Jack Goody, *The Culture of Flowers*, Cambridge: Cambridge University Press, 1993, pp. 291–2.
70. Zenryu Tsukamoto, *A History of Early Chinese Buddhism*, 2 vols, Tokyo: Kodansha International, 1985, p. 889.
71. H. Kern (ed.), *The Saddharma-Pundarika Sutra*, Sacred Books of the East, Vol. X, New York: Scribner, 1901.
72. *Ibid.*, p. 54.
73. *Ibid.*, p. 302.
74. Thomas Cleary (ed.), *The Flower Ornament Scripture*, 3 vols, Boulder and London: Shambhala, 1984.
75. Sung-peng Hsü, *A Buddhist Leader in Ming China*, Philadelphia: Pennsylvania University Press, 1979; Chün-fa Yü, *The Renewal of Buddhism in China*, New York: Columbia University Press, 1981.
76. Cleary, *Flower Ornament Scripture*, Vol. I, pp. 203, 205, 206.
77. *Ibid.*, pp. 361, 364.
78. *Ibid.*, Vol. III, pp. 365–6.
79. Heiko Augustinus Oberman, *The Harvest of Medieval Theology: Gabriel Biel and Late Medieval Nominalism*, Cambridge, Mass.: Harvard University Press, 1963, pp. 281–322.

80. Goody, *The Culture of Flowers*, pp. 156–7.
81. St Alphonsus de Liguori, *The Glories of Mary*, Brooklyn, New York: Redemptorist Fathers, 1931, p. 676.
82. *Ibid.*, pp. 37–38, 200.
83. Gervase Rosser, 'Les fraternités urbaines anglaises à la fin du Moyen Age', *Annales, Économies, Sociétés, Civilisations*, 48(5), September–October 1993, pp. 1127–43.

Bibliography

Adshead, S. A. M., 'An Energy Crisis in Early Modern China', *Ch'ing-shih wen-t'i*, 3(2), December 1974, pp. 20–8.

Aggarwal, S. C., *The Salt Industry in India*, New Delhi: Government of India, 1976.

Albion, Robert Greenhalgh, *Forests and Seapower. The Timber Problem of the Royal Navy 1652–1862*, Cambridge, Mass.: Harvard University Press, 1926.

Alphonsus de Liguori, St, *The Glories of Mary*, Brooklyn, New York: Redemptorist Fathers, 1931.

Amouretti, Marie Claire, 'L'attelage dans l'Antiquité, Le Prestige d'une erreur scientifique', *Annales, Économies, Sociétés, Civilisations*, 46(1), January–February 1991, pp. 219–32.

Anderson, E. N., *The Food of China*, New Haven: Yale University Press, 1988.

Ashtor, E., 'Essai sur l'alimentation des diverses classes sociales dans l'Orient médiéval', *Annales, Économies, Sociétés, Civilisations*, 25(5), September–October 1968, pp. 1017–53.

Aubin, Françoise, 'Chinese Islam: In Pursuit of its Sources', *Central Asian Survey*, 5(2), 1986, pp. 73–80.

Austen, Jane, *Northanger Abbey*, London: Macdonald, 1961.

Bagnall, Roger S., *Egypt in Late Antiquity*, Princeton, New Jersey: Princeton University Press, 1993.

Balard, Michel, *La Romanie Genoise (XIIe-debut de XVe siècles)*, 2 vols, Rome: École Française de Rome, 1978.

Balazs, Etienne, *Chinese Civilization and Bureaucracy*, New Haven: Yale University Press, 1964.

Bardet, J. P., Chaunu, P., Désert, G., Gouthier, P. and Neveux, H. *Le Bâtiment: Enquête d'Histoire Économique 14e–19e siècles*, Tome I, *Maisons rurales et urbaines dans la France traditionnelle*, Paris: Mouton, 1971.

Barfield, Thomas J., *The Perilous Frontier: Nomadic Empires and China, 221 BC to AD 1757*, Oxford: Blackwell, 1992.

Barker, Godfrey, 'Wealth, Unhealthy and Unwise', *Spectator*, 10 April 1993, pp. 21–3.

Barrow, John D. and Tipler, Frank J., *The Anthropic Cosmological Principle*, Oxford: Oxford University Press, 1986.

Barry, Jonathan, 'Identité Urbaine et Classes Moyennes dans L'Angleterre Moderne', *Annales, Économies, Sociétés, Civilisations*, 48(4), July–August 1993, pp. 853–83.

Beattie, Hilary J., *Land and Lineage in China, A Study of T'ung-Ch'eng county, Anhwei in the Ming and Ch'ing dynasties*, Cambridge: Cambridge University Press, 1979.

Bennassar, Bartolomé, *Valladolid au Siècle d'Or*, Paris: Mouton, 1967.

Bennassar, Bartolomé and Lucile, *Les Chrétiens d'Allah. L'histoire extraordinaire des renégats, XVIe–XVIIe siècles*, Paris: Perrin, 1989.

259

Bergier, Jean-François, *Une Histoire du Sel*, Fribourg: Presses Universitaires de France, 1982.

Bergson, Henri, *Creative Evolution*, trans. Arthur Mitchell, London: Macmillan, 1912.

Berkeley, George, *The Works of George Berkeley, Bishop of Cloyne*, ed. A. A. Luce and T. E. Jessup, Vol. V, *Siris, A Chain of Philosophical Reflections and Inquiries concerning the virtues of Tar-water and diverse other Subjects connected together and arising One from Another*, London: Nelson, 1953.

Biget, J-L, Boissière, J. and Hervé, J.-C. (eds), *Le Bois et La Ville du Moyen Age au XXe siècle*, Saint-Cloud: École Normale Supérieure de Fontenay, 1991.

Bouyer, Louis, *The Cistercian Heritage*, London: Mowbray, 1958.

Boyle, Robert, *The Sceptical Chemist*, 1661, facsimile, London: Dawsons, 1965.

Bradley, F. H., *The Principles of Logic*, 2 vols, London: Oxford University Press, 1992.

Braudel, Fernand, *Civilisation matérielle et capitalisme, destins du monde XVe–XVIIIe siècles*, Paris: Armand Colin, 1967.

Braudel, Fernand, *Capitalism and Material Life*, London: Fontana/Collins, 1974.

Britton, Roswell S., *The Chinese Periodical Press 1800–1912*, Shanghai: Kelly and Walsh, 1933.

Busbecq, Ogier Giselin de, *The Turkish Letters*, Oxford: Clarendon Press, 1968.

Cahiers des Annales de la Propagande de la Foi, 1820–29.

Cartier, Michel, 'Aux Origines de l'Agriculture intensive du Bas Yangzi', *Annales, Économies, Sociétés, Civilisations*, 46(5), September–October 1991, pp. 1009–19.

Chan, Hok-lam, 'Liu Ping-chung (1216–74), A Buddhist-Taoist statesman at the court of Khubilai Khan', *T'oung Pao*, 53(1–3), 1967, pp. 98–146.

Chang, Hsin-pao, *Commissioner Lin and the Opium War*, Cambridge, Mass.: Harvard University Press, 1964.

Chang, K. C. (ed.), *Food in Chinese Culture*, New Haven and London: Yale University Press, 1977.

Chapman, J. H. and Chapman, Brian, *The Life and Times of Baron Haussmann*, London: Weidenfeld and Nicolson, 1957.

Chayet, Anne, *Les Temples de Jehol et Leurs Modèles Tibetains*, Paris: Éditions Recherche sur les Civilisations, 1985.

Chen, Yung et al., *The Great Tangshan Earthquake of 1976*, Oxford: Pergamon, 1988.

China, Imperial Maritime Customs, *Salt: Production and Taxation*, Shanghai, 1906.

China, Industrial Handbooks, *Chekiang*, Shanghai: Ministry of Industry, 1935.

Clark, Hugh R., 'Quanzhou (Fujian) during the Tang-Song Interregnum, 879–978', *T'oung Pao*, 68(1–3), 1982, pp. 132–49.

Clark, Peter, *The English Alehouse, A Social History 1200–1850*, London: Longman, 1983.

Cleary, Thomas (ed.), *The Flower Ornament Scripture*, 3 vols, Boulder and London: Shambhala, 1984.

Clunas, Craig, *Superfluous Things: Material Culture and Social Status in Early Modern China*, Cambridge: Polity Press, 1991.

Cottret, Bernard, 'Pour une Sémiotique de la Réforme: Le Consensus Tigurinus (1549) et *La Brève Resolution* (1555) de Calvin', *Annales, Économies, Sociétés,*

Civilisations, 39(2), March–April 1984, pp. 265–85.

Cowan, C. D. (ed.), *The Economic Development of China and Japan*, London: Allen and Unwin, 1964.

Cox, E. H. M., *Plant-Hunting in China*, London: Collins, 1945.

Cranmer-Byng, J. L. (ed.), *An Embassy to China*, London: Longman, 1962.

Crone, Patricia and Cook, Michael, *Hagarism: The Making of the Islamic World*, Cambridge: Cambridge University Press, 1977.

Crow, Carl, *Foreign Devils in the Flowery Kingdom*, London: Hamish Hamilton, 1941.

Davies, C. Stella (ed.), *A History of Macclesfield*, Manchester: Manchester University Press, 1961.

Delille, Gérard, *Famille et Propriété dans Le Royaume de Naples (XV–XIX siècles)*, Rome: École Française de Rome, 1985.

Delort, Robert, *Le Commerce des Fourrures en Occident à la fin du Moyen Age*, 2 vols, Rome: École Française de Rome, 1978.

Delumeau, Jean, *Vie Économique et Sociale de Rome dans la seconde moitié du XVIᵉ siècle*, 2 vols, Paris: Boccard, 1957–9.

Delumeau, Jean, *L'Alum de Rome XVᵉ–XIXᵉ siècle*, Paris: S.E.V.P.E.N., 1962.

Delumeau, Jean, *Reassurer et Protéger, Le Sentiment de Securité dans l'Occident d'autrefois*, Paris: Fayard, 1989.

Dermigny, Louis, *La Chine et L'Occident: Le Commerce à Canton au XVIIIᵉ siècle 1719–1833*, 4 vols, Paris: S.E.V.P.E.N., 1962–4.

Dessert, Daniel, *Argent, Pouvoir et Société au Grand Siècle*, Paris: Fayard, 1984.

Dewerpe, Alain, *L'Industrie aux Champs*, Rome: C.E.F.R., 1985.

Dogget, H., *Sorghum*, Harlow, Essex: Longman, 1988.

Eisenstein, Elizabeth L., *The Printing Press as an Agent of Change: Communications and Cultural Transformations in Early Modern Europe*, 2 vols, Cambridge: Cambridge University Press, 1979.

Elman, Benjamin A., *From Philosophy to Philology: Intellectual and Social Aspects of Change in Late Imperial China*, Cambridge, Mass.: Harvard University Press, 1984.

Elman, Benjamin A., *Classicism, Politics and Kinship: The Ch'ang-chou School of New Text Confucianism in Late Imperial China*, Berkeley: University of California, 1990.

Esherick, Joseph W., *The Origins of the Boxer Uprising*, Berkeley: University of California Press, 1987.

Fairbank, John K. (ed.), *The Cambridge History of China*, Vol. X, *Late Ch'ing, 1800–1911*, Part I, Cambridge: Cambridge University Press, 1978.

Faure, Bernard, *Chan Insights and Oversights*, Princeton, New Jersey: Princeton University Press, 1993.

Finane, Antonia, 'Prosperity and Decline under the Ching: Yangzhou and its Hinterland, 1644–1810', Ph.D. thesis, Canberra: Australian National University, 1985.

Fleming, Peter, *One's Company*, London: Cape, 1940.

Flügel, J. C., *The Psychology of Clothes*, London: Hogarth, 1930.

Fontaine, Patrice, *Le Tapis Persan ou Le Jardin de l'éternel Printemps*, Paris: Éditions Recherche sur les Civilisations, 1990.

Foust, Clifford M., *Rhubarb: The Wondrous Drug*, Princeton, New Jersey: Princeton University Press, 1992.

Fukuyama, Francis, *The End of History and the Last Man*, London: Hamish Hamilton, 1992.

Fu-shun hsien-chih, 1931 edition, Taipei, 1967.

Gadamer, Hans-Georg, *Truth and Method*, New York: Seabury, 1975.

Gamble, Sydney D., *Peking. A Social Survey*, New York: Doran, 1921.

Garden, Maurice, *Lyon et les Lyonnois au XVIIIe siècle*, Paris: Belles Lettres, 1970.

Gari, Margit, *Le Vinaigre et le Fiel*, Paris: Plon, 1983.

Gascon, Richard, *Grand Commerce et Vie Urbaine au XVIe siècle, Lyon et ses marchands (environ de 1520 – environ de 1580)*, 2 vols, Paris: Mouton, 1971.

Gaubil, Antoine, *Correspondence de Pékin 1722–1759*, Geneva, Droz, 1970.

Gay, Peter, *Freud, A Life for Our Time*, London, Dent, 1988.

Gazagnadou, Didier, *La Poste à Relais: Le Diffusion d'une technique de Pouvoir à travers L'Eurasie*, Paris: Éditions Kime, 1994.

Gemelli Careri, John Francis, *A Voyage round the World*, London, 1745.

Gernet, Jacques, *Les Aspects Économiques du Boudhisme dans la Société Chinoise du Ve au Xe siècle*, Saigon: École Française d'Extrême Orient, 1956.

Gernet, Jacques, *Daily Life in China on the Eve of the Mongol Invasion 1250–1276*, London: Allen and Unwin, 1962.

Goodrich, Thomas D., *The Ottoman Turks and the New World*, Wiesbaden: Harrassowitz, 1990.

Goody, Jack, *The Development of the Family and Marriage in Europe*, Cambridge: Cambridge University Press, 1983.

Goody, Jack, *The Interface between the Written and the Oral*, Cambridge: Cambridge University Press, 1987.

Goody, Jack, *The Culture of Flowers*, Cambridge: Cambridge University Press, 1993.

Goubert, Jean-Pierre, *La Conquête de l'Eau*, Paris: Lafant, 1986.

Graham, A. C., *Two Chinese Philosophers*, London: Lund Humphries, 1958.

Grist, D. H., *Rice*, Harlow, Essex: Longman, 1986.

Gu, Gongxu et al., *Catalogue of Chinese Earthquakes (1831 BC – 1969 AD)*, Beijing: Science Press, 1989.

Guy, John S., *Oriental Trade Ceramics in South-East Asia: Ninth to Sixteenth Centuries*, Singapore: Oxford University Press, 1986.

Hanson, Bert, *Nicole Oresme and the Marvels of Nature*, Toronto: Pontifical Institute of Medieval Studies, 1985.

Hayami, Akira and Tsubouchi, Yoshiburo (eds), *Economic and Demographic Development in Rice Producing Societies*, Leuven: Leuven University Press, 1990.

Hayek, F. A., *Law, Legislation and Liberty*, Vol. I, *Rules and Order*, London: Routledge and Kegan Paul, 1973.

Hayes, James, *The Rural Communities of Hong Kong*, Hong Kong: Oxford University Press, 1983.

Hortubise, Pierre, 'La Table d'un Cardinal de la Renaissance: Aspects de la Cuisine et de l'Hospitalité à Rome au milieu du XVIe siècle', *Melanges de L'École Française de Rome*, Tome 92, 1980, 1, pp. 249–82.

Hosie, Alexander, *Report by Consul-General Hosie on the Province of Ssu-*

ch'uan, British Parliamentary Papers, China, No. 5, 1904.

Hsü, Kuang-ch'i, 'T'un-t'ien su-kao', *Tseng-ting Hsü wen-ting kung-chi*, Taipei, 1962.

Hsü, Sung-peng, *A Buddhist Leader in Ming China*, Philadelphia: Pennsylvania University Press, 1979.

Huang, Philip C. C., *The Peasant Economy and Social Change in North China*, Stanford: Stanford University Press, 1985.

Huang, Philip C. C., *The Peasant Family and Rural Development in the Yangzi Delta, 1350–1988*, Stanford: Stanford University Press, 1990.

Hubert, Étienne, *Espace Urbain et Habitat à Rome du Xe siècle à la fin du XIIIe siècle*, Rome: Ecole Française de Rome, 1990.

Huetz de Lemps, Alain and Jean-Robert Pitte (eds), *Les Restaurants dans le monde et à travers les âges*, Grenoble: Éditions Glénat, 1990.

Hume, David, *An Inquiry Concerning Human Understanding*, Indianapolis: Bobbs-Merrill, 1955.

Ip, Manying, *The Life and Times of Zhang Yuanji 1867–1959*, Peking: The Commercial Press, 1985.

Jaki, Stanley, Rochester Lecture, University of Canterbury, New Zealand, 23 July 1992.

Japan Fisheries Association, *Fisheries of Japan*, Tokyo, 1987.

Jashemski, Wilhelmina F., *The Gardens of Pompeii, Herculaneum and the Villas destroyed by Vesuvius*, New York: Caratzos, 1979.

Jenks, Robert Darrah, *The Miao Rebellion, 1854–1872*, Harvard dissertation, University Microfilms, 1988.

John-Paul II, *Centesimus Annus*, London: Catholic Truth Society, 1991.

Johnston, Reginald F., *Twilight in the Forbidden City*, London: Gollancz, 1934.

Jung, C. G., *The Practice of Psychotherapy*, London: Routledge and Kegan Paul, 1954.

Jung, C. G., *Mysterium Conjunctionis*, London: Routledge and Kegan Paul, 1963.

Kahn, E. J., Jr., *The Staffs of Life*, Boston: Little Brown, 1985.

Keightley, Dvaid N. (ed.), *The Origins of Chinese Civilization*, Berkeley: University of California Press, 1983.

Kern, H. (ed.), *The Saddharma-Pundarika Sutra*, Sacred Books of the East, Vol. X, New York: Scribner, 1901.

Kircher, Athanasius, *Mundus Subterraneus*, Amsterdam, 1665.

Kraus, Richard A., *Cotton and Cotton Goods in China, 1918–1936*, New York: Garland, 1980.

Kuhn, Albert J., 'Glory or Gravity: Hutchinson vs Newton', *Journal of the History of Ideas*, 22, 1961, pp. 303–22.

Kuhn, Philip A., *Soul Stealers: The Chinese Sorcery Scare of 1768*, Cambridge, Mass.: Harvard University Press, 1990.

Kultur Chronik, no. 4, 1986.

Lam, Peter Y. K., *A Ceramic Legacy of Asia's Maritime Trade*, Singapore: Oxford University Press, 1985.

Landes, David S., *Revolution in Time: Clocks and the Making of the Modern World*, Cambridge, Mass.: Harvard University Press, 1983.

Lane, E. W., *Manners and Customs of the Modern Egyptians*, London: Dent, 1954.

Latham, James E., *The Religious Symbolism of Salt*, Paris: Beauchesne, 1982.

Laver, James, *Costume and Fashion: A Concise History*, London: Thames and Hudson, 1988.

Lee, Robert H. G., *The Manchurian Frontier in Ch'ing History*, Cambridge, Mass.: Harvard University Press, 1970.

Leibniz, G. W., *Philosophical Writings*, London: Dent, 1951.

Leonard, Jane Kate, *Wei Yüan and China's Rediscovery of the Maritime World*, Cambridge, Mass.: Harvard University Press, 1984.

Le Roy Ladurie, Emmanuel, *Montaillou, Village Occitan de 1294 à 1324*, Paris: Gallimard, 1975.

Lévi-Strauss, Claude, *Mythologiques II: Du Miel aux Cendres*, Paris: Plon, 1966.

Lévi-Strauss, Claude, *Mythologiques III: L'Origine des Manières de Table*, Paris: Plon, 1968.

Lévi-Strauss, Claude, *Totemism*, Harmondsworth: Penguin, 1969.

Lévi-Strauss, Claude, *The Raw and the Cooked*, London: Jonathan Cape, 1970.

Lévi-Strauss, Claude, *Mythologiques IV: L'Homme Nu*, Paris: Plon, 1971.

Lévi-Strauss, Claude, *Tristes Tropiques*, Harmondsworth: Penguin, 1976.

Levine, Stephen I., *Anvil of Victory. The Communist Revolution in Manchuria, 1945–1948*, New York: Columbia University Press, 1987.

Levy, Howard S., *The Lotus Lovers: The Complete History of the Curious Erotic Custom of Footbinding in China*, Buffalo: Prometheus, 1966.

Lipovetsky, Gilles, *L'Empire de l'Éphémère, la mode et son destin dans les sociétés modernes*, Paris: Gallimard, 1987.

Loewe, Michael, *Everyday Life in Early Imperial China*, London: Batsford, 1968.

Lombard, Denys, *Le Carrefour Javanais, Essai d'histoire globale*, 3 vols, Paris: École des Hautes Etudes en Sciences Sociales, 1990.

Lombard-Salmon, Claudine, *Un Exemple d' Acculturation Chinoise: La Province de Gui Zhou au XVIIIᵉ siècle*, Paris: École Française d'Extrême Orient, 1972.

Lurie, Alison, *The Language of Clothes*, New York: Random House, 1981.

Mackeras, Colin P. M., *The Rise of the Peking Opera: Social Aspects of the Theatre in Manchu China*, Oxford: Clarendon Press, 1972.

Mancall, Mark, 'The Kiakhta Trade', in C. D. Cowan (ed.), *The Economic Development of China and Japan*, London: Allen and Unwin, 1964, pp. 19–48.

Mancall, Mark, *Russia and China: Their Diplomatic Relations to 1728*, Cambridge, Mass.: Harvard University Press, 1971.

Manning, Henry Edward, *Miscellanies*, 2 vols, London: Burns and Oates, 1877.

Mansur, Gerhard, *Imperial Berlin*, London: Routledge and Kegan Paul, 1971.

Mauro, Frédéric, *Histoire du Café*, Paris: Éditions Desjonquères, 1991.

May, Jenny, 'The Late Roman Villa: The Relationship between Architectural Form and Social Structure', unpublished paper, Department of Classics, University of Canterbury, 1993.

Meacham, William, 'Origins and Development of Yüeh Coastal Neolithic: A Microcosm of Cultural Change on the Mainland of East Asia', in David Keightley (ed.), *The Origins of Chinese Civilization*, Berkeley: University of California Press, 1983.

Menzies, Nicholas Kaye, 'Trees, Fields and People: The Forests of China from the Seventeenth to the Nineteenth Centuries', Ph.D. thesis, Berkeley: University of California, 1988.

Merlin, Mark David, *On the Trail of the Ancient Opium Poppy*. London and Toronto: Fairleigh Dickinson, 1984.

Micksie, John N., 'Traditional Sumatran Trade', *Bulletin de l'École Française d'Extrême Orient*, 74, 1985, pp. 423–69.

Mintz, Sidney W., *Sweetness and Power: The Place of Sugar in Modern History*, New York: Viking, 1985.

Mokyr, Joel, *Industrialization in the Low Countries 1795–1850*, New Haven and London: Yale University Press, 1976.

Mollat, Michel (ed.), *Le Rôle du Sel dans L' Histoire*, Paris: Presses Universitaires de France, 1968.

Mollat, Michel (ed.), *Histoire des Pêches Maritimes en France*, Paris: Privat, 1987.

Morazé, Charles, *Essai sur la Civilisation d'Occident: L'Homme*, Paris: Armand Colin, 1950.

Morse, H. B., *The Trade and Administration of the Chinese Empire*, London: Longman, 1908.

Morse, H. B., *The Chronicles of the East India Company trading to China 1635–1834*, 5 vols, Oxford, 1926–9.

Multhauf, Robert P., *Neptune's Gift: A History of Common Salt*, Baltimore: Johns Hopkins, 1978.

Musallam, B. F., *Sex and Society in Islam*, Cambridge: Cambridge University Press, 1983.

Musil, Robert, *The Man Without Qualities*, 3 vols, London: Pan, 1979.

Musset, Alain, 'De Tlaloc à Hippocrate: L'Eau et L'Organisation de L'Espace dans le Bassin de Mexico (XVIe–XVIIIe siècles)', *Annales, Économies, Sociétés, Civilisations*, 46(2), March–April 1991, pp. 261–98.

Needham, Joseph, *Science and Civilisation in China*, Vol. IV, *Physics and Physical Technology*, Part II, *Mechanical Engineering*, Cambridge: Cambridge University Press, 1964.

Needham, Joseph, *Science and Civilisation in China*, Vol. IV, *Physics and Physical Technology*, Part III, *Civil Engineering and Nautics*, Cambridge: Cambridge University Press, 1971.

Needham, Joseph, *Science and Civilisation in China*, Vol. V, *Chemistry and Chemical Technology*, Part I, *Paper and Printing*, by Ts'en Tsuen-hsuin, Cambridge: Cambridge University Press, 1983.

Needham, Joseph, *Science and Civilisation in China*, Vol. VI, *Biology and Biological Technology*, Part I, *Botany*, Cambridge: Cambridge University Press, 1986.

Needham, Joseph, Wang Ling, and Sola Price, D. J. de, *Heavenly Clockwork*, Cambridge: Cambridge University Press, 1960.

Nef, J. U., *The Rise of the British Coal Industry*, 2 vols, London: Routledge and Kegan Paul, 1932.

Nef, J. U., *War and Human Progress: An Essay on the Rise of Industrial Civilization*, London: Routledge and Kegan Paul, 1950.

Nicholl, Charles, *The Reckoning: The Murder of Christopher Marlowe*, London: Picador, 1993.

Novak, Michael, 'Two Moral Ideals for Business', IEA Second Annual Hayek Memorial Lecture, 22 June 1993.

Oberman, Heiko Augustinus, *The Harvest of Medieval Theology: Gabriel Biel and Late Medieval Nominalism*, Cambridge, Mass.: Harvard University Press, 1963.

Oresme, Nicole, *Le Livre du Ciel et du Monde*, ed. Albert D. Menut and Alexander J. Denomy CSB, Madison: University of Wisconsin Press, 1968.

Packer, J. I. and Duffield, G. E. (eds), *The Works of Thomas Cranmer*, Appleford, Berkshire: Sutton Courtney, 1965.

Panzac, Daniel, *La Peste dans L'Empire Ottoman 1700–1850*, Louvain: Peeters, 1985.

Penrose, Roger, *The Emperor's New Mind*, London: Vintage, 1990.

Petroski, Henry, *The Pencil: A History of Design and Circumstance*, London: Faber, 1990.

Pezeu-Massabuau, Jacques, 'La maison Japonaise: standardisation de l'espace habité et harmonie sociale', *Annales, Économies, Sociétés, Civilisation*, 32(4), July–August 1977, pp. 670–701.

Pitte, Jean-Robert, *Gastronomie Française: Histoire et Géographie d'une Passion*, Paris: Fayard, 1991.

Polo, Marco, *Travels*, ed. Ronald Latham, Harmondsworth: Penguin, 1958.

Poni, Carlo, 'Archéologie de la Fabrique: la diffusion des moulins à soie *"alla bolognese"* les états dans vénetiens au XVIᵉ au XVIIIᵉ siècles', *Annales, Économies, Sociétés, Civilisations*, 27(6), November–December 1972, pp. 1475–96.

Popper, Karl, *Unended Quest: An Intellectual Biography*, Glasgow: Fontana/Collins, 1976.

Popper, Karl R., *The Open Universe, An Argument for Indeterminism*, London: Hutchinson, 1982.

Prigogine, Ilya and Stengers, Isabelle, *Entre Le Temps et L'Éternité*, Paris: Fayard, 1988.

Punch, *Mr Punch's Cavalcade, A Revue of Thirty Years*, London: The Educational Book Company Ltd, 1930.

Rahner, Karl, *Spirit in the World*, London and Sydney: Sheed and Ward, 1968.

Rawski, Evelyn Sakakida, *Education and Popular Literacy in Ch'ing China*, Ann Arbor: University of Michigan Press, 1979.

Reid, Anthony, *Southeast Asia in the Age of Commerce 1450–1680*, Vol. I, *The Lands Below the Winds*, New Haven: Yale University Press, 1988.

Richthofen, Baron F. von, *Letters 1870–1872*, Shanghai: North China Herald, 1903.

Robertson, Robert H. S., *Fuller's Earth. A History of Calcium Montmorillonite*, Hythe, Kent: Volturna, 1986.

Roche, Daniel, *La Culture des Apparences, une histoire du vêtement, XVIIᵉ–XVIII siècles*, Paris: Fayard, 1989.

Roden, Claudia, *Coffee*, Harmondsworth: Penguin, 1981.

Rosser, Gervase, 'Les fraternités urbaines anglaises à la fin du Moyen Age', *Annales, Économies Sociétés, Civilisations*, 48(5), September–October 1993, pp. 1127–43.

Rowe, William T., *Hankow: Commerce and Society in a Chinese City 1796–1889*, Stanford: Stanford University Press, 1984.

Royal Commission on Opium 1894–5.

Ruffié, J. and Sournia, J. C. *Les Épidémies dans l'Histoire de l'Homme*, Paris: Flammarion, 1984.

Ruitenbeek, Klaas, *Carpentry and Building in Late Imperial China*, Leiden: Brill, 1993.

Rumer, Boris Z., *Soviet Central Asia: 'A Tragic Experiment'*, Boston: Unwin Hyman, 1990.

Sabban, Françoise, 'Le Système des Cuissons dans la Tradition Culinaire Chinoise', *Annales, Économies, Sociétés, Civilisations*, 38(2), March–April 1985, pp. 341–68.

Saenger, Paul, 'Physiologie de la lecture et Séparation des mots', *Annales, Économies, Sociétés, Civilisations*, 44(4), July–August 1989, pp. 939–52.

Schafer, Edward H., *The Golden Peaches of Samarkand, A Study of T'ang Exotics*, Berkeley and Los Angeles: University of California Press, 1963.

Schama, Simon, *The Embarassment of Riches: An Interpretation of Dutch Culture in the Golden Age*, London: Fortuna, 1991.

Semedo, F. Alvarez, *The History of That Great and Renowned Monarchy of China*, London: John Great, 1655.

Sheldrake, Rupert, *A New Science of Life*, London: Paladin, 1984.

Sigaut, François, 'La Chine, L'Europe et les techniques agricoles', *Annales, Économies, Sociétés, Civilisations*, 44(1), January–February 1989, pp. 207–16.

Simon, J. L., *The Ultimate Resource*, Princeton: Princeton University Press, 1981.

Smith, Paul J., *Taxing Heaven's Storehouse*, Cambridge, Mass.: Harvard University Press, 1991.

Smith, R. E. F. and Christian, David, *Bread and Salt, A Social and Economic History of Food and Drink in Russia*, Cambridge: Cambridge University Press, 1984.

Smith, Richard J., *Fortune Tellers and Philosophers: Divination in Traditional Chinese Society*, Boulder: Westview, 1991.

Stockard, Janice E., *Daughters of the Canton Delta. Marriage Patterns and Economic Strategies in South China, 1860–1930*, Stanford: California University Press, 1989.

Stover, Leon E., *The Cultural Ecology of Chinese Civilization*, New York: Mentor, 1974.

Teng, T'o, 'Les mines de charbon de Men-t'ou k'ou', *Annales, Économies, Sociétés, Civilisation*, 22(1), January–February 1967, pp. 50–87.

Tichane, Robert, *Ching-te-chen*, New York: New York State Institute of Glaze Research, 1983.

Toubert, Pierre, *Les Structures du Latium Médiéval*, 2 vols, Rome: École Française de Rome, 1973.

Trevor-Roper, H. R., *Historical Essays*, London: Macmillan, 1957.

Trevor-Roper, H. R., 'Review: *David Hume: Politico e Storico* by Giuseppe Giarizzo, Einaudi, Turin, 1962', *History and Theory*, 3(2), 1964, pp. 381–9.

Trevor-Roper, Hugh, *Renaissance Essays*, London: Secker and Warburg, 1985.

Trevor-Roper, Hugh, *From Counter-Reformation to Glorious Revolution*, London: Secker and Warburg, 1992.

Tsukamoto, Zenryu, *A History of Early Chinese Buddhism*, 2 vols, Tokyo: Kodansha International, 1985.

Turgeon, Laurier, 'Le temps des pêches lointaines', in Michel Mollat (ed.), *Histoire des Pêches Maritimes en France*, Paris: Privat, 1987, pp. 133–81.

Unschuld, Paul U., *Medical Ethics in Imperial China. A Study in Historical Anthropology*, Berkeley: University of California Press, 1979.

Unschuld, Paul U., *Medicine in China: A History of Pharmaceutics*, Berkeley: University of California Press, 1986.

Verley, Patrick, 'La révolution industrielle anglaise: une révision', *Annales, Économies, Sociétés, Civilisations*, 46(3), May–June 1991, pp. 735–55.

Vogel, Hans Ulrich, 'The Great Well of China', *Scientific American*, June 1993, pp. 86–91.

Wagner, Donald E., *Dabieshan, Traditional Chinese Iron-production Techniques practised in Southern Henan in the Twentieth Century*, London and Malmö: Curzon, 1985.

Wakeman, Frederic, Jr., 'The Canton Trade and the Opium War', in John K. Fairbank (ed.), *The Cambridge History of China*, Vol. X, *Late Ch'ing, 1800–1911, Part I*, Cambridge: Cambridge University Press, 1978, pp. 163–212.

Waldron, Arthur, *The Great Wall of China: From History to Myth*, Cambridge: Cambridge University Press, 1990.

Wang, Gung-wu, 'Feng Tao: An Essay in Confucian Loyalty', in Arthur F. Wright and Denis Twitchett (eds), *Confucian Personalities*, Stanford: Stanford University Press, 1962, pp. 122–45.

Wang, Shixiang, *Classical Chinese Furniture*, USA: China Books and Periodicals, Inc., 1986.

Wang, Zhongshu, *Han Civilization*, New Haven: Yale University Press, 1982.

Warren, Kenneth, *Chemical Foundations: The Alkali Industry in Britain to 1926*, Oxford: Clarendon Press, 1980.

Wilde, C. B., 'Hutchinsonianism, Natural Philosophy and Religious Controversy in Eighteenth Century England', *History of Science*, 18, 1980, pp. 1–24.

Wilde, C. B., 'Matter and Spirit as Natural Symbols in Eighteenth Century British Natural Philosophy', *British Journal for the History of Science*, 15, 1982, pp. 91–131.

Will, Pierre-Etienne, *Bureaucratie et Famine en Chine au 18e siècle*, Paris: Mouton, 1980.

Will, Pierre-Etienne, 'Un Cycle Hydraulique en Chine: La Province du Hupei du XVIe au XIXe siècles', *Bulletin de l'École Française d'Extrême Orient*, 68, 1980, pp. 261–98.

Williams, Basil, *The Life of William Pitt, Earl of Chatham*, London: Longman, 1915.

Wilson, E. H., *A Naturalist in Western China*, London: Cadogan, 1986.

Winter, Michael, *Society and Religion in Early Ottoman Egypt*, New Brunswick: Transaction Books, 1982.

Wisdom, John Oulton, *The Unconscious Origins of Berkeley's Philosophy*, London: Hogarth, 1953.

Wise, Mark, *The Common Fisheries Policy of the European Community*, London: Methuen, 1984.

Wittfogel, Karl A., *Oriental Despotism. A Comparative Study of Total Power*, New Haven: Yale University Press, 1957.

Wolf, Arthur P. and Huang Chieh-shan, *Marriage and Adoption in China 1845–1945*, Stanford: Stanford University Press, 1980.

Wolf, Janet, *The Social Production of Art*, London: Macmillan, 1981.

Wright, Arthur F. and Twitchett, Denis (eds), *Confucian Personalities*, Stanford: Stanford University Press, 1962.

Yang, Lien-sheng, *Studies in Chinese Institutional History*, Cambridge, Mass.: Harvard University Press, 1961.

Young, George, *A History of Whitby and Streoneshalh Abbey*, 2 vols, Whitby: Clark and Mudd, 1817.

Yü, Chün-fa, *The Renewal of Buddhism in China*, New York: Columbia University Press, 1981.

Index